Philosophy & Sex

Philosophy & Sex

edited by

Robert Baker & Frederick Elliston

ℙ₿ *Prometheus Books*
BUFFALO, N.Y. 14215

Published 1975 by Prometheus Books
700 East Amherst Street, Buffalo, New York 14215

Fifth Printing

Library of Congress Card Number 75-21670
ISBN 0-87975-055-3

Printed in the United States of America

Contents

v

THE MORALITY OF MARRIAGE

The Tradition

Monogamy

Adultery and Promiscuity

THE LOGIC OF DEVIATION

FEMINISM AND ABORTION

Preface

In this book we have collected a number of recent philosophical essays on sex. Our purpose is twofold: first, to aid, abet, document, and describe a background for the recent philosophical interest in the subject; and second, to make the written evidence of this interest available to non-philosophers.

We would like to express our appreciation to Paul Kurtz and Prometheus Books for publishing this anthology at a time when anthologies that do not come presold as textbooks are finding it increasingly difficult to find publishers.

A word about the essays themselves: It is traditional in anthologies for the editors to explain their selections to their readers. We feel no need to do this. We will introduce the subject, explore its history, and indicate its significance in our introduction to this volume. It is our view that wherever possible essays in normative ethics should be as accessible to the intelligent layperson as they are to the trained philosopher. This principle has guided our selection of essays, so that they are self-explanatory. For the rest, we trust that the various headings in the topical outline will suffice to explain the logic of their argument.

The philosophical literature, while undoubtedly meager, is no doubt richer than our introduction and bibliography admits. We would therefore be grateful to learn of any citations that should be added to the bibliography. We should also be interested in receiving essays, published or unpublished, on the philosophy of sex—partly out of curiosity, but mostly in the hope that we might act as a conduit, making unpublished and inaccessible materials available to philosophers working in the area.

Robert Baker
Frederick Elliston

Robert Baker
and Frederick Elliston

Introduction

In the "war" between philosophers and poets, the philosophers have all too willingly relinquished the field of sex to the poets. Their retreat is puzzling when one considers that all of us are born into this world as biological males or females, and that the attendant gender roles boy/girl, man/woman, husband/wife, father/mother, adulterer/adulteress mediate and perhaps even determine our lives. If anatomy is not all of destiny, sex and sexuality—especially in the institutionalized forms of courtship, marriage, and the family—are crucial in molding individuals and cultures. Surely then, intellectuals who are committed to living the examined life should not fail to devote a goodly part of their work to the analysis of sex, sexuality, and gender.

Why then have philosophers surrendered sex to the poets? In part, their refusal to deal with sex can be traced to the tradition of rejecting the body and all things corporeal. For example, in the dialogue in which Plato

1

introduces the "war" between the philosophers and the poets, he has the Prophetess advise Socrates that the contemplation of pure beauty "is the life for men to live." She goes on to say that he "will esteem [this pure beauty] far beyond . . . those lovely persons whom you and many others now gaze on with astonishment. . . ." Love between persons is contaminated with "the intermixture of human flesh and colors, and all other idle and unreal shapes attendant upon morality"; whereas pure beauty is "simple, pure and uncontaminated."[1]

Writing in a similar vein, Epictetus argued that rationality and sexuality are incompatible, and hence that there is no room for sex in the truly philosophical life.

> Every habit is confirmed and strengthened by corresponding acts. . . . So, if you lie in bed for ten days and then get up and try to take a fairly long walk, you will see how your legs lose their power. . . . When you yield to carnal passion you must take account not only of this one defeat, but of the fact that you fed your incontinence and strengthened it. . . .
>
> Today when I saw a handsome woman I did not say "Would that she were mine!" and "Blessed is her husband!". . . Nor do I picture the next scene: the woman present and disrobing and reclining by my side. . . . And if the woman, poor thing, is willing and beckons, and sends to me, and even touches me and comes close to me, I still hold aloof and conquer; the refutation of this argument is something greater than the argument of "the Liar" or the "Resting" argument. This is a thing really to be proud of. . . .
>
> The man who truly trains is he who disciplines himself to face such impressions. . . . Great is the struggle, divine the task; the stake is a Kingdom, freedom, peace, an unruffled spirit. . . . Can any storm be greater than that which springs from violent impressions to drive out reason?[2]

Except when planning utopias, the ancient philosophers tended to abandon sex to the poets because of the felt conflict between their commitment to reason and the inherent unreasonableness of sexual passion, because of a tendency to regard the sensual world as unworthy of philosophical contemplation, and—on a more personal level—because they tended to regard abnegation and the suppression of libido as intrinsically praiseworthy. For the most part the history of the philosophy of sex has been little more than a footnote to the ancients. Yet, a brief glance at this history is not altogether unrewarding.

In living their lives the great medieval philosophers Augustine and Aquinas followed the antisexual precedent of Plato and Epictetus. And while their writings form a somewhat different tradition, these medievals would undoubtedly have dismissed sex as quickly and disdainfully as their pagan predecessors if their inclinations had not been checked by the Biblical commandment to "increase and multiply and fill the earth."[3] This "blessing of fecundity," even more than St. Paul's grudging concession that marriage is better than hell, led them to consider, analyze, and defend the institution of monogamous marriage—thereby providing us not only with one of the very few bodies of philosophical literature dealing with sex, but also with a series of expositions and arguments that still shape contemporary views.

As is so frequently the case, the typical expression of medieval thought is found in the works of Thomas Aquinas, who developed what might be called the traditional eightfold truth on the subject: (1) seminal discharge defines the essence of sexual intercourse; (2) the only moral function of sexual intercourse is procreation (hence the emission of semen in any way that in itself prevents procreation is unnatural and immoral); (3) procreation naturally completes itself in the generation of an adult; (4) those who engage in sexual intercourse should provide whatever is necessary to rear any creature they procreate; (5) an unadulterous monogamous marriage is the best environment for rearing offspring to become adults; (6) females are inferior to males; (7) the male acts as the female's governor in marriage;[4] (8) divorce is improper (note that the seventh proposition renders it unjust for a male to divorce a female, while the sixth proposition makes female generated divorces inappropriate).

It would be difficult to overestimate the significance of these eight theses for the subject of this book—indeed for the very nature of our society. To accept or reject any one of them, even the most innocuous, is to accept or reject a significant feature of one's culture. Consider proposition 1. If ever a proposition appeared to be a metaphysical irrelevancy, it does. Yet this seemingly superfluous bit of abstraction can—and possibly does—have the mundane and tragically real effect of ruining the sex life of half of the population.[5] If the implications of proposition 1 are somewhat subtle, those of the remaining seven are not. Between them they describe a monogamous, sexually inequitable, paternalistic patriarchy that proscribes divorce and alternative marital and sexual relationships, including recreational and nonprocreative sexual intercourse—for example, masturbation, contraception, oral intercourse, homosexual intercourse, and sodomy.

Contemporary society is not as rigidly traditional as the one described above, but it partakes of the tradition to a greater extent than might be apparent. This point can be underlined by considering what a society that rejects Thomas' eightfold truth might be like.

At the heart of the tradition lies the belief that sex is essentially procreative; a contratraditional view belies this "truth." So let us imagine a society that takes the essence of sex to be erotic fulfillment and that considers sex moral only to the extent that it is fulfilling. (We need not stop to consider whether this "fulfillment" is essentially self-centered, other-directed, or interactive, since this is a rough sketch rather than a blueprint.) Perhaps the most significant difference between the erotic and the procreative conceptions of sex is that if procreation is linked with parental responsibility it provides grounds for believing in a relatively stable relationship with a fair degree of permanence (and generates arguments for sexual exclusivity, and so forth); by contrast, erotic fulfillment has little need of permanence. Hence, in contratraditional society there would be no reason for linking parenthood (or, rather, what might be called "parenting"—that is, the activity of rearing a child) with sexual partnership. Such a society would be free to deny proposition 4 and to allow children to be parented by the state, by private charities, by individual volunteers, or by tribes of volunteers. The erotic act itself could be unburdened of the onus of possible parenthood by socially encouraged policies of sterilization, contraception, and abortion.

While the family has many functions in our society, its two primary functions are to provide for and protect an exclusive sexual relationship between a man and a woman and to provide for the parenting of children. Neither of these functions would be required of sex partners in contratraditional society. In such a society sex partners might be permanent "bachelors," impermanent trios, or tribes; "marriage" might exist in some vestigial form, but since there would be no sexual exclusivity and no sexually determined parenting, there would be no daughters, no sons, no husbands, no wives, no mothers, no fathers, no sisters, no brothers—at least not in the accepted sense. Sexual relations might occur in specially provided places in public buildings (say, in rooms located between the telephone booth and the toilet), or out in the open where everyone could enjoy them as either participant or spectator; or perhaps they might be restricted to more-ritual occasions or more-private locations. But sex-dictated residences, such as the family-oriented dwellings that have been a feature of Western culture since prehistoric times, would be superfluous. Contratraditional society might be the communalistic world of Plato's *Republic*, the libertine world of the Marquis de Sade, or the Harmonian world of Charles Fourier's passional phalansteries. But it would be a postmarital culture, a society without families; as such it would be different from any culture that has played a significant role in any civilization known to history.

Having sketched the possible outlines of postmarital society, we should like to suggest that however radical this society may appear, the contratraditional transfiguration of Western culture is possible—perhaps even probable—within the next few decades. And that change is the subject of this book. While no one essay deals with all aspects of this transfiguration, together they consider the advisability of rejecting the tradition. Yet, if a tradition is to be transformed rationally, it must first be understood.

The following is a selection of passages from Thomas in which he develops the eightfold tradition:

> Now, it is good for each person to attain his end, whereas it is bad for him to serve away from his proper end. Now, this should be considered applicable to the parts, just as it is to the whole being; for instance, each and every part of man, and every one of his acts, should attain the proper end. Now, though the male semen is superfluous in regard to the preservation of the individual, it is nevertheless necessary in regard to the propagation of the species. Other superfluous things, such as excrement, urine, sweat, and such things, are not at all necessary; hence, their emission contributes to man's good. Now, this is not what is sought in the case of semen, but, rather, to emit it for the purpose of generation, to which purpose the sexual act is directed. But man's generative process would be frustrated unless it were followed by proper nutrition, because the offspring would not survive if proper nutrition were withheld. Therefore, the emission of semen ought to be so ordered that it will result in both the production of the proper offspring and in the upbringing of this offspring.
>
> It is evident from this that every emission of semen, in such a way that generation cannot follow, is contrary to the good for man. And if this be done deliberately, it must be a sin. Now, I am speaking of a way from which, *in itself*, generation could not result; such would be any emission of semen apart from the natural union of male and female. For which reason, sins of this type are called *contrary to nature*. But, if by accident generation cannot result from the emission of semen, then this is not a reason for it being against nature, or a sin; as for instance, if the woman happens to be sterile.
>
> Likewise, it must also be contrary to the good for man if the semen be emitted under conditions such that generation could result but the proper upbringing would be prevented. We should take into consideration the fact that, among some animals where the female is able to take care of the upbringing of offspring, male and female do not remain together for any time after the act of generation. This is obviously the case with dogs. But in the case of animals of which the female is not able to provide for the upbringing

of offspring, the male and female do stay together after the act of generation as long as is necessary for the upbringing and instruction of the offspring. . . .

Now, it is abundantly evident that the female in the human species is not at all able to take care of the upbringing of offspring by herself, since the needs of human life demand many things which cannot be provided by one person alone. Therefore, it is appropriate to human nature that a man remain together with a woman after the generative act, and not leave her immediately to have such relations with another woman, as is the practice with fornicators. . . .

Now, we call this society *matrimony*. Therefore, matrimony is natural for man, and promiscuous performance of the sexual act, outside matrimony, is contrary to man's good. For this reason, it must be a sin.

Nor, in fact, should it be deemed a slight sin for a man to arrange for the emission of semen apart from the proper purpose of generating and bringing up children, on the argument that it is either a slight sin, or none at all, for a person to use a part of the body for a different use than that to which it is directed by nature (say, for instance, one chose to walk on his hands, or to use his feet for something usually done with the hands) because man's good is not much opposed by such inordinate use. However, the inordinate emission of semen is incompatible with the natural good; namely, the preservation of the species. Hence, after the sin of homicide whereby a human nature already in existence is destroyed, this type of sin appears to take next place, for by it the generation of human nature is precluded.

Moreover, these views which have just been given have a solid basis in divine authority. That the emission of semen under conditions in which offspring cannot follow is illicit is quite clear. There is the text of Leviticus (18:22-23): "thou shalt not lie with mankind as with womankind . . . and thou shalt not copulate with any beast." And in I Corinthians (6:10): "Nor the effeminate, nor liers with mankind . . . shall possess the Kingdom of God."

Also, that fornication and every performance of the act of reproduction with a person other than one's wife are illicit is evident. For it is said: "There shall be no whore among the daughters of Israel, nor whoremonger among the sons of Israel" (Deut[eronomy] 23:17); and in Tobias (4:13): "Take heed to keep thyself from all fornication, and beside thy wife never endure to know a crime"; and in I Corinthians (6:18): "Fly fornication."

By this conclusion we refute the error of those who say that there is no more sin in the emission of semen than in the emission of any other superfluous matter, and also of those who state that fornication is not a sin.

If one will make a proper consideration, the preceding reasoning will be seen to lead to the conclusion not only that the society of man and woman of the human species, which we call matrimony, should be long lasting, but even that it should endure throughout an entire life.

Indeed, possessions are ordered to the preservation of natural life, and since natural life, which cannot be preserved perpetually in the father, is by a sort of succession preserved in the son in its specific likeness, it is naturally fitting for the son to succeed also to the things which belong to the father. So, it is natural that the father's solicitude for his son should endure until the end of the father's life. Therefore, if even in the case of birds the solicitude of the father gives rise to the cohabitation of male and female, the natural order demands that father and mother in the human species remain together until the end of life.

It also seems to be against equity if the aforesaid society be dissolved. For the female needs the male, not merely for the sake of generation, as in the case of other animals, but also for the sake of government, since the male is both more perfect in reasoning and stronger in his powers. In fact, a woman is taken into man's society for the needs of generation; then, with the disappearance of a woman's fecundity and beauty, she is prevented from association with another man. So, if any man took a woman in the time of her youth, when beauty and fecundity were hers, and then sent her away after she had reached an advanced age, he would damage that woman contrary to natural equity.

Again, it seems obviously inappropriate for a woman to be able to put away her husband, because a wife is naturally subject to her husband as governor, and it is not within the power of a person subject to another to depart from his rule. So, it would be against the natural order if a wife were able to abandon her husband. Therefore, if a husband were permitted to abandon his wife, the society of husband and wife would not be an association of equals, but, instead, a sort of slavery on the part of the wife.

Besides, there is in men a certain natural solicitude to know their offspring. This is necessary for this reason: the child requires the father's direction for a long time. So, whenever there are obstacles to the ascertaining of offspring they are opposed to the natural instinct of the human species. But, if a husband could put away his wife, or a wife her husband, and have sexual relations with another person, certitude as to offspring would be precluded, for the wife would be united first with one man and later with another. [6]

In the seventeenth and eighteenth centuries most of the philosophers were bachelor males dedicated to the life of reason who viewed sex as an antirational distraction unworthy of serious comment. Insofar as they addressed themselves to sexual issues at all, it was only to reinforce the traditional view of marriage. In "Of Polygamy and Divorces," for example, David Hume defends the classic Western marriage ("an engagement entered into by mutual consent and has for its end the propagation of the species"), argues that polygamy and divorce are inimical to these ends, and concludes that "the exclusion of polygamy and divorce sufficiently recommend our present European practices with regard to marriage."[7]

Kant, too, concludes his brief remarks on sex and marriage by defending the tradition. In his precritical work *Observations on the Feeling of the Beautiful and the Sublime* (1763)[8] he takes the stance of an aesthete and extolls the virtues of femininity while decrying the education of women ("her philosophy is not to reason but to sense") as a perversion by which males, who are weakened by the power of women ("a single sly glance sets them more in confusion than the most difficult problem of science"), seek to alter the situation to their own advantage. Kant argues that since women are naturally irrational, while morality is essentially rational, they will avoid the wicked "not because it is unright, but because it is ugly." Reaffirming the traditional procreative view of the nature of sexual intercourse, Kant contends that whatever feelings or fascinations may appear to motivate us in sexual matters, "Nature pursues its great purpose, and all refinements that join together, though they may appear to stand as far from that as they will, are only trimmings and borrow their charm ultimately from that very source." Finally, he concludes that this great procreative purpose is best served by nonadulterous monogamous marriage, because promiscuity "degenerates into excess and dissoluteness." In matrimonial life the united pair should constitute a single moral person animated and governed by the understanding of the man and the taste of the wife.

In Kant's later (critical) work *Lectures on Ethics* the aesthete turns rationalist. Many of his earlier conclusions are retained, but the analyses that buttress them are radically different. He eschews the traditional conception of sexual intercourse as procreation marred by lust and reconceptualizes sex as mutual masturbation salvageable by human love. In a few key passages he originates the concept of a *sex object*. He argues that from the participants' point of view the purpose of coition is not procreation but orgasm, and develops the view that coition is essentially mutual masturbation—that is, that each participant uses the other as a *means* for attaining his own sexual satisfaction and hence does not treat the other as a full human being, as an *end* in himself. Since, for Kant, treating someone as a means rather than as an end is the essence of immorality, he has developed a rational proof of St. Paul's belief that coition is intrinsically evil. Like St. Paul, Kant allows one condition under which coition is morally permissible—nonadulterous monogamous marriage. For in marriage two persons become united as one in all things, and neither uses the other for his own purposes, but each gives himself over to the other. In other words, marriage transubstantiates immoral sexual intercourse into morally permissible human copulation by transforming a manipulative masturbatory relationship into one of altruistic unity.

Human love is good-will, affection, promoting the happiness of others and finding joy in their happiness. But it is clear that, when a person loves another purely from sexual desire, none of these factors enter into the love. Far from there being any concern for the happiness of the loved one, the lover, in order to satisfy his desire and still his appetite, may even plunge the loved one into the depths of misery. Sexual love makes of the loved person an Object of appetite; as soon as that appetite has been stilled, the person is cast aside as one casts away a lemon which has been sucked dry. Sexual love can, of course, be combined with human love and so carry with it the characteristics of the latter, but taken by itself and for itself, it is nothing more than appetite. Taken by itself it is a degradation of human nature; for as soon as a person becomes an Object of appetite for another, all motives of moral relationship cease to function, because as an Object of appetite for another a person becomes a thing and can be treated and used as such by every one. This is the only case in which a human being is designed by nature as the Object of another's enjoyment. Sexual desire is at the root of it; and that is why we are ashamed of it, and why all strict moralists, and those who had pretensions to be regarded as saints, sought to suppress and extirpate it. . . .

Because sexuality is not an inclination which one human being has for another as such, but is an inclination for the sex of another, it is a principle of the degradation of human nature, in that it gives rise to the preference of one sex to the other, and to the dishonoring of that sex through the satisfaction of desire. The desire which a man has for a woman is not directed towards her because she is a human being, but because she is a woman; that she is a human being is of no concern to the man; only her sex is the object of his desires. Human nature is thus subordinated. Hence it comes that all men and women do their best to make not their human nature but their sex more alluring and direct their activities and lusts entirely towards sex. Human nature is thereby sacrificed to sex. If then a man wishes to satisfy his desire, and a woman hers, they stimulate each other's desire; their inclinations meet, but their object is not human nature but sex, and each of them dishonors the human nature of the other. They make of humanity an instrument for the satisfaction of their lusts and inclinations, and dishonor it by placing it on a level with animal nature. Sexuality, therefore, exposes mankind to the danger of equality with the beasts. But as man has this desire from nature, the question arises how far he can properly make use of it without injury to his manhood. . . .

The sole condition on which we are free to make use of our sexual desire depends upon the right to dispose over the person as a whole—over the welfare and happiness and generally over all the circumstances of that person. If I have the right over the whole person, I have also the right over the part and so I have the right to use that person's *organa sexualia* for the satisfaction of sexual desire. But how am I to obtain these rights over the whole person? Only by giving that person the same rights over the whole of myself.

This happens only in marriage. Matrimony is an agreement between two persons by which they grant each other equal reciprocal rights, each of them undertaking to surrender the whole of their person to the other with a complete right of disposal over it. We can now apprehend by reason how a *commercium sexuale* is possible without degrading humanity and breaking the moral laws. Matrimony is the only condition in which use can be made of one's sexuality. If one devotes one's person to another, one devotes not only sex but the whole person; the two cannot be separated. If, then, one yields one's person, body and soul, for good and ill and in every respect, so that the other has complete rights over it, and if the other does not similarly yield himself in return and does not extend in return the same rights and privileges, the arrangement is one-sided. But if I yield myself completely to another and obtain the person of the other in return, I win myself back; I have given myself up as the property of another, but in turn I take that other as my property, and so win myself back again in winning the person whose property I have become. In this way the two persons become a unity of will. Whatever good or ill, joy or sorrow befall either of them, the other will share in it. Thus sexuality leads to a union of human beings, and in that union alone its exercise is possible.[9]

Whether Kant's conception of marriage and sexual intercourse is defensible, or indeed whether it even makes sense, is a question for Kant scholars. What interests us is Kant's reconceptualization of the nature of sexual intercourse, which alters the tradition in at least three significant ways: first, coition has become an essentially hedonic and self-interested act, rather than a procreative one; second, the sexual act is analyzed in terms of the manipulation of an object by a subject; and, third, sexual intercourse (even sexual intercourse entered into with procreative intent) is considered to be moral only if it is done as part of an altruistic union of two human beings. As will shortly become apparent, each of those three alterations had significant influence on later philosophical writings on sex.

If Thomas Aquinas and Kant are the most influential sexual philosophers, Arthur Schopenhauer is unique in being the first Western philosopher to recognize the significance of the subject as such and to contrast the loquaciousness of the poets to the silence of the philosophers.

We are accustomed to see poets principally occupied with describing the love of the sexes....
    ... no one can doubt either the reality or the importance of the matter; and therefore, instead of wondering that a philosophy should also for once make its own this constant theme of all poets, one ought rather to be surprised that a thing which plays throughout so important a part in human life has hitherto practically been disregarded by philosophers altogether, and

lies before us a raw material. The one who has most concerned himself with it is Plato, especially in the "Symposium" and the "Phaedrus." Yet what he says on the subject is confined to the sphere of myths, fables and jokes, and also for the most part concerns only the Greek love of youths. The little that Rousseau says upon our theme in the *Discours sur l'inégalité* is false and insufficient. Kant's explanation of the subject in the third part of the essay, *Über das Gefühl des Schönen und Erhabenen* is very superficial and without practical knowledge, therefore it is also partly incorrect. . . . On the other hand, Spinoza's definition, on account of its excessive näiveté, deserves to be quoted for the sake of amusement: *"Amor est titillatio, concomitante idea causae externae"* ["Love is joy with the accompanying idea of an external cause"]. (*Eth.* iv., prop. 44, dem.) Accordingly I have no predecessors either to make use of or to refute.[10]

Schopenhauer's scholarship is not all that one might have hoped it to be. He may be forgiven for having overlooked a page or so of Bishop Berkeley's *The Querist*; but his omission of Kant's critical reconceptualization of coition in the *Lectures on Ethics* and *The Philosophy of Law* and Johann Gottlieb Fichte's defense of the inequality of women in *The Science of Rights* (1795) is more serious. No less significant (but perhaps more understandable) was Schopenhauer's failure to mention William Godwin's call for the abolition of marriage in *Political Justice* (1793) and Mary Wollstonecraft's defense of the rights of women in *A Vindication of the Rights of Women* (1793).

Nonetheless, Schopenhauer's point was well taken: "one ought to be surprized," given the importance of sex and its attendant institutions, that it has been "disregarded by philosophers altogether." In reviewing the works of the major philosophers of the seventeenth and eighteenth centuries—Hobbes, Descartes, Spinoza, Leibniz, Malebranche, Locke, Berkeley, Rousseau, Fichte, Godwin, Hume, and Kant—one discovers that their writings on sex and its attendant institutions occupies less than twenty octavo-size pages, and almost all of that is by the last five philosophers named. A look at Lewis Selby-Bigge's classical anthology *British Moralists: Being Selections from Writers Principally of the Eighteenth Century*[11] makes clear that in their major essays on ethics the British moralists from Ralph Cudworth to Jeremy Bentham did not consider sexual intercourse, gender roles, marriage, or parental roles to be topics worthy of discussion. So while Schopenhauer was wrong to claim that he had no predecessors, he was essentially correct in holding that both modern and ancient philosophers had hitherto largely abandoned sex to the poets. What then does Schopenhauer have to say in his "pioneering" work on the subject? First, that "all love, however ethereally it may bear itself, is rooted in the sexual impulse alone . . . "; second, that when we consider the power of love and love affairs, not only in our art and fiction but also in life, where it "constantly lays claim to half the powers and thoughts of the younger portion of mankind . . . embarrasses for a while even the greatest minds, [and] demands the sacrifice even of life and health," we are forced to conclude that what is involved in love and sex is more than a "trifle." Why is sexual love so significant? Because it is essentially procreative: it involves the will to life—not of individuals, but of generations. Love, Schopenhauer maintains, is a mechanism whereby the species manipulates the individual for its own ends and whereby individuals deceive themselves—not only as to their role as perpetuators of the species, but also in their relations with each other.

> . . . the sexual impulse, although in itself a subjective need, knows how to assume very skilfully the mask of an objective admiration, and thus to deceive our consciousness; for nature requires this strategem to attain its ends. But yet that in every case of falling in love, however objective and sublime this admiration may appear, what alone is looked to is the production of an individual of a definite nature. [This] is primarily confirmed by the fact that the essential matter is not the reciprocation of love, but possession, i.e., the physical enjoyment. The certainty of the former can therefore by no means console us for the want of the latter; on the contrary, in such a situation many a man has shot himself. On the other hand, persons who are deeply in love, and can obtain no return of it, are contented with possession, i.e., with the physical enjoyment. This is proved by all forced marriages, and also by the frequent purchase of the favor of a woman, in spite of her dislike, by large presents or other sacrifices, nay, even by cases of rape. That this particular child shall be begotten is, although unknown to the parties concerned, the true end of the whole love story; the manner in which it is attained is a secondary consideration.[12]

In terms of the philosophical tradition, Schopenhauer is arguing Kant's point that although sexual intercourse is objectively procreative in nature, subjectively it is essentially hedonic and manipulative, and that, moreover, the objective aspect of sex ennobles and controls the subjective, giving it both its direction and its meaning.

> . . . every lover will experience a marvellous disillusion after the pleasure he has at last attained, and will wonder that what was so longingly desired accomplishes nothing more than every other sexual satisfaction; so that he does not see himself much benefited by it. That wish was related to all other wishes as the species is related to the individual, thus as the infinite to

the finite. The satisfaction, on the other hand, is really only for the benefit of the species, and thus does not come within the consciousness of the individual, who, inspired by the will of the species, here served an end with every kind of sacrifice, which was not his own end at all. Hence, then, every lover, after the ultimate consummation of the great work, finds himself cheated; for the illusion has vanished by means of which the individual was here the dupe of the species.[13]

He concludes his analysis of love by indicating its relationship to marriage.

Happy marriages are well known to be rare; just because it lies in the nature of marriage that its chief end is not the present but the coming generation. However, let me add, for the consolation of tender, loving natures, that sometimes passionate sexual love associates itself with a feeling of an entirely different origin—real friendship based upon agreement of disposition, which yet for the most part only appears when sexual love proper is extinguished in its satisfaction. This friendship will then generally spring from the fact that the supplementing and corresponding physical, moral, and intellectual qualities of the two individuals, from which sexual love arose, with reference to the child to be produced, are, with reference also to the individuals themselves, related to each other in a supplementary manner as opposite qualities of temperament and mental gifts, and thereby form the basis of a harmony of disposition.[14]

For all Schopenhauer's self-proclaimed iconoclasm, he does not really challenge any of the eight theses associated with the traditional view of sex and marriage: he agrees with all those he specifically mentions, and differs from Thomas only by emphasizing a point previously noted by Kant—the hedonic nature of sex when viewed subjectively. On this point Thomas is silent, but since he readily allows the importance of the concupiscible appetite, it seems doubtful that he would be prone to quarrel—or even to cavil. Indeed, with the exception of Plato (who argues that males and females are morally and intellectually equal and who embraces the ideal of communal marriage), all the philosophers considered thus far have been content to justify the indigenous practice current when they penned their analyses. Since Schopenhauer does much the same thing in his essay, there seems to be little call for noting disagreements. But the situation changes in the nineteenth century.

Centuries are shaggy creatures. The social and intellectual movements of one century tend to originate in the eighties or nineties of the previous one and to spill over into half the next. Thus, with a typical disdain for the aesthetics of chronology, the basic sexual issues of the nineteenth century start in the 1790s. And to further complicate matters, Hegel's writings of 1821 and Schopenhauer's essay of 1844 sit more easily with the "eighteenth-century" essays of Kant and Hume than with the "nineteenth century" works of Condorcet, Wollstonecraft, Godwin, Fichte, Mill, and Nietzsche. Why do we claim this? It seems significant that despite the existence of libertine lifestyles the philosophers of the seventeenth and eighteenth centuries did not seriously question the traditional view of sex and marriage, whereas, with the exceptions of the early Schopenhauer and of Hegel, the nineteenth-century writers either had serious reservations about the traditional conception of sex, gender roles, and marriage, or defended the tradition in the face of objections of critics. The polemical nature of these "later" works sets them apart in such a way that they form a "school" if not a "century."

Much of the polemic of the nineteenth-century writers had its roots in feminism, which surfaced as a political movement in France with the publication of *The Petition of the Women of the Third Estate to the King* (1789) and was quickly defended by Condorcet, who pointed out the absurdity of males crying out for equality, yet ignoring these same cries when they issued from the mouths of females. The first feminist manifesto, *Declaration of the Rights of Women*, published by Olympe des Gouges (Marie Gouze) in 1791, called for total equality between the genders ("Woman is born free and her rights are the same as those of men"), education for women, and the abolition of "the trade in women." Traditional marriage ("the tomb of trust and love") was to be replaced with a liberated marriage in which property was owned in common for the duration of the marriage, and in which bastards had full rights if acknowledged by either parent. (In nineteenth-century French law both legitimacy and property were entirely in the province of the male.)

By 1793 the political climate of France changed, causing, among other things, a strong political reaction against feminism. Olympe des Gouges was guillotined and the nascent feminist organizations withered. The ideals of feminism migrated across the channel, to be articulated and developed by Mary Wollstonecraft (and later disseminated by her daughter, Mary Shelley). By the mid-nineteenth century feminism returned to France to be espoused by Charles Fourier, Saint-Simon, and other socialists. It was embraced by Karl Marx and Friedrich Engels and accepted by all communist parties after the Second International.[15] The first self-conscious purely feminist political movement was organized in 1848 when 250 women met at Seneca Falls, New York, to found the American Women's Rights Movement. (Interestingly, most of the women were abolitionists — the impetus for the meeting was the exclusion of Lucretia Mott and Elizabeth Cady Stanton from the proceedings of the 1840 World Anti-Slavery Convention, in London.)

Although feminist arguments changed somewhat in the years between Des Gouges and John Stuart Mill, the basic position remained the same—equality of gender roles through equal education; equal property rights; equal rights in marriage; and above all, absolute legal equality. Legal equality was stressed not because it was more significant but because it seemed to be the prerequisite of everything else. As Mill put this, his central point, in *On the Subjection of Women,* "the principle which regulates the existing relations between the two sexes—the legal subordination of one sex to the other—is wrong in itself, and now one of the chief hindrances to human improvement; and . . . it ought to be replaced by a principle of perfect equality, admitting to no power or privilege on the one side, nor disability on the other."[16]

Revolutions and counterrevolutions go hand in glove, and, not surprisingly, a counterrevolutionary antifeminism quickly developed. For the most part the ideology of the counterrevolution can be described as either traditional or libertine. Perhaps the most powerful antifeminist essay ever published in the traditionalist vein was penned by Johann Gottlieb Fichte as an appendix to his *The Science of Right,* under the title "Fundamental Principles of the Rights of the Family" (1795). In the "Principles" he attempts to deal with the questions posed by the various feminist manifestos of the 1770s: "Has woman the same rights in the state which man has?" Noting that the answer to this question was "never a more urgent problem than in our days," he argues that since both males and females are equally endowed with freedom and reason, the genders do indeed have equal rights. Their apparent inequality arises because it is questionable "how far the female sex *can desire* to exercise these rights."

Fichte's doubts derive from a theory of the nature of males and females that has its roots in Aristotelean biology. In the *Generation of Animals*[17] Aristotle argued that the female is a passive receptacle in procreation, while the male is the active generative principle. Fichte not only accepted this view of procreation but endowed it with a special significance, since he also held (on independent grounds) that (1) "the individual is permanent only as a tendency to form the species"[18] and that (2) an individual is essentially a rational, self-realizing, active agent.[19] If proposition 1 is true, then, Fichte thought, it is also true (1 a) that since individuals can give form to species only as a couple, complete individuals can exist only in a coupled relationship of the two sexes (for example, a married couple); and (1 b) that since the natural role of individuals (both complete and incomplete) is to form a species, the nature of each is determined by its sexual role. Since Fichte accepted the Aristotelean view that the female sexual role is essentially passive and since (by proposition 1 a) in order to complete themselves females (and males) will couple (or marry), it follows (by proposition 1 b) that females will be led through their coupling to an essentially passive role. But passivity is irrational and suicidal for rational agents, since (by proposition 2) rationality is essentially active. Thus, the female sexual role appears to be self-annihilating.

> The character of reason is absolute self-activity; pure passivity for the sake of passivity contradicts reason, and utterly cancels it. Hence, it is not against reason that the one sex should propose to itself the satisfaction of its sexual impulse as an end in itself, since it can be satisfied through activity; but it is absolutely against reason that the other sex should propose to itself the satisfaction of its sexual impulse as an end, because in that case it would make a pure passivity its end. Hence, the female sex is either not rational even in its tendencies, which contradicts our presupposition that all men should be rational, or this tendency can not be developed in that sex in consequence of its peculiar nature, which is a self-contradiction, since it assumes a tendency in nature which nature does not accept; or, finally, that sex can never propose to itself the satisfaction of its sexual impulse as its end. Such an end and rationality utterly cancel each other in that sex.
>
> Nevertheless, the sexual impulse of this female sex, as well as its manifestation and satisfaction, are part of the plan of nature. Hence it is necessary that the sexual impulse should manifest itself in woman under another form; and, in order to be conformable to reason, it must appear as an impulse to activity; and as a characteristic impulse of nature, it must appear as an activity exclusively appertaining to the female sex.[20]

How does the sexual impulse appear to women? Or, given proposition 1 b, what is Fichte's view of the nature of the female gender?

> Woman can not confess to herself that she gives herself up—and since, in a rational being, everything is only in so far as it arises in consciousness— woman can not give herself up to the sexual impulse merely to satisfy her own impulse. But since she can give herself up only in obedience to an impulse, this impulse must assume in woman the character of an impulse to satisfy the man. Woman becomes, in this act, the means for the end of another, because she can not be her own end without renouncing her ulti-

mate end—the dignity of reason! This dignity she maintains, although she becomes means, because she voluntarily makes herself means in virtue of a noble natural impulse—*love*!

Love, therefore, is the form in which the sexual impulse appears to woman. But love is, to sacrifice one's self for the sake of another not in consequence of a reasoning, but in consequence of a feeling. Mere sexual impulse should never be called love; to do so is a vulgar abuse of language, calculated to cause all that is noble in human nature to be forgotten. In fact, my opinion is that nothing should be called love but what we have just now described. Man *originally* does not feel love, but sexual impulse; and love in man is not an original, but a *communicated, derived* impulse, namely, an impulse developed through connection with a loving woman; and has, moreover, quite a different form in man to what it has in woman. Love, the noblest of all natural impulses, is unborn only in woman; and only through woman does it, like many other social impulses, become the common property of mankind. The sexual impulse received this moral form of love in woman, because in its original form it would have canceled all morality in woman. Love is the closest point of union of nature and reason; it is the only link wherein nature connects with reason, and hence it is the most excellent of all that is natural. The Moral Law requires that man should forget himself in the other; but love even sacrifices itself to the other.

Let me state it concisely: In an uncorrupted woman the sexual impulse does not manifest itself at all, but only love; and this love is the natural impulse of a woman to satisfy a man. It is certainly an impulse which urgently requires to be satisfied, but its being thus satisfied is not the satisfaction of the woman. On the contrary, it is the satisfaction of the man, and for woman it is only the satisfaction of her heart. Her only requirement is to love and to be loved. Only thus does the impulse which the woman feels to sacrifice receive that character of freedom and activity which it must have in order to be rational. Perhaps there does not exist a man who does not feel the absurdity to turn this around and to assume in man a similar impulse to satisfy a need of woman; a need, in fact, which he can neither presuppose in woman nor consider himself as its tool without feeling himself disgraced to the innermost depths of his soul.

Hence, also, woman in the sexual union is not in every sense means for the object of the man. She is means for her own end, to satisfy her heart; and she is means for the end of the man only in so far as physical satisfaction is concerned.[21]

Although Fichte does not accept the Kantian view that sexual intercourse is mutual masturbation, his asymmetrical analysis reveals intercourse to be problematic, not only because the female is used by the male merely as a means, but also because to be so used she must reject rationality. On a superficial level Fichte's solution to the problem of the immoral nature of sexual intercourse is similar to Kant's: for both philosophers the moral salvation of copulation is achieved by the marital union of a dominant rational male and a sensitive loving female. Yet, though the rather conventional outward forms of their solutions are identical, the substance is radically different. For Kant, marital union makes moral the essentially manipulative (and hence inherently immoral) nature of intercourse because the very fact of union dissolves the possibility of manipulation. One person can use another only if there is both a one and an other, a user and a used. But if a fusion of the one and the other truly exists, if there is but one entity and hence neither user nor used, then the very possibility of using an *other* as a means no longer exists. Thus Kant's resolution of the dilemma turns on the cataclysmic power of love to transform a coupling into a unity called a couple.

For Fichte, on the other hand, a marital union is very much a *duo*. As such, it does not eliminate the possibility of manipulation but rather provides the opportunity for reciprocal manipulation—a quid pro quo whereby each partner uses the other. The female accepts her status as a sex object in return for the male's acquiescence in his role as a love object. The function of union is to allow each to use the other for his or her own ends. Presumably this reciprocity will ensure the morality of the exchange. (Of course, this exchange would be just only if the role of love object was as desirable—or as undesirable—as that of sex object; the point of much feminist literature is that while it is not altogether unattractive to be a love object, the status of sex object is quite repellent.)

The modern reader might be tempted to dismiss Fichte as obscure, antiquated, and, hence, uninteresting. But however dated the form of his analysis may be, the substance is both contemporary and radical. For Fichte argues that women are intrinsically the equal of men and that the female gender role (feminity) is essentially antihuman. So far, his analysis is consistent with radical feminism. Like the radical feminist, he sees the situation as one in which a woman must sacrifice her femininity to her humanity or her humanity to her femininity. He opted for the latter alternative because he held the not uncommon view that the interests of the species override those of its members; hence given the species' compelling interest in preserving itself, procreation demands the sacrifice of women's humanity to their femininity. Interestingly, as radical feminists have been quick to point out, revolutionary biological innovations such as cloning, parthenogenesis, and artificial placentas are on the verge of rendering obsolete the species' interest in womankind's acquiescence in femininity. Moreover, the most radical feminists concur with Fichte's view that "man does not originally feel love, but only sexual impulse," agree with him in rejecting the female sexual role as antihuman, and hence view the nascent biological revolution as heralding a post-sexual or, perhaps, lesbian or homosexual society. Thus, had the biology of one hundred years ago been more advanced, Fichte might have been remembered as the (perhaps inadvertent) grandfather of radical feminism rather than as the godfather of male chauvinism.

Yet another ironic aspect of Fichte's work is that while he was the first philosopher to establish a cogent justification for exclusive monogamous marriage without parenting, the structure of his argumentation is basically the same as that used by Fourier to justify sexual communes and by Robert Rimmer and Nena and George O'Neill to justify open marriage (a "marriage" between cohabiting sexual partners who may share parenting but who deny any commitment to sexual exclusivity on the part of either partner). That is, Fichte was the first to advance the argument that the value of marriage is inherent in the relationship itself, and not merely, as the tradition held, a function of procreative responsibility.[22] For Fichte, as for Fourier, Rimmer, and Nena and George O'Neill, the value of marriage lay in the fact that only through marriage could one become a whole person, a full human being capable of both love and reason.

> Philosophers have hitherto considered it necessary to assign some end to marriage, and have specified that end variously. But marriage has no other end than itself; it is its own end. The marriage relation is the true mode of existence of grown persons of both sexes, required even by nature. In this relation all man's faculties develop; but out of it many, and among them the most remarkable faculties of man, remain uncultivated. Precisely as the whole existence of man has no relation to any sensuous end, so neither has its necessary mode, marriage.
>
> Marriage is a union between *two* persons—*one* man and *one* woman. A woman who has given herself up to one, can not give herself up to a second, for her whole dignity requires that she should belong only to this one. Again, a man who has to observe the slightest wish of one woman can not conform to the contradictory wishes of many. Polygamy presupposes that women are not rational beings like men, but merely willess and lawless means to gratify man. Such is, indeed, the doctrine of the religious legislation which tolerates polygamy. This religion has—probably without being clearly conscious of the grounds—drawn onesided conclusions from the destination of woman to remain passive.[23]

As we pointed out earlier, Fichte's writings on sexual philosophy were basically addressed to the question of the political rights of women. And here again he develops the classic male-chauvinist position.

> As a rule, woman is either a maid or married. If a maid, she is still under the care of her father, precisely as the unmarried young man. Herein both sexes are perfectly equal. Both become free by marriage, and in regard to their marriage both are equally free; . . .
>
> If she is *married*, her whole dignity depends upon her being completely subjected, and seeming to be so subjected, to her husband. Let it be well observed, what my whole theory expresses, but what it is perhaps necessary to repeat once more emphatically—woman is not subjected to her husband in such a manner as to give him a *right of compulsion* over her; she is subjected through her own continuous necessary wish—a wish which is the condition of her morality—to be so subjected. She has the *power* to withdraw her freedom, if she could have the *will* to do so; but that is the very point: she can not rationally will to be free. Her relation to her husband being publicly known, she must, moreover, will to appear to all whom she knows as utterly subjected to, and utterly lost in, the man of her choice.
>
> Her husband is, therefore, the administrator of all her rights in consequence of her own necessary will; and she wishes those rights asserted and exercised only in so far as *he* wishes it. He is her natural representative in the state and in the whole society. This is her *public* relation to society. She can not even allow herself to think for a moment that she should exercise herself her rights in the state.
>
> So far as her *private* and *internal* relation in the house is concerned, *the tenderness of the husband necessarily restores to her all and more than she has lost*. The husband will not relinquish her rights, because they are his own; and because, if he did so, he would dishonor himself and his wife before society. The wife has also rights in public affairs, for she is a citizen. I consider it the duty of the husband—in states which give to the citizen a vote on public matters—not to vote without having discussed the subject with his wife, and allowed her to modify his opinion through her own. His vote will then be the result of their common will. The father of a family, who represents not only his own but also the interests of his wife and children, ought indeed to have a greater influence and a more decisive vote in a commonwealth, than the citizen who represents only his own interests. The manner of arranging this is a problem for the science of politics.
>
> Women, therefore, do really exercise the right of suffrage—not immediately, however, in their own person, because they can not wish to do so without lowering their dignity, but—through the influence which results from the nature of the marriage relation.[24]

Nineteenth-century antifeminism exhibited itself in the works of philosophical libertines as well as in the writings of traditionalists. The Magna Carta of libertinism is *Justine*, by the Marquis de Sade, a work that contains the defining theme of the libertine tradition—the view that in sexual matters the natural determines the moral, with a correlative rejection of social restraints on coition and sexuality. In the words of its greatest exponent, libertinism calls upon one to "break those bonds" of social constraint: "nature wills it; for a bridle have nothing but your inclinations, for laws your desires, for morality Nature's alone. . . ." Libertinism per se need not be antifeminist. Godwin's variety is certainly profeminist (see *Social Justice*, 1793), and even de Sade's version has notable profeminist elements, for example, the call for houses intended for women's libertinage and the advocacy of state institutions to relieve women of the labors of parenting. Nonetheless, it is reasonably clear that for de Sade nature dictates a somewhat lesser role for females than for males.

> It is certain, in a state of Nature, that women are born *vulguivaguous*, that is to say, are born enjoying the advantages of other female animals and belonging, like them and without exception, to all males; such were, without any doubt, both the primary laws of Nature and the only institutions of those earliest societies into which men gathered. *Self-interest, egoism,* and *love* degraded these primitive attitudes. . . .
>
> Never may an act of possession be exercised upon a free being; the exclusive possession of a woman is no less unjust than the possession of slaves; all men are born free, all have equal rights: never should we lose sight of those principles; according to which never may there be granted to one sex the legitimate right to lay monopolizing hands upon the other, and never may one of these sexes, or classes, arbitrarily possess the other. Similarly, a woman existing in the purity of Nature's laws cannot allege, as justification for refusing herself to someone who desires her, the love she bears another, because such a response is based upon exclusion, and no man may be excluded from the having of a woman as of the moment it is clear she definitely belongs to all men. The act of possession can only be exercised upon a chattel or an animal, never upon an individual who resembles us, and all the ties which can bind a woman to a man are quite as unjust as illusory.
>
> If then it becomes incontestable that we have received from Nature the right indiscriminately to express our wishes to all women, it likewise becomes incontestable that we have the right to compel their submission, not exclusively, for I should then be contradicting myself, but temporarily. It cannot be denied that we have the right to decree laws that compel woman to yield to the flames of him who would have her; violence itself being one of that right's effects, we can employ it lawfully. Indeed! has Nature not proven that we have that right, by bestowing upon us the strength needed to bend women to our will? [25]

The later nineteenth-century philosophical libertines tended to accept de Sade's view that nature dictates the bending of the female to the will of the male, without conceding that justice mandated some profeminist revisions of the status quo. Perhaps the purest example of libertine antifeminism is Schopenhauer's essay *On Women*, which was written after, and in partial reaction to, the feminist aspects of the libertarian revolutionary movements of 1848. This essay differs markedly from his treatise of 1844. Whereas *The Metaphysics of Sexual Love* was a traditionalist defense of a monogamous union of a rational, dominant male with a sensitive, loving, submissive female, the later work bears all the earmarks of libertinism—the assimilation of the natural to the proper and the concomitant call for the revision of "unnatural" norms. In addition it is informed by a bitter misogyny and takes the radical libertine stance of rejecting monogamy as an unnatural perversion. For nature, he argues, has determined that the female is merely a mechanism by which *man*kind reproduces himself; since monogamy limits man's ability to reproduce himself, it must be replaced by polygamy.

It is only the man whose intellect is clouded by his sexual impulses that could give the name of *the fair sex* to that undersized, narrow-shouldered, broad-hipped, and short-legged race; for the whole beauty of the sex is bound up with this impulse. Instead of calling them beautiful, there would be more warrant for describing women as the unaesthetic sex. . . .

And since women exist in the main solely for the propagation of the species, and are not destined for anything else, they live, as a rule, more for the species than for the individual. . . .

They form the *sexus sequior*—the second sex, inferior in every respect to the first; their infirmities should be treated with consideration; but to show them great reverence is extremely ridiculous, and lowers us in their eyes. When Nature made two divisions of the human race, she did not draw the line exactly through the middle. These divisions are polar and opposed to each other, it is true; but the difference between them is not qualitative merely, it is also quantitative.

This is just the view which the ancients took of a woman, and the view which people in the East take now; and their judgment as to her proper position is much more correct than ours, with our old French notions of gallantry and our preposterous system of reverence—that highest product of Teutonico-Christian stupidity.

The laws of marriage prevailing in Europe consider the woman as the equivalent of the man—start, that is to say, from a wrong position. In our part of the world where monogamy is the rule, to marry means to halve one's rights and double one's duties. Now, when the laws gave woman equal rights with man, they ought also to have endowed her with a masculine intellect. But the fact is that just in proportion as the honors and privileges which the laws accord to women, exceed the amount which nature gives, is there a diminution in the number of women who really participate in these privileges; and all the remainder are deprived of their natural rights by just so much as is given to the others over and above their share. For the institution of monogamy, and the laws of marriage which it entails, bestow upon the woman an unnatural position of privilege, by considering her throughout as the full equivalent of the man, which is by no means the case; and seeing this, men who are shrewd and prudent very often scruple to make so great a sacrifice and to acquiesce in so unfair an arrangement.

Consequently, whilst among polygamous nations every woman is provided for, where monogamy prevails the number of married women is limited; and there remains over a large number of women without stay or support, who, in the upper classes, vegetate as useless old maids, and in the lower succumb to hard work for which they are not suited; or else become *filles de joie*, whose life is as destitute of joy as it is of honor. But under the circumstances they become a necessity; and their position is openly recognized as serving the special end of warding off temptation from those women favored by fate, who have found, or may hope to find, husbands. In London alone there are eighty thousand prostitutes. What are they but the women, who, under the institution of monogamy have come off worse? Theirs is a dreadful fate: they are human sacrifices offered up on the altar of monogamy. The women whose wretched position is here described are the inevitable set-off to the European lady with her arrogance and pretension. Polygamy is therefore a real benefit to the female sex if it is taken as a whole. And, from another point of view, there is no true reason why a man whose wife suffers from chronic illness, or remains barren, or has gradually become too old for him, should not take a second. The motives which induce so many people to become converts to Mormonism appear to be just those which militate against the unnatural institution of monogamy.[26]

In Schopenhauer's work there is a devolution of the status of woman from the deceived but sublime ladies of *The Metaphysics of Sexual Love* to the basically supine in *On Women,* while the evolution of his conception of the male role is ever upward. In the works of the third libertine we shall consider, Friedrich Nietzsche, the subsidiary procreative role of women is a constant. The themes of libertinism abound in Nietzsche's works. Nature, albeit a nature much tempered by the "evolutionary laws" of the survival of the fittest, determines morality, and traditions that are unnatural must be rejected. Thus, since nature determines that woman's sole role is the propagation of the species, any other activity by females is perverse: "When a woman has scholarly inclinations there is generally something wrong with her sexual nature; barrenness itself conduces to a certain virility of taste; man, if I may say so, is the barren animal."[27]

If women are naturally incapable of creative intellectual endeavor, and if as essentially herd creatures they threaten to mire males in herd mentality (and hence must be subdued), they are nonetheless capable of fulfilling their procreatve function in the service of evolution.

"Much hath Zarathustra spoken also to us women, but never spake he unto us concerning woman."

And I answered her: "Concerning woman, one should only talk unto men."

"Talk also unto me of woman," said she; "I am old enough to forget it presently."

And I obliged the old woman and spake thus unto her:

Everything in woman is a riddle, and everything in woman hath one solution—it is called pregnancy.

Man is for woman a means: the purpose is always the child. But what is a woman for man?

Two different things wanteth the true man: danger and diversion. Therefore wanteth he woman, as the most dangerous plaything.

Man shall be trained for war, and woman for the recreation of the warrior; all else is folly.

Too sweet fruits—these the warrior liketh not. Therefore liketh he woman;—bitter is even the sweetest woman.

Better than man doth woman understand children, but man is more childish than woman.

In the true man there is a child hidden: it wanteth to play. Up then, ye women, and discover the child in man!

A plaything let woman be, pure and fine like the precious stone, illumined with the virtues of a world not yet come.

Let the beam of a star shine in your love! Let your hope say: "May I bear the Superman."[28] . . .

Not only onward shalt thou propagate thyself, but upward! For that purpose may the garden of marriage help thee!

A higher body shalt thou create, a first movement, a spontaneously rolling wheel—a creating one shalt thou create.

Marriage: so call I the will of the twain to create the one that is more than those who created it. The reverence for one another, as those exercising such a will, call I marriage.

Let this be the significance and the truth of thy marriage. But that which the many-too-many call marriage, those superfluous ones—ah, what shall I call it?

Ah, the poverty of soul in the twain! Ah, the faith of soul in the twain! Ah, the pitiable self-complacency in the twain!

Marriage they call it all; and they say their marriages are made in heaven.

Well, I do not like it, that heaven of the superfluous! No, I do not like them, those animals tangled in the heavenly toils!

Far from me also be the God who limpeth thither to bless what he hath not matched!

Laugh not at such marriages! What child hath not had reason to weep over its parents? ...

"Lo! now hath the world become perfect!"—thus thinketh every woman when she obeyeth with all her love.

Obey, must the woman, and find a depth for her surface. Surface is woman's soul, a mobile, stormy film on shallow water.

"Man's soul, however, is deep, its current gusheth in subterranean caverns: woman surmiseth its force, but comprehendeth it not.—

Then answered me the old woman: "Many fine things hath Zarathustra said, especially for those who are young enough for them.

Strange! Zarathustra knoweth little about woman, and yet he is right about them! Doth this happen, because with women nothing is impossible?

And now accept a little truth by way of thanks! I am old enough for it!

Swaddle it up and hold its mouth: otherwise it will scream too loudly, the little truth."

"Give me, woman, thy little truth!" said I. And thus spake the old woman:

"Thou goest to women? Do not forget thy whip!"—
Thus spake Zarathustra.[29]

Nietzsche finished speaking in 1888 but actually died in 1900. Twentieth-century sexual philosophy opens with, and is almost immediately dominated by, Bertrand Russell—whose syncretic blend of feminism, libertinism, and traditionalism (best expounded in *Marriage and Morals*) constitutes virtually the entire philosophical literature on the subject until Jean-Paul Sartre's analysis in *Being and Nothingness* (1943; chapter three, section two). Aside from the works of Russell and Sartre, the only other major contributions were Ortega y Gasset's *On Love* (1939), Simon de Beauvoir's *The Second Sex* (1949), and the chapter on "The Body in Its Sexual Being" in Merleau-Ponty's *The Phenomenology of Perception* (1945). The views of these philosophers are too contemporary, too significant—and, above all, too interrelated with the essays we have anthologized —to receive the sort of summary historical treatment accorded to the works we have hitherto discussed. Unfortunately, to present their work in an appropriate manner would expand this introduction to such an extent that it would crowd out some of the works we would like to include. We believe that the least unsatisfactory resolution of this dilemma is to refrain from commenting on pre-1968 modern work on sexual philosophy and to refer interested readers to D. P. Verene's *Sexual Love and Western Morality*,[30] which contains a fine selection of and introduction to this literature.

Why do we speak of *pre-1968* literature? To appreciate the significance of the date it is important to take cognizance of the fact that of the major twentieth-century philosophers not previously mentioned—Austin, Carnap, Heidegger, Husserl, James, Peirce, Whitehead, and Wittgenstein —not one wrote on sexual philosophy. *The Encyclopedia of Philosophy* (published in 1967) has no entries under "adultery," "contraception," "engagement," "marriage," "femininism," "libertinism," "monogamy," "perversion," "procreation," "sex," or "women." *The Philosopher's Index* indicates that no articles were published on these topics in 1967. Yet in the very next year articles began to appear in philosophical journals— hence the significance of the date. But why did this begin to happen in 1968?

One hypothesis is that if the time lag between inspiration and publication is taken into account, the two primary causes were the newly emergent feminist movement, which dates from the foundation of NOW in 1965, and the almost simultaneous rebirth of libertinism in the countercultural revolution of the late sixties (for example, the "Hippie" movement). In this the genesis of the newly renascent literature on sexual philosophy seems to follow the precedent of its nineteenth-century forbears, although they are unlike most of their nineteenth-century predecessors in their inclination to be favorable toward the feminist movement. Also, two new factors that influence the literature are gay liberation and the ecology movement.

This new literature is not only a response to changing social conditions but to a new philosophical climate as well. By 1968 the "linguistic turn" had been executed and logical positivism had spent itself, leaving Anglo-American philosophers receptive to refocusing philosophical inquiry. By contrast, the existential-phenomenological tradition of Husserl, Heidegger, Sartre, Merleau-Ponty, Marcel, Ricoeur, and Ortega had retained its preoccupation with man's concrete existence. The translations of their works into English, which began to appear in the late fifties and early sixties, increasingly challenged the "analytic" tradition to address itself to mundane realities such as sex. This challenge was taken up explicitly by Thomas Nagel in his pioneering essay of 1969 "Sexual Perversion," and others have since joined the discussion.

In the present volume we have attempted to bring together essays that reflect the most significant aspects of the post-1968 literature. We have acted in the belief that sex, gender, and parenting are too significant to be the exclusive domain of the poets and too important to be left to the pragmatics of revolutionary politics. For the sexual revolution is in our midst, and philosophers have only belatedly begun to contemplate it.

NOTES

1. Plato, *Symposium,* trans. Percy Shelley (New York: Peter Pauper Press, 1967), pp. 64-65, Steph. 211-12.
2. Epictetus, *The Discourse and Manual,* trans. P. E. Matheson, (Oxford: Clarendon Press, 1916), Book 2, chap. 18, pp. 208-09.
3. Genesis 8:17.
4. Cf. Genesis 3:16.
5. Cf. Janice Moulton, "Sex and Reference," herein, pp. 34-44.
6. Thomas Aquinas, *On the Truth of the Catholic Faith,* Book 3: Providence, pt. 1, trans. Vernon J. Bourke (New York: Doubleday, 1956).
7. David Hume, *Essays Moral, Political and Literary,* vol. 1, ed. T. H. Green and T. H. Grose (London: Longmans, Green, 1875), pp. 231-39.
8. Immanuel Kant, *Observations on the Feeling of the Beautiful and the Sublime,* trans. John T. Goldthwait (Berkeley and Los Angeles: University of California Press, 1960). All quotes are from section three.
9. Immanuel Kant, *Lectures on Ethics,* trans. Louis Infield (London: Methuen and Co., Ltd., 1930), pp. 162-71.
10. Arthur Schopenhauer, "Metaphysics of the Love and the Sexes," in Edman, *The Philosophy of Schopenhauer* (New York: Random House, Modern Library), p. 334.
11. Oxford, 1893.
12. In Edman, *The Philosophy of Schopenhauer,* pp. 342-43.
13. Ibid., pp. 349-50.
14. Ibid., pp. 373-74.
15. For an exposition of the views of Fourier and Marx see David Palmer, "The Consolation of the Wedded," herein, pp. 178-89.
16. John Stuart Mill, "The Subjection of Women" (1869), reprinted in *Three Essays by J. S. Mill* (London: Oxford University Press, World Classics Series, 1966), p. 427.
17. Book 1, chaps. 20-23.
18. *The Science of Rights* (Philadelphia: Lippincott, 1869), chap. 1, sec. 1.
19. This is the argument of Book 1 of *The Science of Rights* (Philadelphia: Lippincott, 1869).
20. Fichte, *The Science of Rights,* p. 394.
21. Ibid., sec. 4, pp. 398-401.
22. Cf. Thomas' propositions 3-5.
23. Fichte, *The Science of Rights,* pp. 406-07.
24. Ibid., pp. 440-42.
25. Marquis de Sade, *The Complete Justine* (New York: Grove Press, 1965), p. 318.

26. *Essays on Women* (New York: Simon & Schuster, Philosophers Library, 1928), pp. 450-55.

27. "Beyond Good and Evil," sec. 144 in *The Philosophy of Nietzsche* (New York: Random House, Modern Library, 1970), pp. 465-66.

28. "Child and Marriage," chap. 28 of "Thus Spake Zarathustra," trans. Thomas Common, in ibid., pp. 72-73.

29. "Old and Young Women," chap. 18 of "Thus Spake Zarathustra," in ibid., pp. 68-69.

30. New York: Harper & Row, 1972.

THE SEMANTICS OF SEX

Barbara Lawrence

Four-Letter Words Can Hurt You

Why should any words be called obscene? Don't they all describe natural human functions? Am I trying to tell them, my students demand, that the "strong, earthy, gut-honest"—or, if they are fans of Norman Mailer, the "rich, liberating, existential"—language they use to describe sexual activity isn't preferable to "phony-sounding, middle-class words like 'intercourse' and 'copulate'"? "Cop You Late!" they say with fancy inflections and gagging grimaces. "Now, what is *that* supposed to mean?"

Well, what is it supposed to mean? And why indeed should one group of words describing human functions and human organs be acceptable in ordinary conversation and another, describing presumably the same organs and functions, be tabooed—so much so, in fact, that some of these

This article is reprinted from the *New York Times*, October 27, 1973 (© 1973 by the New York Times Company. Reprinted by permission.)

words still cannot appear in print in many parts of the English-speaking world?

The argument that these taboos exist only because of "sexual hang-ups" (middle-class, middle-age, feminist), or even that they are a result of class oppression (the contempt of the Norman conquerors for the language of their Anglo-Saxon serfs), ignores a much more likely explanation: the sources and functions of the words themselves.

The best known of the tabooed sexual verbs, for example, comes from the German *flicken*, meaning "to strike"; combined, according to Eric Partridge's etymological dictionary *Origins*, with the Latin sexual verb *futuere*; associated in turn with the Latin *fustis*, "a staff or cudgel"; the Celtic *buc*, "a point, hence to pierce"; the Irish *bot*, "the male member"; the Latin *battuere*, "to beat"; the Gaelic *batair*, "a cudgeller"; the Early Irish *bualaim*, "I strike"; and so forth. It is one of what etymologists sometimes call "the sadistic group of words for the man's part in copulation."

The brutality of this word, then, and its equivalents ("screw," "bang," and so forth) is not an illusion of the middle class or a crotchet of Women's Liberation. In their origins and imagery these words carry undeniably painful, if not sadistic, implications, the object of which is almost always female. Consider, for example, what a screw actually does to the wood it penetrates; what a painful, even mutilating, activity this kind of analogy suggests. "Screw" is particularly interesting in this context, since the noun, according to Partridge, comes from words meaning "groove," "nut," "ditch," "breeding sow," "scrofula," and "swelling," while the verb, besides its explicit imagery, has antecedent associations to "write on," "scratch," "scarify," and so forth—a revealing fusion of a mechanical or painful action with an obviously denigrated object.

Not all obscene words, of course, are as implicitly sadistic or denigrating to women as these, but all that I know seem to serve a similar purpose: to reduce the human organism (especially the female organism) and human functions (especially sexual and procreative) to their least organic, most mechanical dimension; to substitute a trivializing or deforming resemblance for the complex human reality of what is being described.

Tabooed male descriptives, when they are not openly denigrating to women, often serve to divorce a male organ or function from any significant interaction with the female. Take the word "testes," for example, suggesting "witnesses" (from the Latin *testis*) to the sexual and procreative strengths of the male organ; and the obscene counterpart of this word, which suggests little more than a mechanical shape. Or compare almost any of the "rich," "liberating" sexual verbs, so fashionable today among male writers, with that much-derided Latin word "copulate" ("to bind or join together"), or even to those two four-letter Anglo-Saxon words (which seem to have had no trouble surviving the Norman Conquest) "make love."

How arrogantly self-involved the tabooed words seem in comparison to either of the other terms, and how contemptuous of the female partner. Understandably so, of course, if she is only a "skirt," a "broad," a "chick," a "pussycat" or a "piece." If she is, in other words, no more than her skirt, or what her skirt conceals; no more than a breeder, or the broadest part of her; no more than a piece of a human being or a "piece of tail."

The most severely tabooed of all the female descriptives, incidentally, are those like "piece of tail," which suggest (either explicitly or through antecedents) that there is no significant difference between the female channel through which we are all conceived and born and the anal outlet common to both sexes—a distinction that pornographers have always enjoyed obscuring.

This effort to deny women their biological identity, their individuality, their humanness, is such an important aspect of obscene language that one can only marvel at how seldom, in an era preoccupied with definitions of obscenity, this fact is brought to our attention. One problem, of course, is that many of the people in the best position to do this (critics, teachers, writers) are so reluctant today to admit that they are angered or shocked by obscenity. Bored, maybe, unimpressed, aesthetically displeased, but— no matter how brutal or denigrating the material—never angered, never shocked.

And yet, how eloquently angered, how piously shocked many of these same people become if denigrating language is used about any minority group other than women; if the obscenities are racial or ethnic, that is, rather than sexual. Words like "coon," "kike," "spic," "wop," after all, deform identity, deny individuality and humanness in almost exactly the same way that sexual vulgarisms and obscenities do.

No one that I know, least of all my students, would fail to question the values of a society whose literature and entertainment rested heavily on racial or ethnic pejoratives. Are the values of a society whose literature and entertainment rest as heavily as ours on sexual pejoratives any less questionable?

Janice Moulton

Sex and Reference

I

In this essay I shall discuss the infrequency of female orgasms in sexual intercourse. I shall claim that concern about this infrequency embodies a confusion about the concept of sexual intercourse. The confusion is reflected in our language and in other widespread, although factually unsubstantiated, beliefs about sexual intercourse.[1]

Hardly anyone today denies that women are capable of orgasms, even as capable as men when sufficiently stimulated. Kinsey says: "In general females and males appear to be equally responsive to the whole range of physical stimuli which may initiate erotic reactions ... and the specific data show that the average female is no slower in response than the average male when she is sufficiently stimulated and when she is not inhibited in her activity."[2] The key words are "sufficiently stimulated." Although women have the same capacity for orgasm as men, they reach orgasm far less frequently during sexual intercourse.[3]

Invariably, suggestions for increasing the possibility of female orgasms focus on releasing inhibitions of the female, prolonging intercourse, or stimulating the female before intercourse. However, these methods often create new problems. Direct stimulation of the female before intercourse usually ceases when intercourse begins. If these procedures fail, the woman may be considered sexually inadequate, or the man sexually incompetent. Sexual activity, instead of being a source of pleasure and enjoyment, is treated as a complicated and difficult skill, something not to be enjoyed, but mastered. Often the female is advised to fake orgasm (men, the marriage manuals point out, obviously cannot fake it and so could never be under an obligation to try).[4] Faking relieves the obligations of the male but certainly does not solve the problems of the female. The old disparity between the frequency of male and female orgasms remains, to which the need for deception has been added.

In spite of this disparity, many people who are interested in orgasm for the female still rely on sexual intercourse as the main or only method of interpersonal sexual stimulation.[5] The continued belief, despite the facts, that intercourse is the appropriate sexual activity to bring about the orgasms of both male and female involves a conceptual confusion. Sexual intercourse is an activity in which male arousal is a necessary condition, and male satisfaction, if not also a necessary condition, is the primary aim. Despite this, sexual intercourse is thought by many to be an activity that involves (or ought to) both male and female equally. But female arousal and satisfaction, although they may be concomitant events occasionally, are not even constituents of sexual intercourse.

II

Our language mirrors this confusion. Grammatically, polite expressions for sexual intercourse tend to be symmetric, giving the impression that what A does to B, B likewise does to A. Yet their definitions give a different picture. Although both male and female genitals are mentioned, the activity is characterized solely in terms of the *male* responses that constitute it.

Most expressions for sexual intercourse have the symmetry of other relations, like "shaking hands with," "being a sibling of" and "dancing with."[6] If a woman has sexual intercourse with a man, then it follows from the meaning of the terms that he has had sexual intercourse with her. If he has gone all the way with her, then, logically, she has gone all the way with him. Since so many of the expressions for intercourse exhibit this symmetry, one might be led to expect that he and she are equally involved in this activity. Thus, if a male orgasm is a primary aim and usual constituent of the activity, it would seem that a female orgasm should be an aim and constituent too.

The exceptions, the expressions for sexual intercourse that are not symmetric, are significant in that they are vulgar. If he fucked her, it does not follow that she has fucked him, but only that she has been fucked by him. The grammar of the word "fuck" does not imply that he and she are equally involved in the activity.[7]

Acceptable expressions for sexual intercourse are symmetric; unacceptable expressions usually are not. Thus the grammar reflects the expectation of many people that if sexual intercourse is considered a decent and nice thing to do, men and women are likely to find it equally satisfying; and if it is considered a vulgar, dirty experience, they will not. This contrast reinforces the idea that a man and a woman *should*, if they are decent and nice, find this activity equally pleasurable. The belief is further reinforced by the slang use of the vulgar expressions such as "fuck" and "screw" to mean take advantage of, deceive, and injure. Thus, the grammar of these expressions invites us to believe that sexual intercourse, if it does not involve deceit and injury, is an activity that pertains to both parties equally. Viewed as an activity in genetics, sexual intercourse does involve both parties equally. But as an activity for producing pleasure, it is not an equal-opportunity experience.

III

What purports to be a mutually pleasurable activity, what is politely expressed in terms of a symmetric relation, in fact results in far fewer orgasms for women than for men. The reasons for this become obvious when we consider the definitions of expressions for sexual intercourse.

For sexual subjects dictionaries are usually barren sources. However, *Webster's Third New International Dictionary of the English Language* gives a definition under "coitus," and refers one to this word for all synonymous expressions. Coitus is defined as "the act of conveying the male semen to the female reproductive tract involving insertion of the penis in the vaginal orifice followed by ejaculation."[8] If we look up "ejaculation" we find: "the sudden or spontaneous discharging of a fluid (as semen in orgasm) from a duct"; and for "orgasm": "the climax of sexual excitement typically occurring toward the end of coitus."

According to these definitions the male orgasm is a necessary condition for sexual intercourse (coitus). To many people the only necessary condition of sexual intercourse is penetration; *coitus interruptus* is still coitus. But male orgasm is such a regular and expected part of sexual intercourse that the *Webster's Third* definition is widely accepted. For example, the law, which defines rape in terms of penetration, requires the presence of semen in the vaginal tract as *evidence* of the penetration. (Of course, this is because the testimony of the victim is not considered sufficient. If the law thought victims of other crimes were as likely to be liars, it might require other evidence to substantiate the charge. Significantly, for this paper, although many people object to the way rape victims are treated by the law, to my knowledge no one has objected to the semen test on the grounds that male orgasm is not an invariable aspect of rape.)

Thus, although there are exceptions, sexual intercourse is widely accepted as a process that is brought to a conclusion by the male orgasm. Physiologically it is usually impossible to continue intercourse after male orgasm. Thus, any discussion of the female orgasm during sexual intercourse is actually a discussion of the female orgasm before or during the male orgasm. Once the male orgasm occurs, sexual intercourse ends. This puts an arbitrary restriction on the period during which the female orgasm may occur. In addition, sexual intercourse formally begins when the primary focus for sexual stimulation in the male (the penis) is inserted in a container particularly well suited to bring about the male orgasm (the vaginal orifice). Although the dictionary merely says that sexual intercourse "involves" this insertion, anything prior to this insertion is termed "foreplay" or "preliminaries"; the real thing does not begin until the insertion occurs.[9]

The important point to notice is that this activity, which is described by verbs that are logically symmetrical, is in fact *defined* exclusively in terms of *male* stimulation by contact with the female, leading to (or at least aiming at) *male* orgasm. Thus, discussions of the female orgasm during sexual intercourse amount to discussions of the female orgasm after the source of *male* stimulation is placed in its container and before or during the *male* orgasm. The female locus of stimulation and the female orgasm are not even part of the definition of sexual intercourse. From this view, one might wonder why anyone ever thought the female orgasm had anything to do with sexual intercourse, except as an occasional and accidental co-occurrence. Sometimes the telephone rings, too.

IV

Some claims about the nature of sexual behavior can be seen as attempts to explain the asymmetry between male and female orgasms. Ignoring the definition of sexual intercourse, they assume that sexual intercourse would ordinarily involve the mutual pleasure of both male and female, and blame the inadequacies of the participants when it does not.

The claim about vaginal orgasms says, in effect, that for sexual intercourse to be a mutually pleasurable activity, the anatomical source of female stimulation must be the container that stimulates the male, and if it is not, there is something wrong with the female. The claim does not deny that women have orgasms for which the clitoris is the anatomical source. But such orgasms, it is claimed, (1) are not very good and (2) indicate immaturity.[10] In childhood masturbation the anatomical source may be the clitoris, but in sexual intercourse it should become the vagina. Significantly, no analogous difference between the locus of stimulation in masturbation and intercourse is claimed for the male. Nor is it claimed that a male must mature to experience an intense orgasm during intercourse.

The claim about vaginal orgasms contradicts physiological evidence. All female orgasms share the same physiological characteristics: all may result in contractions of the vagina, but direct stimulation of the clitoral area produces more intense and rapid orgasms.[11]

It might be argued against this evidence that orgasm is not mainly a physiological, but a psychological, state. However, psychological (introspective) data are not allowed as falsifications by this claim for the superiority of vaginal orgasms. If a woman denies having orgasms produced by vaginal stimulation, her report can be discredited by the claim that she is fixated in childhood and does not experience a real orgasm because of her lack of sexual maturity. If a woman reports that vaginal orgasms are less intense than clitorally oriented ones, according to the claim, she does not know what a vaginal orgasm is. If it is less intense than a clitoral orgasm, it could not be a vaginal orgasm, which by definition is the more intense.

Psychologically the above claim is untestable; physiologically it is groundless. What purpose does this myth serve? It gives an account that hails sexual intercourse as a mutually pleasurable activity despite the facts against it. It also gives an explanation for this discordance with the facts: the female may still be more interested in the childish, self-centered sexual pleasures of masturbation and not mature enough to enjoy intercourse. The supposed symmetry of sexual intercourse presupposes this maturity; the facts are sometimes otherwise.

Another such claim is that in the best sexual experiences the male and female orgasms occur stimultaneously. There is little specific physiological evidence to support this. In fact there is a loss of perceptual awareness that accompanies orgasm.[12] Thus, with simultaneous orgasms, neither participant is very aware of what is happening to the other. Part of the reason for interpersonal sexual activity is to enjoy the pleasure given to the other person. But with simultaneous orgasms one is less able to appreciate the partner's experience because one is overwhelmed by one's own.

What rationale supports this widely believed claim about simultaneous orgasms?[13] Sexual intercourse is an event that regularly and expectedly culminates in the male orgasm. So if the female orgasm happened at the same time, then intercourse would have culminated in a female orgasm too. Simultaneous orgasms would provide the female's orgasm with the same status as the male's and would guarantee that sexual intercourse really had been a mutual activity. If people only did it right, sexual intercourse would merit the symmetry of its polite expressions.

V

Once it is recognized that sexual intercourse is an activity characterized in terms of male arousal and orgasm, for which female arousal and orgasm is irrelevant, the disparity between male and female orgasms in sexual intercourse should not be a problem. The disparity would be reduced if the standard sexual activity were a process characterized by the arousal and satisfaction of both sexes, rather than, as it is now, the process of sexual intercourse.[14] When sexual intercourse occurs, the male must be sexually aroused and regularly is orgasmic. If this activity included the same responses for the female, everything would be fine. But, as we know, it does not. The whole problem arises from trying to produce a female orgasm as a useful by-product of a process aimed at producing the male orgasm. And this attempt arises from the belief that the process will be, or should be, a mutually pleasurable activity involving both partners equally.

VI

One might object to blaming a conceptual confusion for the infrequency of female orgasms in sexual intercourse. It may be agreed that for most people sexual intercourse begins with stimulation of the male and ends with the male orgasm. But the objection would claim that this is the result of a male-oriented society. The contrast between grammar and definition may exist, but that too is the result of a male-oriented culture.

If the discrepancy in orgasm attainment were simply the result of male orientation, sexual intercourse could be represented as something to be initiated and carried out solely by the male for his own pleasure, with or without the use of the female. No one would be concerned about female orgasms at all.

It might be diplomatic to misrepresent sexual intercourse as a mutually pleasurable activity, a pretense that would help keep women in their place. One would not expect such deception to fool anyone acquainted with the facts. Yet many people (both male and female) believe that sexual activity should provide maximum satisfaction for both parties, recognize that women reach orgasm in intercourse far less often than men, and yet, thinking that sexual intercourse is a symmetric activity, continue to believe that it should provide the same sort of satisfaction for both sexes. If there were no conceptual confusion, then those who were only concerned with male satisfaction in sexual activity between males and females could restrict that activity to intercourse, while those concerned with female satisfaction as well would not be so restricted.

VII

Perhaps the nature of the confusion can be best brought out by an analogy. Let us imagine a culture in which the women prepared all the food and spoon-fed it to the men, but fed none to themselves. And suppose this feeding activity was described as if it were a mutual activity, that is, by expressions that indicated symmetric relations. This custom would be described by expressions such as "have feeding behavior with." Logically it would follow that if he had feeding behavior with her, then she had feeding behavior with him. Despite this symmetry and the universal and frequent practice of feeding behavior, a great many women in this culture suffered from malnutrition. Instead of changing or expanding the custom, so that women got a chance to eat too, the society attributed the malnutrition to biological differences. It was argued that women's bodies were not as able to be nourished as were men's. Malnutrition was considered a consequence of a sex-linked congenital defect. Experts claimed that women, unlike men, could not be satisfied with mere hunger-satiation anyway. Instead, the satisfaction women derived from feeding behavior was in the warmth and closeness of a meaningful relationship.

Educated women introduced variations of feeding behavior that included spoon-licking while cooking. This was called "foretaste." Men often encouraged it, although it was rarely continued when feeding behavior began. Other women relied on self-feeding to survive, but this was frowned on by the whole community as perverted, antisocial behavior. The influence of custom was so strong that few believed that women in the kitchen together might feed each other. It was commonly thought that women who fed each other did so only because they could not get men to feed. No one ever thought they did it to get food.

Gourmet cookbooks claimed that in truly gourmet feeding both male and female got nourished together. However, since only one spoon was used in feeding behavior, simultaneous nourishment was very unusual. Even when it was managed most of the food spilled and neither party got very much.

Nutrition manuals argued that since feeding behavior *should* be a mutual activity, the female *should* receive nourishment through the spoon that feeds the male, and if she did not there was something inadequate about her. The books did not deny that a female could be nourished through her mouth. But such nourishment, they claimed, (1) is not very satisfying and (2) indicates immaturity. In childhood self-feeding, the focus of feeding satisfaction may be the mouth, but in mature feeding behavior, it should become the spoon. Of course, the locus of nourishment in the male was not thought to be different in mature feeding behavior from that of childhood self-feeding.

In this imaginary culture the problem of how to provide nourishment for the female during feeding behavior is beset with the same conceptual difficulties as the problem in our culture of how to provide orgasm for the female during sexual intercourse. Attributing either problem to basic anatomic differences between men and women is absurd. It is not anatomic differences that account for female malnutrition in the feeding-behavior culture. The female is just not getting enough food. Note that a larger female would not get enough food just by getting the same amount of food as a smaller male. What counts as "enough" varies with the individual.

Similarly, it is not anatomical differences that account for lack of female orgasms during sexual intercourse. The female is just not getting enough stimulation.

VIII

It is often said that for women the sympathy and understanding expressed in sexual relations is more satisfying than an orgasm.[15] Many critics of physiological research claim that it ignores these psychological aspects of sexual behavior. Now of course these psychological aspects are important. They are the whole reason for engaging in interpersonal sexual activity rather than masturbation. But if a woman spends the time and energy to produce someone else's orgasm, with the understanding that she is participating in a mutual activity, it is only fair that her partner do the same for her. If she has to be satisfied with sympathy and understanding alone, then so should her partner.

IX

Sexual activities, as with most social behaviors, are stylized, deriving much of their immutability from the language that describes them. For each new generation of humans, lacking the instinctual control of other species, the "rediscovery" of sexual activity is greatly influenced by information carried by spoken and written language. There is a big difference between pointing out a conceptual confusion and its remedy and actually changing the behavior that the confusion helps maintain. To do the latter it is necessary to change the concept of the standard sexual activity to one that involves the arousal and satisfaction of all participants. That involves changing the romantic looks and smiles that now convey "I'm interested in sexual intercourse with you" so that they convey "I'm interested in our both having a satisfying sexual experience together."

NOTES

1. This essay does not question the sociological data of Kinsey or Masters and Johnson. Nor does it raise any epistemological questions concerning their data, since I assume that knowledge about the sexual pleasure of others is just as possible as knowledge about any other feelings. And I assume that women are just as able as men to know about their own feelings of sexual pleasure.

2. Alfred Kinsey et al., *Sexual Behavior in the Human Female* (Philadelphia: W. R. Saunders, 1953), p. 163.

3. According to Kinsey's research "something between 36 and 44 per cent of the females in the sample had responded to [experienced] orgasm in a part but not all of their coitus in marriage. About one-third of those females had responded only a small part of the time, and the other third had responded a major portion of the time, even though it was not a hundred per cent of the time . . ." (ibid., p. 375). That is, fewer than 14 percent managed to have orgasms a major portion of the time, while over 56 percent had never had an orgasm during coitus. Objections to Kinsey's statistics (cf. Abram Kardiner, *Sex and Morality* [London: Routledge & Kegan Paul, 1955], p. 73) claim that his percentages of female orgasms during intercourse are much too *high*, giving women expectations that could never be met. Yet men, with rare exceptions, experience orgasms in sexual intercourse every time, without special techniques or partner skill.

4. Eustace Chesser, *An Outline of Human Relationships* (London: William Heinemann, Ltd., 1959), p. 66: ". . . the misfortune of premature [preceeding the female's orgasm] ejaculation is extremely common. It cannot be too strongly emphasized that intercourse is more beset with difficulties for a man than a woman. A woman may take no pleasure in it for a variety of reasons, but if she cares deeply for her husband, she can pretend."

5. The popularity of David Rubin's book *Any Woman Can* [have an orgasm in intercourse] shows that (1) it is widely known that many women do not have orgasms, and (2) many people who are interested in orgasm for the female think of sexual intercourse as the appropriate sexual activity.

6. A selection of verbs and verb phrases for sexual intercourse from the *Dictionary of American Slang* and from *Webster's Third New International Dictionary* include the taboo: "screw," "lay," "fuck," and "ball"; the slang: "do it (with)," "make," "make it (with)," "go all the way," and "give it to"; more acceptable expressions: "mate," "copulate," "couple," "have sex," "engage in coitus," and "sleep with"; expressions for intercourse outside marriage: "fornicate," "commit adultery"; and expressions for intercourse on a regular basis: "have an affair," "shack up," "have a relationship."

7. It has even been claimed that it is ungrammatical for "fuck" to have a female subject (cf. Robert Baker, "'Pricks' and 'Chicks': A Plea for 'Persons,'" herein, pp. 45-64). However, the *Dictionary of American Slang* says about "lay": "As most taboo words, this is primarily used by, but not restricted to use by, males" (p. 313). My experience supports the latter source.

8. Even this definition is incorrect. If the male semen is deliberately prevented by a condom from entering the female reproductive tract, it would still be an act of

coitus. A more accurate definition might be: That act involving insertion of the penis in the vaginal orifice followed by ejaculation.

9. In the standard coital position sexual stimulation of the penis actually prevents similar stimulation of the primary area of sexual stimulation of the female. (William Masters and Virginia Johnson, *Human Sexual Response* [Boston: Little, Brown, and Co., 1966], p. 60).

10. Kardiner, p. 67; Noel Lamare, *Love and Fulfillment in Woman* (New York: Macmillan, 1957), p. 21; Sigmund Freud, "The Transformation of Puberty," in *The Basic Writings of Sigmund Freud*, trans. A. A. Brill (New York: Random House, 1938), pp. 613-14; and Freud, "Female Sexuality," in *Collected Papers*, vol. 5, ed. J. V. Strachey (London: Hogarth Press, 1953), p. 252.

11. Masters and Johnson, *Human Sexual Response*, pp. 59, 66-67.

12. Ibid., p. 135.

13. After orgasm the genital areas of both sexes may become oversensitive, so that continued stimulation is painful. Simultaneous orgasms would avoid this problem, but at the cost of delicate and difficult timing that often diminishes the intensity of the orgasm. More important, I suspect, is that the loss of awareness actually encourages the support for simultaneity, as it provides an ideal time for the faking recommended by the marriage manuals. The male is excused from not knowing and can ask "Did you?" when at any other time the answer would be obvious to him.

14. For some people this change might result in no variation of physical behavior. This is not a recommendation for any particular sort of physical behavior—let that be the province of physiologists—but a recommendation that the physical behavior engaged in, whatever it is, fit (or try to) this description: a process that involves the arousal and satisfaction of all participants equally.

15. Eustace Chesser, *Is Chastity Outmoded?* (London: William Heinemann, Ltd., 1960), p. 88.

Robert Baker

"Pricks" and "Chicks":
A Plea for "Persons"

There is a school of philosophers who believe that one starts philosophizing not by examining whatever it is one is philosophizing about but by examining the words we use to designate the subject to be examined. I must confess my allegiance to this school. The import of my confession is that this is an essay on women's liberation.

There seems to be a curious malady that affects those philosophers who in order to analyze anything must examine the way we talk about it; they seem incapable of talking about anything without talking about their talk about it—and, once again, I must confess to being typical. Thus I shall argue, first, that the way in which we identify something reflects our conception of it; second, that the conception of women embedded in our language is male chauvinistic; third, that the conceptual revisions proposed by the feminist movement are confused; and finally, that at the root of the problem are both our conception of sex and the very structure of sexual identification.

IDENTIFICATION AND CONCEPTION

I am not going to defend the position that the terms we utilize to identify something reflect our conception of it; I shall simply explain and illustrate a simplified version of this thesis. Let us assume that any term that can be (meaningfully) substituted for x in the following statements is a term used to identify something: "Where is the x?" "Who is the x?" Some of the terms that can be substituted for x in the above expressions are metaphors; I shall refer to such metaphors as metaphorical identifications. For example, southerners frequently say such things as "Where did that girl get to?" and "Who is the new boy that Lou hired to help out at the filling station?" If the persons the terms apply to are adult Afro-Americans, then "girl" and "boy" are metaphorical identifications. The fact that the metaphorical identifications in question are standard in the language reflects the fact that certain characteristics of the objects properly classified as boys and girls (for example, immaturity, inability to take care of themselves, need for guidance) are generally held by those who use identifications to be properly attributable to Afro-Americans. One might say that the whole theory of southern white paternalism is implicit in the metaphorical identification "boy" (just as the rejection of paternalism is implicit in the standardized Afro-American forms of address, "man" and "woman," as in, for example, "Hey, man, how are you?").

Most of what I am going to say in this essay is significant only if the way we metaphorically identify something is not a superficial bit of conceptually irrelevant happenstance but rather a reflection of our conceptual structure. Thus if one is to accept my analysis he must understand the significance of metaphorical identifications. He must see that, even though the southerner who identifies adult Afro-American males as "boys" feels that this identification is "just the way people talk"; but for a group to talk that way it must think that way. In the next few paragraphs I shall adduce what I hope is a persuasive example of how, in one clear case, the change in the way we identified something reflected a change in the way we thought about it.

Until the 1960s, Afro-Americans were identified by such terms as "Negro" and "colored" (the respectable terms) and by the more disreputable "nigger," "spook," "kink," and so on. Recently there has been an unsuccessful attempt to replace the respectable identifications with such terms as "African," and "Afro-American," and a more successful attempt to replace them with "black." The most outspoken champions of this linguistic reform were those who argued that nonviolence must be abandoned for Black Power (Stokely Carmichael, H. Rap Brown), that integration must be abandoned in favor of separation (the Black Muslims: Malcolm X, Muhammad Ali), and that Afro-Americans were an internal colony in the alien world of Babylon who must arm themselves against the possibility of extermination (the Black Panthers: Eldridge Cleaver, Huey Newton). All of these movements and their partisans wished to stress that Afro-Americans were different from other Americans and could not be merged with them because the differences between the two was as great as that between black and white. Linguistically, of course, "black" and "white" are antonyms; and it is precisely this sense of oppositeness that those who see the Afro-American as alienated, separated, and nonintegratable wish to capture with the term "black." Moreover, as any good dictionary makes clear, in some contexts "black" is synonymous with "deadly," "sinister," "wicked," "evil," and so forth. The new militants were trying to create just this picture of the black man—civil rights and Uncle Tomism are dead, the ghost of Nat Turner is to be resurrected, Freedom Now or pay the price, the ballot or the bullet, "Violence is as American as cherry pie." The new strategy was that the white man would either give the black man his due or pay the price in violence. Since conceptually a "black man" was an object to be feared ("black" can be synonymous with "deadly," and so on), while a "colored man" or a "Negro" was not, the new strategy required that the "Negro" be supplanted by the "black man." White America resisted the proposed linguistic reform quite vehemently, until hundreds of riots forced the admission that the Afro-American was indeed black.

Now to the point: I have suggested that the word "black" replaced the word "Negro" because there was a change in our conceptual structure. One is likely to reply that while all that I have said above is well and good, one had, after all, no choice about the matter. White people are identified in terms of their skin color as whites; clearly, if we are to recognize what is in reality nothing but the truth, that in this society people are conscious of skin color, to treat blacks as equals is merely to identify them by their skin color, which is black. That is, one might argue that while there was a change in words, we have no reason to think that there was a parallel conceptual change. If the term "black" has all the associations mentioned above, that is unfortunate; but in the context the use of the term "black" to identify the people formerly identified as "Negroes" is natural, inevitable, and, in and of itself, neutral; black is, after all, the skin color of the people in question. (Notice that this defense of the natural-inevitable-and-neutral conception of identification quite nicely circumvents the possible use of such seemingly innocuous terms as "Afro-American" and "African" by suggesting that in this society it is *skin color* that is the relevant variable.)

The great flaw in this analysis is that the actual skin color of virtually all of the people whom we call "black" is not black at all. The color tones range from light yellow to a deep umber that occasionally is literally black. The skin color of most Afro-Americans is best designated by the word "brown." Yet "brown" is not a term that is standard for identifying Afro-Americans. For example, if someone asked, "Who was the brown who was the architect for Washington, D.C.?" we would not know how to construe the question. We might attempt to read "brown" as a proper name ("Do you mean Arthur Brown, the designer?"). We would have no trouble understanding the sentence "Who was the black (Negro, colored guy, and so forth) who designed Washington, D.C.?" ("Oh, you mean Benjamin Banneker"). Clearly, "brown" is not a standard form of identification for Afro-Americans. I hope that it is equally clear that "black" has become the standard way of identifying Afro-Americans not because the term was natural, inevitable, and, in the context, neutral, but because of its occasional synonymy with "sinister" and because as an antonym to "white" it best fitted the conceptual needs of those who saw race relations in terms of intensifying and insurmountable antonymies. If one accepts this point, then one must admit that there is a close connection between the way in which we identify things and the way in which we conceive them —and thus it should be also clear why I wish to talk about the way in which women are identified in English.[1] (Thus, for example, one would expect Black Muslims, who continually use the term "black *man*"—as in "the black *man*'s rights"—to be more male chauvinistic than Afro-Americans who use the term "black *people*" or "black *folk*.")

WAYS OF IDENTIFYING WOMEN

It may at first seem trivial to note that women (and men) are identified sexually; but conceptually this is extremely significant. To appreciate the significance of this fact it is helpful to imagine a language in which proper names and personal pronouns do not reflect the sex of the person designated by them (as they do in our language). I have been told that in some oriental languages pronouns and proper names reflect social status rather than sex, but whether or not there actually exists such a language is irrelevant, for it is easy enough to imagine what one would be like. Let us then imagine a language where the proper names are sexually neutral (for example, "Xanthe"), so that one cannot tell from hearing a name whether the person so named is male or female, and where the personal pronouns in the language are "under" and "over." "Under" is the personal pronoun appropriate for all those who are younger than thirty, while "over" is appropriate to persons older than thirty. In such a language, instead of saying such things as "Where do you think *he* is living now?" one would say such things as "Where do you think *under* is living now?"

What would one say about a cultural community that employed such a language? Clearly, one would say that they thought that for purposes of intelligible communication it was more important to know a person's age grouping than the person's height, sex, race, hair color, or parentage. (There are many actual cultures, of course, in which people are identified by names that reflect their parentage; for example, Abu ben Adam means Abu son of Adam.) I think that one would also claim that this people would not have reflected these differences in the pronominal structure of their language if they did not believe that the differences between unders and overs was such that a statement would frequently have one meaning if it were about an under and a different meaning if it were about an over. For example, in feudal times if a serf said, "My lord said to do this," that assertion was radically different from "Freeman John said to do this," since (presumably) the former had the status of a command while the latter did not. Hence the conventions of Middle English required that one refer to people in such a way as to indicate their social status. Analogously, one would not distinguish between pronominal references according to the age differences in the persons referred to were there no shift in meaning involved.

If we apply the lesson illustrated by this imaginary language to our own, I think that it should be clear that since in our language proper nouns and pronouns reflect sex rather than age, race, parentage, social status, or religion, we believe one of the most important things one can know about a person is that person's sex. (And, indeed, this is the first thing one seeks to determine about a newborn babe—our first question is almost invariably "Is it a boy or a girl?") Moreover, we would not reflect this important difference pronominally did we not also believe that statements frequently mean one thing when applied to males and something else when applied to females. Perhaps the most striking aspect of the conceptual discrimination reflected in our language is that man is, as it were, essentially human, while woman is only accidentally so.

This charge may seem rather extreme, but consider the following synonyms (which are readily confirmed by any dictionary). "Humanity" is synonymous with "mankind" but not with "womankind." "Man" can be substituted for "humanity" or "mankind" in any sentence in which the terms "mankind" or "humanity" occur without changing the meaning of the sentence, but significantly, "woman" cannot. Thus, the following expressions are all synonymous with each other: "humanity's great achievements," "mankind's great achievements," and "man's great achievements." "Woman's great achievements" is not synonymous with any of these. To highlight the degree to which women are excluded from humanity, let me point out that it is something of a truism to say that "man is a rational animal," while "woman is a rational animal" is quite debatable. Clearly, if "man" in the first assertion embraced both men and women, the second assertion would be just as much a truism as the first.[2] Humanity, it would seem, is a male prerogative. (And hence, one of the goals of women's liberation is to alter our conceptual structure so that someday "mankind" will be regarded as an improper and vestigial ellipsis for "humankind," and "man" will have no special privileges in relation to "human being" that "woman" does not have.[3])

The major question before us is, How are women conceived of in our culture? I have been trying to answer this question by talking about how they are identified. I first considered pronominal identification; now I wish to turn to identification through other types of noun phrases. Methods of nonpronominal identification can be discovered by determining which terms can be substituted for "woman" in such sentences as "Who is that woman over there?" without changing the meaning of the sentence. Virtually no term is interchangeable with "woman" in that sentence for all speakers on all occasions. Even "lady," which most speakers would accept as synonymous with "woman" in that sentence, will not do for a speaker who applies the term "lady" only to those women who display manners, poise, and sensitivity. In most contexts, a large number of students in one or more of my classes will accept the following types of terms as more or less interchangeable with "woman." (An asterisk indicates interchanges acceptable to both males and females; a plus sign indicates terms restricted to black students only. Terms with neither an asterisk nor a plus sign are accepted by all males but are not normally used by females.)

A. NEUTRAL TERMS: *lady, *gal, *girl (especially with regard to a coworker in an office or factory), *+sister, *broad (originally in the animal category, but most people do not think of the term as now meaning pregnant cow)

B. ANIMAL: *chick, bird, fox, vixen, filly, bitch (Many do not know the literal meaning of the term. Some men and most women construe this use as pejorative; they think of "bitch" in the context of "bitchy," that is, snappy, nasty, and so forth. But a large group of men claim that it is a standard nonpejorative term of identification—which may perhaps indicate that women have come to be thought of as shrews by a large subclass of men.)

C. PLAYTHING: babe, doll, cuddly

D. GENDER (association with articles of clothing typically worn by those in the female gender role): skirt, hem

E. SEXUAL: snatch, cunt, ass, twat, piece (of ass, and so forth), lay, pussy (could be put in the animal category, but most users associated it with slang expression indicating the female pubic region), +hammer (related to anatomical analogy between a hammer and breasts). There are many other usages, for example, "bunny," "sweat hog," but these were not recognized as standard by as many as 10 percent of any given class.

The students in my classes reported that the most frequently used terms of identification are in the neutral and animal classifications (although men in their forties claim to use the gender classifications quite a bit) and that the least frequently used terms of identification are sexual. Fortunately, however, I am not interested in the frequency of usage but only in whether the use is standard enough to be recognized as an identification among some group or other. (Recall that "brown" was not a standardized term of identification and hence we could not make sense out of "Who was the brown who planned Washington, D.C.?" Similarly, one has trouble with "Who was the breasts who planned Washington, D.C.?" but not with "Who was the babe (doll, chick, skirt, and so forth) who planned Washington, D.C.?")

Except for two of the animal terms, "chick" and "broad"—but note that "broad" is probably neutral today—women do not typically identify themselves in sexual terms, in gender terms, as playthings, or as animals; *only males use nonneutral terms to identfy women.* Hence, it would seem that there is a male conception of women and a female conception. Only males identify women as "foxes," "babes," "skirts," or "cunts" (and since all the other nonneutral identifications are male, it is reasonable to assume that the identification of a woman as a "chick" is primarily a male conception that some women have adopted).

What kind of conception do men have of women? Clearly they think that women share certain properties with certain types of animals, toys, and playthings; they conceive of them in terms of the clothes associated with the female gender role; and, last (and, if my classes are any indication, least frequently), they conceive of women in terms of those parts of their anatomy associated with sexual intercourse, that is, as the identification "lay" indicates quite clearly, as sexual partners.

The first two nonneutral male classifications, animal and plaything, are prima facie denigrating (and I mean this in the literal sense of making one like a "nigger"). Consider the animal classification. All of the terms listed, with the possible exception of "bird," refer to animals that are either domesticated for servitude (to *man*) or hunted for sport. First, let us consider the term "bird." When I asked my students what sort of birds might be indicated, they suggested chick, canary (one member, in his forties, had suggested "canary" as a term of identification), chicken, pigeon, dove, parakeet, and hummingbird (one member). With the exception of the hummingbird, which like all the birds suggested is generally thought to be diminutive and pretty, all of the birds are domesticated, usually as pets (which reminds one that "my pet" is an expression of endearment). None of the birds were predators or symbols of intelligence or nobility (as are the owl, eagle, hawk, and falcon); nor did large but beautiful birds seem appropriate (for example, pheasants, peacocks, and swans). If one construes the bird terms (and for that matter, "filly") as applicable to women because they are thought of as beautiful, or at least pretty, *then there is nothing denigrating about them*. If, on the other hand, the common properties that underlie the metaphorical identification are domesticity and servitude, then they are indeed denigrating (as for myself, I think that both domesticity and prettiness underlie the identification). "Broad," of course, is, or at least was, clearly denigrating, since nothing renders more service to a farmer than does a pregnant cow, and cows are not commonly thought of as paradigms of beauty.

With one exception all of the animal terms reflect a male conception of women either as domesticated servants or as pets, or as both. Indeed, some of the terms reflect a conception of women first as pets and then as servants. Thus, when a pretty, cuddly little chick grows older, she becomes a very useful servant—the egg-laying hen.

"Vixen" and "fox," variants of the same term, are the one clear exception. None of the other animals with whom women are metaphorically identified are generally thought to be intelligent, aggressive, or independent—but the fox is. A chick is a soft, cuddly, entertaining, pretty, diminutive, domesticated, and dumb animal. A fox too is soft, cuddly, entertaining, pretty, and diminutive, but it is neither dependent nor dumb. It is aggressive, intelligent, and a minor predator—indeed, it preys on chicks —and frequently outsmarts ("outfoxes") men.

Thus the term "fox" or "vixen" is generally taken to be a compliment by both men and women, and compared to any of the animal or plaything terms it is indeed a compliment. Yet, considered in and of itself, the conception of a woman as a fox is not really complimentary at all, for the major connection between *man* and fox is that of predator and prey. The fox is an animal that men chase, and hunt, and kill for sport. If women are conceived of as foxes, then they are conceived of as prey that it is fun to hunt.

In considering plaything identifications, only one sentence is necessary. *All the plaything identifications are clearly denigrating since they assimilate women to the status of mindless or dependent objects.* "Doll" is to male paternalism what "boy" is to white paternalism.

Up to this point in our survey of male conceptions of women, every male identification, without exception, has been clearly antithetical to the conception of women as human beings (recall that "man" was synonymous with "human," while "woman" was not). Since the way we talk of things, and especially the way we identify them, is the way in which we conceive of them, any movement dedicated to breaking the bonds of female servitude must destroy these ways of identifying and hence of conceiving of women. Only when both sexes find the terms "babe," "doll," "chick," "broad," and so forth, as objectionable as "boy" and "nigger" will women come to be conceived of as independent *human beings.*

The two remaining unexamined male identifications are gender and sex. There seems to be nothing objectionable about gender identifications per se. That is, women are metaphorically identified as skirts because in this culture, skirts, like women, are peculiarly female. Indeed, if one accepts the view that the slogan "female and proud" should play the same role for the women's liberation movement that the slogan "Black is beautiful" plays for the black-liberation movement, then female clothes should be worn with the same pride as Afro clothes. (Of course, one can argue that the skirt, like the cropped-down Afro, is a sign of bondage, and hence both the item of clothing and the identification with it are to be rejected—that is, cropped-down Afros are to Uncle Tom what skirts are to Uncle Mom.)

The terms in the last category are obviously sexual, and frequently vulgar. For a variety of reasons I shall consider the import and nature of these identifications in the next section.

MEN OUGHT NOT TO THINK OF WOMEN AS SEX OBJECTS

Feminists have proposed many reforms, and most of them are clearly desirable, for example, equal opportunity for self-development, equal pay for equal work, and free day-care centers. One feminist proposal, however, is peculiarly conceptual and deeply perplexing. I call this proposal peculiarly conceptual because unlike the other reforms it is directed at getting people to think differently. The proposal is that *men should not think of women (and women should not think of themselves) as sex objects*. In the rest of this essay I shall explore this nostrum. I do so for two reasons: first, because the process of exploration should reveal the depth of the problem confronting the feminists; and second, because the feminists themselves seem to be entangled in the very concepts that obstruct their liberation.

To see why I find this proposal puzzling, one has to ask what it is to think of something as a sex object.

If a known object is an object that we know, an unidentified object is an object that we have not identified, and a desired object is an object that we desire, what then is a sex object? Clearly, a sex object is an object we have sex with. Hence, to think of a woman as a sex object is to think of her as someone to have sexual relations with, and when the feminist proposes that men refrain from thinking of women in this way, *she is proposing that men not think of women as persons with whom one has sexual relations.*

What are we to make of this proposal? Is the feminist suggesting that women should not be conceived of in this way because such a conception is "dirty"? To conceive of sex and sex organs as dirty is simply to be a prude. "Shit" is the paradigm case of a dirty word. It is a dirty word because the item it designates is taboo; it is literally unclean and untouchable (as opposed to something designated by what I call a curse word, which is not untouchable but rather something to be feared—"damn" and "hell" are curse words; "piss" is a dirty word). If one claims that "cunt" (or "fuck") is a dirty word, then one holds that what this term designates is unclean and taboo; thus one holds that the terms for sexual intercourse or sexual organs are dirty, one has accepted puritanism. If one is a puritan and a feminist, then indeed one ought to subscribe to the slogan *men should not conceive of women as sexual objects.* What is hard to understand is why anyone but a puritan (or, perhaps, a homosexual) would promulgate this slogan; yet most feminists, who are neither lesbians nor puritans, accept this slogan. Why?

A word about slogans: Philosophical slogans have been the subject of considerable analysis. They have the peculiar property (given a certain seemingly sound background story) of being obviously true, yet obviously false. "Men should not conceive of women as sex objects" is, I suggest, like a philosophical slogan in this respect. The immediate reaction of any humanistically oriented person upon first hearing the slogan is to agree with it—yet the more one probes the meaning of the slogan, the less likely one is to give one's assent. Philosophical analysts attempt to separate out the various elements involved in such slogans—to render the true-false slogan into a series of statements, some of which are true, some of which are false, and others of which are, perhaps, only probable. This is what I am trying to do with the slogan in question. I have argued so far that one of the elements that seems to be implicit in the slogan is a rejection of women as sexual partners for men and that although this position might be proper for a homosexual or puritanical movement, it seems inappropriate to feminism. I shall proceed to show that at least two other interpretations of the slogan lead to inappropriate results; but I shall argue that there are at least two respects in which the slogan is profoundly correct—even if misleadingly stated.

One plausible, but inappropriate, interpretation of "men ought not to conceive of women as sex objects" is that men ought not to conceive of women *exclusively* as sexual partners. The problem with this interpretation is that everyone can agree with it. Women are conceived of as companions, toys, servants, and even sisters, wives, and mothers—and hence not exclusively as sexual partners. Thus this slogan loses its revisionary impact, since even a male chauvinist could accept the slogan without changing his conceptual structure in any way—which is only to say that men do not usually identify or conceive of woman as sexual partners (recall that the sexual method of identification is the least frequently used).

Yet another interpretation is suggested by the term "object" in "sex object," and this interpretation too has a certain amount of plausibility.

Men should not treat women as animate machines designed to masturbate men or as conquests that allow men to "score" for purposes of building their egos. Both of these variations rest on the view that to be treated as an object is to be treated as less than human (that is, to be treated as a machine or a score). Such relations between men and women are indeed immoral, and there are, no doubt, men who believe in "scoring." Unfortunately, however, this interpretation—although it would render the slogan quite apt—also fails because of its restricted scope. When feminists argue that men should not treat women as sex objects they are not *only* talking about fraternity boys and members of the Playboy Club; they are talking about all males in our society. The charge is that in our society men treat women as sex objects rather than as persons; it is this universality of scope that is lacking from the present interpretation. *Nonetheless, one of the reasons that we are prone to assent to the unrestricted charge that men treat women as sex objects is that the restricted charge is entirely correct.*

One might be tempted to argue that the charge that men treat women as sex objects is correct since such a conception underlies the most frequently used identifications, as animal and plaything; that is, these identifications indicate a sexual context in which the female is used as an object. Thus, it might be argued that the female fox is chased and slayed if she is four-legged, but chased and layed if she is two. Even if one admits the sexual context *implicit* in *some* animal and plaything identifications, one will not have the generality required; because, for the most part, the plaything and animal identifications themselves are nonsexual—most of them do not involve a sexual context. A pregnant cow, a toy doll, or a filly are hardly what one would call erotic objects. Babies do not normally excite sexual passion; and anyone whose erotic interests are directed toward chicks, canaries, parakeets, or other birds is clearly perverse. The animals and playthings to whom women are assimilated in the standard metaphorical identifications are not symbols of desire, eroticism, or passion (as, for example, a bull might be).

What is objectionable in the animal and plaything identifications is not the fact that some of these identifications reflect a sexual context but rather that—regardless of the context—these identifications reflect a conception of women as mindless servants (whether animate or inanimate is irrelevant). The point is not that men ought not to think of women in sexual terms but that they ought to think of them as human beings; and the slogan *men should not think of women as sex objects* is only appropriate when a man thinking of a woman as a sexual partner automatically conceives of her as something less than human. It is precisely this antihuman-ism implicit in the male concept of sex that we have as yet failed to uncover —but then, of course, we have not yet examined the language we use to identify sexual acts.

OUR CONCEPTION OF SEXUAL INTERCOURSE

There are two profound insights that underlie the slogan "men ought not conceive of women as sexual objects"; both have the generality of scope that justifies the universality with which the feminists apply the slogan; neither can be put as simply as the slogan. The first is that the conception of sexual intercourse that we have in this culture is antithetical to the con-ception of women as human beings—as persons rather than objects. (Re-call that this is congruent with the fact we noted earlier that "man" can be substituted for "humanity," while "woman" cannot.)

Many feminists have attempted to argue just this point. Perhaps the most famous defender of this view is Kate Millett,[4] who unfortunately faces the problem of trying to make a point about our conceptual structure without having adequate tools for analyzing conceptual structures.

The question Millett was dealing with was conceptual—Millett, in effect, asking about the nature of our conception of sexual roles. She tried to answer this question by analyzing novels; I shall attempt to answer this question by analyzing the terms we use to identify coitus, or more techni-cally, in terms that function synonymously with "had sexual intercourse with" in a sentence of the form "A had sexual intercourse with B." The following is a list of some commonly used synonyms (numerous others that are not as widely used have been omitted, for example, "diddled," "laid pipe with"):

> screwed
> laid
> fucked
> had
> did it with (to)
> banged
> balled
> humped
> slept with
> made love to

Now, for a select group of these verbs, names for males are the subjects of sentences with active constructions (that is, where the subjects are said to be doing the activity); and names for females require passive constructions (that is, they are the recipients of the activity—whatever is done is done to them). Thus, we would not say "Jane did it to Dick," although we would say "Dick did it to Jane." Again, Dick bangs Jane, Jane does not bang Dick; Dick humps Jane, Janes does not hump Dick. In contrast, verbs like "did it with" do not require an active role for the male; thus, "Dick did it with Jane, and Jane with Dick.'" Again, Jane may make love to Dick, just as Dick makes love to Jane; and Jane sleeps with Dick as easily as Dick sleeps with Jane. (My students were undecided about "laid." Most thought that it would be unusual indeed for Jane to lay Dick, unless she played the masculine role of seducer-aggressor.)

The sentences thus form the following pairs. (Those nonconjoined singular noun phrases where a female subject requires a passive construction are marked with a cross. An asterisk indicates that the sentence in question is not a sentence of English if it is taken as synonymous with the italicized sentence heading the column.[5])

> *Dick had sexual intercourse with Jane*
> Dick screwed Jane†
> Dick laid Jane†
> Dick fucked Jane†
> Dick had Jane†
> Dick did it to Jane†
> Dick banged Jane†
> Dick humped Jane†
> Dick balled Jane(?)
> Dick did it with Jane
> Dick slept with Jane
> Dick made love to Jane
>
> *Jane had sexual intercourse with Dick*
> Jane was banged by Dick
> Jane was humped by Dick
> *Jane was done by Dick
> Jane was screwed by Dick
> Jane was laid by Dick
> Jane was fucked by Dick
> Jane was had by Dick

Jane balled Dick (?)
Jane did it with Dick
Jane slept with Dick
Jane made love to Dick
*Jane screwed Dick
*Jane laid Dick
*Jane fucked Dick
*Jane had Dick
*Jane did it to Dick
*Jane banged Dick
*Jane humped Dick

These lists make clear that within the standard view of sexual intercourse, males, or at least names for males, seem to play a different role than females, since male subjects play an active role in the language of screwing, fucking, having, doing it, and perhaps, laying, while female subjects play a passive role.

The asymmetrical nature of the relationship indicated by the sentences marked with a cross is confirmed by the fact that the form "—ed with each other" is acceptable for the sentences not marked with a cross, but not for those that require a male subject. Thus:

Dick and Jane had sexual intercourse with each other
Dick and Jane made love to each other
Dick and Jane slept with each other
Dick and Jane did it with each other
Dick and Jane balled with each other (*?)
*Dick and Jane banged with each other
*Dick and Jane did it to each other
*Dick and Jane had each other
*Dick and Jane fucked each other
*Dick and Jane humped each other
*(?) Dick and Jane laid each other
*Dick and Jane screwed each other

It should be clear, therefore, that our language reflects a difference between the male and female sexual roles, and hence that we conceive of the male and female roles in different ways. The question that now arises is, What difference in our conception of the male and female sexual roles requires active constructions for males and passive for females?

One explanation for the use of the active construction for males and the passive construction for females is that this grammatical asymmetry merely reflects the natural physiological asymmetry between men and women: the asymmetry of "to screw" and "to be screwed," "to insert into" and "to be inserted into." That is, it might be argued that the difference between masculine and feminine grammatical roles merely reflects a difference naturally required by the anatomy of males and females. This explanation is inadequate. Anatomical differences do not determine how we are to conceptualize the relation between penis and vagina during intercourse. Thus one can easily imagine a society in which the female normally played the active role during intercourse, where female subjects required active constructions with verbs indicating copulation, and where the standard metaphors were terms like "engulfing"—that is, instead of saying "he screwed her," one would say "she engulfed him." It follows that the use of passive constructions for female subjects of verbs indicating copulation does not reflect differences determined by human anatomy but rather reflects those generated by human customs.

What I am going to argue next is that the passive construction of verbs indicating coitus (that is, indicating the female position) can *also* be used to indicate that a person is being harmed. I am then going to argue that the metaphor involved would only make sense if we conceive of the female role in intercourse as that of a person being harmed (or being taken advantage of).

Passive constructions of "fucked," "screwed," and "had" indicate the female role. They also can be used to indicate being harmed. Thus, in all of the following sentences, Marion plays the female role: "Bobbie fucked Marion"; "Bobbie screwed Marion"; "Bobbie had Marion"; "Marion was fucked"; "Marion was screwed"; and "Marion was had." All of the statements are equivocal. They might literally mean that someone had sexual intercourse with Marion (who played the female role); or they might mean, metaphorically, that Marion was deceived, hurt, or taken advantage of. Thus, we say such things as "I've been screwed" ("fucked," "had," "taken," and so on) when we have been treated unfairly, been sold shoddy merchandise, or conned out of valuables. Throughout this essay I have been arguing that metaphors are applied to things only if what the term *actually* applies to shares one or more properties with what the term *metaphorically* applies to. Thus, the female sexual role must have something in common with being conned or being sold shoddy merchandise.

The only common property is that of being harmed, deceived, or taken advantage of. *Hence we conceive of a person who plays the female sexual role as someone who is being harmed* (that is, "screwed," "fucked," and so on).

It might be objected that this is clearly wrong, since the unsignated terms do not indicate someone's being harmed, and hence we do not conceive of having intercourse as being harmed. The point about the unsignated terms, however, is that they can take both females and males as subjects (in active constructions) and thus *do not pick out the female role.* This demonstrates that we conceive of sexual roles in such a way that only females are thought to be taken advantage of in intercourse.

The best part of solving a puzzle is when all the pieces fall into place. If the subjects of the passive construction are being harmed, presumably the subjects of the active constructions are doing harm, and, indeed, we do conceive of these subjects in precisely this way. Suppose one is angry at someone and wishes to express malevolence as forcefully as possible without actually committing an act of physical violence. If one is inclined to be vulgar one can make the sign of the erect male cock by clenching one's fist while raising one's middle finger, or by clenching one's fist and raising one's arm and shouting such things as "screw you," "up yours," or "fuck you." In other words, one of the strongest possible ways of telling someone that you wish to harm him is to tell him to assume the female sexual role relative to you. Again, to say to someone "go fuck yourself" is to order him to harm himself, while to call someone a "mother fucker" is not so much a play on his Oedipal fears as to accuse him of being so low that he would inflict the greatest imaginable harm (fucking) upon that person who is most dear to him (his mother).

Clearly, we conceive of the male sexual role as that of hurting the person in the female role—but lest the reader have any doubts, let me provide two further bits of confirming evidence: one linguistic, one nonlinguistic. One of the English terms for a person who hurts (and takes advantage of) others is the term "prick." This metaphorical identification would not make sense unless the bastard in question (that is, the person outside the bonds of legitimacy) was thought to share some characteristics attributed to things that are literally pricks. As a verb, "prick" literally means "to hurt," as in "I pricked myself with a needle"; but the usage in question is as a noun. As a noun, "prick" is a colloquial term for "penis." Thus, the question before us is what characteristic is shared by a penis and a person who harms others (or, alternatively, by a penis and by being stuck by a

needle). Clearly, no physical characteristic is relevant (physical characteristics might underlie the Yiddish metaphorical attribution "schmuck,"
but one would have to analyze Yiddish usage to determine this); hence the
shared characteristic is nonphysical; the only relevant shared nonphysical
characteristic is that both a literal prick and a figurative prick are agents
that harm people.

Now for the nonlinguistic evidence. Imagine two doors: in front of
each door is a line of people; behind each door is a room; in each room is a
bed; on each bed is a person. The line in front of one room consists of
beautiful women, and on the bed in that room is a man having intercourse
with each of these women in turn. One may think any number of things
about this scene. One may say that the man is in heaven, or enjoying himself at a bordello; or perhaps one might only wonder at the oddness of it
all. One does not think that the man is being hurt or violated or degraded
—or at least the possibility does not immediately suggest itself, although
one could conceive of situations where this was what was happening (especially, for example, if the man was impotent). Now, consider the other
line. Imagine that the figure on the bed is a woman and that the line consists of handsome, smiling men. The woman is having intercourse with
each of these men in turn. It immediately strikes one that the woman is
being degraded, violated, and so forth—"that poor woman."

When one man fucks many women he is a playboy and gains status;
when a woman is fucked by many men she degrades herself and loses
stature.

Our conceptual inventory is now complete enough for us to return to
the task of analyzing the slogan that men ought not to think of women as
sex objects.

I think that it is now plausible to argue that the appeal of the slogan
"men ought not to think of women as sex objects," and the thrust of much
of the literature produced by contemporary feminists, turns on something
much deeper than a rejection of "scoring" (that is, the utilization of sexual
"conquests" to gain esteem) and yet is a call neither for homosexuality nor
for puritanism.

The slogan is best understood as a call for a new conception of the
male and female sexual roles. If the analysis developed above is correct,
our present conception of sexuality is such that to be a man is to be a person capable of brutalizing women (witness the slogans "The marines will
make a man out of you!" and "The army builds *men*!" which are widely
accepted and which simply state that learning how to kill people will make

a person more manly). Such a conception of manhood not only bodes ill for a society led by such men, but also is clearly inimical to the best interests of women. It is only natural for women to reject such a sexual role, and it would seem to be the duty of any moral person to support their efforts—to redefine our conceptions not only of fucking, but of the fucker (man) and the fucked (woman).

This brings me to my final point. We are a society preoccupied with sex. As I noted previously, the nature of proper nouns and pronouns in our language makes it difficult to talk about someone without indicating that person's sex. This convention would not be part of the grammar of our language if we did not believe that knowledge of a person's sex was crucial to understanding what is said about that person. Another way of putting this point is that sexual discrimination permeates our conceptual structure. Such discrimination is clearly inimical to any movement toward sexual egalitarianism and virtually defeats its purpose at the outset. (Imagine, for example, that black people were always referred to as "them" and whites as "us" and that proper names for blacks always had an "x" suffix at the end. Clearly any movement for integration as equals would require the removal of these discriminatory indicators. Thus at the height of the melting-pot era, immigrants Americanized their names: "Bellinsky" became "Bell," "Burnstein" became "Burns," and "Lubitch" became "Baker.")

I should therefore like to close this essay by proposing that contemporary feminists should advocate the utilization of neutral proper names and the elimination of gender from our language (as I have done in this essay); and they should vigorously protest any utilization of the third-person pronouns "he" and "she" as examples of sexist discrimination (perhaps "person" would be a good third-person pronoun)—for, as a parent of linguistic analysis once said, "The limits of our language are the limits of our world."

NOTES

1. The underlying techniques used in this essay were all developed (primarily by Austin and Strawson) to deal with the problems of metaphysics and epistemology. All I have done is to attempt to apply them to other areas; I should note, however, that I rely rather heavily on metaphorical identifications, and that first philosophy tends not to require the analysis of such superficial aspects of language. Note also that it is an empirical matter whether or not people do use words in a certain way.

In this essay I am just going to assume that the reader uses words more or less as my students do; for I gathered the data on which words we use to identify women, and so on, simply by asking students. If the reader does not use terms as my students do, then what I say may be totally inapplicable to him.

2. It is also interesting to talk about the technical terms that philosophers use. One fairly standard bit of technical terminology is "trouser word." J. L. Austin invented this bit of jargon to indicate which term in a pair of antonyms is important. Austin called the important term a "trouser word" because "it is the use which wears the trousers." Even in the language of philosophy, to be important is to play the male role. Of course, the antifeminism implicit in the language of technical philosophy is hardly comparable to the male chauvinism embedded in commonplaces of ordinary discourse.

3. Although I thought it inappropriate to dwell on these matters in the text, it is quite clear that *we* do *not* associate many positions with females—as the following story brings out. I related this conundrum both to students in my regular courses and to students I teach in some experimental courses at a nearby community college. Among those students who had not previously heard the story, only native Swedes invariably resolved the problem; less than half of the students from an upper-class background would get it (eventually), while lower-class and black students virtually never figured it out. Radical students, women, even members of women's liberation groups fared no better than anyone else with their same class background. The story goes as follows: A little boy is wheeled into the emergency room of a hospital. The surgeon on emergency call looks at the boy and says, "I'm sorry I cannot operate on this child; he is my son." The surgeon was not the boy's father. In what relation did the surgeon stand to the child? Most students did not give any answer. The most frequent answer given was that the surgeon had fathered the boy illegitimately. (Others suggested that the surgeon had divorced the boy's mother and remarried and hence was not legally the boy's father.) Even though the story was related as a part of a lecture on women's liberation, at best only 20 percent of the written answers gave the correct and obvious answer—the surgeon was the boy's mother.

4. *Sexual Politics* (New York: Doubleday, 1971); but see also *Sisterhood Is Powerful*, ed. Robin Morgan (New York: Vintage Books, 1970).

5. For further analysis of verbs indicating copulation see "A Note on Conjoined Noun Phrases," *Journal of Philosophical Linguistics*, vol. 1, no. 2, Great Expectations, Evanston. Ill. Reprinted with "English Sentences Without Overt Grammatical Subject," in Zwicky, Salus, Binnick, and Vanek, eds., *Studies Out in Left Field: Defamatory Essays Presented to James D. McCawley* (Edmonton: Linguistic Research, Inc., 1971). The puritanism in our society is such that both of these articles are pseudoanonymously published under the name of Quang Phuc Dong; Mr. Dong, however, has a fondness for citing and criticizing the articles and theories of Professor James McCawley, Department of Linguistics, University of Chicago. Professor McCawley himself was kind enough to criticize an earlier draft of this essay. I should also like to thank G. E. M. Anscombe for some suggestions concerning this essay.

Marilyn Frye

Male Chauvinism:
A Conceptual Analysis

Some years ago the new feminist rhetoric brought into common use the term "male chauvinist."[1] The term found ready acceptance among feminists, and it seems to wear its meaning on its sleeve. But many males to whom it has been applied have found it rather puzzling. This puzzlement cannot properly be dismissed as a mere expression of defensiveness. In the first place, the term is frequently used as though it were interchangeable with the term "sexist," with the consequence that it can be difficult to see clearly that there may be different kinds of sin here. In the second place, a bit of analysis of the phenomenon called male chauvinism shows that it is not likely to work in male psychology quite as a chauvinism should work, though it may bear considerable resemblance to a chauvinism when viewed from the position of the female. As if this were not enough to cloud the picture, male chauvinism involves self-deception, and thus it is bound to escape notice on the first round of self-examination. So for this reason also it is difficult for a male chauvinist, even one eager to repent, clearly to discern the nature of his offense and the extent of his guilt.

One of my tasks here is to disentangle the notions of a male chauvinist and a sexist. The other is to provide the outlines of an analysis of male chauvinism itself. I shall to some extent be describing feminist usage and theory as I understand it and to some extent be developing and improving upon it. There is no sharp line here between description and improvisation.

SEXISM

The term "sexist" in its core and perhaps most fundamental meaning is a term that characterizes anything whatever that creates, constitutes, promotes, or exploits any irrelevant or impertinent marking of the distinctions between the sexes. I borrow the term "mark" here from a use in linguistics. Different distinctions may be "marked" in different languages. For example, the distinction between continuous and instantaneous present action is marked in some languages and not in others, that is, some do and some do not have different syntactic or semantic forms corresponding to this distinction. Behavior patterns very frequently mark the distinction between the sexes. For instance, behavior required in polite introductions differs according to the sexes of the participants. This means, curiously enough, that one must know a person's genital configuration before one has made that person's acquaintance, in order to know *how* to make her or his acquaintance. In general, "correct" or "appropriate" behavior, both nonlinguistic and linguistic, so frequently varies with (that is, marks) the sexes of the persons involved that it is of the utmost importance that a person's sex be immediately obvious upon the briefest encounter, even in conditions relatively unfavorable to observation. Hence our general need for abundant redundancy in sex marking.

The term "sexist" can be, and sometimes is, used in such a way that it is neutral with respect to what, if any, advantage or favor is associated with the marking of the distinction between the sexes and whether such advantage is enjoyed by the female or the male. But it is not standardly used in this neutral sense. As it is standardly used, the unqualified term denotes only those impertinent markings of the sexes that are in some way or sense associated with advantage to the male. To refer to such markings when they are associated with advantage to the female, one standardly must qualify the noun, using some such phrase as "reverse sexism." There is a kind of irony here with which one is now depressingly familiar. The word "sexist" is itself male-centered—one may perhaps say sexist. Nonetheless, for present purposes, I shall use and refer to the term "sexist" in its male-centered sense.

Although the term "sexist" is commonly applied to specific acts or behavior or to certain institutional processes, laws, customs, and so forth when they irrelevantly mark the distinction between the sexes, these uses seem to me to be relatively unproblematic, and I shall not directly discuss them. I shall focus instead on the characterization of persons as sexists—the notion of *a sexist*.

THREE KINDS OF SEXISTS AND AN IMPOSTER

One would standardly characterize a person as a sexist in virtue of his sexist beliefs, opinions, convictions, and principles.[2] A person might also be called a sexist in virtue of his acts and practices, but in general only if they are seen as associated with sexist beliefs. There may be people whose sexist behavior is nothing but an unthinking adoption of the habits of those around them, for instance, a door-opening habit whose genesis is like that of peculiarities of dishwashing or driving techniques picked up from one's parents. If a person's sexist behavior consisted solely of such habits, perhaps he would be found innocent of sexist belief. In that case I think that though his behavior might be labeled sexist (and he might reasonably be expected to change it), one should probably refrain from labeling *him* sexist.[3] Actually, it is a bit difficult to imagine someone having many such habits and not developing sexist beliefs to link the habits to each other and to various aspects of social life. Perhaps much of our sexist training takes this route, from unthinking habit to conviction.

Speaking quite generally, sexists are those who hold certain sorts of general beliefs about sexual differences and their consequences. They hold beliefs that would, for instance, support the view that physical differences between the sexes must always make for significant social and economic differences between them in any human society, such that males and females will in general occupy roles at least roughly isomorphic to those they now occupy in most extant human societies. In many cases, of course, these general beliefs might more accurately be represented by the simple proposition: Males are innately superior to females.

It is central to most feminist views that these general beliefs (assuming they are beliefs and not mere sentiments) are to be viewed as theories subject to the test of evidence and in principle falsifiable. And one kind of sexist is one who shares this attitude with respect to the epistemological status of such beliefs and differs from the feminist primarily in taking one version or another of them to be true, while the feminist holds that all such theories are false.[4] I call this person a *doctrinaire sexist*. When the feminist and the doctrinaire sexist are both fairly sophisticated, their debates tend to focus on preferred modes of empirical testing and the weights of various kinds of evidence.

There is another kind of sexist who would cheerfully assent to the same sorts of sexist propositions as those accepted by the doctrinaire sexist but who does not view them as mere theories. Such people, whom I call *primitive sexists*, are committed to these propositions as a priori truths, or ultimate metaphysical principles. A value-laden male/female dualism is embedded in their conceptual schemes more or less as a value-laden mind/body dualism is embedded in the conceptual schemes of many people of our culture. Looking at things from the point of view of the primitive sexist, these beliefs or principles cannot simply be refuted by empirical evidence, for they are among the principles of interpretation involved in *taking in* evidence. Even so, there is a point in challenging and haranguing the primitive sexist, for the turmoil of attack and defense may generate a reorganization of his conceptual scheme, changing the role of his sexist beliefs. One may be able to convert the primitive sexist to doctrinaire sexism, which is vulnerable to evidence and argument. (I am inclined to think that much of what feminists think of as unconscious sexism may really be primitive sexism.)

Borrowing a Quinean analogy, we might say that the sexist beliefs of the doctrinaire sexist are relatively near the periphery of his conceptual net, and that those of the primitive sexist have a central position. Sexist beliefs may indeed be anywhere between the center and the periphery of a conceptual net, and accordingly, sexists come in all shades, from empirical to metaphysical.

The stances of the doctrinaire and primitive sexists mark ends of a spectrum. Another spectrum of cases differs from the doctrinaire position in the degree to which a person's sexist beliefs are internally coherent and distinct from sundry other beliefs. Certainly, many people would assent (unless the new social pressure inhibited them) to quite a variety of statements the doctrinaire sexist would make; yet they could not in conscience be said to be adherents of a theory. There are those in whom such beliefs are scattered helter-skelter among religious persuasions, racist notions, beliefs and uncertainties about their own excellences and flaws, and so on. These sexist beliefs, though perhaps empirical enough, are not sufficiently organized or distinct from other networks of beliefs to constitute something so dignified as a theory. Sexists such as these I call *operational sexists*. They live pretty much as though they were doctrinaire sexists, but they are not so academic about it. Like the primitive sexist, the operational sexist may be more receptive to persuasion if first educated to the doctrinaire position.

There are other sorts of sexists that would have to be mentioned if we were striving for a complete catalog of members of the species according to the status of their sexist beliefs, but enough has been said to indicate the gist of the list. One other creature, however, should not go unmentioned—the *Opportunist*. The Opportunist is an impostor: he either has no particular beliefs about sexual differences and their consequences or in one degree or another accepts feminist claims about them, but he pretends to sexist convictions in order to gain the privileges and advantages associated with their acceptance by others. Regularly carrying on as though it is one's natural destiny to have some woman tend to one's laundry has, in the context of our present lives, a tendency to bring about the regular appearance of clean and mended clothes without effort on one's own part. Such opportunities abound in our society and are not missed by many persons of normal intelligence and normal distaste for distasteful tasks. (Many of us should recall here that in our youth we took advantage of such opportunities with respect to the rich variety of services our mothers were expected to perform but which we could well have performed for ourselves.) The Opportunist, furthermore, can share not only the advantages but also the excuses of the genuine sexists. The privilege attendant upon the opportunistic pretense of sexism can often be protected by availing oneself of the excuses and sympathy available to the genuine sexist—sexism is, after all, deeply ingrained in our society and in our individual lives, and who can blame the poor soul if the cannot rid himself of it overnight? One may well wonder how many of the people we identify as sexists are really cynical impostors; and while one's speculation on this question may place one on an optimist-pessimist spectrum, it is unfortunately not obvious which end of the spectrum is which.[5]

To accuse a person of being a sexist is to accuse him of having certain false beliefs and, in some cases, of having tendencies to certain reprehensible behavior presumed to be related in one way or another to such beliefs. Those justly accused of being sexists may or may not be blameworthy in this matter; personal responsibility for holding false beliefs varies greatly with persons and circumstances.

MALE CHAUVINISM

The accusation of male chauvinism is a deeper matter than the accusation of sexism. "Male chauvinism" is one of the strongest terms in feminist rhetoric; "male chauvinist pig," which to some ears sounds pleonastic, belongs to a vocabulary of stern personal criticism. In the more extreme instances, persons called male chauvinists are not seen as ignorant or stupid, nor as hapless victims of socialization, but as wicked—one might almost say, perverted. They are accused of something whose relation to belief and action is like that of a defect of character, or a moral defect—a defect that might partially account for an otherwise reasonable and reasonably virtuous and self-critical person holding beliefs that are quite obviously false and behaving in ways that are obviously reprehensible. I believe the defect in question is a particularly nasty product of closely related moral failure and conceptual perversity.

Prior to its new association with the term "male," the concept of chauvinism was connected primarily, perhaps exclusively, with excessive and blind patriotism and closely similar phenomena. Patriotism seems at a glance to be an identification of some kind with one's country. One is personally affronted if one's country is criticized, and one takes personal pride in the country's real or imagined strengths and virtues. A national chauvinism is an exaggerated version of this identification, in which the righteousness and intolerance are extreme. Other chauvinisms will presumably be similar identifications with other sorts of groups, such as religious sects. In any of these cases the chauvinist will be convinced of the goodness, strength, and virtue—in general, the superiority—of his nation, sect, or so on, and will have some sort of psychological mechanisms linking this virtue with his own goodness, strength, and virtue—his own superiority.

Given roughly this view of chauvinisms, it might seem that if we could analyze and understand the mechanisms linking the supposed virtue and superiority of the nation or sect to the supposed personal virtue and superiority of the chauvinist, we could then transfer that understanding to the case of the male chauvinist to see how he is accused of ticking.

But there is a serious obstacle to pursuing this course. An analogy between national and male chauvinisms will not hold up because the objects of the identifications are not relevantly similar. Whatever the mechanisms of national and religious chauvinism might turn out to be, they are mechanisms that associate a person with an entity that is pseudo-personal. Nations and sects act and are responsible for their actions; they are therefore pseudo-persons. Identification with such an entity is identification with a pseudo-person, and its mechanisms therefore will presumably be similar in some fairly important and enlightening ways to those of identifications with persons. Now, if we take the label "male chauvinism" at face value, male chauvinism should be an identification with the group consisting of all male human beings from which the chauvinist derives heightened self-esteem. But the group of all male human beings is not a pseudo-person: it does not have an internal structure that would give it an appropriate sort of unity; it does not act as a unit; it does not relate pseudo-personally to any other pseudo-persons; it is not virtuous or vicious. There cannot be a self-elevating identification with the group of all males the mechanisms of which would be like those of a national or sectarian chauvinism. The group with which the person supposedly identifies is the wrong sort of entity; in fact, one might say it is not an entity at all.

These reflections point to the conclusion that the phenomenon called male chauvinism is not in fact a chauvinism—a conclusion that should not be surprising. There clearly is some kind of mental set in which a male's knowledge that he is male[6] is closely connected with his self-esteem and with the perception and treatment of females as "other," or "alien." But to picture this as a chauvinism is quite obviously odd. So diverse, varied, and amorphous a group as that consisting of all male members of the species *homo sapiens* is an implausible peg on which to hang self-esteem. I do think, however, that this phenomenon, like a chauvinism, critically involves an identification through which one gains support of one's self-esteem. Drawing on a prevalent current in feminist thought, I suggest it is at bottom a version of a self-elevating identification with Humanity or Mankind —a twisted version in which mankind is confused with malekind. Superficially it looks somewhat like a chauvinism, and a female's experience in confronting it is all too much like that of an Algerian in France; but actually the feminist is accusing the so-called male chauvinist not of improperly identifying with some *group* but of acting as though what really is *only* a group of human beings were all there is to the human race. Since that is not a chauvinism and calling it such can only be misleading, I shall hereafter refer to it as *phallism*.

PHALLISM

Feminists have always been sensitive to the tendency to conflate and confuse the concepts of Man and male. We tend (we are explicitly taught) to think of distinctively human characteristics as distinctively masculine and to credit distinctively human achievements like culture, technology, and science, to men, that is, to males. This is one element of phallism: a picture of humanity as consisting of males. Blended with this, there is a (distinctively human?) tendency to romanticize and aggrandize the human species and to derive from one's rosy picture of it a sense of one's individual specialness and superiority.

Identifying with the human race, with the species, seems to involve a certain consciousness of the traits or properties one has qua member of the species. In this, we generally focus on those specific differences that we can easily construe as marking our elevation above the rest of the animal kingdom, among which the powers of speech and reason and moral sentiment are prime. Being the highest animals, the crowning achievement of evolution, we feel it morally acceptable to treat members of other species with contempt, condescension, and patronage. We supervise their safety, we decide what is best for them, we cultivate and train them to serve our needs and please us, we arrange that they shall be fed and sheltered as we please and shall breed and have offspring at our convenience (and often our concern for their welfare is sincere and our affection genuine). Every single human being, simply qua human being and regardless of personal virtues, abilities, or accomplishments, has these rights and, in some cases, duties with respect to members of any other species. All human beings can be absolutely confident of their unquestionable superiority over every creature of other species, however clever, willful, intelligent, or independently capable of survival.

We are all familiar enough with this self-serving arrogance. It might suitably be called *humanism*. It is just this sort of arrogance and assumption of superiority that is characteristic of the phallist. It is an assumption of superiority, with accompanying rights and duties, that is not seen as needing to be justified by personal virtue or individual merit, and is seen as justifying a contemptuous or patronizing attitude toward certain others.

What the phallist does, generally, is to behave toward women with humanist contempt and patronage. The confusion of "man" with lowercase "m" and "Man" with uppercase "m" is revealed when the attitudes with which a man meets a lower amimal are engaged in the male man's encounter with the female man.

It will be noted by the alert liberal that women are not the only human creatures that are not, or not generally, treated with the respect apparently due members of so elevated a species as ours. This is, of course, quite true. An arrogation of rights and duties fully analogous to humanism is carried out also in relation to infants, the aged, the insane, the criminal, the retarded, and other sorts of outcasts. It turns out that only certain of the creatures that are human (as opposed to equine, canine, and so on) are taken to be blessed with the superiority natural to the species; others are defective or underdeveloped and are not to be counted among the superior "us." The point here is just that phallists place females of the species in just this latter category. The words "defective" and "underdeveloped" and similar terms actually are used, with deadly seriousness, in descriptions of female psychology and anatomy broadcast by some of those assumed to have professional competence in such things.

With this degree of acquaintance with the phallist, I think one can see quite clearly why women complain of not being treated as persons by those who have been called male chauvinists. Those human creatures that we approach and treat with not the slightest trace of humanistic contempt are those we recognize unqualifiedly as fully actualized, fully normal, morally evaluable *persons*. The phallist approaches females with a superiority and condescension that we all take to be more or less appropriate to encounters with members of other species and with defective or underdeveloped members of our own. In other words, phallists do not treat women as persons.

I speak here of "the slightest trace of humanist contempt" and "fully actualized, fully normal, morally evaluable persons." These heavy qualifications are appropriate because much of our behavior suggests that there are degrees of personhood. But for now I wish to avoid this matter of degrees. I propose to simplify things by concentrating on unqualified fully actualized personhood. When in the rest of this essay I speak of persons or of the treatment or recognition of someone as a person, it is "full" personhood that I have in mind. Anything less than that, in any dimension, is covered by phrases like "not a person" or "not as a person." I shall also confine my attention to females and males who are not very young nor generally recognized as criminal or insane.

THE PHALLIST FANTASY— I

The phallist does not treat women as persons. The obvious question is, Does he withhold this treatment in full awareness that women are persons? Are we dealing with simple malice? I have no doubt that there are cases of this transparent wickedness, but it may be more common for a person to shrink from such blatant immorality, guarding his conscience with a protective membrane of self-deception. The phallist can arrange things so that he does not experience females as persons in the first place, and thus will not have to justify to himself his failure to treat them as persons. In this and the succeeding section, I shall sketch out the phallist's characteristic strategies.

What makes a human creature a person is its possession of a range of abilities and traits whose presence is manifest in certain behavior under certain circumstances. Sacrificing elegance to brevity, I shall refer to these traits and abilities as person-abilities and to the behavior in which they are manifest as person-behavior. As with abilities in general, and their manifestations in behavior, certain circumstances are, and others are not, suitable for the manifestation of person-abilities in person-behavior.

Given this general picture one can easily see that the possibilities for self-deceptive avoidances of attributing personhood are plentiful. (1) One can observe a creature that is in fact person-behaving and deceive oneself straight out about the facts before one; one can come away simply denying that the behavior took place. (2) One can observe certain behavior and self-deceptively take it as a manifestation of a lower degree or smaller range of abilities than it in fact manifests. (3) One may self-deceptively judge circumstances that are adverse to the manifestation of the abilities to have been optimal and then conclude from the fact that the abilities were not manifest that they are not present. I have no doubt that persons anxious to avoid perceiving females as persons use all of these devices, singly and in combination. But another, more vicious device is at hand. It is not a matter of simple misinterpretation of presented data but a matter of rigging the data and then self-deceptively taking them at face value.

Person-abilities are manifest only in certain suitable circumstances; so one can ensure that an individual will seem not to have these abilities by arranging for the false appearance that the individual has been in suitable circumstances for their manifestation. The individual will not in fact have been in suitable circumstances, which guarantees that the abilities will not be manifest; but it will seem that the individual was in suitable circumstances and the deceived observer will sensibly perceive the individual to lack the abilities in question. Then to wrap it up, one can deceive oneself about having manipulated the data, take the position of the naive observer, and conclude for oneself that the individual lacks the abilities. Parents are often in a position to do this. Presenting their daughters with unsuitable learning situations self-deceptively arranged to appear suitable, they convince themselves that they have discovered the children's inability to learn those things. A simple but illuminating example is frequently acted out in a father's attempt to teach his daughter to throw a baseball. He goes through various superficial maneuvers and declares failure—her failure—without having engaged anything like the perseverence and ingenuity that he would have engaged in the training of his son.

But even this does not exhaust the tricks available to the phallist. A critical central range of the traits and abilities that go into a creature's being a person are traits and abilities that can be manifest only in circumstances of interpersonal interaction wherein another person maintains a certain level of communicativeness and cooperativeness. One cannot, for instance, manifest certain kinds of intelligence in interactions with a person who has a prior conviction of one's stupidity, lack of insight, absence of wit; one cannot manifest sensitivity or loyalty in interactions with someone who is distrustful and will not share relevant information. It is this sort of thing that opens up the possibility for the most elegant of the self-deceptive moves of the phallist, one that very nicely combines simplicity and effectiveness. He can avoid seeing the critical central range of a woman's person-abilities simply by being uncooperative and uncommunicative and can, at the same time, do it without knowing he has done it by self-deceptively believing he has been cooperative and communicative. The ease with which one can be uncooperative and uncommunicative while believing oneself to be the opposite is apparent from the most casual acquaintance with common interpersonal problems. The manipulation of the circumstances is easy, the deception is easy, and the effects are broad and conclusive.

The power and rigidity of the phallist's refusal to experience women as persons is exposed in a curious perceptual flip he performs when he is forced or tricked into experiencing as a person someone who is in fact female. Those of her female characteristics that in another woman would irresistibly draw his attention go virtually unnoticed, and she becomes "one of the boys." Confronted with the dissonant appearance of a female person in a situation where he is unable to deny that she is a person, he denies that she is female.

The frustration of trying to function as a person in interaction with someone who is self-deceptively exercising this kind of control over others and over his own perceptions is one of the primary sources of feminist rage.

THE PHALLIST FANTASY—II

It has been assumed in the preceding section that it is obvious that women are persons. Otherwise, failure to perceive women as persons would not have to involve self-deception. Some women, however, clearly think there is some point in asserting that they are persons, and some women's experience is such that they are inclined to say that they are denied personhood.

To some, there seems to be a certain silliness about the assertion that women are persons, which derives from the fact that almost everybody, female and male alike, seems to *agree* that women are people. But in many instances this constitutes no more than an acceptance of the fact that females are biologically human creatures with certain linguistic capacities and emotional needs; in accepting this, one is committed to no more than the belief that women should be treated humanely, as we are enjoined to treat the retarded and the elderly. But the personhood of which I am speaking here is "full" personhood. I am speaking of unqualified participation in the radical superiority of the species, without justification by individual virtue or achievement—unqualified membership of that group of beings that may approach all other creatures with humanist arrogance. Members of this group are to be treated not humanely but with respect. It is plain that not everybody, not even almost everybody, agrees that women belong to this group. The assertion that they do is hardly the assertion of something so generally deemed obvious as to be unworthy of assertion.

The other claim—that women are denied personhood—also seems strange to some people. But it by no means emerges parthenogenetically from feminine fantasy. To some, the concept of a person seems somewhat like the concepts that are sometimes called "institutional," such as the concepts of a lawyer or a knight. To some it seems that "person" denotes a social or institutional role and that one may be allowed or forbidden to adopt that role. It seems that we (persons) have some sort of power to admit creatures to personhood. I do not find this view plausible, but it surely recommends itself to some, and it must be attractive to the phallist, who would fancy the power to create persons. His refusal to perceive women as persons could then be taken by him as an exercise of this power. Some phallists give every sign of accepting this or a similar view, and some women seem to be taken in by it too. Hence, some women are worked into the position of asking to be granted personhood. It is a peculiar position for a person to be in, but such are the almost inevitable effects of phallist magic on those not forewarned. Of course, one cannot make what is a person not a person by wishing it so. And yet some vague impression lingers that phallists do just that—and it is not without encouragement that it lingers.

Even apart from the cases of institutional concepts, there is in the employment of concepts, as in the employment of words, a certain collective subjectivity. Every concept has some standard use or uses in some community—the "conceptual community" whose usage fixes its correct application. While admitting that various hedges and qualifications should be made here, one may say that, generally, if everyone in the community where the concept Y is in general use declares Xs to be Ys, then Xs are Ys. For concepts employed only by specialists or, say, used only within certain neighborhoods, the relevant conceptual communities consist of those specialists or the residents of those neighborhoods. In general, the conceptual community whose use of a concept fixes its correct application simply consists of all the people who use it. To determine its correct application, one identifies the people who use it and then describes or characterizes their use of it.

The concept of a person is a special case here. To discover the range of application of the concept of a person, one might identify the conceptual community in which that concept is used. It consists, of course, of all the persons who use the concept. To identify that conceptual community, one must decide which human creatures are persons, for one will not want to take into account the usages of simply any and every human creature which shows the slightest sign of using concepts. The upshot is that the phallist who self-deceptively adjusts the range of application of the concept of a person is also manipulating appearances with respect to the constitution of the conceptual community. Males who live their lives under the impression that only males are persons (and in the belief that this impression is shared by other males) will see *themselves* (the persons) as completely constituting the conceptual community and thence take *their* agreement in the (overt) application of the concept of a person as fixing its correct application, much as we all take our agreement in the application of the concept of a tree as fixing its correct application. We do not have the power to make what is a tree not a tree, but the collective subjectivity of conceptual correctness can be mistaken to mean that we do. Nor could the phallists, if they did constitute the conceptual community, thereby have the power to make what is a person not a person. But it is here, I think, that one finds the deepest source of the impression that women are *denied* personhood.

The self-deceptive denial that women are (full) persons adds up to an attempt to usurp the community's control over concepts in general by denying females membership in the conceptual community, or rather, by failing to see that they are members of the conceptual community. The effect is not simply the exclusion of females from the rights and duties of full persons but is a conceptual banishment that ensures that their complaints about this exclusion simply do not fit into the resulting conceptual scheme. Hence the phallist's almost incredible capacity for failure to understand what on earth feminists are talking about. His self-deception is locked into his conceptual framework, not simply as his analytic or a priori principles are, but in the underlying determinants of its entire structure and content. The self-deception fixes his conception of the constitution of the conceptual community whose existence makes conceptualization possible and whose collective perceptions determine in outline its progress.

The rejection of females by phallists is both morally and conceptually profound. The refusal to perceive females as persons is conceptually profound because it excludes females from that community whose conceptions of things one allows to influence one's own concepts—it serves as a police-lock on a closed mind. Furthermore, the refusal to treat women with the respect due to persons is in itself a violation of a moral principle that seems to many to be *the* founding principle of all morality. This violation of moral principle is sustained by an active manipulation of circumstances that is systematic and habitual and self-deceptively unacknowledged. The exclusion of women from the conceptual community simultaneously excludes them from the moral community. So the self-deception here is designed not just to dodge particular applications of moral principles but to narrow the moral community itself, and is therefore particularly insidious. It is the sort of thing that leavens the moral schizophrenia of the gentle, honest, god-fearing racist monster, the self-anointed *über-*

mensch, and other moral deviates. The phallist is confined with the worst of moral company in a self-designed conceptual closet—and he has taken great pains to ensure that this escape will not be abetted by any woman.

Postscript: It may seem that I have assumed here that all sexists and phallists are male. I do assume that in the paradigm cases phallists are male, but the suggestion that all sexists and all phallists are male arises innocently from the standard English usage of personal pronouns. "He," "him," and "his" are of course to be understood in their generic sense.

NOTES

1. I am heavily indebted to Carolyn Shafer, with whom I thoroughly and profitably discussed all parts of this essay at all stages of its development; her contribution is substantial. I also profited from discussion with an audience of philosophers and others at Michigan State University, and an audience at a meeting of the Eastern Division of the Society of Women in Philosophy, in April 1974, at Wellesley College.

2. I will refer to beliefs, opinions, convictions, and principles all indifferently as "beliefs." Not that it does not make any difference; a fuller analysis of sexism would take these distinctions into account.

3. This might be seen as an instance when we condemn the sin but not the sinner.

4. It should be noted that such theories are sexist only if they are false; for if true, they would not count as marking the sexes irrelevantly or impertinently. Consequently my own use of the terms "sexist" and "sexism" in connection with such theories constitutes a certain commitment in this regard.

5. Women are warmly encouraged to view belief in the ubiquity of Opportunists as paranoia. In this connection I refer the reader to a speech by William Lloyd Garrison, included under the title "Intelligent Wickedness" in *Feminism: The Essential Historical Writings*, edited by Miriam Schneir (New York: Vintage Books, 1972). He points out that men "manifest their guilt to a demonstration, in the manner in which they receive this movement [feminism] . . . they who are only ignorant, will never rage, and rave, and threaten, and foam, when the light comes. . . ." One cannot but believe that there are also some who, well aware of the point Garrison makes, prudently refrain from foaming in public.

6. I am not attending to pathological cases in this essay, so I here ignore cases of females who fancy they are males.

SEX AND MORALITY

Sara Ruddick

Better Sex

It might be argued that there is no specifically sexual morality.[1] We have, of course, become accustomed to speaking of sexual morality, but the "morality" of which we speak has a good deal to do with property, the division of labor, and male power, and little to do with our sexual lives. Sexual experiences, like experiences in driving automobiles, render us liable to specific moral situations. As drivers we must guard against infantile desires for revenge and excitement. As lovers we must guard against cruelty and betrayal, for we know sexual experiences provide special opportunities for each. We drive soberly because, before we get into a car, we believe that it is wrong to be careless of life. We resist temptations to adultery because we believe it wrong to betray trust, whether it be a parent, a sexual partner, or a political colleague who is betrayed. As lovers and drivers we act on principles that are particular applications of general moral principles. Moreover, given the superstitions from which sexual experience has suffered, it is wise to free ourselves, as lovers, from any moral concerns, other than those we have as human beings. There is no specifically sexual morality, and none should be invented. Or so it might be argued.

When we examine our moral "intuitions," however, the analogy with driving fails us. Unburdened of *sexual* morality, we do not find it easy to apply general moral principles to our sexual lives. The "morally average" lover can be cruel, violate trust, and neglect social duties with less opprobrium precisely *because* he is a lover. Only political passions and psychological or physical deprivation serve as well as sexual desire to excuse what would otherwise be seriously and clearly immoral acts. (Occasionally, sexual desire is itself conceived of as a deprivation, an involuntary lust. And there is, of course, a tradition that sees sexual morality as a way of controlling those unable to be sexless: "It is better to marry than to burn.") Often, in our sexual lives, we neither flout nor simply apply general moral principles. Rather, the values of sexual experience themselves figure in the construction of moral dilemmas. The conflict between better sex (more complete, natural, and pleasurable sex acts) and, say, social duty is not seen as a conflict between the immoral and compulsive, on one hand, and the morally good, on the other, but as a conflict between alternative moral acts.

Our intuitions vary but at least they suggest we can use "good" sex as a positive weight on some moral balance. What is that weight? Why do we put it there? How do we, in the first place, evaluate sexual experiences? On reflection, should we endorse these evaluations? These are the questions whose answers should constitute a specifically sexual morality.

In answering them, I will first consider three characteristics that have been used to distinguish some sex acts as better than others—greater pleasure, completeness, and naturalness. Other characteristics may be relevant to evaluating sex acts, but these three are central. If they have *moral* significance, then the sex acts characterized by them will be better than others not so characterized.

After considering those characteristics in virtue of which some sex acts are allegedly better than others, I will ask whether the presence of those characteristics renders the acts *morally* superior. I will not consider here the unclear and overused distinction between the moral and the amoral, nor the illegitimate but familiar distinction between the moral and the prudent. I hope it is sufficient to set out dogmatically and schematically the moral notions I will use. I am confident that better sex is morally preferable to other sex, but I am not at all happy with my characterization of its moral significance. Ultimately, sexual morality cannot be considered apart from a "prudential" morality in which it is shown that what is good is good for us and what is good for us makes us good. In such a morality, not only sex, but art, fantasy, love, and a host of other intellectual and emotional enterprises will regain old moral significances and acquire new ones. My remarks here, then, are partial and provisional.

A characteristic renders a sex act morally preferable to one without that characteristic if it gives, increases, or is instrumental in increasing the "benefit" of the act for the person engaging in it. Benefits can be classified as peremptory or optional. Peremptory benefits are experiences, relations, or objects that anyone who is neither irrational nor anhedonic will want so long as he wants anything at all. Optional benefits are experiences, relations, or objects that anyone, neither irrational nor anhedonic, will want so long as he will not thereby lose a peremptory benefit. There is widespread disagreement about which benefits are peremptory. Self-respect, love, and health are common examples of peremptory benefits. Arms, legs, and hands are probably optional benefits. A person still wanting a great deal might give up limbs, just as she would give up life, when mutilation or death is required by self-respect. As adults we are largely responsible for procuring our own benefits and greatly dependent on good fortune for success in doing so. However, the moral significance of benefits is most clearly seen not from the standpoint of the person procuring and enjoying them but from the standpoint of another *caring* person, for example, a lover, parent, or political leader responsible for procuring benefits for specific others. A benefit may then be described as an experience, relation, or object that anyone who properly cares for another is obliged to attempt to secure for him. Criteria for the virtue of care and for benefit are reciprocally determined, the virtue consisting in part in recognizing and attempting to secure benefits for the person cared for, the identification of benefit depending on its recognition by those already seen to be properly caring.

In talking of benefits I shall be looking at our sexual lives from the vantage point of hope, not of fear. The principal interlocutor may be considered to be a child asking what he should rightly and reasonably hope for in living, rather than a potential criminal questioning conventional restraints. The specific question the child may be imagined to ask can now be put: In what way is better sex beneficial or conducive to experiences or relations or objects that are beneficial?

A characteristic renders a sex act morally preferable to one without that characteristic if either the act is thereby more just or the act is thereby likely to make the person engaging in it more just. Justice includes giving others what is due them, taking no more than what is one's own, and giving and taking according to prevailing principles of fairness.

A characteristic renders a sex act morally preferable to one without that characteristic if because of the characteristic the act is more virtuous or more likely to lead to virtue. A virtue is a disposition to attempt, and an ability to succeed in, good acts—acts of justice, acts that express or produce excellence, and acts that yield benefits to oneself or others.

SEXUAL PLEASURE

Sensual experiences give rise to sensations and experiences that are paradigms of what is pleasant. Hedonism, in both its psychological and ethical forms, has blinded us to the nature and to the benefits of sensual pleasure by overextending the word "pleasure" to cover anything enjoyable or even agreeable.[2] The paradigmatic type of pleasure is sensual. Pleasure is a temporally extended, more or less intense quality of particular experiences. Pleasure is enjoyable independent of any function pleasurable activity fulfills. The infant who continues to suck well after he is nourished, expressing evident pleasure in doing so, gives us a demonstration of the nature of pleasure.[3]

As we learn more about pleasant experiences we not only apply but also extend and attenuate the primary notion of "pleasure." But if pleasure is to have any nonsophistical psychological or moral interest, it must retain its connections with those paradigm instances of sensual pleasure that give rise to it. We may, for example, extend the notion of pleasure so that particular episodes in the care of children give great pleasure; but the long-term caring for children, however intrinsically rewarding, is not an experience of pleasure or unpleasure.

Sexual pleasure is a species of sensual pleasure with its own conditions of arousal and satisfaction. Sexual acts vary considerably in pleasure, the limiting case being a sexual act where no one experiences pleasure even though someone may experience affection or "relief of tension" through orgasm. Sexual pleasure can be considered either in a context of deprivation and its relief or in a context of satisfaction. Psychological theories have tended to emphasize the frustrated state of sexual desire and to construe sexual pleasure as a relief from that state. There are, however, alternative accounts of sexual pleasure that correspond more closely with our experience. Sexual pleasure is "a primary distinctively poignant pleasure experience that manifests itself from early infancy on. . . . Once experienced it continues to be savored. . . ."[4] Sexual desire is not experienced as frustration but as part of sexual pleasure. Normally, sexual desire transforms itself gradually into the pleasure that appears, misleadingly, to be an aim extrinsic to it. The natural structure of desire, not an inherent quality of frustration, accounts for the pain of an aroused but unsatisfied desire.

Sexual pleasure, like addictive pleasure generally, does not, except very temporarily, result in satiety. Rather, it increases the demand for more of the same while sharply limiting the possibility of substitutes. The experience of sensual pleasures, and particularly of sexual pleasures, has a pervasive effect on our perceptions of the world. We find bodies inviting, social encounters alluring, and smells, tastes, and sights resonant because our perception of them includes their sexual significance. Merleau-Ponty has written of a patient for whom "perception had lost its erotic structure, both temporally and physically."[5] As the result of a brain injury the patient's capacity for sexual desire and pleasure (though not his capacity for performing sexual acts) was impaired. He no longer sought sexual intercourse of his own accord, was left indifferent by the sights and smells of available bodies, and if in the midst of sexual intercourse his partner turned away, he showed no signs of displeasure. The capacity for sexual pleasure, upon which the erotic structure of perception depends, can be accidentally damaged. The question that this case raises is whether it would be desirable to interfere with this capacity in a more systematic way than we now do. With greater biochemical and psychiatric knowledge we shall presumably be able to manipulate it at will.[6] And if that becomes possible, toward what end should we interfere? I shall return to this question after describing the other two characteristics of better sex—completeness and naturalness.

COMPLETE SEX ACTS

The completeness of a sexual act depends upon the *relation* of the participants to their own and each other's *desire*. A sex act is complete if each partner allows himself to be "taken over" by an active desire, which is desire not merely for the other's body but also for his active desire. Completeness is hard to characterize, though complete sex acts are at least as natural as any others—especially, it seems, among those people who take them casually and for granted. The notion of "completeness" (as I shall call it) has figured under various guises in the work of Sartre, Merleau-Ponty, and more recently Thomas Nagel. "The being which desires is consciousness making itself body."[7] "What we try to possess, then, is not just a body, but a body brought to life by consciousness."[8] "It is important that the partner be aroused, and not merely aroused, but aroused by the awareness of one's desire."[9]

The precondition of complete sex acts is the "embodiment" of the participants. Each participant submits to sexual desires that take over consciousness and direct action. It is sexual desire and not a separable satisfaction of it (for example, orgasm) that is important here. Indeed, Sartre finds pleasure external to the essence of desire, and Nagel gives an example of embodiment in which the partners do not touch each other. Desire is pervasive and "overwhelming," but it does not make its subject its involuntary victim (as it did the Boston Strangler, we are told), nor does it, except at its climax, alter capacities for ordinary perceptions, memories, and inferences. Nagel's embodied partners can presumably get themselves from bar stools to bed while their consciousness is "clogged" with desire. With what, then, is embodiment contrasted?

Philosophers make statements that when intended literally are evidence of pathology: "Human beings are automata"; "I never really see physical objects"; "I can never know what another person is feeling." The clearest statement of disembodiment that I know of is W. T. Stace's claim: "I become aware of my body in the end chiefly because it insists on accompanying me wherever I go."[10] What "just accompanies me" can also stay away. "When my body leaves me/I'm lonesome for it./ . . . body/goes away I don't know where/and it's lonesome to drift/above the space it/fills when it's here."[11] If "the body is felt more as one object among other objects in the world than as the core of the individual's own being,"[12] then what appears to be bodily can be dissociated from the "real self." Both a generalized separation of "self" from body and particular disembodied experiences have had their advocates. The attempt at disembodiment has also been seen as conceptually confused and psychologically disastrous.

We may often experience ourselves as relatively disembodied, observing or "using" our bodies to fulfill our intentions. On some occasions, however, such as in physical combat, sport, physical suffering, or danger, we "become" our bodies; our consciousness becomes bodily experience of bodily activity.[13] Sexual acts are occasions for such embodiment; they may, however, fail for a variety of reasons, for example, because of pretense or an excessive need for self-control. If someone is embodied by sexual desire, he submits to its direction. Spontaneous impulses of desire become his movements—some involuntary, like gestures of "courting behavior" or physical expressions of intense pleasure, and some deliberate. His consciousness, or "mind," is taken over by desire and the pursuit of its object, in the way that at other times it may be taken over by an intellectual problem or by obsessive fantasies. But unlike the latter takeovers, this one is bodily. A desiring consciousness is flooded with specifically sexual feelings that eroticize all perception and movement. Consciousness "becomes flesh."

Granted the precondition of embodiment, complete sex acts occur when each partner's embodying desire is active and actively responsive to the other's. This second aspect of complete sex constitutes a "reflexive mutual recognition" of desire by desire.[14]

The partner *actively* desires another person's desire. Active desiring includes more than embodiment, which might be achieved in objectless masturbation. It is more, also, than merely being aroused by and then taken over by desire, though it may come about as a result of deliberate arousal. It commits the actively desiring person to her desire and requires her to identify with it—that is, to recognize herself as a sexual agent as well as respondent. (Active desiring is less encouraged in women, and probably more women than men feel threatened by it.)

The other recognizes and responds to the partner's desire. Merely to recognize the desire as desire, not to reduce it to an itch or to depersonalize it as a "demand," may be threatening. Imperviousness to desire is the deepest defense against it. We have learned from research on families whose members tend to become schizophrenic that such imperviousness, the refusal to recognize a feeling for what it is, can force a vulnerable person to deny or to obscure the real nature of his feelings. Imperviousness tends to deprive even a relatively invulnerable person of his efficacy. The demand that our feelings elicit a response appropriate to them is part of a general demand that *we* be recognized, that our feelings be allowed to make a difference.

There are many ways in which sexual desire may be recognized, countless forms of submission and resistance. In complete sex, desire is recognized by a responding and active desire that commits the other, as it committed the partner. Given responding desire, both people identify themselves as sexually desiring the other. They are neither seducer nor seduced, neither suppliant nor benefactress, neither sadist nor victim, but sexual agents acting sexually out of their recognized desire. Indeed, in complete sex one not only welcomes and recognizes active desire, one desires it. Returned and endorsed desire becomes one of the features of an erotically structured perception. Desiring becomes desirable. (Men are less encouraged to desire the other's active and demanding desire, and such desiring is probably threatening to more men than women.)

In sum, in complete sex two persons embodied by sexual desire actively desire and respond to each other's active desire. Although it is difficult to write of complete sex without suggesting that one of the partners is the initiator, while the other responds, complete sex is reciprocal sex. The partners, whatever the circumstances of their coming together, are equal in activity and responsiveness of desire.

Sexual acts can be partly incomplete. A necrophiliac may be taken over by desire, and a frigid woman may respond to her lover's desire without being embodied by her own. Partners whose sexual activities are accompanied by private fantasies engage in an incomplete sex act. Consciousness is used by desire but remains apart from it, providing it with stimulants and controls. Neither partner responds to the other's desire, though each may appear to. Sartre's "dishonest masturbator," for whom masturbation is the sex act of choice, engages in a paradigmatically incomplete sex act: "He asks only to be slightly distanced from his own body, only for there to be a light coating of otherness over his flesh and over his thoughts. His personae are melting sweets. . . . The masturbator is enchanted at never being able to feel himself sufficiently another, and at producing for himself alone the diabolic appearance of a couple that fades away when one touches it. . . . Masturbation is the derealisation of the world and of the masturbator himself."[15]

Completeness is more difficult to describe than incompleteness, for it turns on precise but subtle ways of responding to a particular person's desire with specific expressions of impulse that are both spontaneous and responsive.

There are many possible sex acts that are pleasurable but not complete. Sartre, Nagel, and Merleau-Ponty each suggest that the desire for the responsive desire of one's partner is the "central impulse" of sexual desire.[16] The desire for a sleeping woman, for example, is possible only "in so far as this sleep appears on the ground of consciousness."[17] This seems much too strong. Some lovers desire that their partners resist, others like them coolly controlled, others prefer them asleep. We would not say that there was anything abnormal or less fully sexual about desire. Whether or not complete sex is preferable to incomplete sex (the question to which I shall turn shortly), incompleteness does not disqualify a sex act from being fully sexual.

SEXUAL PERVERSION

The final characteristic of allegedly better sex acts is that they are "natural" rather than "perverted." The ground for classifying sexual acts as either natural or unnatural is that the former type serve or could serve the evolutionary and biological function of sexuality—namely, reproduction. "Natural" sexual desire has as its "object" living persons of the opposite sex, and in particular their postpubertal genitals. The "aim" of natural sexual desire—that is, the act that "naturally" completes it—is genital intercourse. Perverse sex acts are deviations from the natural object (for example, homosexuality, fetishism) or from the standard aim (for example, voyeurism, sadism). Among the variety of objects and aims of sexual desire, I can see no other ground for selecting some as natural, except that they are of the type that can lead to reproduction.[18]

The connection of sexual desire with reproduction gives us the criterion but not the motive of the classification. The concept of perversion depends on a disjointedness between our experience of sexual desire from infancy on and the function of sexual desire—reproduction. In our collective experience of sexuality, perverse desires are as natural as nonperverse ones. The sexual desire of the polymorphously perverse child has many objects—for example, breasts, anus, mouth, genitals—and many aims—for example, autoerotic or other-directed looking, smelling, touching, hurting. From the social and developmental point of view, natural sex is an achievement, partly biological, partly conventional, consisting in a dominant organization of sexual desires in which perverted aims or objects are subordinate to natural ones. The concept of perversion reflects the vulnerability as much as the evolutionary warrant of this organization.

The connection of sexual desire with reproduction is not sufficient to yield the concept of perversion, but it is surely necessary. Nagel, however, thinks otherwise. There are, he points out, many sexual acts that do not lead to reproduction but that we are not even inclined to call perverse—for example, sexual acts between partners who are sterile. Perversion, according to him, is a psychological concept while reproduction is (only?) a physiological one. (Incidentally, this view of reproduction seems to me the clearest instance of male bias in Nagel's paper.)

Nagel is right about our judgments of particular acts, but he draws the wrong conclusions from those judgments. The perversity of sex acts does not depend upon whether they are intended to achieve reproduction. "Natural" sexual desire is for heterosexual genital activity, not for reproduction. The ground for classifying that desire as natural is that it is so organized that it *could* lead to reproduction in normal physiological circumstances. The reproductive organization of sexual desires gives us a *criterion* of naturalness, but the *virtue* of which it is a criterion is the "naturalness" itself, not reproduction. Our vacillating attitude toward the apparently perverse acts of animals reflects our shifting from criterion to virtue. If, when confronted with a perverse act of animals, we withdraw the label "perverted" from our own similar acts rather than extend it to theirs, we are relinquishing the reproductive criterion of naturalness, while retaining the virtue. Animals cannot be "unnatural." If, on the other hand, we "discover" that animals can be perverts too, we are maintaining our criterion, but giving a somewhat altered sense to the "naturalness" of which it is a criterion.

Nagel's alternative attempt to classify acts as natural or perverted on the basis of their completeness fails. "Perverted" and "complete" are evaluations of an entirely different order. The completeness of a sex act depends upon qualities of the participants' experience and upon qualities of their relation—qualities of which they are the best judge. To say a sex act is perverted is to pass a conventional judgment about characteristics of the act, which could be evident to any observer. As one can pretend to be angry but not to shout, one can pretend to a complete, but not to a natural, sex act (though one may, of course, conceal desires for perverse sex acts or shout in order to mask one's feelings). As Nagel himself sees, judgments about particular sex acts clearly differentiate between perversion and completeness. Unadorned heterosexual intercourse where each partner has private fantasies is clearly "natural" and clearly "incomplete," but there is nothing prima facie incomplete about exclusive oral-genital intercourse or homosexual acts. If many perverse acts are incomplete, as Nagel claims, this is an important fact *about* perversion, but it is not the basis upon which we judge its occurrence.

IS BETTER SEX REALLY BETTER?

Some sex acts are, allegedly, better than others insofar as they are more pleasurable, complete, and natural. What is the moral significance of this evaluation? In answering this question, official sexual morality sometimes appeals to the social consequences of particular types of better sex acts. For example, since dominantly perverse organizations of sexual impulses limit reproduction, the merits of perversion depend upon the need to limit or increase population. Experience of sexual pleasure may be desirable if it promotes relaxation and communication in an acquisitive society, undesirable if it limits the desire to work or, in armies, to kill. The social consequences of complete sex have not received particular attention,because the quality of sexual experience has been of little interest to moralists. It might be found that those who had complete sexual relations were more cooperative, less amenable to political revolt. If so, complete sexual acts would be desirable in just and peaceable societies, undesirable in unjust societies requiring revolution.

The social desirability of types of sexual acts depends on particular social conditions and independent criteria of social desirability. It may be interesting and important to assess particular claims about the social desirability of sex acts, but this is not my concern. What is my concern is the extent to which we will allow our judgments of sexual worth to be influenced by social considerations. But this issue cannot even be raised until we have a better sense of sexual worth.

THE BENEFIT OF SEXUAL PLEASURE

To say that an experience is pleasant is to give a self-evident, terminal reason for seeking it. We can sometimes "see" that an experience is pleasant. When, for example, we observe someone's sensual delight in eating, his behavior can expressively characterize pleasure. We can only question the benefit of such an experience by referring to other goods with which it might conflict. Though sensual pleasures may not be sufficient to warrant giving birth or to deter suicide, so long as we live they are self-evidently benefits to us.

The most eloquent detractors of sexual experience have admitted that it provides sensual pleasures so poignant that once experienced they are repeatedly, almost addictively, sought. Yet, unlike other appetites, such as hunger, sexual desire can be permanently resisted, and resistance has been advocated. How can the prima facie benefits of sexual pleasure appear deceptive?

There are several grounds for complaint. Sexual pleasure is ineradicably mixed, frustration being part of every sexual life. The capacity for sexual pleasure is unevenly distributed, cannot be voluntarily acquired, and diminishes through no fault of its subject. If such a pleasure were an intrinsic benefit, benefit would in this case be independent of moral effort. Then again, sexual pleasures are not serious. Enjoyment of them is one of life's greatest recreations, but none of its business. And finally, sexual desire has the defects of its strengths. Before satisfaction, it is, at the least, distracting; in satisfaction, it "makes one little roome, an everywhere." Like psychosis, sexual desire turns us from "reality"—whether the real be God, social justice, children, or intellectual endeavor. This turning away is more than a social consequence of desire, though it is that. Lovers themselves feel that their sexual desires are separate from their "real" political, domestic, ambitious, social selves.

If the plaintiff is taken to argue that sensual pleasures are not peremptory benefits, he is probably right. We can still want a good deal and forego sexual pleasures. We often forego pleasure just because we want something incompatible with it, for example, a good marriage. We must distinguish between giving up some occasions for sexual pleasure and giving up sexual pleasure itself. When all circumstances of sexual pleasure seem to threaten a peremptory benefit, such as self-respect, then the hope and the possibility of sexual pleasure may be relinquished. Since sexual pleasure is such a great, though optional, benefit, its loss is a sad one.

In emphasizing the unsocial, private nature of sexual experiences, the plaintiff is emphasizing a morally important characteristic of them. But his case against desire, as I have sketched it, is surely overstated. The mixed, partly frustrated character of any desire is not particularly pronounced for sexual desire, which is in fact especially plastic, or adaptable to changes (provided perverse sex acts have not been ruled out). Inhibition, social deprivation, or disease make our sexual lives unpleasant, but that is because they interfere with sexual desire, not because the desire is by its nature frustrating. More than other well-known desires (for example, desire for knowledge, success, or power), sexual desire is simply and completely satisfied upon attaining its object. Partly for this reason, even if we are overtaken by desire during sexual experience, our sexual experiences do not overtake us. Lovers turn away from the world while loving, but return—sometimes all too easily—when loving is done. The moralist rightly perceives sexual pleasure as a recreation, and those who upon realizing its benefits make a business of its pursuit appear ludicrous. The capacity for recreation, however, is surely a benefit that any human being rightly hopes for who hopes for anything. Indeed, in present social and economic conditions we are more likely to lay waste our powers in work than in play. Thus, though priest, revolutionary, and parent are alike in fearing sexual pleasure, this fear should inspire us to psychological and sociological investigation of the fearing rather than to moral doubt about the benefit of sexual pleasure.

THE MORAL SIGNIFICANCE OF PERVERSION

What is the moral significance of the perversity of a sexual act? Next to none, so far as I can see. Though perverted sex may be "unnatural" both from an evolutionary and developmental perspective, there is no connection, inverse or correlative, between what is natural and what is good. Perverted sex is sometimes said to be less pleasurable than natural sex. We have little reason to believe that this claim is true and no clear idea of the kind of evidence on which it would be based. In any case, to condemn perverse acts for lack of pleasure is to recognize the worth of pleasure, not of naturalness.

There are many other claims about the nature and consequences of perversion. Some merely restate "scientific" facts in morally tinged terminology. Perverse acts are, by definition and according to psychiatric theory, "immature" and "abnormal," since natural sex acts are selected by criteria of "normal" sexual function and "normal" and "mature" psychological development. But there is no greater connection of virtue with maturity and normality than there is of virtue with nature. The elimination of a village by an invading army would be no less evil if it were the expression of controlled, normal, natural, and mature aggression.

Nagel claims that many perverted sex acts are incomplete, and in making his point, gives the most specific arguments that I have read for the inferiority of perverted sex. But as he points out, there is no reason to think an act consisting solely of oral-genital intercourse is incomplete; it is doubtful whether homosexual acts and acts of buggery are especially liable to be incomplete; and the incompleteness of sexual intercourse with animals is a relative matter depending upon their limited consciousness. And again, the alleged inferiority is not a consequence of perversion but of incompleteness, which can afflict natural sex as well.

Perverted acts might be thought to be inferior because they cannot result in children. Whatever the benefits and moral significance of the procreation and care of children (and I believe they are extensive and complicated), the virtue of proper care for children neither requires nor follows from biological parenthood. Even if it did, only a sexual life consisting solely of perverse acts rules out conception.

If perverted sex acts did rule out normal sex acts, if one were *either* perverted *or* natural, then certain kinds of sexual relations would be denied some perverts—relations that are benefits to those who enjoy them. It seems that sexual relations with the living and the human would be of greater benefit than those with the dead or with animals. But there is no reason to think that heterosexual relations are of greater benefit than homosexual ones. It might be that children can only be raised by hetero-sexual couples who perform an abundance of natural sex acts. If so (though it seems unlikely), perverts will be denied the happiness of parent-hood. This would be an *indirect* consequence of perverted sex and might yield a moral dilemma: How is one to choose between the benefits of children and the benefits of more pleasurable, more complete sex acts?

Some perversions are immoral on independent grounds. Sadism is the obvious example, though sadism practiced with a consenting masochist is far less evil than other, more familiar forms of aggression. Voyeurism may seem immoral because, since it must be secret to be satisfying, it violates others' rights to privacy.[19] Various kinds of rape can constitute perversion if rape, rather than genital intercourse, is the aim of desire. Rape is ser-iously immoral, a vivid violation of respect for persons. Sometimes doubly perverse rape is doubly evil (the rape of a child), but in other cases (the rape of a pig) its evil is halved. In any case, though rape is always wrong, it is only perverse when raping becomes the aim and not the means of desire.

Someone can be dissuaded from acting on his perverse desires either from moral qualms or from social fears. Although there may be ample basis for the latter, I can find none for the former except the possible indirect loss of the benefits of child care. I am puzzled about this since re-flective people who do not usually attempt to legislate the preferences of others think differently. There is no doubt that beliefs in these matters in-volve deep emotions that should be respected. But for those who do in fact have perverted desires, the first concern will be to satisfy them, not to divert or to understand them. For sexual pleasure is intrinsically a benefit, and complete sex acts, which depend upon expressing the desires one in fact has, are both beneficial and conducive to virtue. Therefore, barring extrinsic moral or social considerations, perverted sex acts are preferable to natural ones if the latter are less pleasurable or less complete.

THE MORAL SIGNIFICANCE OF COMPLETENESS

Complete sex consists in mutually embodied, mutually active, responsive desire. Embodiment, activity, and mutual responsiveness are instrumentally beneficial because they are conducive to our psychological well-being, which is an intrinsic benefit. The alleged pathological consequences of disembodiment are more specific and better documented than those of perversity.[20] To dissociate oneself from one's actual body, either by creating a delusory body or by rejecting the bodily, is to court a variety of ill effects, ranging from self-disgust to diseases of the will, to faulty mental development, to the destruction of a recognizable "self," and finally to madness. It is difficult to assess psychiatric claims outside their theoretical contexts, but in this case I believe that they are justified. Relative embodiment is a stable, *normal* condition that is not confined to cases of complete embodiment. But psychiatrists tell us that exceptional physical occasions of embodiment seem to be required in order to balance tendencies to reject or to falsify the body. Sexual acts are not the only such occasions, but they do provide an immersion of consciousness in the bodily, which is pleasurable and especially conducive to correcting experiences of shame and disgust that work toward disembodiment.

The mutual responsiveness of complete sex is also instrumentally beneficial. It satisfies a general desire to be recognized as a particular "real" person and to make a difference to other particular "real" people. The satisfaction of this desire in sexual experience is especially rewarding, its thwarting especially cruel. Vulnerability is increased in complete sex by the active desiring of the partners. When betrayal, or for that matter, tenderness or ecstasy, ensues, one cannot dissociate oneself from the desire with which one identified and out of which one acted. The psychic danger is real, as people who attempt to achieve a distance from their desires could tell us. But the cost of distance is as evident as its gains. Passivity in respect to one's own sexual desire not only limits sexual pleasure but, more seriously, limits the extent to which the experience of sexual pleasure can be included as an experience of a coherent person. With passivity comes a kind of irresponsibilty in which one can hide from one's desire, even from one's pleasure, "playing" seducer or victim, tease or savior. Active sexual desiring in complete sex acts affords an especially threatening but also especially happy occasion to relinquish these and similar roles. To the extent that the roles confuse and confound our intimate relations, the benefit from relinquishing them in our sexual acts, or the loss from adhering to them then, is especially poignant.

In addition to being beneficial, complete sex acts are morally superior for three reasons. They tend to resolve tensions fundamental to moral life; they are conducive to emotions that, if they become stable and dominant, are in turn conducive to the virtue of loving; and they involve a preeminently moral virtue—respect for persons.

In one of its aspects, morality is opposed to the private and untamed. Morality is "civilization," social and regulating; desire is "discontent" resisting the regulation. Obligation, rather than benefit, is the notion central to morality so conceived, and the virtues required of a moral person are directed to preserving right relations and social order. Both the insistence on natural sex and the encouragement of complete sex can be looked upon as attempts to make sexual desire more amenable to regulation. But whereas the regulation of perverted desires is extrinsic to them, those of completeness modify the desires themselves. The desiring sensual body that in our social lives we may laugh away or disown becomes our "self" and enters into a social relation. Narcissism and altruism are satisfied in complete sex acts in which one gives what one receives by receiving it. Social and private "selves" are unified in an act in which impersonal, spontaneous impulses govern an action that is responsive to a particular person. For this to be true we must surmount our social "roles" as well as our sexual "techniques," though we incorporate rather than surmount our social selves. We must also surmount regulations imposed in the name of naturalness if our desires are to be spontaneously expressed. Honestly spontaneous first love gives us back our private desiring selves while allowing us to see the desiring self of another. Mutually responding partners confirm each others' desires and declare them good. Such occasions, when we are "moral" without cost, help reconcile us to our moral being and to the usual mutual exclusion between our social and private lives.

The connection between sex and certain emotions—particularly love, jealousy, fear, and anger—is as evident as it is obscure. Complete sex acts seem more likely than incomplete pleasurable ones to lead toward affection and away from fear and anger, since any guilt and shame will be extrinsic to the act and meliorated by it. It is clear that we need not feel for someone any affection beyond that required (if any is) simply to participate with him in a complete sex act. However, it is equally clear that sexual pleasure, especially as experienced in complete sex acts, is conducive to many feelings—gratitude, tenderness, pride, appreciation, dependency, and others. These feelings magnify their object who occasioned them, making him unique among men. When these magnifying feelings become stable and habitual they are conducive to love—not universal love, of course, but love of a particular sexual partner. However, even "selfish" love is a virtue, a disposition to care for someone as her interests and demands would dictate. Neither the best sex nor the best love require each other, but they go together more often than reason would expect—often enough to count the virtue of loving as one of the rewards of the capacity for sexual pleasure exercised in complete sex acts.

It might be argued that the coincidence of sex acts and several valued emotions is a cultural matter. It is notoriously difficult to make judgments about the emotional and, particularly, the sexual lives of others, especially culturally alien others. There is, however, some anthropological evidence that at first glance relativizes the connection between good sex and valued emotion. For example, among the Manus of New Guinea, it seems that relations of affection and love are encouraged primarily among brother and sister, while easy familiarity, joking, and superficial sexual play is expected only between cross-cousins. Sexual intercourse is, however, forbidden between siblings and cross-cousins but required of married men and women, who are as apt to hate as to care for each other and often seem to consider each other strangers. It seems, however, that the Manus do not value or experience complete or even pleasurable sex. Both men and women are described as puritanical, and the sexual life of women seems blatantly unrewarding. Moreover, their emotional life is generally impoverished. This impoverishment, in conjunction with an unappreciated and unrewarding sexual life dissociated from love or affection, would argue for a connection between better sex and valued emotions. If, as Peter Winch suggests, cultures provide their members with particular possibilities of making sense of their lives, and thereby with possibilities of good and evil, the Manus might be said to deny themselves one possibility both of sense and of good—namely the coincidence of good sex and of affection and love. Other cultures, including our own, allow this possibility, whose realization is encouraged in varying degrees by particular groups and members of the culture.[21]

Finally, as Sartre has suggested, complete sex acts preserve a respect for persons. Each person remains conscious and responsible, a "subject" rather than a depersonalized, will-less, or manipulated "object." Each actively desires that the other likewise remain a "subject." Respect for persons is a central virtue when matters of justice and obligation are at issue. Insofar as we can speak of respect for persons in complete sex acts, there are different, often contrary requirements of respect. Respect for persons, typically and in sex acts, requires that *actual present* partners participate, partners whose desires are recognized and endorsed. Respect for persons typically requires taking a distance from both one's own demands and those of others. But in sex acts the demands of desire take over, and equal distance is replaced by mutual responsiveness. Respect typically requires refusing to treat another person merely as a means to fulfilling demands. In sex acts, another person is so clearly a means to satisfaction that she is always on the verge of becoming merely a means ("intercourse counterfeits masturbation"). In complete sex acts, instrumentality vanishes only because it is mutual and mutually desired. Respect requires encouraging, or at least protecting, the autonomy of another. In complete sex, autonomy of will is recruited by desire, and freedom from others is replaced by frank dependence on another person's desire. Again the respect consists in the reciprocity of desiring dependence, which bypasses rather than violates autonomy.

Despite the radical differences between respect for persons in the usual moral contexts and respect for persons in sex acts, it is not, I think, a mere play on words to talk of respect in the latter case. When, in any sort of intercourse, persons are respected, their desires are not only, in fair measure, fulfilled. In addition, their desires are active and determine, in fair measure, the form of intercourse and the manner and condition of desire's satisfaction. These conditions are not only met in sexual intercourse when it is characterized by completeness; they come close to defining completeness.

Sartre is not alone in believing that just because the condition of completeness involves respect for persons, complete sex is impossible. Completeness is surely threatened by pervasive tendencies to fantasy, to possessiveness, and to varieties of a sadomasochistic desire. But a complete sex act, as I see it, does not involve an heroic restraint on our sexual interpulses. Rather, a complete sex act is a normal mode of sexual activity expressing the natural structure and impulses of sexual desire.

While complete sex is morally superior because it involves respect for persons, incomplete sex acts do not necessarily involve immoral disrespect for persons. They may, depending upon the desires and expectations of the partners; but they may involve neither respect nor disrespect. Masturbation, for example, allows only the limited completeness of embodiment and often fails of that. But masturbation only rarely involves disrespect to anyone. Even the respect of the allegedly desirable sleeping woman may not be violated if she is unknowingly involved in a sex act. Disrespect, though likely, may be obviated by her sensibilities and expectations that she has previously expressed and her partner has understood. Sex acts provide one context in which respect for persons can be expressed. That context is important both because our sexual lives are of such importance to us and because they are so liable to injury because of the experience and the fear of the experience of disrespect. But many complete sex acts in which respect is maintained makes other casual and incomplete sex acts unthreatening. In this case a goodly number of swallows can make a summer.

In sum, then, complete sex acts are superior to incomplete ones. First, they are, whatever their effects, better than various kinds of incomplete sex acts because they involve a kind of "respect for persons" in acts that are otherwise prone to violation of respect for, and often to violence to, persons. Second, complete sex acts are good because they are good for us. They are conducive to some fairly clearly defined kinds of psychological well-being that are beneficial. They are conducive to moral well-being because they relieve tensions that arise in our attempts to be moral and because they encourage the development of particular virtues.

To say that complete sex acts are preferable to incomplete ones is not to court a new puritanism. There are many kinds and degrees of incompleteness. Incomplete sex acts may not involve a disrespect for persons. Complete sex acts only *tend* to be good for us, and the realization of these tendencies depends upon individual lives and circumstances of sexual activity. The proper object of sexual desire is sexual pleasure. It would be a foolish ambition indeed to limit one's sexual acts to those in which completeness was likely. Any sexual act that is pleasurable is prima facie good, though the more incomplete it is—the more private, essentially autoerotic, unresponsive, unembodied, passive, or imposed—the more likely it is to be harmful to someone.

ON SEXUAL MORALITY: CONCLUDING REMARKS

There are many questions we have neglected to consider because we have not been sufficiently attentive to the quality of sexual lives. For example, we know little about the ways of achieving better sex. When we must choose between inferior sex and abstinence, how and when will our choice of inferior sex damage our capacity for better sex? Does, for example, the repeated experience of controlled sexual disembodiment ("desire which takes over will take you too far") that we urge (or used to urge) on adolescents damage their capacity for complete sex? The answers to this and similar questions are not obvious, though unfounded opinions are always ready at hand.

Some of the traditional sexual vices might be condemned on the ground that they are inimical to better sex. Obscenity, or repeated public exposure to sexual acts, might impair our capacity for pleasure or for response to desire. Promiscuity might undercut the tendency of complete sex acts to promote emotions that magnify their object. Other of the traditional sexual vices are neither inimical nor conducive to better sex, but are condemned because of conflicting nonsexual benefits and obligations. For example, infidelity qua infidelity neither secures nor prevents better sex. The obligations of fidelity have many sources, one of which may be a past history of shared complete sex acts, a history that included promises of exclusive intimacy. Such past promises are as apt to conflict with as to accord with a current demand for better sex. I have said nothing about how such a conflict would be settled. I hope I have shown that where the possibility of better sex conflicts with obligations and other benefits, we have a *moral dilemma*, not just an occasion for moral self-discipline.

The pursuit of more pleasurable and more complete sex acts is, among many moral activities, distinguished not for its exigencies but for its rewards. Since our sexual lives are so important to us, and since, whatever our history and our hopes, we are sexual beings, this pursuit rightly engages our moral reflection. It should not be relegated to the immoral, nor to the "merely" prudent.

NOTES

1. An earlier version of this paper was published in *Moral Problems*, edited by James Rachels (New York: Harper & Row, 1971). I am grateful to many friends and students for their comments on the earlier version, especially to Bernard Gert, Evelyn Fox Keller, and James Rachels.

2. This may be a consequence of the tepidness of the English "pleasant." It would be better to speak of lust and its satisfaction if our suspicion of pleasure had not been written into that part of our language.

3. The example is from Sigmund Freud, *Three Essays on Sexuality*, standard ed., vol. 7 (London: Hogarth, 1963), p. 182. The concept of pleasure I urge here is narrower but also, I think, more useful than the popular one. It is a concept that, to paraphrase Wittgenstein, we (could) learn when we learn the language. The idea

of paradigmatic uses and subsequent more-or-less-divergent, more-or-less-"normal" uses also is derived from Wittgenstein.

4. George Klein, "Freud's Two Theories of Sexuality," in L. Berger, ed., *Clinical-Cognitive Psychology: Models and Integrations* (Englewood Cliffs, N.J.: Prentice-Hall, 1969), pp. 131-81. This essay gives a clear idea of alternative psychological accounts of sexual pleasure.

5. Maurice Merleau-Ponty, *Phenomenology of Perception*, trans. Colin Smith (London: Routledge & Kegan Paul, 1962), p. 156.

6. See Kurt Vonnegut, Jr., "Welcome to the Monkey House," in *Welcome to the Monkey House* (New York: Dell, 1968), which concerns both the manipulation and the benefit of sexual pleasure.

7. Jean-Paul Sartre, *Being and Nothingness*, trans. Hazel E. Barnes (New York: Philosophical Library, 1956), p. 389.

8. Merleau-Ponty, *Phenomenology of Perception*, p. 167.

9. Thomas Nagel, "Sexual Perversion," *The Journal of Philosophy* 66, no. 1 (January 16, 1969): 13; herein, pp. 255-56. My original discussion of completeness was both greatly indebted to and confused by Nagel's. I have tried here to dispel some of the confusion.

10. W. T. Stace, "Solipsism," from *The Theory of Knowledge and Existence*; reprinted in Tillman, Berofsky, and O'Connor, eds. *Introductory Philosophy* (New York: Harper & Row, 1967), p. 113.

11. Denise Levertov, "Gone Away," in *O Taste and See* (New York: New Directions, 1962), p. 59. Copyright by Denise Levertov Goodman, New Directions Publishing Corporation, New York.

12. R. D. Laing, *The Divided Self* (Baltimore: Pelican Books, 1965), p. 69.

13. We need not become our bodies on such occasions. Pains, muscular feelings, and emotions can be reduced to mere "sensations" that may impinge on "me" but that I attempt to keep at a distance. Laing describes the case of a man who when beaten up felt that any damage to his body could not really hurt *him*. See *The Divided Self*, p. 68.

14. Nagel, "Sexual Perversion," p. 254.

15. Jean-Paul Sartre, *Saint Genet* (New York: Braziller, 1963), p. 398; cited and translated by R. D. Laing, *Self and Others* (New York: Pantheon, 1969), pp. 39-40.

16. Ibid., p. 13.

17. Sartre, *Being and Nothingness*, p. 386.

18. See, in support of this point, Sigmund Freud, *Introductory Lectures on Psychoanalysis*, standard ed., vol. 26 (London: Hogarth, 1963), chaps. 20, 21.

19. I am indebted to Dr. Leo Goldberger for this example.

20. See, for example, R. D. Laing, *The Divided Self*; D. W. Winnicott, "Transitional Objects and Transitional Phenomena," *International Journal of Psychoanalysis* 34 (1953): 89-97; Paul Federn, *Ego Psychology and the Psychoses* (New York: Basic Books, 1952); Phyllis Greenacre, *Trauma, Growth, and Personality* (New York: International Universities Press, 1969); Paul Schilder, *The Image and Appearance of the Human Body* (New York: International Unversities Press, 1950); Moses Laufer, "Body Image and Masturbation in Adolescence," *The Psychoanalytic Study of the Child* 23 (1968): 114-46. Laing's work is most specific

about both the nature and consequences of disembodiment, but the works cited, and others similar to them, give the clinical evidence upon which much of Laing's workd depends.

21. The evidence about the life of the Manus comes from Margaret Mead, *Growing Up in New Guinea* (Harmondsworth, Eng.: Penguin Books, 1942). Peter Winch's discussion can be found in his "Understanding a Primitive Society," *American Philosophical Quarterly* 1 (1964): 307-34.

D. P. Verene

Sexual Love and Moral Experience

In contemporary society human sexuality and the questions of sexual morality that are thought to surround it are widely discussed. Much of this discussion, like much contemporary discussion of social and moral issues generally, is unconnected with historical views and is theoretically vague. It approaches the issues of sex and morality in terms of analyses of opinions, social statistics, reflections on personal experience, journalistic commonplaces about human nature and human good, and broad arguments that stem from no systematic theory of man. We confront these approaches almost daily, in the public press, in national magazines, in books on sexual relations and the advertisements for them, and in the views continually expressed on television interviews and talk shows. When sex is discussed in terms that are less immediate in form, the approach tends to be medical (for example, the research of Masters and Johnson) or social scientific (for example, Kinsey's studies of sexual behavior, and the work of the Institute for Sex Research) or psychoanalytic. Although medical, social, and psychological studies of sex are of great value, little attention is given sex as a philosophical and ethical problem. One of the reasons for this is that philosophy is thought by the public to be generally divorced from the forces that can and do shape the ongoing stream of social experience. Another reason is that philosophers themselves have come to regard their enterprise as a technical one not primarily directed to the normative discussion of specific human activities. Philosophical and ethical thought has generally lost touch with the sphere of direct human problems. This is not true of the thought of many figures in the history of philosophy. Philosophers such as Plato, Aristotle, Augustine, Thomas Aquinas, Hume, Kant, Schopenhauer, and Marx devoted substantial attention to questions concerning sexual love and the relations between the sexes.[1]

My aim in this essay is to consider what may be said from a philosophical point of view about the nature of sexual love and relations between the sexes. It is not my intention to say all that can be said on the subject, nor even to indicate in principle all that would be necessary for a full or systematic account of it. I wish to suggest several issues that I take to be central to a philosophical and ethical understanding of human sexuality in contemporary life. I will consider three questions: (1) To what extent is there something that can be called "sexual ethics," and to what extent is ethical analysis as traditionally conceived relevant to human sexual activity? (2) What accounts for the fact that we in contemporary Western civilization regard human sexuality as having moral questions intrinsically connected with it? (3) What are the features of contemporary consciousness that act to make sexual love a fundamentally problematic activity?

The first of these questions is related to the problem of whether there is a dimension of human moral experience that can be labeled "sexual morality" and that contains such unique moral problems and principles of conduct as to warrant the conception of a special division of ethical theory that can be called "sexual ethics." Such an area of inquiry might be conceived in terms of an analogy with other areas of special activity, such as "business ethics" or "legal ethics." Seen from this perspective sexual activity would seem to involve the possibility of codes of conduct for how one should act in various types of sexual situations, how one's sexual partner or partners should be treated, and so forth. Such an approach, if it is desirable at all in relation to sexual activity, would not constitute a philosophical inquiry into sex. This "sexual-morality" and "sexual-ethics" approach is what we frequently encounter in the advice columns of news-papers and in articles in popular magazines. The task of philosophical ethics has never truly been that of giving advice on matters of moral eti-quette, even in such private and esoteric areas as sexual relations. Sexual activity as an ethical problem would appear to begin where this concern leaves off.

There is a second sense in which sexual ethics can be conceived. This is the notion that sexual activity is in itself so sufficiently unique and significant a human activity as to pose special problems for the general analysis of human moral conduct. Here the question is not one of coming to understand what is socially acceptable behavior in sexual matters. It is the question of developing intellectual criteria whereby sexual activity can be understood in terms of conceptions of moral good or right. It is the attempt to determine what ought to prevail for persons in relation to the sexual dimension of their humanity. The ethical understanding of sexual-ity in this sense can either proceed from specific problems seen as present in human sexuality, and reason toward general ethical principles and criteria, or it can begin from the perspective of some general ethical view and work toward understanding human sexual activity as a special case to which the principles of this general view apply. Thus, in the latter case, one can begin from, say, the position of utilitarianism or hedonism or the Kantian categorical imperative and attempt to derive some specific ethical understanding of sex. It is also possible to employ an analysis of sexual activity as a means to raise difficulties for, or show the failure of, one or more of such classical ethical points of view when it is used to account for the nature of sexual activity. It is my contention that from whatever gen-eral direction such ethical analysis is conducted it is basically criteria-oriented.[2] Such an approach is oriented not only toward understanding the principles by which sexual activity can be related to the concept of good or right or proper, but also toward distinguishing between forms of sexual activity that are "moral" or "natural" or "desirable" and those that are not. In doing this the results produced may endorse or be at odds with those that predominate in the larger social order or various groups within it.

It is my contention that the criteria approach just described is not especially illuminating for understanding in philosophical terms the mean-ing of sexual activity and relations between the sexes. Any analysis of sex-uality as a special ethical problem either assumes or consciously employs some general theory of human morality. The particular relations that are found through such analysis to occur between humans in sexual activity, or the relation any individual has to his own sexual being, either will be seen as an illustration of the meaning of the principles of such a theory or will be seen as the basis for a critical challenge of them. The logic of this traditional kind of approach is one involving a method of reflection and the application of the principles discovered in reflection as criteria for evaluating the phenomena in question. It is a method that is largely argumentative and formula-like and which in fact always leaves the phenomena untouched.

My point is that contemporary philosophical thought about sexuality must not begin and end its analysis within the circle of traditional ethical analysis concerned with principles, maxims, and evaluation. This method, which may have its strengths in relation to ethical questions conceived in general terms, pales before the concrete. After having gone through a set of arguments about moral principles and criteria in relation to a concrete phenomena such as sex, we may feel that we have been intellectually broadened, but we find it has done very little for us in relation to our understanding ourselves as sexual beings. At the end of such analysis we still lack a perspective on the normative character of our own sexuality. The arguments seem to exist apart from the intrinsic structure of sexual activity that we directly experience. The analysis exists in one realm and the activity as we actually encounter it exists in another. The exchanges in the arguments function as matters of cognitive assertion and production of evidence, whereas sex itself functions as an activity within the concrete structures of our particular period of history, culture, and society, all of which operate as forces on our sexual acts. To apply standard ethical analysis to such experience certainly offers us something of a perspective on human sexuality and sexual morality, but it by no means offers us a route of primary access to them. It never loses its a priori status as it stands before them.

The second question I originally posed has to do with the possibility of a method of approaching the question of the moral dimension of human sexuality in terms of a concept of its origin.[3] The method I have described above has its beginning in the simple assertion that a problem exists that is regarded by most as ethical in character and it then proceeds to reason about it, applying to it general standards of logic and evidence and the insights and general forms of reasoning that have been developed in classical and recent ethical theory. But from the perspective I wish to suggest, the first and most fundamental question that must be raised concerning the morality of sexual activity is that of why we have moral questions about it at all. Does human sexuality involve moral questions by its very nature? Or do we think of it as involving moral questions because of the particular period in which we live?

Human sexuality is not the cause of activity that by its very nature involves moral questions in any greater or more special sense than any number of other basic human activities. Sex was not a moral issue for the ancient Greeks, at least not in anything of the same sense that it is for us.[4] Sexual morality is a problem for us because we are the inheritors of the Judeo-Christian tradition. It is in St. Paul and the early fathers of the Christian church, not in Plato, that we find the view that "it is well for a man not to touch a woman" and "a wife is bound to her husband as long as he lives."[5] In Plato's *Republic* the proposal that in the ideal society women shall hold highest office and share education equally with men was revolutionary, particularly since Greek society kept women largely in seclusion.[6] But what would be truly scandalous from the standpoint of the mentality of St. Paul is the companion proposal that the guardian class of the ideal state from which the officeholders are to come are to "have wives and children in common," even though sexual relations are to be closely controlled under a system of eugenics. It is not that in the works of Plato, and in the thought of the ancient world generally, sex and sexual relations are not discussed and discussed in ethical and philosophical terms; it is that for the ancient mind the very notion of morality itself is not tied to one's sexual conduct.

It is in connection with Christian thought and what has become the Judeo-Christian tradition of Western society that the notion of moral character is portrayed to the individual through his sexual nature and his existence as a body with senses. Thus we find Augustine, in the *City of God*, taking considerable pains to argue at length concerning the nature of lust or the "stirrings of obscene heat." It is of great concern to him that even though the sex act may be properly performed within the framework of marriage and with the intention of procreation, this act necessary to the continuance of the species depends upon the sexual organs being moved by the lust of the body. In other instances of bodily activity, such as moving an arm or leg, the will can exercise control over the body. But we cannot move our sexual organs into action at will. They seem completely moved by bodily stimulations (it should also be noted that throughout his analysis Augustine approaches the question from the standpoint of the male body, an approach that is reinforced by the Judeo-Christian conception of marriage with the male as dominant active agent and the female as passive receptacle). The Christian can resist with his will the illicit sexual relations toward which his bodily appetites may incline him. But he must submit to them if he is to engage in the sex act in its licit form of having children in marriage. The true Christian, Augustine states, "would prefer to beget children without this kind of lust."[7] From the classic Judeo-Christian perspective the body becomes the element of original sin to be overcome. From this perspective sex becomes a moral issue of extraordinary magnitude, since it is in sexual activity that the body seems to take over the person and the will. In the sexual act the senses seem to command the body in total frenzy.

It is this basic view of sexuality—that human sexuality is morally problematic in and of itself and that acts in which the body is used for purely sensual purposes are illicit—that one finds stated and restated within the tradition of Western morality. Thinkers such as Hume and Kant, who in their criticisms of the ideas that formed the bases of traditional epistemology and metaphysics changed the direction of Western thought, simply reflect the standard views of the Judeo-Christian tradition when they turn their attention to questions of marriage and sexuality. Hume's discussion of the value of monogamous marriage in *Essays Moral, Political, and Literary*[8] and Kant's analysis of the sexual impulse and "crimes against nature" in his *Lectures on Ethics*, given between 1775 and 1781,[9] appear as largely unoriginal restatements of the Judeo-Christian conception of sex and the sexes. It is difficult to believe that the former work is by the same mind that wrote the *Treatise of Human Nature* and the latter by the one that wrote the *Critique of Pure Reason*. But when our attention is turned to concrete ethical problems, the Judeo-Christian ethic exerts a powerful influence.

Even as society becomes secularized in the modern period this attitude that human sexuality intrinsically involves moral questions and the moral disposition of individual character comes to be written into the structure of our ordinary moral consciousness. Thus we immediately conjure up a sexual referent when someone says of another, "He has questionable morals." To allege that someone's morals are questionable—except in academic discussion or classroom ethics, where perhaps the notion of morality is already being taken in a wider sense—connotes something about the person's sexual behavior. To say that a person's morals are questionable does not call to mind questions about his possible honesty or his sense of duty to his country or family. To report that someone was arrested on a "morals charge" is clearly to indicate that he was arrested on some charge relating to his sexual conduct. In common speech and consciousness sexual conduct and attitudes come to function as the indicator of the moral character of the person. This response is offset by the challenge to the traditional Judeo-Christian view of sex as sin that has its origin in the work of Freud and psychoanalysis. Freud's analysis of human sexuality points to the unnaturalness of the Judeo-Christian ethic. [10] From such a perspective sexuality is no longer seen on the metaphor of a disease to be cured by proper exercise of the will; it is regarded as a natural and dynamic force in human affairs and a basic motivation of the psyche. In contemporary life the individual is in fact caught between these two perspectives—that of the Judeo-Christian ethic, which forms the basis of the customs and laws of Western society, and that of the notion that proper relationships must exist between the individual and the society to insure the freedom of his sexual being. The ability of the individual to explore the dimensions of his sexual being rather than restrictions of it is seen as the key to enlightened social practice and the health of the individual psyche.

The third of my initial questions points to the fact that although sex appears to us as a moral problem through the tension between the Judeo-Christian ethic and widespread perspectives on human sexuality that have developed from the wellspring of modern psychoanalytic and social-scientific thought, the true source of its problematic character lies elsewhere. It lies in the very form that contemporary life takes. In the contemporary world the question facing the individual is not so much, How can one develop criteria to evaluate sexual activity? but, How can one experience sexual love at all? It is my contention that love, and specifically sexual love, is an important force that is connected to human creativity and creativity in human relations. On this view, in order for man to conceive of himself as ethical he must have experience of himself as a creative agent. I wish to suggest that sexual love, which has at its center the sexual act, is the fundamental act wherein the individual makes contact with the erotic, and it is a feeling for the erotic that underlies the creation of ethical and aesthetic forms. The teleological direction that is established in experience by the ethical or aesthetic ideal is grasped at the most fundamental human level in the physical and emotional production of the climax. Sexual activity is our primary access as individuals to the erotic and thus to that power that underlies the ability of consciousness to act in terms of a created ideal. The sexual act, no matter what particular form it may take, is a primary way in which human consciousness encounters the *eros* that is requisite for the orientation of human activity under an ideal.

It is not possible here to explore at length the view I am suggesting. What I want to emphasize is that in considering the relationship between morality and sexuality, the fundamental question is not whether sexual activity can or cannot be judged in certain moral terms. The more interesting and important aspect of the relationship between human morality and human sexuality is the sense in which sex can be understood as itself the basis for the impetus to moral ideals and human value. The basic problem for a philosophy of sexuality is not to reflect on sexual activity and to attempt to produce moral principles adequate to its nature; rather it is to see the sense in which sexual activity is itself responsible for moral experience. Once this ordering of the relationship is seen, the reason that the Judeo-Christian ethic so strongly desires to control sexual activity can also be seen. If the primary form of the erotic in experience is the sexual act and if the erotic is an element necessary for consciousness to orient itself in terms of an ideal, it is just this factor that any such ethic must control. It appears to it as something uncontrolled. The erotic itself is always potentiality, ready to strike new chords, to stimulate imaginative power. It is not accidental, then, that the Judeo-Christian ethic seeks so systematically to bound the sexual act with moral principles, for in so doing it achieves through a displacement of the *eros* of the sexual act the force necessary to the generation of its own *ethos*. To approach the problem of sex and morality in terms of the process of ethical argumentation, even if it is undertaken to criticize the Judeo-Christian standpoint, is never in fact to depart from its relationship to *eros*. In fact, in such a process of argumentation and analysis the erotic is never truly opposed or endorsed. It is left philosophically untouched.

The central problem involving sexuality and morality today is not one of deciding which moral principles are true but one of discovering how the eroticism of sexual love can be recovered as an act between individuals and within the social world. One of the paradoxes of contemporary sexual life that Rollo May calls attention to in *Love and Will* [11] is that never before have persons been more informed about the techniques of "sexual fulfillment"; yet coupled with this is widespread uncertainty by individuals as to whether they have achieved erotic experience in the sex act, or even pleasure. There exists today almost a totality of sexual information available to most persons throughout most of Western society. The

techniques of sexual love are commonplace knowledge; yet sexual love remains problematic. The point I wish to suggest is that we have a problem
with the *reality* of sexual love and that we have the problem because we
have a problem with the reality of *eros,* or the erotic. Contemporary society
is technological in form.[12] Human consciousness functions in the contemporary world through technique. It experiences its own activity
through the medium of technique: that which is real is that which is
capable of formulation as technique. Sex is no exception and its reality becomes for us the reality of technique. All that is needed on the part of the
individual sexual actor, from the viewpoint of technological consciousness,
is the knowledge of sexual technique and the physical coordination to act
in terms of this knowledge. This is not to say that technique is not important in sexual matters. Technique as such has always been of great importance to people who have pursued sexually erotic lives, such as Casanova and Madame de Pompadour, and has had a prominent place in
erotic literature such as Ovid's *Art of Love* or the *Kama Sutra.* But the
important feature of such examples is that for Casanova and Madame de
Pompadour, for Ovid or the *Kama Sutra,* sexual technique is an extension
of the erotic reality of sexual activity. Any particular sexual act derives its
erotic reality from the fact that the world itself is perceived as erotic.
Ovid's work and the *Kama Sutra,* like all ancient works on the techniques
of sexual love, involve a view of the entire world as sexual.[13]

Sexual activity in the contemporary world is no longer a route to stir-
ring erotic experience in the individual because the *eros* of the particular
sexual act requires that the world itself be experienced as erotic. The eros
of the sexual act and the eros of the world are codeterminative.[14] By transforming nature into a system of instrumentalities through technique, and
by transforming society into a system of interlocking techniques of human
organization, the realities to which the *eros* of the sex act has been connected are de-eroticized. Thus in the contemporary world the sex act
becomes simply pleasurable, or at least potentially pleasurable, but not
erotic. The pleasurable and the erotic become equated and sex becomes the
quest for the best techniques to induce pleasure in one's partner and in
oneself. Ethical inquiry into sexual activity becomes an activity of discovering the limits that may or may not be set for the extension of this quest.
Thus moral debate occurs concerning the limits of sexual practice—
whether, for example, flagellation or sexual masochism are ethically justifiable, or whether they are in all cases perversions. The antinomous char-

acter of all conclusions reached in such debate mirrors in the intellectual sphere the loss of *eros* that is a constant feature of contemporary sexual life itself.

To recapitulate my point, the question that is fundamental when considering the relationship beteen sex and morality is that of how it is possible to recover in the sex act the experience of *eros*, in terms of which the world can be felt as alive. I have suggested that there is a connection between *eros* and the creation of values and that the creativity necessary for the formation of ideals arises out of the basic experience of the manipulation of the senses and the sensuous body that occurs in the sex act and the production of the climax. The contemporary problem of sexuality must not begin with moral critique but with thought about how it is that the sexual act can be experienced as a basis for recovering the kind of feelings about the world that have been lost in the technological shaping of nature and modern society.

NOTES

1. For a treatment of the portions of the works by these and other philosophers that deal with sexuality, see D. P. Verene, *Sexual Love and Western Morality: A Philosophical Anthology* (New York: Harper Torchbooks, 1972).

2. A work that I would take to fall under the general classification I am describing but that I also take to be an important exception to the type of moral abstraction ordinarily involved in this approach is John Wilson, *Logic and Sexual Morality* (Baltimore: Penguin Books, 1965). See especially Wilson's discussion of the "fallacy of discrimination," p. 59 f.

3. It is not my intention here to actually trace a philosophical history of the conception of sex as a moral issue, but I do wish to adhere to the methodological importance of understanding the nature of a problem through the nature of its origin, especially in the treatment of questions of an ethical or social nature. I take this mode of understanding to originate with Vico. I regard his view that "doctrines must take their beginning from that of the matters of which they treat" to be a much overlooked methodological insight. See *The New Science of Giambattista Vico*, rev. trans. Thomas Goddard Bergin and Max Harold Fisch (Ithaca, N.Y.: Cornell University Press, 1968), par. 314.

4. See, for example, Paul Brandt [Hans Licht, pseud.], *Sexual Life in Ancient Greece*, trans. J. H. Freese and ed. Lawrence W. Dawson (London: Routledge & Kegan Paul, 1932).

5. 1 Corinthians 7:1, 39.

6. *The Republic of Plato*, trans. F. M. Cornford (New York and London: Oxford University Press, 1945), p. 144. See also Werner Jaeger's comments in *Paideia: The Ideals of Greek Culture*, trans. Gilbert Highet (New York: Oxford University

Press, 1944), vol. 2, pp. 242-46.

7. For Augustine's discussion of these questions see *City of God*, trans. Philip Levine (Cambridge, Mass.: The Loeb Classical Library, Harvard University Press, 1966), IV, pp. 345-401. Augustine carries his argument as far as to maintain that humans as God originally designed them for the state of Paradise could move their sexual organs by will and without need of lust. He presents an a posteriori argument for this that must be among the most curious arguments in the history of philosophy, involving as evidence of the will's control over the body the ability of some people to wiggle their ears ("either one at a time or both together") and to wiggle their scalps, to swallow and regurgitate objects, to imitate perfectly the calls of animals and birds, to deliberately perspire and shed tears, and to "produce at will without any stench such rhythmical sounds from their fundament that they appear to be making music even from that quarter"!

8. "Of Polygamy and Divorces," *Essays Moral, Political, and Literary*, ed. T. H. Green and T. H. Grose (London: Longmans, Green, 1875), vol. 2, pp. 231-39.

9. Trans. Louis Infield (London: Methuen & Co., 1930), pp. 162-71.

10. I have in mind specifically Freud's paper "'Civilized' Sexual Morality and Modern Nervous Illness," in *The Standard Edition of the Complete Works of Sigmund Freud*, ed. James Strachey, rev. ed. (London: Hogarth Press, 1959), vol. 9, pp. 187-204.

11. New York: W. W. Norton, 1969, pp. 37-48.

12. The view of technique that I am here employing is that of the French thinker, Jacques Ellul, principally from his work *The Technological Society*, trans. John Wilkinson (New York: Knopf, 1964).

13. For a contemporary statement of this perspective see Henry Miller, *The World of Sex* (New York: Grove Press, 1965).

14. For an account of the role of the sexually erotic in the structuring of consciousness and the self see Michael Kosok, "The Phenomenology of Fucking," *Telos* (Summer 1971): 64-76.

Bernard H. Baumrin

Sexual Immorality Delineated

Human sexual interaction is essentially manipulative—physically, psychologically, emotionally, and even intellectually. On different occasions of such interaction or anticipated interaction, different weights, emphases, and significance will be given to these factors; so the analysis of their relative force in any given sexual interaction is exceedingly complicated. It will not be my task here to present even a general taxonomy or analysis of these factors (though this is where, in my view, the most fruitful discoveries will be made); rather I shall use this information only in order to delineate the realm of immoral sexual interaction, if there is one.

I start with the thesis that human sexual interaction is essentially manipulative for several reasons. (1) If one were to suppose that the Kantian dictum "never treat anyone as a means only but always as an end"[1] implies that one should never use anyone as a means and that manipulating another for one's own purpose is using another as a means, then every instance of sexual manipulation would be immoral; and that, it seems to me, would perhaps make every human sexual interaction immoral. There seem to me to be several weaknesses in this view, not the least of which is the fact that virtually no one believes the conclusion to be true—that is, that every human sexual interaction involving the manipulation of another for one's own (sexual) ends is immoral. Another perhaps not less important point is that Kant's dictum does not mean that one should never treat anyone in *any* respect as a means, but rather that one should never treat anyone in *every* respect as a means, or not as an end as well as a means. In this form the dictum might be true and useful; otherwise it is piously empty, for it bids us to refrain from the unavoidable.

I dwell on this point only because if there is any sexual immorality, one interpretation of Kant's view seems most straitaway to establish what it is—the manipulation of others for one's own ends. It seems to me that this must be wrong, since sex is manipulation, is using others as means to one's own ends, and I take it as indisputable that nothing that virtually everyone thinks is not immoral is in fact immoral.

(2) A second reason for beginning with the thesis that sex is essentially manipulative is that it eliminates, in gross, any number of quite silly views that espouse the mythology of perfect sexual harmony, of two minds (in the manner of *The Prophet*) conceptually indistinguishable, of two hearts beating as one, of two bodies locked together like bronze equestrian sculptures. It is not that I think these are merely rare occurrences and thus bad bases on which to erect theories and make recommendations; rather I think that they are impossible occurrences and that any theories that rest on or press for them must perforce be mistaken. Thus, I begin (as moralists sometimes do) by admitting the most damaging facts—for they are, in my view, facts—that any theory of sexual immorality must countenance, and then look about to see what is left. For this reason I expand a bit on what I consider the facts to be.

However inherently attractive, desirable, and satisfying to others we think we may be, so much of our thought and action shaped by such thought is concerned with enhancing these characteristics, with making them noticeable or perhaps even remarkable, that it is painfully clear that all of us think of ourselves often enough as awkward, ugly, repulsive, detestable, inept, and laughable to others. The primary point here is that we are frequently taking ourselves in hand, not leaving totally to the chance conjunction of emotional storms the success of our mating instincts. We do not (often) behave as statues sought for their inherent qualities—sexual interaction is a bundle of disparate activities that we try to manage, devoting to it a great deal of energy, foresight, and care. Even when hoping for the perfect spontaneous interaction we at least try to do what will not thwart it. We invite attention and manage what attention we attract. Often we do this ineptly and need to review our errors to understand from them what not to do in the future, and so sacrifice with advancing age and growing wisdom the possibility of the perfect spontaneous interaction. We change the focus of our desire to satisfaction or naturalness or pleasure or some other piece of the ideal sexual interaction that is promulgated in our sexual mythology. But all along from the primping and swaggering teenager to whatever age the reader is, memories of the management of one's encounters charm or horrify. Perhaps no one has ever had a perfectly spontaneous sexual interaction, but everyone has spoken to cajole, shifted eyes to charm, acquiesced to trick, clothed to attract, touched to try to thrill, waited for the moment, played on a known weakness, looked for a sign of one's initial success to move the game along. We use our own emotions sexually to change the emotions of others. We seek to know the inner psyche of our partners to enhance at least for ourselves our interaction with them; we want to know their physical responsiveness, their likes and dislikes, for use now or in the future. Who supposes that our interest in such information is scientific, medical, artistic, or philosophic? Who supposes that our interest in such information is sought by us solely to benefit our partner? Is it not patent that even if we wish to benefit a sexual partner, we seek such knowledge at least also for our own benefit, and possibly only for our own benefit.

There appears to be no plausible theory[2] on the basis of which we could justify the use of someone[3] sexually exclusively as a means. This fact does not merely imply that we should never so treat them; it also implies that to some extent we ought to treat them as non-means—that is, it is a positive duty of every sexual interaction that each person treat every other not merely as a means to the satisfaction of their own desires but as someone to whom one owes this positive duty and who has a right to expect implementation of it. This point may not seem to be altogether clear as stated; so I shall restate it in two other ways. First, if a person X has a particular duty D toward someone else Y, it is always appropriate to infer that Y has a right with respect to X that X fulfill D. X's duties to Y exist only if Y has rights; Y has rights against X only if X has duties to Y. A negative duty of X's toward Y implies that Y has a right to expect X not to do whatever the duty forbids; a positive duty of X's toward Y implies that Y has a right to expect X to do whatever the duty calls for.

But not all apparently negative duties are genuinely negative. While I have a genuinely negative duty not to kill anyone, Y has only a right to expect me to engage in behavior that avoids the likelihood of my killing him. He does not have the right to expect me to do this in any particular way, or even in cognizance of his existence. I may do it quite well by avoiding him. But in sexual interaction my behavior involves interaction with another, and I cannot engage in the action in a purely negative way. I am, as it were, constrained to act with someone, and thus all the rights that that person has and all the duties that I have toward that person coexist during that interaction. All the negative duties may be dischargeable by not infringing the other's rights, but the positive duties cannot be satisfied without some other-directed behavior being done that the other has a right to expect. My duty is only apparently negative since my choosing to interact sexually at all creates rights in the other, just as their choosing to so interact creates rights in me.

The second way of putting the point is this: If I have a duty in a sexual interaction to treat Y as other than a non-means, then the class of such non-means treatment is a class of behaviors permissible to me; Y has a right to expect that at least some of my behavior will come from this class, and the implementation by me of at least one such behavior is a positive duty that I have toward Y. My failure to perform or appear to try to perform some behavior in the class may properly be regarded by Y as a failure to perform my duty, or a violation of Y's rights.

Let me sum up this point by saying that the voluntary choices by X and Y to engage in a sexual interaction creates in both X and Y new positive duties and rights, and failure by either to do that which fulfills the former violates the latter and is immoral.

But what exactly is this class of permissible treatment of another, some of which each person has a duty to do and some of which each has a right to expect. The class in question has only the following criteria to delineate it thus far: (1) the persons involved must in some positive respect treat each other as non-means; (2) each person properly expects some such treatment; (3) that expectation is based on the apparently voluntary choice of the other to engage in this kind of activity, that is, sexual interaction.

While these factors delineate the class of permissible sexual treatment, they do not do so with sufficient precision, since they exist as well in other than sexual contexts. They can be found in normal contractual situations, for example, undertaking to have someone repair one's car or ordering a meal from a waiter. Nor would it be sufficient merely *to say* that these are the crucial factors in *sexual* situations, since that would leave "sexual" unspecified and thus fail to tell us anything more about what creates specifically sexual rights and duties. What we need to specify for sexual interactions are just those additional factors that differentiate sexual interactions from other similar interpersonal interactions. Those additional factors are: (4) behavior reasonably apprehendable by one person as being intended by another to form an offer of some form or level of sexual interaction creates in the initiating agent a duty to perform in that form or at that level should the offer be explicitly or implicitly accepted; (5) accordingly, the apparent acceptance of such an offer creates a duty toward the initiating agent to perform at least at the behavioral level or in the behavioral form of the acceptance (not necessarily in the form or at the level of the offer).

Thus the initiating agent creates a right in the other properly to accept the offered performance, if the initiative is accepted without modification.

The accepting party may accept, but only with modification, which therefore might entirely discharge the offering party of any further duty.

There is, however, one further factor that is of central importance. The initiating agent, through his or her behavior, implicitly offers the following proposal (this holds even if there are simultaneous offers): (6) *I wish to use you as an instrument for my sexual purposes and therefore undertake to make myself the instrument of your sexual purposes to the extent that you accept my proposal.* Thus, on this view, the crucial element in creating specifically sexual rights and duties is the desire to use another as a means for a certain kind of end and the willingness to offer oneself to that person as an inducement to form a voluntary arrangement. What one is offering is to make oneself the other's means for the satisfaction of their desires. Otherwise one would in fact not be making an offer at all, or at least not a sexual one, since one would merely be behaving in a peculiar way or forcing one's attentions on the other. In either case, the immorality of one's behavior would be obvious. Consider the following examples: (1) A approaches B and suggests charmingly that due to B's attractive characteristics, A would like to make love to B. In response, B invites A to B's home. On arrival A shakes B's hand and leaves. (2) C approaches B and suggests that due to B's attractive characteristics C would like to make love to B. B says no. C becomes more demonstrative. B attempts to leave. C locks the door and proceeds to shower B with attention, while B spends the evening trying to extricate himself. (3) The particulars are the same as in case 1 except that on arriving at B's home B shakes A's hand and goes inside alone.

I think it is clear that the six factors I have set down are interrelated, and although they provide a clear enough test of sexual immorality of the grosser sorts, it is not altogether clear what their force is on a more intimate level. It is to this subject that I now turn.

If it is immoral to propose to use someone else as a sexual instrument without at the same time being prepared to be used by them as their instrument, then it is also immoral to use someone else as a sexual instrument without permitting oneself to be so used. While the immorality of the unilateral proposal is derived from intending to use someone only as a means, the immorality of the behavior is derived from the actual depersonalization of the other.

To illustrate, let us suppose that A wishes to engage in a specific kind of sexual activity and manipulates B, for example, emotionally and physically, to that end. All along, B anticipates the later occurrence of another kind of sexual activity that B wants, and B's wishes are known all along by A; but A nevertheless avoids doing what B wants. On the view stated above, A's behavior is immoral. It makes no difference that A loves B in some way (otherwise quite satisfactory); if A, knowing what B wishes, nevertheless knowingly fails to do what B wishes and B has done what A wished, then A is immoral. This is so because A has failed to be what he has undertaken to be—namely, an instrument of B's satisfaction.

A would of course not be immoral (that is, would not have violated B's rights) if A had *tried* to do what A reasonably believed B wished; but if A did not try, then A did not discharge the duty owed to B. A has no right to use B without B's having a right to use A; therefore, if A will not let B use A, then to that extent A previously had no right to use B.

Now, one might object that the situations of A and B are not parallel since A manipulated B and A stands ready to be manipulated but is not ready to volunteer. This objection (which arises domestically not infrequently) rests on a confusion: if A knows that B wishes A to do Q and Q is the kind of behavior that must be volunteered by A, then what A must do in order to be B's instrument is Q; for if B is required to manipulate A to engage in the sexual acts included in Q, it is no longer Q that A will do, because part of the definition of Q is that it emanates voluntarily from A. Thus, if A knows that B wishes Q and B knows that A wishes R, then if B engages in R, A is obliged to do Q.

We might speculate that one who never or rarely initiates sexual activity may simply not wish to create duties for himself or rights in others. There might be some psychological explanatory power in such an analysis of the origin of sexual passivity, frigidity, and impotence.

The central point is that if one offers to be used within certain bounds, then if one's offer is accepted, the other person determines what use is to be made of one within those bounds. If one does not intend to be used, one is neither genuinely making nor accepting an offer of sexual interaction, despite the appearances. One might, however, be morally bound anyway to perform as expected because the appearances seemed to create an offer or an acceptance, and might thus put one under a duty to satisfy the good-faith expectations of the other created by one's own behavior. This arises, for example, when one has created the appearances deliberately while knowing more or less how they would be interpreted.

It is, of course, perfectly permissible for one who accepts an offer not to wish to use another. This is not an uncommon occurrence, and I think it springs in part from the frequent failure to realize that rights are created by interpersonal transactions, and not just the ones we have been discussing. Probably part of this unconsciousness of one's rights (as well as of one's duties) comes from the now quite ancient tradition of considering sexual interaction as a romance between feelings, where feelings have been elevated to a sacrosanct position. Thus it appears that many believe that if one's positive feelings change, one is relieved of the burden of responding to overtures based on the now mistaken belief that those positive feelings still exist. Similarly, some believe that if one performs under the influence of a feeling, one's behavior is excusable, as well as explainable. What is especially implausible about views of this sort is that no analysis has as yet been made of feeling that shows it to be of a higher value than any other psychological entity; nor has any analysis been made that shows that behavior caused by feeling has any comparatively privileged position that makes it immune from praise or blame. Of course one might argue that behavior caused by feeling is uncontrollable; but why should that fact, if indeed it is one, make such behavior more valuable than merely rational or calculative or habitual behavior. One can well understand someone's being driven by his feelings to do something he might otherwise not do; but surely there is nothing specially laudable or natural in such action. The intellectual picture of sexuality that we have had for quite some time applauds the natural, the pastoral, the uninhibited, the silent communion of souls; it treats the contrived, the cultured, the controlled, and the merely carnal as contemptible. This legacy of romanticism has endured in our thinking about sex, while all of the intellectual paraphernalia that supported it has long since been swept away by clear thinking and rational criticism.

One might be curious to see what this analysis has to say about the immorality of such sexual interactions as adultery, incest, and rape. Ordinary rape is easily enough dealt with, since its immorality stems from the lack of voluntary participation of one of the parties, thus giving the other no rights and making the rapist's behavior a violation of other rights of the involuntary participant. There are, however, two kinds of rape cases that are more complicated. First, there is the case where the rapist has a good-faith belief that he has received an offer of sexual interaction and views his behavior as the implementation of his acceptance. Such cases depend for their resolution on a careful analysis of the actual behavior of the person raped and what reasonable people would have interpreted it to mean (this problem will be dealt with in more detail later).

Second, there is the possible case of a person who believes that (1) there is a class of persons who can achieve sexual fulfillment only if raped, that (2) he is a person gifted in perceiving who these persons are, and that (3) his activities in this regard are a social duty (I suppose he is also a utilitarian). This case is complicated because number 1 seems true and number 3 is self-supporting; so only number 2 is open to criticism. But if he believes that he is gifted in perceiving those persons who can achieve sexual fulfillment only if raped, then it may be the case that we cannot show him that he is wrong. Thus, if he rapes someone not in the class in question, he is doing both what he believes to be his duty and something immoral. I think there are ways of handling this apparent difficulty, but since it is not especially a problem for my view, I leave it here unresolved.

Adultery, it seems to me, presents no special problems since its immorality, *when* it is immoral qua adultery, springs from the violation by one or more parties of a prior agreement with some other person(s) to preserve some degree of exclusive access. Thus in adultery the very fact of the interaction's existence might be immoral even though no part of the interaction is itself immoral.

There seems to be nothing sexually immoral about incest that is not accounted for by the immorality that springs, on one hand, from adultery and, on the other, from constructive (or statutory) rape. This implies that adult-sibling incest is not immoral and that incest is in general not sexually immoral, even though such interactions might be immoral on other grounds.

When I began to rethink this subject some years ago I approached it from an entirely different direction and uncovered for myself a wealth of complications. In deference to those complications, I have here almost entirely omitted even tangential reference to the domain of directive communication (except in our discussion of rape). However, something needs to be said of it, even if all too schematically. A good deal of the communication of offer, acceptance, counteroffer, scope, seriousness, and detail in sexual transactions occurs by means of customary and special-convention gestures—that is, by behavior whose primary purpose is to transmit information. Gestural communication with or without attendant verbal communication is used in preference to mere verbal communication for a wide variety of purposes and for different sorts of reasons. One of the most interesting is that gestures are by nature ambiguous, both as to what the user intends and the interpreter understands. When used in sexual transactions (as they very often are), they court misunderstanding. Nevertheless, they also preserve the possibility of innovation, of a new agreement, of new levels of behavior. They also permit the avoidance of embarrassments and permit us to overcome our mistakes almost as quickly as we make them. In short, they facilitate the management of our interpersonal relations with less friction, less recrimination, and less pain than if we were relegated to the use only of language stripped of nonverbal behavior.

But it should be remembered as well that gestures and gesturally enriched talk easily lends itself to misperception, and misperception lends itself to disappointment. It is here that we so often fail each other without being immoral; for our duty is to act on what we perceive the other to wish, and the other has only a right to expect us to act on what we perceive and not on what he or she wishes in fact. Our perceptions create the particular character of our duties; thus we may do what we in good faith believe is required of us without doing what is wished. Such sexual failure stems from miscommunication and not immorality.

AN APPENDIX ON UTILITARIANISM AND EGOISM

I think it is obvious that sexually self-interested behavior is not always immoral; so clearly the question is whether it is ever immoral and, if so, when and why. One might begin by seeing whether any clear direction can be given by any standard popular ethical theory. Whatever the merits of utilitarianism are, this is one area where, if there are merits, they are quite obscure. Certainly a sexual interaction might increase the sum total of pleasure or happiness or even good in the world, but certainly not for very many people, and not necessarily for any. And the long-range consequences of the interaction for increasing pleasure, happiness, or good are unprojectible. But even were these difficulties easily set to rest, sexual interaction is not so clearly more beneficial for mankind than is sexual abstinence, unless one were constrained to argue that it has to be engaged in so as to provide future generations who would enjoy a balance of a valued property over a disvalued property. (If it is believed that the future will in fact be worse than the past in regard to the property in question, then the argument would have the opposite thrust—that is, that one should discourage the production of future generations.) Finally, and perhaps most importantly, ought one to engage in sexual interactions (acts of class S) in order to increase the amount of the valued property? Is it in fact a moral duty to do acts of the class S, and if so, ought one do them to increase the amount of the valued property, or just do them simply? This question is of some importance, for it must be asked not only of utilitarians. Suppose that S represents the class of all sexual acts. Then, whether or not one wishes finally to say some S ought not be done, one must ask whether some S ought to be done. That is, are some sexual acts morally obligatory? Utilitarianism, to its credit, does seem to imply that S's that would increase the balance of pleasure over pain (P/p) in the world should be done, and if the opportunity is available, one should do that S that would have this result (in fact one should do that S that *maximizes* this result). But the question remains for utilitarians: Should one do what one does *in order to* increase the balance of P/p? Is increasing P/p the criterion for S's obligatoriness and also the reason why one ought to do S? Would one be immoral for doing S for some other reason? Would sexual immorality for a utilitarian be doing what one ought, but not for the reason one ought, or would it be merely not doing what one ought? The latter answer supposes that the agent not only knows that he ought to do S, but also that he does not think on utilitarian grounds that he ought to do some other act, T. Suppose he believes (on utilitarian grounds) that T will increase the balance of P/p more than S will. Then (on utilitarian grounds) he should do T, unless S will in fact increase the balance more than T. But if he believes T will increase the balance of P/p more than S will he should do T anyway, since he believes (on utilitarian grounds) that S is not as obligatory as T.

Now suppose he believes (on utilitarian grounds) he ought to do S; then it follows that he must believe that S will enhance the balance of P/p more than T. Therefore, if he ought to do S, then he ought to do S *because* it will enhance P/p, and he cannot be said to have a moral duty to do S unless he first determines that S will enhance P/p. If he does S without making this prior determination, he cannot know that doing S is his moral duty; and so he cannot be doing S, if he then does it because it is his moral duty.

It is clear, then, that if utilitarianism is used to support the view that some acts of the class S ought to be done, it is committed to the view that they must be done from the motive to increase the balance of the desired property over its contrary. If this conclusion is correct, then both utilitarianism and Kantianism are pretty much in the same canoe—namely, they share the view that all sexual acts, if they ought to be done, ought to be done from the belief that it is one's duty to do them. And further, any such act not so done might for that very reason be immoral.

I have dwelt on this small point because it seems to me that besides being counterintuitive, it is inconsistent with the view that the manipulative acts I cited at the beginning are not always immoral. This, I think, accounts in part for the fact that neither utilitarians nor Kantians seem to have had much to say about human sexual interaction. They have thought that by sweeping all human activity together they can deal neatly with sex in the same package as lying, assault, and the distribution of bonbons. But this is quite wrong. One does not primp, swagger, wink, cajole, or importune out of duty, nor for the general production in the long or short run of an enhanced balance of P/p; and it is not obviously immoral to do so. It is not obvious that it is immoral to act as we do thoughtlessly, ineptly or irrelevantly; but it is just as obvious that a lightly considered provocative wink whose principal effect is to create pained jealously in another is probably immoral for both utilitarians and Kantians, and either we are much more evil than we think, or these views are just wrong.

Are we then driven at last into the waiting embrace of egoism? Is the final arbitration of sexual morality to be found in a principle that bids us to act only for the enhancement of what we believe to be what we want? Or, put differently, is there nothing sexually immoral save what hinders or thwarts our reaching what we perceive to be what we desire? Versions of an egoistic sexual morality are not difficult to state, but however stated, they seem open to a flaw that militates against their plausibility. That flaw arises from the fact that often (though perhaps not always) sexual gratification, satisfaction, enjoyment, pleasure, and success involves the cooperation (sometimes even the enthusiastic cooperation) of others. Unlike any number of other characteristically moral situations, it is difficult to envision sexual partners as merely passive recipients or victims of our behavior —which we can easily do with, for example, lying, killing, being kind, or being charitable.

In order to have that cooperation that seems desirable (perhaps even necessary), one cannot always do what one desires to do, for fear of alienating the other or of reducing or eliminating the desired cooperation. Whether one then does other than one would dissemblingly (or insincerely) or in a genuine attempt to encourage the desired cooperation, one's behavior is being determined as much by what one perceives the other to wish or desire—or at least not be displeased with—as by what one genuinely desires to do. Thus the egoist (as anyone else similarly situated) is often constrained to behave in accordance with the desires of others in order to try to fulfill his own desires. On his own principles, an immoral act of his would be to do that which he perceives to be counterproductive to fulfilling his goals, and anything offensive to the other might thus be immoral.[4] Thus the only acts that serve self are those that are accepted by the other as serving self as well. The egoist in sex, then, gains little from his or her egoism, for here, as perhaps elsewhere as well, it is not the individual himself who determines what is moral or immoral for him to do, but others who determine it for him. And, of course, they may make that determination on principles quite alien to egoism.

So my criticism of egoism in regard to sexual morality is not that what serves only self is immoral because it is like a kind of theft or deceit, where the services of another are gained by a dissembling larceny; rather, my criticism is that the egoist cannot serve self successfully without serving others successfully. Thus his moral theory does not serve at all as a guide for action, nor even as much of a guide for moral criticism. In short, my view is that whatever the other merits of egoism might be, in sexual matters, it is largely, perhaps entirely, irrelevant.

NOTES

1. "Act so that you treat humanity, whether in your own person or in that of another, always as an end and never as a means only." Kant, *Grundlegung*, IV, p. 429; translated as *Foundations of the Metaphysics of Morals*, L. W. Beck, trans. (Indianapolis, Ind.: Library of Liberal Arts Press), p. 87.

2. The arguments for this conclusion are set out in an appendix to this article, where the two most popular kinds of moral theory, utilitarianism and egoism, are analyzed.

3. I exclude here dead people, animals, and objects of voyeurism, on the theory that we are talking about human sexual interaction and not merely the exercise of one's genitalia or imagination.

4. Cf. Aristotle E.N. IX, 1, 1164a 5-15; IX, 8, 1165b 1-10.

THE MORALITY OF MARRIAGE

The Tradition
Monogamy
Adultery and Promiscuity

Pope Paul VI

Humanae Vitae

To the venerable Patriarchs, Archbishops and other local ordinaries in peace and communion with the Apostolic See, to priests, the faithful and to all men of good will.

Venerable brothers and beloved sons:

THE TRANSMISSION OF LIFE

1. The most serious duty of transmitting human life, for which married persons are the free and responsible collaborators of God the Creator, has always been a source of great joys to them, even if sometimes accompanied by not a few difficulties and by distress.

At all times the fulfillment of this duty has posed grave problems to

The encyclical *Humanae Vitae* was issued July 29, 1968, at Rome. This official translation is reprinted by permission of the National Catholic News Service.

the conscience of married persons, but, with the recent evolution of society, changes have taken place that give rise to new questions which the Church could not ignore, having to do with a matter which so closely touches upon the life and happiness of men.

1. NEW ASPECTS OF THE PROBLEM AND COMPETENCY OF THE MAGISTERIUM

New Formulation of the Problem

2. The changes which have taken place are in fact noteworthy and of varied kinds. In the first place, there is the rapid demographic development. Fear is shown by many that world population is growing more rapidly than the available resources, with growing distress to many families and developing countries, so that the temptation for authorities to counter this danger with radical measures is great. Moreover, working and housing conditions, as well as increased exigencies both in the economic field and in that of education, often make the proper education of a large number of children difficult today. A change is also seen both in the manner of considering the person of woman and her place in society, and in the value to be attributed to conjugal love in marriage, and also in the appreciation to be made of the meaning of conjugal acts in relation to that love.

Finally and above all, man has made stupendous progress in the domination and rational organization of the forces of nature, such that he tends to extend this domination to his own total being: to the body, to psychical life, to social life and even to the laws which regulate the transmission of life.

3. This new state of things gives rise to new questions. Granted the conditions of life today, and granted the meaning which conjugal relations have with respect to the harmony between husband and wife and to their mutual fidelity, would not a revision of the ethical norms, in force up to now, seem to be advisable, especially when it is considered that they cannot be observed without sacrifices, sometimes heroic sacrifices?

And again: by extending to this field the application of the so-called "principle of totality," could it not be admitted that the intention of a less abundant but more rationalized fecundity might transform a materially sterilizing intervention into a licit and wise control of birth? Could it not be admitted, that is, that the finality of procreation pertains to the ensemble of conjugal life, rather than to its single acts? It is also asked whether, in view of the increased sense of responsibility of modern man, the moment has not come for him to entrust to his reason and his will, rather than to the biological rhythms of this organism, the task of regulating birth.

Competency of the Magisterium

4. Such questions required from the teaching authority of the Church a new and deeper reflection upon the principles of the moral teaching on marriage: a teaching founded on the natural law, illuminated and enriched by divine revelation.

No believer will wish to deny that the teaching authority of the Church is competent to interpret even the natural moral law. It is, in fact, indisputable, as our predecessors have many times declared,[1] that Jesus Christ, when communicating to Peter and to the Apostles His divine authority and sending them to teach all nations His commandments,[2] constituted them as guardians and authentic interpreters of all the moral law, not only, that is, of the law of the Gospel, but also of the natural law, which is also an expression of the will of God, the faithful fulfillment of which is equally necessary for salvation.[3]

Conformable to this mission of hers, the Church has always provided —and even more amply in recent times—a coherent teaching concerning both the nature of marriage and the correct use of conjugal rights and the duties of husband and wife.[4]

Special Studies

5. The consciousness of that same mission induced us to confirm and enlarge the study commission which our predecessor Pope John XXIII of happy memory had instituted in March, 1963. That commission which included, besides several experts in the various pertinent disciplines, also married couples, had as its scope the gathering of opinions on the new questions regarding conjugal life, and in particular on the regulation of births, and of furnishing suitable elements of information so that the magisterium could give an adequate reply to the expectation not only of the faithful, but also of world opinion.[5]

The work of these experts, as well as the successive judgments and counsels spontaneously forwarded by or expressly requested from a good number of our brothers in the episcopate, have permitted us to measure exactly all the aspects of this complex matter. Hence with all our heart we express to each of them our lively gratitude.

Reply of the Magisterium

6. The conclusions at which the commission arrived could not, nevertheless, be considered by us as definitive, nor dispense us from a personal examination of this serious question; and this also because, within the commission itself, no full concordance of judgments concerning the moral norms to be proposed had been reached, and above all because certain criteria of solutions had emerged which departed from the moral teaching of marriage proposed with constant firmness by the teaching authority of the Church.

Therefore, having attentively sifted the documentation laid before us, after mature reflection and assiduous prayers, we now intend, by virtue of the mandate entrusted to us by Christ, to give our reply to these grave questions.

II. DOCTRINAL PRINCIPLES

A Total Vision of Man

7. The problem of birth, like every other problem regarding human life, is to be considered, beyond partial perspectives—whether of the biological or psychological, demographic or sociological orders—in the light of an integral vision of man and of his vocation, not only his natural and earthly, but also his supernatural and eternal vocation. And since, in the attempts to justify artificial methods of birth control, many have appealed to the demands both of conjugal love and of "responsible parenthood," it is good to state very precisely the true concept of these two great realities of married life, referring principally to what was recently set forth in this regard, and in a highly authoritative form, by the Second Vatican Council in its pastoral constitution *Gaudium et Spes*.

Conjugal Love

8. Conjugal love reveals its true nature and nobility, when it is considered in its supreme origin, God, who is love,[6] "the Father, from whom every

family in heaven and on earth is named."[7]

Marriage is not, then, the effect of chance or the product of evolution of unconscious natural forces; it is the wise institution of the Creator to realize in mankind His design of love. By means of the reciprocal personal gift of self, proper and exclusive to them, husband and wife tend towards the communion of their beings in view of mutual personal perfection, to collaborate with God in the generation and education of new lives.

For baptized persons, moreover, marriage invests the dignity of a sacramental sign of grace, inasmuch as it represents the union of Christ and of the Church.

Its Characteristics

9. Under this light, there clearly appear the characteristic marks and demands of conjugal love, and it is of supreme importance to have an exact idea of these.

This love is first of all fully human, that is to say, of the senses and of the spirit at the same time. It is not, then, a simple transport of instinct and sentiment, but also, and principally, an act of the free will, intended to endure and to grow by means of the joys and sorrows of daily life, in such a way that husband and wife become only one heart and only one soul, and together attain their human perfection.

Then, this love is total, that is to say, it is a very special form of personal friendship, in which husband and wife generously share everything, without undue reservations or selfish calculations. Whoever truly loves his marriage partner loves not only for what he receives, but for the partner's self, rejoicing that he can enrich his partner with the gift of himself.

Again, this love is faithful and exclusive until death. Thus in fact, do bride and groom conceive it to be on the day when they freely and in full awareness assume the duty of the marriage bond. A fidelity, this, which can sometimes be difficult, but is always possible, always noble and meritorious, as no one can deny. The example of so many married persons down through the centuries shows, not only that fidelity is according to the nature of marriage, but also that it is a source of profound and lasting happiness and finally, this love is fecund for it is not exhausted by the communion between husband and wife, but is destined to continue, raising up new lives. "Marriage and conjugal love are by their nature ordained toward the begetting and educating of children. Children are really the supreme gift of marriage and contribute very substantially to the welfare of their parents."[8]

Responsible Parenthood

10. Hence conjugal love requires in husband and wife an awareness of their mission of "responsible parenthood," which today is rightly much insisted upon, and which also must be exactly understood. Consequently it is to be considered under different aspects which are legitimate and connected with one another.

In relation to the biological processes, responsible parenthood means the knowledge and respect of their functions; human intellect discovers in the power of giving life biological laws which are part of the human person.[9]

In relation to the tendencies of instinct or passion, responsible parenthood means that necessary dominion which reason and will must exercise over them.

In relation to physical, economic, psychological and social conditions, responsible parenthood is exercised, either by the deliberate and generous decision to raise a large family, or by the decision, made for grave motives and with due respect for the moral law, to avoid for the time being, or even for an indeterminate period, a new birth.

Responsible parenthood also and above all implies a more profound relationship to the objective moral order established by God, of which a right conscience is the faithful interpreter. The responsible exercise of parenthood implies, therefore, that husband and wife recognize fully their own duties towards God, towards themselves, towards the family and towards society, in a correct hierarchy of values.

In the task of transmitting life, therefore, they are not free to proceed completely at will, as if they could determine in a wholly autonomous way the honest path to follow; but they must conform their activity to the creative intention of God, expressed in the very nature of marriage and of its acts, and manifested by the constant teaching of the Church.[10]

Respect for the Nature and Purpose of the Marriage Act

11. These acts, by which husband and wife are united in chaste intimacy, and by means of which human life is transmitted, are, as the council re-

called, "noble and worthy,"[11] and they do not cease to be lawful if, for
causes independent of the will of husband and wife, they are foreseen to be
infecund, since they always remain ordained towards expressing and con-
solidating their union. In fact, as experience bears witness, not every conjugal act is followed by a new life. God has widely disposed natural laws
and rhythms of fecundity which, of themselves, cause a separation in the
succession of births. Nonetheless the Church, calling men back to the observance of the norms of the natural law, as interpreted by their constant
doctrine, teaches that each and every marriage act (*quilibet matrimonii
usus*) must remain open to the transmission of life.[12]

Two Inseparable Aspects: Union and Procreation

12. That teaching, often set forth by the magisterium, is founded upon the
inseparable connection, willed by God and unable to be broken by man on
his own initiative, between the two meanings of the conjugal act: the unitive meaning and the procreative meaning. Indeed, by its intimate structure, the conjugal act, while most closely uniting husband and wife, em-
powers them to generate new lives, according to laws inscribed in the very
being of man and of woman. By safeguarding both these essential aspects,
unitive and procreative, the conjugal act preserves in its fullness the sense
of true mutual love and its ordination towards man's most high calling to
parenthood. We believe that the men of our day are particularly capable of
seizing the deeply reasonable and human character of this fundamental
principle.

Faithfulness to God's Design

13. It is in fact justly observed that a conjugal act imposed upon one's
partner without regard for his or her condition and lawful desires is not a
true act of love, and therefore denies an exigency of right moral order in
the relationships between husband and wife. Hence, one who reflects well
must also recognize that a reciprocal act of love, which jeopardizes the responsibility to transmit life which God the Creator, according to particular
laws, inserted therein is in contradiction with the design constitutive of
marriage, and with the will of the Author of life. To use this divine gift
destroying, even if only partially, its meaning and its purpose is to contradict the nature both of man and of woman and of their most intimate re-

lationship, and therefore, it is to contradict also the plan of God and His will. On the other hand, to make use of the gift of conjugal love while respecting the laws of the generative process means to acknowledge oneself not to be the arbiter of the sources of human life, but rather the minister of the design established by the Creator. In fact, just as man does not have unlimited dominion over his body in general, so also, with particular reason, he has no such dominion over his generative faculties as such, because of their intrinsic ordination towards raising up life, of which God is the principle. "Human life is sacred," Pope John XXIII recalled; "from its very inception it reveals the creating hand of God." [13]

Illicit Ways of Regulating Birth

14. In conformity with these landmarks in the human and Christian vision of marriage, we must once again declare that the direct interruption of the generative process already begun, and, above all, directly willed and procured abortion, even if for therapeutic reasons, are to be absolutely excluded as licit means of regulating birth. [14]

Equally to be excluded, as the teaching authority of the Church has frequently declared, is direct sterilization, whether perpetual or temporary, whether of the man or of the woman. [15] Similarly excluded is every action which, either in anticipation of the conjugal act, or in its accomplishment, or in the development of its natural consequences, proposes, whether as an end or as a means, to render procreation impossible. [16]

To justify conjugal acts made intentionally infecund, one cannot invoke as valid reasons the lesser evil, or the fact that such acts would constitute a whole together with the fecund acts already performed or to follow later, and hence would share in one and the same moral goodness. In truth, if it is sometimes licit to tolerate a lesser evil in order to avoid a greater evil or to promote a greater good [17] it is not licit, even for the gravest reasons, to do evil so that good may follow therefrom, [18] that is, to make into the object of a positive act of the will something which is intrinsically disordered, and hence unworthy of the human person, even when the intention is to safeguard or promote individual, family, or social well-being. Consequently it is an error to think that a conjugal act which is deliberately made infecund and so is intrinsically dishonest could be made honest and right by the ensemble of a fecund conjugal life.

Licitness of Therapeutic Means

15. The Church, on the contrary, does not at all consider illicit the use of those therapeutic means truly necessary to cure diseases of the organism, even if an impediment to procreation, which may be foreseen, should result therefrom, provided such impediment is not, for whatever motive, directly willed.[19]

Licitness of Recourse to Infecund Periods

16. To this teaching of the Church on conjugal morals, the objection is made today, as we observed earlier, that it is the prerogative of the human intellect to dominate the energies offered by irrational nature and to orientate them towards an end conformable to the good of man. Now, some may ask: in the present case, is it not reasonable in many circumstances to have recourse to artificial birth control if, thereby, we secure the harmony and peace of the family, and better conditions for the education of the children already born? To this question it is necessary to reply with clarity: the Church is the first to praise and recommend the intervention of intelligence in a function which so closely associates the rational creature with his Creator; but she affirms that this must be done with respect for the order established by God.

If, then, there are serious motives to space out births, which derive from the physical or psychological condition of husband and wife, or from external conditions, the Church teaches that it is then licit to take into account the natural rhythms immanent in the generative functions, for the use of marriage in the infecund periods only, and in this way to regulate birth without offending the moral principles which have been recalled earlier.[20]

The Church is consistent with herself when she considers recourse to the infecund periods to be licit, while at the same time condemning, as being always illicit, the use of means directly contrary to fecundation, even if such use is inspired by reasons which may appear honest and serious. In reality, there are essential differences between the two cases; in the former, the married couple make legitimate use of a natural disposition; in the latter, they impede the development of natural processes. It is true that, in the one and the other case, the married couple are in agreement in the positive will of avoiding children for plausible reasons, seeking the certainty that offspring will not arrive; but it is also true that only in the former case are they able to renounce the use of marriage in the fecund periods when, for just motives, procreation is not desirable, while making use of it during infecund periods to manifest their affection and to safe-guard their mutual fidelity. By so doing, they give proof of a truly and integrally honest love.

Grave Consequences of Methods of Artificial Birth Control

17. Upright men can even better convince themselves of the solid grounds on which the teaching of the Church in this field is based, if they care to re-flect upon the consequences of methods of artificial birth control. Let them consider, first of all, how wide and easy a road would thus be opened up towards conjugal infidelity and the general lowering of morality. Not much experience is needed in order to know human weakness, and to un-derstand that men—especially the young, who are so vulnerable on this point—have need of encouragement to be faithful to the moral law, so that they must not be offered some easy means of eluding its observance. It is also to be feared that the man, growing used to the employment of anti-conceptive practices, may finally lose respect for the woman and, no longer caring for her physical and psychological equilibrium, may come to the point of considering her as a mere instrument of selfish enjoyment, and no longer as his respected and beloved companion.

Let it be considered also that a dangerous weapon would thus be placed in the hands of those public authorities who take no heed of moral exigencies. Who could blame a government for applying to the solution of the problems of the community those means acknowledged to be licit for married couples in the solution of a family problem? Who will stop rulers from favoring, from even imposing upon their peoples, if they were to con-sider it necessary, the method of contraception which they judge to be most efficacious? In such a way men, wishing to avoid individual, family, or social difficulties encountered in the observance of the divine law, would reach the point of placing at the mercy of the intervention of public authorities the most personal and most reserved sector of conjugal intimacy.

Consequently, if the mission of generating life is not to be exposed to the arbitrary will of men, one must necessarily recognize unsurmountable limits to the possibility of man's domination over his own body and its functions; limits which no man, whether a private individual or one in-vested with authority, may licitly surpass. And such limits cannot be determined otherwise than by the respect due to the integrity of the human organism and its functions, according to the principles recalled earlier, and also according to the correct understanding of the "principle of totality" illustrated by our predecessor Pope Pius XII. [21]

The Church Guarantor of True Human Values

18. It can be foreseen that this teaching will perhaps not be easily received by all: Too numerous are those voices—amplified by the modern means of propaganda—which are contrary to the voice of the Church. To tell the truth, the Church is not surprised to be made, like her divine founder, a "sign of contradiction," [22] yet she does not because of this cease to proclaim with humble firmness the entire moral law, both natural and evangelical. Of such laws the Church was not the author, nor consequently can she be their arbiter; she is only their depositary and their interpreter, without ever being able to declare to be licit that which is not so by reason of its intimate and unchangeable opposition to the true good of man.

In defending conjugal morals in their integral wholeness, the Church knows that she contributes towards the establishment of a truly human civilization; she engages man not to abdicate from his own responsibility in order to rely on technical means; by that very fact she defends the dignity of man and wife. Faithful to both the teaching and the example of the Saviour, she shows herself to be the sincere and disinterested friend of men, whom she wishes to help, even during their earthly sojourn, "to share as sons in the life of the living God, the Father of all men." [23]

III. PASTORAL DIRECTIVES

The Church Mater et Magistra

19. Our words would not be an adequate expression of the thought and solicitude of the Church, mother and teacher of all peoples, if, after having recalled men to the observance and respect of the divine law regarding matrimony, we did not strengthen them in the path of honest regulation of birth, even amid the difficult conditions which today afflict families and peoples. The Church, in fact, cannot have a different conduct towards men than that of the Redeemer: She knows their weaknesses, has compassion on the crowd, receives sinners; but she cannot renounce the teaching of the law which is, in reality, that law proper to a human life restored to its original truth and conducted by the spirit of God. [24]

Possibility of Observing the Divine Law

20. The teaching of the Church on the regulation of birth, which promulgates the divine law, will easily appear to many to be difficult or even impossible of actuation. And indeed, like all great beneficent realities, it demands serious engagement and much effort, individual, family, and social effort. More than that, it would not be practicable without the help of God, who upholds and strengthens the good will of men. Yet, to anyone who reflects well, it cannot but be clear that such efforts ennoble man and are beneficial to the human community.

Mastery of Self

21. The honest practice of regulation of birth demands first of all that husband and wife acquire and possess solid convictions concerning the true values of life and of the family, and that they tend towards securing perfect self-mastery. To dominate instinct by means of one's reason and free will undoubtedly requires ascetical practices, so that the affective manifestations of conjugal life may observe the correct order, in particular with regard to the observance of periodic continence. Yet this discipline which is proper to the purity of married couples, far from harming conjugal love, rather confers on it a higher human value. It demands continual effort yet, thanks to its beneficent influence, husband and wife fully develop their personalities, being enriched with spiritual values. Such discipline bestows upon family life fruits of serenity and peace, and facilitates the solution of other problems; it favors attention for one's partner, helps both parties to drive out selfishness, the enemy of true love; and deepens their sense of responsibility. By its means, parents acquire the capacity of having a deeper and more efficacious influence in the education of their offspring; little children and youths grow up with a just appraisal of human values, and in the serene and harmonious development of their spiritual and sensitive faculties.

Creating an Atmosphere Favorable to Chastity

22. On this occasion, we wish to draw the attention of educators, and of all who perform duties of responsibility in regard to the common good of human society, to the need of creating an atmosphere favorable to education

in chastity, that is, to the triumph of healthy liberty over license by means of respect for the moral order.

Everything in the modern media of social communications which leads to sense excitation and unbridled habits, as well as every form of pornography and licentious performances, must arouse the frank and unanimous reaction of all those who are solicitous for the progress of civilization and the defense of the common good of the human spirit. Vainly would one seek to justify such depravation with the pretext of artistic or scientific exigencies,[25] or to deduce an argument from the freedom allowed in this sector by the public authorities.

Appeal to Public Authorities

23. To Rulers, who are those principally responsible for the common good, and who can do so much to safeguard moral customs, we say: Do not allow the morality of your peoples to be degraded; do not permit that by legal means practices contrary to the natural and divine law be introduced into that fundamental cell, the family. Quite other is the way in which public authorities can and must contribute to the solution of the demographic problem: namely the way of a provident policy for the family, of a wise education of peoples in respect of moral law and the liberty of citizens.

We are well aware of the serious difficulties experienced by public authorities in this regard, especially in the developing countries. To their legitimate preoccupations we devoted our encyclical letter *Populorum Progressio*. But with our predecessor Pope John XXIII, we repeat: No solution to these difficulties is acceptable "which does violence to man's essential dignity" and is based only on an utterly materialistic conception of man himself and of his life. The only possible solution to this question is one which envisages the social and economic progress both of individuals and of the whole of human society, and which respects and promotes of true human values.[26] Neither can one, without grave injustice, consider divine providence to be responsible for what depends, instead, on a lack of wisdom in government, on an insufficient sense of social justice, on selfish monopolization, or again on blameworthy indolence in confronting the efforts and the sacrifices necessary to ensure the raising of living standards of a people and of all its sons.[27]

May all responsible public authorities—as some are already doing so laudably—generously revive their efforts. And may mutual aid between all the members of the great human family never cease to grow. This is an almost limitless field which thus opens up to the activity of the great international organizations.

To Men of Science

24. We wish now to express our encouragement to men of science, who "can considerably advance the welfare of marriage and the family, along with peace of conscience, if by pooling their efforts they labor to explain more thoroughly the various conditions favoring a proper regulation of births." [28] It is particularly desirable that, according to the wish already expressed by Pope Pius XII, medical science succeed in providing a sufficiently secure basis for a regulation of birth, founded on the observance of natural rhythms. [29] In this way, scientists and especially Catholic scientists will contribute to demonstrate in actual fact that, as the Church teaches, "a true contradiction cannot exist between the divine laws pertaining to the transmission of life and those pertaining to the fostering of authentic conjugal love." [30]

To Christian Husbands and Wives

25. And now our words more directly address our own children, particularly those whom God calls to serve Him in marriage. The Church, while teaching imprescriptible demands of the divine law, announces the tidings of salvation, and by means of the sacraments opens up the paths of grace, which makes man a new creature, capable of corresponding with love and true freedom to the design of his Creator and Saviour, and of finding the yoke of Christ to be sweet. [31]

Christian married couples, then, docile to her voice, must remember that their Christian vocation, which began at baptism, is further specified and reinforced by the sacrament of matrimony. By it husband and wife are strengthened and as it were consecrated for the faithful accomplishment of their proper duties, for the carrying out of their proper vocation even to perfection, and the Christian witness which is proper to them before the whole world. [32] To them the Lord entrusts the task of making visible to men the holiness and sweetness of the law which unites the mutual love of husband and wife with their co-operation with the love of God, the author of human life.

We do not at all intend to hide the sometimes serious difficulties inherent in the life of Christian married persons; for them as for everyone else, "the gate is narrow and the way is hard, that leads to life."[33] But the hope of that life must illuminate their way, as with courage they strive to live with wisdom, justice and piety in this present time,[34] knowing that the figure of this world passes away.[35]

Let married couples, then, face up to the efforts needed, supported by the faith and hope which "do not disappoint . . . because God's love has been poured into our hearts through the Holy Spirit, who has been given to us."[36] Let them implore divine assistance by persevering prayer; above all, let them draw from the source of grace and charity in the Eucharist. And if sin should still keep its hold over them, let them not be discouraged, but rather have recourse with humble perseverance to the mercy of God, which is poured forth in the sacrament of Penance. In this way they will be enabled to achieve the fullness of conjugal life described by the Apostle: "husbands, love your wives, as Christ loved the Church . . . husbands should love their wives as their own bodies. He who loves his wife loves himself. For no man ever hates his own flesh, but nourishes and cherishes it, as Christ does the Church . . . this is a great mystery, and I mean in reference to Christ and the Church. However, let each one of you love his wife as himself, and let the wife see that she respects her husband."[37]

Apostolate in Homes

26. Among the fruits which ripen forth from a generous effort of fidelity to the divine law, one of the most precious is that married couples themselves not infrequently feel the desire to communicate their experience to others. Thus there comes to be included in the vast pattern of the vocation of the laity a new and most noteworthy form of the apostolate of like to like; it is married couples themselves who become apostles and guides to other married couples. This is assuredly, among so many forms of apostolate, one of those which seem most opportune today.[38]

To Doctors and Medical Personnel

27. We hold those physicians and medical personnel in the highest esteem who, in the exercise of their profession, value above every human interest the superior demands of their Christian vocation. Let them persevere, therefore, in promoting on every occasion the discovery of solutions inspired by faith and right reason, let them strive to arouse this conviction

and this respect in their associates. Let them also consider as their proper professional duty the task of acquiring all the knowledge needed in this delicate sector, so as to be able to give those married persons who consult them wise counsel and healthy direction, such as they have a right to expect.

To Priests

28. Beloved priest sons, by vocation you are the counselors and spiritual guides of individual persons and of families. We now turn to you with confidence. Your first task—especially in the case of those who teach moral theology—is to expound the Church's teaching on marriage without ambiguity. Be the first to give, in the exercise of your ministry, the example of loyal internal and external obedience to the teaching authority of the Church. That obedience, as you know well, obliges not only because of the reasons adduced, but rather because of the light of the Holy Spirit, which is given in a particular way to the pastors of the Church in order that they may illustrate the truth.[39] You know, too, that it is of the utmost importance, for peace of consciences and for the unity of the Christian people, that in the field of morals as well as in that of dogma, all should attend to the magisterium of the Church, and all should speak the same language. Hence, with all our heart we renew to you the heartfelt plea of the great Apostle Paul: "I appeal to you, brethren, by the name of Our Lord Jesus Christ, that all of you agree and that there be no dissensions among you, but that you be united in the same mind and the same judgment."[40]

29. To diminish in no way the saving teaching of Christ constitutes an eminent form of charity for souls. But this must ever be accompanied by patience and goodness, such as the Lord himself gave example of in dealing with men. Having come not to condemn but to save,[41] he was indeed intransigent with evil, but merciful towards individuals.

In their difficulties, many married couples always find, in the words and in the heart of a priest, the echo of the voice and the love of the Redeemer.

Speak out confidently, beloved sons, with the conviction that the Spirit of God, while assisting the Magisterium in propounding doctrine, enlightens internally the hearts of the faithful, and invites them to give their assent. Teach married couples the necessary way of prayer, and prepare them to have recourse frequently and with faith to the sacraments of the Eucharist and Penance, without ever allowing themselves to be disheartened by their weakness.

To Bishops

30. Beloved and venerable brothers in the episcopate, with whom we most intimately share the solicitude of the spiritual good of the people of God, at the conclusion of this encyclical our reverent and affectionate thoughts turn to you. To all of you we extend an urgent invitation. At the head of the priests, your collaborators, and of your faithful, work ardently and incessantly for the safeguarding and the holiness of marriage, so that it may always be lived in its entire human and Christian fullness. Consider this mission as one of your most urgent responsibilities at the present time. As you know, it implies concerted pastoral action in all the fields of human activity, economic, cultural and social; for, in fact, only a simultaneous improvement in these various sectors will make it possible to render the life of parents and of children within their families not only tolerable, but easier and more joyous, to render the living together in human society more fraternal and peaceful, in faithfulness to God's design for the world.

Final Appeal

31. Venerable brothers, most beloved sons, and all men of good will, great indeed is the work of education, of progress and of love to which we call you, upon the foundation of the Church's teaching, of which the successor of Peter is, together with his brothers in the episcopate, the depositary and interpreter. Truly a great work, as we are deeply convinced, both for the world and for the Church, since man cannot find true happiness—towards which he aspires with all his being—other than in respect of the laws written by God in his very nature, laws which he must observe with intelligence and love. Upon this work, and upon all of you, and especially upon married couples, we invoke the abundant graces of the God of holiness and mercy, and in pledge thereof we impart to you all our apostolic blessing.

Given at Rome, from St. Peter's, this 25th day of July, feast of St. James the Apostle, in the year 1968, the sixth of our pontificate.

NOTES

1. Cf. Pius IX, encyc. *Qui Pluribus*, November 9, 1846; in *PII IX P. M. Acta*, I, pp. 9-10; St. Pius X, encyc. *Singulari Quadam*, Sept. 24, 1912; in *AAS* IV (1912), p. 658; Pius XI, encyc. *Casti Connubii*, Dec. 31, 1930; in *AAS* XXI (1930), pp. 579-81; Pius XXI, allocution *Magnificate Dominum* to the episcopate of the Catholic world, Nov. 2, 1954; in *AAS* XLVI (1954), 671-72; John XXIII, encyc. *Mater et Magistra*, May 15, 1961; in *AAS* LIII (1961), p. 457.

2. Cf. Matthew 28:18-19.

3. Cf. Matthew 7:21.

4. Cf. *Catechismus Romanus Concilii Tridentini*, part 2, chap. 8, Leo XIII, encyc. *Arcanum*, Feb. 19, 1880; in *Acta Leonis XIII*, II (1881), pp. 26-29; Pius XI, encyc. *Divini Illius Magistri*, Dec. 31, 1929, in *AAS* XXII (1930), pp. 58-61; encyc. *Casti Connubii*, in *AAS* XXII (1930), pp. 545-46; Pius XII, alloc. to the Italian medicobiological union of St. Luke, Nov. 12, 1944, in *Discorsi e Radiomessaggi*, 6, pp. 191-92; to the Italian Catholic union of midwives, Oct. 29, 1951, in *AAS* XLIII (1951), pp. 857-59; to the seventh Congress of the International Society of Haematology, Sept. 12, 1958, in *AAS* L (1958), pp. 734-35; John XXIII, encyc. *Mater et Magistra*, in *AAS* LIII (1961), pp. 446-47; *Codex Iuris Canonici*, Canon 1067; Can. 1968, S 1, Can. 1066 S 1-2; II Vatican Council, Pastoral Constitution, *Gaudium et Spes*, nos. 47-52.

5. Cf. Paul VI, allocution to the Sacred College, June 23, 1964, in *AAS* LVI (1964), p. 588; to the Commission for Study of Problems of Population, Family and Birth, March 27, 1965, in *AAS* LVII (1965), p. 388; to the National Congress of the Italian Society of Obstetrics and Gynecology, Oct. 29, 1966, in *AAS* LVIII (1966), p. 1168.

6. Cf. I John 4:8.

7. Cf. Ephesians 3:15.

8. Cf. Pastoral Const. *Gaudium et Spes*, no. 50.

9. Cf. St. Thomas, *Summa Theologica*, I-II, q. 94, art. 2.

10. Cf. Pastoral Const. *Gaudium et Spes*, nos. 50, 51.

11. Ibid., no. 49.

12. Cf. Pius XI, encyc. *Casti Connubii*, in *AAS* XXII (1930), p. 560; Pius XII, in *AAS* XLIII (1951), p. 843.

13. Cf. John XXIII, encyc. *Mater et Magistra*, in *AAS* LIII (1961), p. 447.

14. Cf. *Catechismus Romanus Concilii Tridentini*, part 2, chap. 8; Pius XI, encyc. *Casti Connubii*, in *AAS* XXII (1930), pp. 562-64; Pius XII, *Discorsi e Radiomessaggi*, VI (1944), pp. 191-92; *AAS* XLIII (1951), pp. 842-43; pp. 857-59; John XXIII, encyc. *Pacem in Terris*, Apr. 11, 1963, in *AAS* LV (1963), pp. 259-60; *Gaudium et Spes*. no. 51.

15. Cf. Pius XI, encyc. *Casti Connubii*, in *AAS* XXII (1930), p. 565; decree of the Holy Office, Feb. 22, 1940, in *AAS* L (1958), pp. 734-35.

16. Cf. *Catechismus Romanus Concilii Tridentini*, part 2, chap. 8; Pius XI, encyc. *Casti Connubii*, in *AAS* XXII (1930), pp. 559-61; Pius XII, *AAS* XLIII (1951), p. 843; *AAS* L (1958), pp. 734-35; John XXIII, encyc. *Mater et Magistra*, in *AAS* LIII (1961), p. 447.

17. Cf. Pius XII, alloc. to the National Congress of the Union of Catholic Jurists, Dec. 6, 1953, in *AAS* XLV (1953), 798-99.

18. Cf. Romans 3:8.

19. Cf. Pius XII, alloc. to Congress of the Italian Association of Urology, Oct. 8, 1953, in *AAS* XLV (1953), pp. 674-75; *AAS* L (1958), pp. 734-35.

20. Cf. Pius XII, *AAS* XLIII (1951), p. 846.

21. Cf. *AAS* XLV (1953), pp. 674-75; *AAS* XLVIII (1956), pp. 461-62.

22. Cf. Luke 2:34.

23. Cf. Paul VI, encyc. *Populorum Progressio*, March 26, 1967, no. 21.

24. Cf. Romans 8.

25. Cf. II Vatican Council, decree *Inter Mirifica, On the Instruments of Social Communication*, nos. 6-7.

26. Cf. encyc. *Mater et Magistra*, in *AAS* LIII (1961), p. 447.

27. Cf. encyc. *Populorum Progressio*, nos. 48-55.

28. Cf. Pastoral Const. *Gaudium et Spes*, no. 52.

29. Cf. *AAS* XLIII (1951), p. 859.

30. Cf. Pastoral Const. *Gaudium et Spes*, no. 51.

31. Cf. Matthew 11:30.

32. Cf. Pastoral Const. *Gaudium et Spes*, no. 48; II Vatican Council, Dogmatic Const. *Lumen Gentium*, no. 35.

33. Matthew 7:14; cf. Hebrews 11:12.

34. Cf. Titus 2:12.

35. Cf. I Corinthians 7:31.

36. Cf. Romans 5:5.

37. Ephesians 5:25, 28-29, 32-33.

38. Cf. Dogmatic Const. *Lumen Gentium*, nos. 35 and 41; Pastoral Const. *Gaudium et Spes*, nos. 48-49; II Vatican Council, Decree *Apostolicam Actuositatem*, no. 11.

39. Cf. Dogmatic Const. *Lumen Gentium*, no. 25.

40. Cf. I Corinthians 1:10.

41. Cf. John 3:17.

Carl Cohen

Sex, Birth Control, and Human Life

I

The 1968 encyclical letter of Pope Paul VI, *Humanae Vitae*, has caused deep dismay both within and without the Roman Catholic Church. In re-affirming categorically its absolute prohibition of all devices for birth control, the Church creates with this document a new impediment to the slowing of the rate of population growth on earth. Some underdeveloped areas of the planet, where human crowding is now extreme and the need to limit population is already desperate, are greatly influenced by the teachings of the Catholic Church. Where its prohibitions are taken seriously by poverty-stricken masses, *Humanae Vitae* will have as its direct result the discouragement of effective birth-control techniques, and therefore the

This article is reprinted from *Ethics* 79, no. 4 (July 1969), with the permission of the author and the University of Chicago Press.

creation of more new lives than can be decently fed or cared for—a greater number than would be the case if the encyclical had been more enlightened. Indirectly, its foreseeable results will be more of the suffering and misery that overpopulation necessarily imposes. It is an unhappy irony that the document whose name is "human life" will reap human death as its harvest.

My present aim is not to bemoan this encyclical further but to exhibit, through an examination of its argument, the internal weakness of the moral position it presents. The practical consequences of the conclusions of *Humanae Vitae* are simply awful; the argument it provides in defense of these conclusions is equally bad.

II

The argument begins by establishing a foundation of doctrinal principles of a very general sort regarding the nature of marriage and of conjugal love. These principles may well be doubted by one who does not accept the teachings of the Church, but they are not at issue here. Essentially they come to this: that marriage, love, and birth must be viewed not from any narrow perspective but in the light of an integral vision of man and his vocation, both natural and supernatural. Within this vision, conjugal love is understood to flow from God Who is Love, and marriage is the deliberate institution of the Creator realizing in mankind his design of love. Through marriage husband and wife collaborate with God in the generation of new lives. In this perspective, conjugal love is understood to possess certain essential characteristics: first, that it is fully human, love of the senses and of the spirit at the same time; second, that it is an act of the free will, intended to endure and grow, and leading to greater human perfection; third, that it is total in that in it husband and wife share everything without reservation or calculation; fourth, that it is faithful and exclusive until death; and, finally, that it is fecund, destined to raise up new lives. "In the task of transmitting life, therefore," the encyclical concludes, "they [husband and wife] are not free to proceed completely at will, as if they could determine in a wholly autonomous way the honest path to follow; but they must conform their activity to the creative intention of God, expressed in the very nature of marriage and of its acts."[1]

These are the doctrinal foundations. I now propose to show that the specific conclusions of the encyclical regarding birth control are not (as they purport to be) the logical consequences of these general principles.

Even if one does accept the Church's general views on marriage, he is not obliged by reason to accept its dogmas on birth control.

III

Precisely what are the conclusions at issue? Essentially, they reduce to a categorical prohibition of all control of the sex act, once begun, and all efforts or devices whose object is the blocking of conception.

> We must once again declare that the direct interruption of the generative process already begun, and above all, directly willed and procured abortion, even if for therapeutic reasons, are to be absolutely excluded as licit means of regulating birth.
> Equally to be excluded . . . is direct sterilization, whether perpetual or temporary, whether of the man or of the woman. Similarly excluded is every action which, whether in anticipation of the conjugal act, or in its accomplishment, or in the development of its natural consequences, proposes, whether as an end or as a means, to render procreation impossible.[2]

The encyclical does permit as licit, however, the regulation of birth through the scheduling of intercourse for infecund periods only. It is concluded that this rhythm method and sheer abstinence are the only forms of birth control that do not offend against moral principles.

IV

How does one get from the very general doctrine holding marriage to be a free, loving, and fecund relationship to the specific dogmas regarding birth control for which *Humanae Vitae* is so widely condemned? The argument requires certain additional premises; its completed form runs something like this: The love of husband and wife has many aspects, natural and supernatural, physical and spiritual. The act of sexual intercourse between them is the physical manifestation of their spiritual union. The act itself, therefore, has two meanings, *unitive* and *procreative*, both of which inhere in it. Joining in sex as lovers one of another and as the creators of new life one with another are two aspects of the same sexual act. Men have the power to *distinguish* these two aspects of sex, but no human power can rightly separate them, because *the eternal conjunction of unitive and procreative functions is willed by God*. Therefore (it is held) "each and every marriage act must remain open to the transmission of life."[3] Any single instance of sexual intercourse that does not remain open to the conception of life destroys the meaning and purpose of that intercourse, contradicts the nature of man and woman and their love, and serves, therefore, "to contradict the plan of God and His will."[4] Birth control, as it is normally practiced, the encyclical concludes, has just this consequence and must threfore be prohibited and condemned.

The crucial premise, upon which the entire argument of the encyclical depends, is the claim that sexual intercourse and procreation are *universally* and *indivisibly* conjoined. This proposition must be maintained literally and in its strongest form to support the conclusion drawn: that we must condemn "every action which, either in anticipation of the conjugal act, or in its accomplishment, or in the development of its natural consequences, proposes, whether as an end or as a means, to render procreation impossible."[5] This fundamental premise, that the unitive and procreative functions of sex are conjoined in such a way as to be totally inseparable in every case, must be gravely questioned.

About this premise—let us call it the "inseparability" premise—several things need to be said. First, it is without good foundation. Second, it is false. Third, its denial is perfectly consistent with the larger doctrines of the Catholic Church regarding marriage. Fourth, it betrays an unwholesome, essentially instrumental view of sex. Fifth, it is a premise contradicted by the Church's own view of licit birth control. Elaboration upon these claims is called for.

V

How is the inseparability premise defended in *Humanae Vitae?* Rational argument based on the merits of the case is not even attempted. Scriptural authority (even if it were persuasive) cannot be offered because it does not exist. Neither is the principle encountered in any standard version of the natural law, nor in the consciences of most honest men within or without the Catholic Church. The majority report of the Papal Commission on Birth Control could not support it. Dr. John Marshall, a member of that commission, reports that after lengthy inquiry even the four theologians of the minority group, although supporting the prohibition of birth control, acknowledged that they could not demonstrate the intrinsic evil of contraception on the basis of natural law. What then does the premise rest upon? Authority and nothing more. All that is said in its defense is that inseparability has long been part of the teaching of the Church. By accepting that teaching and repeating it, the Pope is spared the need to break from an old tradition.

Papal authority, however persuasive for some Catholics, cannot constitute proof for a moderately rational man. Too often have popes proclaimed as true and binding what has later been admitted (at a time too late to remedy the injury done) to be blatantly false. Pope Boniface VIII could influence an epoch, causing misery and promoting war, with his insistence (in *Unam Sanctam*, 1302) that "it is entirely necessary for salvation that every human creature be subject to the Roman pontiff." One of the major instruments of modern economic growth—the lending and borrowing of money with interest—was condemned by Pope Urban III (in 1185) in his ban against usury; it was, he said, self-evidently immoral. Even the notion that everyone is entitled to freedom of conscience was condemned as "a delirium" and "a pestilential error" by Pope Gregory XVI as recently as 1832.

The Church now recognizes the grave errors in many of its earlier teachings. Those mistaken doctrines did not express the will of God, all now agree, but were only the confused opinions of limited, sometimes narrow-minded men. Yet the frame of mind that leads to such wrong-headedness has not been recognized—a frame of mind in which it is presumed that the Church alone knows what God plans and knows also exactly what instruments He has decided we may use in helping Him to accomplish these plans. In elevating fallible human opinions on controversial issues to the status of divine will, this encyclical, like many before it, makes a false and deceptive appeal, seeking to shield dogma from rational criticism.

The argument of *Humanae Vitae* has precisely that character. Repeatedly Pope Paul appeals to his only available support—past teaching, the magisterium of the Church. The defense of the inseparability premise boils down to this: "It's true because we tell you it is; if you doubt us, note that we have been telling you the same thing for a very long time." Such reiteration has absolutely no probative force.

VI

The inseparability premise is false. It is hard to reach certainty in matters of this sort, of course. But granting, *arguendo*, the twofold "meaning" of sexual intercourse, its procreative and unitive functions, such evidence as experience and reflection provide would strongly suggest that in many instances it is right for these functions to be separated. Very briefly I will try to indicate the ways in which this might be shown.

1. In any utilitarian ethic the falsity of the inseparability premise could be quite convincingly established. The disutility of its consequences is so great, so sure, and so widely understood that the encyclical does not attempt—with some minor exceptions to be discussed shortly—a defense of that premise based on its consequences. Such efforts prove hopeless.

2. Perhaps utilitarian calculi will be flatly rejected by the Church, but its own larger principles cannot be disposed of so easily. On its own principles the inseparability premise is virtually impossible to defend. Recall that the entire argument arises in a context of doctrine concerning the nature of the marriage union and the character of conjugal love. Sexual intercourse in marriage, it is held, must be free and loving. But it cannot be fully so if it is flawed by the fear of a conception the couple cannot afford for reasons of economy or health. Sexual intercourse, it is held, should be total; it is love incarnate and supposes that the partners give to one another without reservations. But reservations are precisely what the inseparability premise forces upon them. They must, if it be true, either hold back in passion or have that passion marred by the awareness that total reciprocity between them risks the well-being of themselves or their family. In short, the larger aims of the Church, which include the most perfect realization of the ideals of marriage that the circumstances permit, are undermined by the conclusions of this encyclical. To oblige as alternatives the acceptance of the hazards of uncontrolled sexual intercourse or the avoidance of ill health and impoverishment through abstinence is to present a pair of options both foolish and cruel. Cruel because the actual consequences of forcing that choice are inhumane and can be rather accurately predicted. Foolish because that obligation runs counter to the highest ideals of the Church itself.

Whatever the origin of the institution of marriage, particular marriages are enriched and deepened when the sexual congress of the partners is free and happy, untroubled and unreserved. The passions and pleasures of sex, manifesting the intense affection of one human being for another, are blessings that ought to be supported by reason, not blemished or curtailed by the deliberate refusal to use reason. The rational control of birth requires the deliberate separation of the procreative from the unitive functions when appropriate. Because this has as consequences the encouragement of satisfying sexual intercourse, and the greater likelihood of contentment, such separation is right conduct if the strength and happiness of the marriage are ruling considerations.

3. But perhaps it will be argued that even these considerations cannot rule when the act in question is intrinsically wrong, a contravention of the will of God. The claim that God's plan is disrupted by the control of birth appears to be based on the notion (not fully explicit in the encyclical) that God intends all natural functions to be completed and that since procreation is the natural completion of sexual intercourse any act that deliberately thwarts procreation is ungodly. Final causes are divinely set; birth is the "final cause" of coition; to block the possibility of birth flowing from coition is to contravene the divine will.

The entire argument is plausible only on the assumption that God's plans and instruments are precisely known—a degree of presumption whose dangers I have remarked upon earlier. Beyond this, it is noteworthy that the principle that morality requires the absolute completion of all sexual acts is one that any rational man will find difficult to maintain, even supposing one knew what "completion" meant in every context. Such a principle would seem to commit one to the view that unless every kiss leads to intercourse God's will is frustrated, or that no attention that is sexually motivated may be given to the child since the fulfillment of that attention would lead to incest. The fact that much of our conduct in daily life is sexually toned is neither avoidable nor wrong. The greatest part of this sexual activity stops far short of consummation, but surely that is not unnatural. No sensible person denies the pervasive influence of sex or supposes that once an act takes on sexual dimensions we are obliged to pursue the relationship to full intercourse. Loving acts, including those that incorporate sexual activity, are worthy in themselves, quite apart from whether they lead to orgasm, or to new lives. There need be no misuse of natural functions or dishonesty of purpose when, deliberately and humanely, we limit the range or techniques of sex play. To insist that such play, once begun, must be pursued to its extremes would be absurd; it is no less absurd to insist that intercourse, once begun, must be pursued to its extremes and that no intelligent limits may be placed upon its techniques or consequences.

The defender of the encyclical might here rejoin that the thrust of the inseparability premise has been misconstrued in the preceding critique. It is not simply the completion of natural functions that is required (he may say) but their integrity that must be respected. It is the distortion of the act as it is being completed, the suppression of an essential aspect of its significance, that contradicts God's will.

Once again one might wonder whether the Church's view of unnatural distortion and God's view of it—if He has one—are altogether in accord and how we find that out. But putting all that aside, it would be well to see the consequences of the general application of the principle invoked here. Moving to another sphere for the sake of illustration, suppose we were to agree that artistic creation has (using terms the Church is likely to find acceptable) at least a twofold meaning. Being an application of the practical intellect, it is necessarily concerned with the quality of the art object produced. Call this its *productive* meaning. Being a satisfaction of the artist's appetite for beauty, it is necessarily concerned with the exercise of his inventive talents. Call this its spontaneous or *originative* meaning. Would we wish to say that artistic activity that is spontaneous and originative but wholly playful and exploratory, having no concern for a product (or even seeking to avoid one), is unnatural or ungodly? Consider the artist who distinguishes the exercise of his creative talents from the perfection of his created objects and pursues now one of these objectives, now the other, sometimes both conjointly. Surely his occasional separation of these functions does not convict him of dishonest or disorderly acts.

Another example, closer to that of sex, may prove more persuasive. Most men will allow that eating, in addition to its *nutritive* function, provides certain intrinsic satisfactions that we may call *gustatory*. A good meal will be rich in protein, carbohydrates, vitamins, and so on, but will also be agreeable to the palate. Eating may fulfill these functions concurrently, but is there any moral fault in eating with the intent to separate them? Sometimes, as when one is ill, we eat for the sake of nutrition, altogether without gusto. Often we eat with the deliberate intention of avoiding additional nutriment, yet relishing the taste of the dish. Many of the foods and flavors we prize are known to be without nutritive value— mushrooms, truffles, a cup of fine tea, for example—but we do not think it wrong to eat them.

In the sphere of sex the case is essentially no different. The pleasures, emotional as well as physical, derived from the satisfaction of an appetite may be separated rationally and without wrongdoing from the fulfillment of organic functions also possible through the satisfaction of that appetite. Whether it is right, or wise, to satisfy an appetite repeatedly without ever fulfilling the organic functions of such satisfaction is a question that may remain moot here. But the force of this encyclical depends upon the claim that such separation is in *every* case immoral. That claim seems plainly false.

VII

The denial of the inseparability premise is perfectly consistent with the larger doctrines of the Church regarding the purpose of marriage. The apparent stumbling block here is the notion of fecundity; every marriage, the Church holds, must be loving and total, free and faithful—and fecund. For a marriage to be fecund, however, it need not be the case that every sexual act within it be potentially so. If the married couple assumes an obligation to raise up new lives (an obligation those outside the Church may question), that obligation may be fully and honestly met without their every sexual union being open to conception. The intelligent use of birth control does not block fecundity or in any way denigrate it; indeed, the importance of fecundity is magnified by control. No honor is done to marriage by forcing fecundity upon the partners willy-nilly or depriving them of sexual satisfaction. The fecundity of human marriage is not the fecundity of animals who bear young at every season of heat because they know not what they do. When the decision to create new life is made deliberately and rationally, out of love and with a full understanding of the consequences, the act of procreation itself is enhanced. Birth is then not an accident beyond human control but the happy outcome of a free act, an act right in its purpose and good in its execution. The life brought into being, rather than being tolerated or resented as a blunder, is then wanted and loved. That is the procreative meaning of conjugal love; that, if anything, may be construed as collaboration with God. The accomplishment of these worthy goals, however, requires that fecundity *not* be tied to every passionate sexual embrace. On the doctrinal principles of the Church itself the marriage of a man and a woman—the moral union of two beings without reservations—is made potentially *more* perfect through the rational use of birth control.

VIII

Embedded in the argument of *Humanae Vitae* is a view of sex as an aspect of human life fundamentally unworthy in itself because essentially instrumental in character. The insistence that every coition be open to conception implicitly supposes that all sex, and every act of love sexually toned, is at bottom a tool for the accomplishment of something else. An uneasy distaste for fleshly things, partly disguised, is revealed in the refusal of the Church to approve of sexual intercourse for its own sake. The intrinsic worth of sexual passion is not precisely denied, but that denial is clearly suggested by insisting that, separated from procreation, the act is dishonest and contravenes God's will. A more generous conception of divine intentions might suppose sex to be a blessing that humans are peculiarly able to understand and appreciate. It might view sex as that animal function most essentially of a loving kind and its practice (whether fecund or not) the closest thing to the incarnation of the religious ideal of love. Such at least is a possible view. In such a view sex might be conceived as an element of our condition having sometimes an instrumental role, sometimes a consummatory role, and often both. Even when not intended to produce new life it may serve to make tangible our union with another human creature. If it makes sense at all to infer the intentions of God, we may reasonably suppose that so rich and delightful a dimension of human life was designed by Him (if He is wise and loving) both as an instrument and as a satisfaction to be enjoyed mutually, for its own and each other's sake. To suppose narrowly that sexual intercourse must serve as an instrument in every circumstance is to demean its designer, if it has one.

That an essentially instrumental view of sex *is* implicit in the argument of *Humanae Vitae* is further evidenced by the very language it adopts in dealing with sex; not as acts of love or of passion—which they are and ought to be—but as the *uses* or *familiarities* of marriage are coital acts discussed in this document. "[Q]*uilibet matrimonii usus*" must, it is proclaimed, "remain open to the transmission of life." But sexual intercourse is not a *use* of marriage; it is one realization of it, and it may serve as that realization whether or not it also serves, on any particular occasion, its further instrumental function.

IX

In approving the so-called rhythm method of birth control, the Church flatly contradicts its own dogmas in this sphere and shows clearly that in its more reflective moments it too denies the "inseparable connection" of sexual intercourse and procreation. *Humanae Vitae* says straightforwardly that it is entirely proper for the married couple to "take into account the natural rhythms immanent in the generative functions, for the use of marriage in the infecund periods only, and in this way to regulate birth without offending the moral principles."[6] This form of birth regulation, the encyclical allows, remains licit *even though the married couple are engaging in sexual intercourse with the deliberate intention of avoiding the creation of new life.*

Earlier, however, the encyclical had condemned birth control in principle, that condemnation based upon the "inseparable connection, willed by God and unable to be broken by man on his own initiative," between the unitive and procreative aspects of sexual congress.[7] Can the permission of deliberate and knowing efforts to effect this very separation by the clever timing of intercourse be logically reconciled with the earlier prohibition of all such efforts? It cannot. Recognizing the difficulty, *Humanae Vitae* seeks to ward off the charge of self-contradiction, but fails.

The Pope argues that, in this matter, the Church "is coherent with herself" because there are essential differences between birth control using natural rhythms and all other common methods of achieving the same result. In fact, an examination of these claimed differences in method shows that they cannot justify the condemnation of separating unitive and procreative functions in the one case while approving it in the other.

The differences specified are only two, and neither can bear the weight the argument puts upon them. One of these amounts to nothing more than a restatement of what the rhythm method is—a system in which husband and wife are "able to renounce the use of marriage in the fecund periods when, for just motives, procreation is not desirable, while making use of it during infecund periods to manifest their affection and to safeguard their mutual fidelity. By so doing they give proof of a truly and integrally honest love."[8] Clearly it is not the manifestation of affection or the safeguarding of fidelity that differentiates the rhythm method from all others. The difference, rather, lies only in the fact that this system relies upon the timing of intercourse and no mechanical or pharmaceutical aids. But this difference has no bearing whatever upon the separability of sex and procreation. In the case of the rhythm method, as with all other methods, the fact is—and the encyclical admits—that "the married couple are concordant in the positive will of avoiding children for plausible reasons, seeking the certainty that offspring will not arrive."[9] It is precisely that will, the will to have sexual intercourse and not conceive, that had earlier been damned as a contradiction of the will of God.

The other difference specified is that upon which all the argument must rest. The claim is that with the rhythm method, the couple makes use of a "natural disposition"; with all other methods "they impede the development of natural processes."[10] The encyclical supposes, but cannot demonstrate, that only the use of timing is a "legitimate use" of nature and that drugs or diaphragms are not legitimate. In what aspect of the latter cases does the claimed illegitimacy lie? All that can be said is that in the one case instruments are not used, in the other case they are. Surely civilization, and with it the Catholic Church, has passed the point where it was considered a disruption of God's plan to accomplish worthwhile objectives with the aid of rational and humane instruments. Is it legitimate to protect health with exercise but illegitimate to do so with vaccination? Is it legitimate to fight illness with nutrition but illegitimate to do so with medicines? Surely the notion that an act is illegitimate only because instruments are used is absurd. The Church agrees unequivocally in matters of personal and public health; its hospitals are among the finest in the world. Why is the notion any less absurd in the sphere of sexual health and family well-being? No reason is or can be given.

If birth control is wrong, it is wrong not because an instrument is used but because of what is being accomplished and the intent to accomplish it. The argument of the encyclical clearly states that the (alleged) evil lies in the immoral separation of sexual love and procreation. But it is freely admitted that that separation *is* permissible to manifest affection and safeguard fidelity. If it is permissible in some cases, then it must be permissible in all cases, unless the difference between the cases distinguished bears upon the intentions with which the act is done. The differences specified do not bear upon such intentions. By simply calling the rhythm method licit and all other methods illicit, the encyclical begs the central question. Why is the one legitimate, the other not? The argument purports to exhibit a morally relevant difference, but never begins to do so.

This inconsistency is not just a minor slip; it is fatal to the entire position of *Humanae Vitae*. For that position depends utterly upon what has here been called the inseparability premise; and it is now clear that, even for the Church, where there are plausible reasons and honest love, a couple may indeed separate their desire for children from their desire for sex with each other. Both fecund and loving the marriage should be, perhaps, but even if true that principle gives no warrant for the prohibition of any humane method of birth control.

X

The leaders of the Catholic Church are far from callous men; they are fully aware of the human misery that flows from uncontrolled population growth. They understand the grave need for the global control of human numbers; hence their approval of the rhythm method. Still they argue that other forms of birth control, being intrinsically wrong, may not be practiced because it is never permissible to do what is wrong, even with a view to some larger good.

> [I]t is not licit, even for the gravest reasons, to do evil so that good may follow therefrom; that is, to make into the object of a positive act of the will something which is intrinsically disorder, and hence unworthy of the human person, even when the intention is to safeguard or promote individual, family, or social well-being. Consequently it is an error to think that a conjugal act which is deliberately made infecund and so is intrinsically dishonest could be made honest and right by the ensemble of a fecund conjugal life.[11]

This argument fails utterly; both of its premises are false. The major premise—that it is never right to do a minor evil in order that a greater good may come of it—will be denied by most reasonable men. But even granting that premise, the condemnation of birth control does not follow. In the first place, if all control of sexual intercourse with the deliberate intent of avoiding birth is dishonest and disorderly, it is so whatever the method employed to reach that end. The argument cuts as strongly against the rhythm method as against any other, since all birth control embodies the positive will to enjoy sex without procreation. More importantly, the argument depends also on the minor premise, that deliberate control of birth *is* intrinsically evil, dishonest, and disorderly. That premise *Humanae Vitae* does not and cannot establish. Even if one accepts the larger doctrinal principles of the Church regarding marriage and its essentially loving, total, faithful, and fecund character, family planning and the intelligent control of sexual intercourse to implement such planning may be approved and encouraged, not as instrumental evils but as acts wholly honest and right.

XI

Finally, *Humanae Vitae* offers, in support of its prohibition of birth control, three arguments of a totally different sort, arguments aiming not to establish the wrongness of birth control in itself but to point out the evils alleged to flow from its employment. This emphasis upon consequences rather than intrinsic quality is not characteristic of the encyclical, not in harmony with its general spirit. Moreover, the arguments appear in abbreviated form, and not the slightest effort is made to show that the consequences alleged would in fact ensue. This pragmatic interlude does not play a major role in the document. Still it is proper to give these arguments the little attention they deserve.

1. Birth-control devices, it is claimed, offer "easy means of eluding" the observance of the moral law by leading to "conjugal infidelity and the general lowering of morality."[12]

The argument is thrice bad: First, there is no evidence to show that birth control would in fact increase the frequency of marital infidelity. Indeed, it is the Church's prohibition, in combination with a couple's inability to care properly for more children, which creates frustration, forces unnatural abstinence, and may lead to extramarital intercourse. This counterclaim is, of course, equally unproved; but of the two positions it appears reasonable that the prohibition of birth control is at least as likely to encourage infidelity as its use would be.

Second, if the moral law is what the Church believes it to be, none of the consequences of the use of birth control, good or bad, are needed to enforce it or able to do so. Obedience to it as a moral law is complete only when compliance is willing and free and not forced by the sanctions of disobedience. Those who deny the existence of that law or wish to flout it can as easily deny or flout the prohibition of birth control as well.

Third, even if the consequence—sexual intercourse more widely enjoyed—were evil, and even if the general use of birth control were shown to have that consequence, it is plainly unjust to force abstinence on faithful married couples, or to compel them to rear more children than is good for them or the community, simply because the instrument that might avoid such hardship could be used improperly by others.

The argument is intolerable.

2. Birth-control devices, it is claimed, give excessive power to public authorities, placing in their hands "a dangerous weapon" that may be easily abused. "Who will stop rulers from favoring, from even imposing upon their peoples, if they were to consider it necessary, the method of contraception which they deem to be most efficacious? In such a way men . . . would reach the point of placing at the mercy of the intervention of public authorities the most personal and most reserved sector of conjugal intimacy."[13]

The scare of this argument is largely fictitious. What, precisely, is the grave danger being hinted at? Is it that governments may play a more active role in stabilizing the size of human population? Such a development would be no bad thing. Or is it that governments might force individual couples to use contraceptive devices they do not wish to use? Considering the circumstances of most sexual intercourse, that would be quite a trick, even for Big Brother. Or might it be that governments ("rulers," as the Pope perceives them) would use their power to encourage or oblige the use of contraceptives in ways contrary to the interests of citizens? There is that danger, of course, if government eludes the control of the people; but such dangers exist now, having been created by the very invention of the instruments in question. The general prohibition by the Church of all use of such instruments reduces that power not one iota. If it is the immoral use of power that we fear, it is not precepts or the banning of instruments but the strengthened control of the people over their government that is called for.

3. The final argument is the most extraordinary of all. The encyclical states: "It is also to be feared that the man, growing used to the employment of anticonceptive practices, may finally lose respect for the woman and, no longer caring for her physical and psychological equilibrium, may come to the point of considering her as a mere instrument of selfish enjoyment, and no longer as his respected and beloved companion."[14] How in the world this consequence is drawn from the use of birth control is never rationally explained, nor could it be. The imagination is staggered by the picture of continuing sexual relations harbored in the minds of the authors of this passage: the males, blinded by lust and potent as satyrs—now freed by birth control—plunge relentlessly into the females, who in spite of their frailty are reduced to instruments of carnal pleasure, to be cast aside when passion's spent. The speculation would be amusing if the circumstances were not serious. One who supposes that sex is essentially a one-sided demand placed by men on women, and that sex separated from procreation leads inevitably to the selfish use of the woman by the man, tells us far more about himself and his sexual fantasies than about birth control in the real world. The complete failure to consider the woman's desire for sex and for the pleasure of it, the implicit distorted picture of what sexual intercourse for its own sake may be, reveal enough about the authors of this document to put their competence in this entire sphere, not to speak of their authority, in gravest doubt.

It is understandable that the encyclical does not rely in any serious way upon the supposed consequences to support its conclusions. For if consequences are relevant at all, the consequences of not using birth-control devices must be weighed against the consequences of using them. And while the latter consequences are at worst controversial and at best happy, the former—the results of population growth uncontrolled or controlled only by timing or abstinence—are famine, sickness, and death for millions. Such suffering is already upon us; with the help of unenlightened dogmatism like that found in *Humanae Vitae*, far worse is in store.

The argument based on consequences the Church is obliged, for the security of its dogma on birth control, to skirt. The argument based on the intrinsic moral quality of the act itself the Church is unable, in behalf of this dogma, to defend. It is time for the dogma to be changed.

NOTES

1. Section 10. All citations in this article are from the official English-language version of the encyclical letter.
2. Section 14
3. Section 11
4. Section 13
5. Section 14
6. Section 16
7. Section 12
8. Section 16
9. Ibid.
10. Ibid.
11. Section 14
12. Section 17
13. Ibid.
14. Ibid.

John McMurtry

Monogamy: A Critique

Remove away that black'ning church
Remove away that marriage hearse
Remove away that man of blood
You'll quite remove the ancient curse.
                    —William Blake

I

Almost all of us have entered or will one day enter a specifically standard-ized form of monogamous marriage. This cultural requirement is so very basic to our existence that we accept it for most part as a kind of intrac-table given—dictated by the laws of God, Nature, Government, and Good Sense all at once. Though it is perhaps unusual for a social practice to be so promiscuously underwritten, we generally find comfort rather than curiosity in this fact and seldom wonder how something could be divinely

This article is reprinted from *The Monist* 56, no. 4 (1972), La Salle, Illinois, with the permission of the author and publisher.

inspired, biologically determined, coerced, and reasoned out all at the same time. We simply take for granted.

Those in society who are officially charged with the thinking function with regard to such matters are no less responsible for this uncritical acceptance than is the man on the street. The psychoanalyst traditionally regards our form of marriage as a necessary restraint on the anarchic id and no more to be queried than civilization itself. The lawyer is as undisposed to questioning the practice as he is to criticizing the principle of private property (this is appropriate, as I shall later point out). The churchman formally perceives the relationship between man and wife to be as inviolable and insusceptible to question as the relationship between the institution he works for and the Christ. The sociologist standardly accepts the formalized bonding of heterosexual pairs as the indispensable basis of social order and perhaps a societal universal. The politician is as incapable of challenging it as he is the virtue of his own continued holding of office. And the philosopher (at least the English-speaking philosopher), as with most issues of socially controversial or sexual dimensions, ignores the question almost altogether.

Even those irreverent adulterers and unmarried couples who seem to be challenging the institution in the most basic possible way, in practice, tend merely to mimic its basic structure in unofficial form. The coverings of sanctities, taboos, and cultural habit continue to hold them with the grip of public clothes.

II

"Monogamy" means, literally, "one marriage." But it would be wrong to suppose that this phrase tells us much about our particular species of official wedlock. The greatest obstacle to the adequate understanding of our monogamy institution has been the failure to identify clearly and systematically the full complex of principles it involves. There are four such principles, each carrying enormous restrictive force and together constituting a massive social-control mechanism that has never, so far as I know, been fully schematized. To come straight to the point, the four principles in question are as follows:

1. *The partners are required to enter a formal contractual relation:* (a) whose establishment demands a specific official participant, certain conditions of the contractors (legal age, no blood ties, and so on), and a standard set of procedures; (b) whose governing terms are uniform for all

and exactly prescribed by law; and (c) whose dissolution may only be legally effected by the decision of state representatives.

The ways in which this elaborate principle of contractual requirement is importantly restrictive are obvious. One may not enter into a marriage union without entering into a contract presided over by a state-investured official.[1] One may not set any of the terms of the contractual relationship by which one is bound for life. And one cannot dissolve the contract without legal action and costs, court proceedings, and in many places actual legislation. (This is the one and only contract in all English-speaking law that is not dissoluble by the consent of the contracting parties.) The extent of control here—over the most intimate and putatively "loving" relationships in all social intercourse—is so great as to be difficult to catalogue without exciting in oneself a sense of disbelief.

Lest it be thought there is always the real option of entering a common-law relationship free of such encumbrances, it should be noted that: (a) these relationships themselves are subject to state regulation, though of a less imposing sort; and (much more important) (b) there are very formidable selective pressures against common-law partnerships, such as employment and job discrimination, exclusion from housing and lodging facilities, special legal disablements,[2] loss of social and moral status (consider such phrases as "living in sin" and "make her an honest woman"), family shame and embarrassment, and so on.

2. *The number of partners involved in the marriage must be two and only two* (as opposed to three, four, five, or any of the almost countless possibilities of intimate union). This second principle of our specific form of monogamy (the concept of "one marriage," it should be pointed out, is consistent with any number of participating partners) is perhaps the most important and restrictive of the four principles we are considering. Not only does it confine us to just one possibility out of an enormous range, but it confines us to that single possibility that involves the least number of people, two. It is difficult to conceive of a more thoroughgoing mechanism for limiting extended social union and intimacy. The fact that this monolithic restriction seems so "natural" to us (if it were truly "natural," of course, there would be no need for its rigorous cultural prescription by everything from severe criminal law[3] to ubiquitous housing regulations) simply indicates the extent to which its hold is implanted in our social structure. It is the institutional basis of what I will call the "binary frame of sexual consciousness," a frame through which all our heterosexual relationships are typically viewed ("two's company, three's a crowd") and

in light of which all larger circles of intimacy seem almost inconceivable.[4]

3. *No person may participate in more than one marriage at a time or during a lifetime* (unless the previous marriage has been officially dissolved by, normally, one partner's death or a divorce). Violation of this principle is, of course, a criminal offense (bigamy) that is punishable by a considerable term in prison. Of various general regulations of our marriage institution, it has experienced the most significant modification, not indeed in principle, but in the extent of flexibility of its "escape hatch" of divorce. The ease with which this escape hatch is opened has increased considerably in the past few years (the grounds for divorce being more permissive than previously) and it is in this regard most of all that the principles of our marriage institution have undergone formal alteration—that is, in plumbing rather than substance.

4. *No married person may engage in any sexual relationship with any person other than the marriage partner.* Although a consummated sexual act with another person alone constitutes an act of adultery, lesser forms of sexual and erotic relationships[5] may also constitute grounds for divorce (for example, cruelty) and are generally proscribed as well by informal social convention and taboo. In other words, the fourth and final principle of our marriage institution involves not only a prohibition of sexual intercourse per se outside one's wedlock (this term deserves pause) but a prohibition of all one's erotic relations whatever outside this bond. The penalties for violation here are as various as they are severe, ranging from permanent loss of spouse, children, chattel, and income to job dismissal and social ostracism. In this way, possibly the most compelling natural force toward expanded intimate relations with others is strictly confined within the narrowest possible circle for (barring delinquency) the whole of adult life.[6] The sheer weight and totality of this restriction is surely one of the great wonders of all historical institutional control.

III

With all established institutions, apologetics for perpetuation are never wanting. Thus it is with our form of monogamous marriage.

Perhaps the most celebrated justification over the years has proceeded from the belief in a Supreme Deity, who secretly utters sexual and other commands to privileged human representatives. Almost as well known a line of defense has issued from a similarly confident conviction that the need for some social regulation of sexuality demonstrates the need for our specific type of two-person wedlock. Although these have been important justifications in the sense of being very widely supported, they are not—having other grounds than reason—susceptible to treatment here.

If we put aside such arguments, we are left, I think, with two major claims. The first is that our form of monogamous marriage promotes a profound affection between the partners that is not only of great worth in itself but invaluable as a sanctuary from the pressures of outside society. Since, however, there are no secure grounds whatever for supposing that such "profound affection" is not at least as easily achievable by any number of *other* marriage forms (that is, forms that differ in one or more of the four principles), this justification conspicuously fails to perform the task required of it.

The second major claim for the defense is that monogamy provides a specially loving context for child-upbringing. However, here again there are no grounds at all for concluding that it does so as, or any more, effectively than other possible forms of marriage. (The only alternative type of upbringing to which it has apparently been shown to be superior is non-family institutional upbringing, which of course is not relevant to the present discussion.) Furthermore, the fact that at least half the span of a normal monogamous marriage involves no child-upbringing at all is overlooked here, as is the reinforcing fact that there is no reference to or mention of the quality of child-upbringing in any of the prescriptions connected with it.

In brief, the second major justification of our particular type of wedlock scents somewhat too strongly of red herring to pursue further.

There is, it seems, little to recommend the view that monogamy specially promotes "profound affection" between the partners or a "loving context" for child-upbringing. Such claims are simply without force. On the other hand, there are several aspects to the logic and operation of the four principles of this institution that suggest that it actually *inhibits* the achievement of these desiderata. Far from uniquely abetting the latter, it militates against them in these ways:

1. Centralized official control of marriage (which the Church gradually achieved through the mechanism of Canon Law after the fall of the Roman Empire[7] in one of the greatest seizures of social power of history) necessarily alienates the partners from full responsibility for and freedom in their relationship. "Profound closeness" between the partners—or at least an area of it—is thereby expropriated rather than promoted and

"sanctuary" from the pressures of outside society prohibited rather than fostered.

2. Limitation of the marriage bond to two people necessarily restricts, in perhaps the most unilateral way possible consistent with offspring survival, the number of adult sources of affection, interest, and material support and instruction for the young. The "loving context for child-up-bringing" is thereby dessicated rather than nourished, providing the structural conditions for such notorious and far-reaching problems as sibling rivalry for scarce adult attention[8] and parental oppression through exclusive monopoly of the child's means of life.[9]

3. Formal exclusion of all others from erotic contact with the marriage partner systematically promotes conjugal insecurity, jealousy, and alienation in several ways. (a) It officially underwrites a literally totalitarian expectation of sexual confinement on the part of one's husband or wife: which expectation is, *ceteris paribus*, inevitably more subject to anxiety and disappointment than one less extreme in its demand and/or cultural-juridical backing.[10] (b) It requires so complete a sexual isolation of the marriage partners that should one violate the fidelity code the other is left alone and susceptible to a sense of fundamental deprivation and resentment. It stipulates such a strict restraint of sexual energies that there are habitual violations of the regulations, frequently if not always attended by willful deception and reciprocal suspicion about the occurrence or quality of the extramarital relationship, anxiety and fear on both sides of permanent estrangement from partner and family, and overt and covert antagonism over the prohibited act in both offender (who feels "trapped") and offended (who feels "betrayed").

The disadvantages of the four principles of monogamous marriage do not, however, end with inhibiting the very effects they are said to promote. There are further shortcomings:

1. The restriction of marriage union to two partners necessarily prevents the strengths of larger groupings. Such advantages as the following are thereby usually ruled out: (a) the security, range, and power of larger socioeconomic units; (b) the epistemological and emotional substance, variety, and scope of more pluralist interactions; (c) the possibility of extra-domestic freedom founded on more adult providers and upbringers as well as more broadly based circles of intimacy.

2. The sexual containment and isolation that the four principles together require variously stimulates such social malaises as: (a) destructive aggression (which notoriously results from sexual frustration); (b) apathy,

frustration, and dependence within the marriage bond; (c) lack of spontaneity, bad faith, and distance in relationships without the marriage bond; (d) sexual fantasizing, perversion, fetishism, prostitution, and pornography in the adult population as a whole.[11]

Taking such things into consideration, it seems difficult to lend credence to the view that the four principles of our form of monogamous marriage constitute a structure beneficial either to the marriage partners themselves or to their offspring (or indeed to anyone else). One is moved to seek for some other ground of the institution, some ground that lurks beneath the reach of our conventional apprehensions.

IV

The ground of our marriage institution, the essential principle that underwrites all four restrictions, is this: *the maintenance by one man or woman of the effective right to exclude indefinitely all others from erotic access to the conjugal partner.*

The first restriction creates, elaborates on, and provides for the enforcement of this right to exclude. And the second, third, and fourth restrictions together ensure that the right to exclude is—respectively—not cooperative, not simultaneously or sequentially distributed, and not permissive of even casual exception.

In other words, the four restrictions of our form of monogamous marriage together constitute a state-regulated, indefinite, and exclusive ownership by two individuals of one another's sexual powers. Marriage is simply a form of private property.[12]

That our form of monogamous marriage is, when the confusing layers of sanctity, apologetic, and taboo are cleared away, another species of private property should not surprise us.[13] The history of the institution is so full of suggestive indicators—dowries, inheritance, property alliances, daughter sales (of which women's wedding rings are a carry-over), bride exchanges, and legitimacy and illegitimacy—that it is difficult not to see some intimate connections between marital and ownership ties. We are better able still to apprehend the ownership essence of our marriage institution, when in addition we consider: (1) that until recently almost the only way to secure official dissolution of consummated marriage was to be able to demonstrate violation of one or both partner's sexual ownership, (that is, adultery); (2) that the imperative of premarital chastity is tantamount to a demand for retrospective sexual ownership by the eventual marriage partner; (3) that successful sexual involvement with a married person is prosecutable as an expropriation of ownership—"alienation of affections"—which is restituted by cash payment; (4) that the incest taboo is an iron mechanism that protects the conjugal ownership of sexual properties, both the husband's and wife's, from the access of affectionate offspring and the offsprings' (who themselves are future marriage partners) from access of siblings and parents;[14] (5) that the language of the marriage ceremony is the language of exclusive possession ("take," "to have and to hold," "forsaking all others and keeping you only unto him/her," and so on, not to mention the proprietary locutions associated with the marital relationship ("he's mine," "she belongs to him," "keep to your own husband," "wife stealer," "possessive husband," and so on).

V

Of course, it would be remarkable if marriage in our society was not a relationship akin to private property. In our socioeconomic system we relate to virtually everything of value by individual ownership: by, that is, the effective right to exclude others from the thing concerned.[15] That we do so as well with perhaps the most highly valued thing of all—the sexual partners' sexuality—is only to be expected. Indeed, it would probably be an intolerable strain on our entire social structure if we did otherwise.

This line of thought deserves pursuit. The real secret of our form of monogamous marriage is not that it functionally provides for the needs of adults who love one another or of the children they give birth to but that it serves the maintenance of our present social system. It is an institution that is indispensable to the persistence of the capitalist order[16] in the following ways:

1. A basic principle of current social relations is that some people legally acquire the use of other people's personal powers, from which they may exclude other members of society. This system operates in the workplace (owners and hirers of all types contractually acquire for their exclusive use workers' regular labor powers) and in the family (husbands and wives contractually acquire for their exclusive use their partner's sexual properties). A conflict between the structures of these primary relations—as would obtain were there a suspension of the restrictions governing our form of monogamous marriage—might well undermine the systemic coherence of present social intercourse.

2. The fundamental relation between individuals and things that

satisfy their needs is, in our present society, that each individual has or does not have the effective right to exclude other people from the thing in question.[17] A rudimentary need is that for sexual relationship(s). Therefore the object of this need must be related to the one who needs it as owned or not owned (that is, via marriage or not-marriage, or approximations thereof) if people's present relationship to what they need is to retain —again—systemic coherence.

3. A necessary condition for the continued existence of the present social formation is that its members feel a powerful motivation to gain favorable positions in it. But such social ambition is heavily dependent on the preservation of exclusive monogamy in that (a) the latter confines the discharge of primordial sexual energies to a single unalterable partner and thus typically compels those energies to seek alternative outlet, such as business or professional success[18] and (b) the exclusive marriage necessarily reduces the sexual relationships available to any one person to absolute (nonzero) minimum, a unilateral promotion of sexual shortage that in practice renders hierarchial achievement essential as an economic and "display" means for securing scarce partners.[19]

4. Because the exclusive marriage necessarily and dramatically reduces the possibilities of sexual-love relationships, it thereby promotes the existing economic system by: (a) rendering extreme economic self-interest —the motivational basis of the capitalistic process—less vulnerable to altruistic subversion; (b) disciplining society's members into the habitual repression of natural impulse required for long-term performance of repetitive and arduous work tasks; (c) developing a complex of suppressed sexual desires to which sales techniques may be effectively applied in creating those new consumer wants that provide indispensable outlets for ever increasing capital funds.

5. The present form of marriage is of fundamental importance to (a) the continued relative powerlessness of the individual family: which, with larger numbers would constitute a correspondingly increased command of social powers; (b) the continued high demand for homes, commodities, and services: which, with the considerable economies of scale that extended unions would permit, would otherwise falter; (c) the continued strict necessity for adult males to sell their labor power and for adult women to remain at home (or vice versa): which strict necessity would diminish as the economic base of the family unit extended; (d) the continued immense pool of unsatisfied sexual desires and energies in the population at large: without which powerful interests and institutions would

lose much of their conventional appeal and force;[20] (e) the continued profitable involvement of lawyers, priests, and state officials in the jurisdictions of marriage and divorce and the myriad official practices and proceedings connected thereto.[21]

VI

If our marriage institution is a linchpin of our present social structure then a breakdown in this institution would seem to indicate a breakdown in our social structure. On the face of it, the marriage institution is breaking down—enormously increased divorce rates, nonmarital sexual relationships, wife-swapping, the Playboy philosophy, and communes. Therefore one might be led by the appearance of things to anticipate a profound alteration in the social system.

But it would be a mistake to underestimate the tenacity of an established order or to overestimate the extent of change in our marriage institution. Increased divorce rates merely indicate the widening of a traditional escape hatch. Nonmarital relationships imitate and culminate in the marital mold. Wife-swapping presupposes ownership, as the phrase suggests. The Playboy philosophy is merely the view that if one has the money one has the right to be titillated—the commercial call to more fully exploit a dynamic sector of capital investment. And communes—the most hopeful phenomenon—almost nowhere offer a *praxis* challenge to private property in sexuality. It may be changing. But history, as the old man puts it, weighs like a nightmare on the brains of the living.

NOTES

1. Any person who presides over a marriage and is not authorized by law to do so is guilty of a criminal offense and is subject to several years imprisonment (for example, Canadian Criminal Code, Sec. 258.) Here and elsewhere, I draw examples from Canadian criminal law. There is no reason to suspect the Canadian code is eccentric in these instances.

2. For example, offspring are illegitimate, neither the wife nor children are legal heirs, and the husband has no right of access or custody should separation occur.

3. "Any kind of conjugal union with more than one person at the same time, whether or not it is by law recognized as a binding form of marriage—is guilty of an indictable offence and is liable to imprisonment for five years" (Canadian Criminal Code, Sec. 257, [1] [a] [ii]). Part 2 of the same section adds: "Where an accused is charged with an offence under this section, no averment or proof of the

method by which the alleged relationship was entered into, agreed to or consented to is necessary in the indictment or upon the trial of the accused, nor is it necessary upon the trial to prove that the persons who are alleged to have entered into the relationship had or intended to have sexual intercourse."

4. Even the sexual revolutionary Wilhelm Reich seems constrained within the limits of this "binary frame." Thus he says: "Nobody has the right to prohibit his or her partner from entering a temporary or lasting sexual relationship with someone else. He has only the right *either to withdraw or to win the partner back*" (Wilhelm Reich, *The Sexual Revolution*, trans. T. P. Wolfe [New York: Farrar, Straus & Giroux, 1970], p. 28. Emphasis added.) The possibility of sexual partners extending their union to include the other loved party (as opposed to one partner having either to "win" against this third party or to "withdraw" altogether) does not seem even to occur to Reich.

5. I will be using "sexual" and "erotic" interchangeably throughout this paper.

6. It is worth noting here that: (*a*) man has by nature the most "open" sexual instinct—year-round operativeness and response to a wide variety of stimuli—of all the species (except perhaps the dolphin); and (*b*) it is a principle of human needs in general that maximum satisfaction involves regular variation in the form of the need-object.

7. "Roman law had no power of intervening in the formation of marriages and there was no legal form of marriage. . . . Marriage was a matter of simple private agreement and divorce was a private transaction" (Havelock Ellis, *Studies in the Psychology of Sex* [New York: Random House, 1963], vol. 2, p. 429).

8. The dramatic reduction of sibling rivalry through an increased number of adults in the house is a phenomenon that is well known in contemporary domestic communes.

9. One of the few other historical social relationships I can think of in which one person holds thoroughly exclusive monopoly over another's means of life is slavery. Thus, as with another's slave, it is a criminal offense to "receive" or "harbor" another's child without "right of possession" (Canadian Criminal Code, Sec. 250).

10. Certain cultures, for example, permit extramarital sexuality by married persons with friends, guests, or in-laws with no reported consequences of jealousy. From such evidence, one is led to speculate that the intensity and extent of jealousy at a partner's extramarital sexual involvement is in direct proportion to the severity of the accepted cultural regulations against such involvements. In short such regulations do not prevent jealousy so much as effectively engender it.

11. It should not be forgotten that at the same time marriage excludes marital partners from sexual contact with others, it necessarily excludes those others from sexual contact with marital partners. Walls face two ways.

12. Those aspects of marriage law that seem to fall outside the pale of sexual property holding—for example, provisions for divorce if the husband fails to provide or is convicted of a felony or is an alcoholic—may themselves be seen as simply prescriptive characterizations of the sort of sexual property that the marriage partner must remain to retain satisfactory conjugal status; a kind of permanent warranty of the "good working order" of the sexual possession.

What constitutes the "good working order" of the conjugal possession is, of course, different in the case of the husband and in the case of the wife: an *asymmetry* within the marriage institution that, I gather, women's liberation movements are anxious to eradicate.

13. It is instructive to think of even the nonlegal aspects of marriage, for example, its sentiments, as essentially private-property structured. Thus the preoccupation of those experiencing conjugal sentiments with expressing how much "my very own," "my precious," the other is, with expressing, that is, how valuable and inviolable the ownership is and will remain.

14. I think the secret to the long-mysterious incest taboo may well be the fact that in all its forms it protects sexual property: not only conjugal (as indicated above) but paternal and tribal as well. This crucial line of thought, however, requires extended separate treatment.

15. Sometimes—as with political patronage, criminal possession, de facto privileges, and so forth—a *power* to exclude others exists with no corresponding "right" (just as sometimes a right to exclude exists with no corresponding power). Therefore, properly speaking, I should here use the phrase "power to exclude," which covers "effective right to exclude" as well as all nonjuridical enablements of this sort.

16. It is no doubt indispensable as well—in some form or other—to any private-property order. Probably (if we take the history of Western society as our data base) the more thoroughgoing and developed the private-property formation is, the more total the sexual ownership prescribed by the marriage institution.

17. Things in unlimited supply—like, presently, oxygen—are not of course related to people in this way.

18. This is, of course, a Freudian or quasi-Freudian claim. "Observation of daily life shows us," says Freud, "that most persons direct a very tangible part of their sexual motive powers to their professional or business activities" (Sigmund Freud, *Dictionary of Psychoanalysis*, ed. Nandor Fodor and Frank Gaynor [New York: Fawcett Publications, Premier Paperback, 1966], p. 139).

19. It might be argued that exclusive marriage also protects those physically less attractive persons who—in an "open" situation—might be unable to secure any sexual partnership at all. The force of this claim depends, I think, on improperly continuing to posit the very principle of exclusiveness that the "open" situation rules out (for example, in the latter situation, X might be less attractive to Y than Z is and yet Z not be rejected, any more than at present an intimate friend is rejected who is less talented than another intimate friend).

20. The sexual undercurrents of corporate advertisements, religious systems, racial propaganda, and so on, are too familiar to dwell on here.

21. It is also possible that exclusive marriage protects the adult-youth power structure in the manner outlined on p. 171.

David Palmer

The Consolation of the Wedded

It will be agreed that all this sanctimonious prudish world . . . that this heap of libertines and intriguers who disguise themselves behind a verbiage of fidelity, is a bigamous, trigamous and polygamous world in every degree.
    Those who hasten to invalidate my thesis will surely be the most guilty in these matters, because false prudes always rise up violently against the vices from which they secretly profit.
        —Charles Fourier, The New Theory of Society.

"With all established institutions," John McMurtry tells us, "apologetics for perpetuation are never wanting."[1] If that is so it is surely because the critics of those institutions are never silent. And, indeed, the criticisms directed at monogamy are many and varied. But in spite of the title of this essay, I enter the discussion as no dogmatist—neither as apologist nor as critic. I propose instead to spend these few pages in investigating some of the kinds of claims and criticisms to which the institution of marriage has been subjected in both the nineteenth and twentieth centuries. If I rise up violently against any vices, I hope that they shall be only the philosophical vices of conceptual confusion or specious argument and that these shall not be vices from which I secretly profit. First, then, what is the nature of the institution that finds such vocal critics and such a profusion of apologists?

Unfortunately, it is not clear that we can do more than list certain fairly common features of marriage. For example, there is usually a temporally extended relationship between (or among) two or more individuals; this usually involves (1) a sexual relationship; (2) the expectation of procreation; (3) certain expectations or even agreements to provide economic, physical, or psychological support for one another; and (4) a ceremonial event recognizing the creation of the marriage. However, none of these is a *necessary* condition of marriage, and if they are logically *sufficient* conditions when taken jointly, it is probably because of the inclusion of feature number 4. And, in effect, number 4 says only that *whatever* is recognized within the social context as a marriage *is* a marriage—that is, that what is sufficient to constitute a marriage is dependent upon the social structure and institutions of the society. But of course this does not constitute a definition.

It is largely because marriage (and monogamy) is so widespread that arriving at a definition of it is so difficult. That is, the practice of marriage transcends our society and its customs, habits, legal systems, social institutions, and ways of life. Any successful attempt to define marriage would have to define it in terms of social institutions or practices that were necessarily present wherever marriage could occur; but as it turns out, there are few, if any, institutions as universal as marriage. In our society marriage may, for example, be first and foremost a legal relationship. But, unfortunately for the attempt to arrive at a definition, there is no reason to think that marriage could not exist in a prelegal society or as a religious and nonlegal relationship. Thus there seem to be no necessary conditions of marriage apart from that of involving (at least) two individuals. The concept of marriage seems to have all the marks of what philosophers call a "primitive," that is, simple or unanalyzable, concept. Hence, with respect to monogamy, we can say only that it is the practice of being married to no more than one person at a time. [2]

Given this very limited amount of essential formal structure involved in monogamous marriage, it is probably inevitable that many critiques of monogamy will turn out to be directed not at monogamy itself but at monogamy of some particular description and in some social context. Indeed, some critiques of marriage or monogamy have taken the form of an attack on one or more of the social or economic concomitants of marriage in one particular setting and thus have little to do with that relationship per se. For example, the undesirable aspects of monogamy or marriage may be a function of religious traditions that make divorce or remarriage after the death of a spouse impossible, or of a legal system of a particular state at a particular time that subordinates one spouse to another or fails to provide for a just property settlement upon termination of a marriage, or of various other social conditions and economic difficulties that are reflected in marriage and the family.

There is, of course, nothing wrong with pointing out the difficulties people face in marriage or the evils of marriage or monogamy *as a special set of customs in a particular setting*, even when those difficulties and evils are a consequence of factors quite extrinsic to marriage or monogamy per se. Yet there is always the danger that the reader, if not the author himself, may become conceptually muddled about the distinction between (1) a certain set of social practices at a certain time and place, and (2) a transplantable institution like monogamy. As a result, he will confuse a justifiable attack on the first with a justifiable attack on the second. That is to say, a monogamous relationship may be damnable either because *monogamy* is bad or because the relationship is surrounded with and contaminated by a variety of other evil and unhappy institutions and practices. Very different conclusions are warranted in one case than in the other.

Karl Marx, to whom many twentieth-century critics of marriage owe a considerable intellectual debt, was often far more careful than his followers have been to recognize this distinction between criticism of the institution of marriage and criticism of the practices and institutions that surround it. In fact, in 1842 Marx wrote approvingly of romantic love and of monogamous relationships between men and women, speaking, for example, of "the sanctification of the sex drive through *exclusiveness*, the restraint of the drive through law, the *ethical beauty* which turns nature's command into an ideal moment of spiritual union—the *spiritual essence* of marriage."[3] And in a later article he opposed the liberalization of divorce laws on the grounds of the importance to children of a family structure that could not be readily dissolved.[4]

Marx's later attacks on this exclusive relationship and the family structure were founded not on any conviction that these early views were fundamentally mistaken but rather on the discovery that love, which should be (and could be) the fundamental principle of family life, had been replaced in that role by the ownership of property.[5] Private property made a family life based on love impossible.[6] With the development of a communal economy, the division of labor, unequal division of the products of labor, and the increasing accumulation of goods, changes were brought about in the nature of the family. In fact, Marx wrestled mightily with the problem of explaining the origin of private property and the emergence of male dominance and of slavery within the family. He hoped to account for these developments in a way that did not support the capitalist economists' view that they were due to an innate desire of man to acquire goods and dominate other people.[7] That is, he hoped to show that there is nothing in the nature of the individual or of the monogamous relationship *as such* that makes monogamous marriage undesirable. He wrote, in 1846, for example, "Assume particular stages of development in production, commerce, and consumption and you will have a corresponding social constitution, a corresponding organization of the family, of order, of classes: in a word, a corresponding civil society."[8] Clearly, Marx himself, perhaps unlike his followers, placed the source of evil not in marriage or monogamy but in other social conditions and developments.

It may be that many people have been misled about the nature of Marx's views on marriage and the family by his calls for an end to marriage and for the substitution of a new set of male-female relationships.[9] However, the suggestion that the institutions of marriage and the family should be destroyed was not based on the inherent evils of these institutions, as many later interpreters of Marx have assumed, but rather on his conviction that this would be a pragmatic means of implementing changes in yet other institutions and practices that were indeed inherently bad. But it must not be thought that the means of social reform necessarily reflect the structure of the evils of society. There may be a causal relationship between the destruction of monogamous marriage and the destruction of other institutions in the society. Yet, it does not follow from this that the evils of monogamous marriage are the cause of the evils of society.[10]

Certainly, not all critiques of monogamy have been limited to the consideration of extrinsic social and economic concomitants of marriage. A notable alternative is the sustained attack on monogamy by the early nineteenth-century French social utopian Charles Fourier. Fourier is especially interesting, not only because of his strong influence on Marx and the relative modernity of his views on society, sex, and the family, but also because his attack on monogamy is designed to show that institution—independent of other social institutions and practices—to be unsatisfactory as a model for human relationships.

Fourier held that the monogamous relationship was essentially an incomplete relationship. A complete unit of the human species in the physical or material sense consists of two individuals, two bodies—one male and one female. But man consists of more than body alone, more than material man. He also consists of soul, personality, or "passional man." And just as no male or female is materially complete alone, so no individual, and indeed no couple, is passionally complete. For, rather than two individuals, as in the case of physical man, it takes 810 individuals—810 distinct character types, in the ratio of 415 men to 395 women, to make up the complete passional man:

> ... if a thousand men were presented to form a human body, we should have to reject 999, and to the one which remained add a woman. Now if ... the integrality of the human body requires two different bodies, should we be surprised that the integrality of the soul may require two or even two thousand souls? ...
>
> When the 810 characters are brought together and fully developed, forming the complete passional man ... it will be seen that in this new order the poorest individual may develop and satisfy more of the passions of the soul than the richest potentate can do in the present day, and the greater the inequalities in fortune, intelligence, etc., the easier will association rise to a general accord, which will be as perfect as the muscles of the body, or the various instruments of a good orchestra—the latter being an image of the human passions, which constitute an orchestra of 810 instruments.[11]

To the extent that Fourier has this metaphysical view of the nature of man, he has a basis for the claim that monogamy and the family are not the social relationships for which man is best suited—a far different kind of criticism of monogamy than we have so far seen. Fourier proposes the creation of Phalansteries—ideal communities composed of the various passional components working together in a tightly knit socialistic unit that would be so economically viable as to be able to provide all its members with a life of luxury and so emotionally harmonious as to be able to provide satisfaction for the sexual desires and emotional needs of all of its members.[12]

But even Fourier's criticism of marriage and the family is not made strictly on metaphysical grounds. If one reads on one finds that his views on marriage were influenced by sixteen other problems that beset marriage at the turn of the nineteenth century in France—all of them institutions and practices and problems not essentially connected with monogamy and many of which no longer exist.

Unfortunately, not everyone criticizing the practice of monogamy, even in this century, has been careful to determine in any clear way what is and what is not an essential part of that institution. The awkward consequence is that what is claimed to be a critique of marriage or monogamy often turns out to be a critique of factors that are essentially independent of the marriage relationship. I believe that Professor McMurtry's critique of monogamy to a large extent contains just this sort of conceptual confusion. There are, in fact, three major points that I should like to make about his critique. First, there is a consistent failure on his part to identify unambiguously the object of his attack. Is it the institution of monogamy or the social problems and practices of some particular group? Second, certain psychological criticisms he makes of monogamy, like Fourier's analysis of the passional man, presuppose, yet utterly lack, supporting empirical data. And third, his ultimate analysis of the nature of monogamous marriage—that it is essentially an ownership relation—is not only false but implausible. I shall discuss these points in order.

McMurtry talks about "our specific species of official wedlock," "our monogamy institution," "our specific form of monogamy," and "our marriage institution," all in the context of attempting to "identify clearly and systematically the full complex of principles it involves."[13] Indeed, in the very process of identifying these principles (which themselves require some critical scrutiny) he makes repeated references to local laws and attitudes making marriage, and perhaps specifically monogamy, *in those circumstances* less desirable than it might otherwise be. Such laws and attitudes include the requirement of a state-investitured official, a formal contractual agreement (about the terms of which the partners have nothing to say and the dissolution of which must be effected by a state representative), certain specific laws concerning rights of inheritance from common-law marriage, public hostility to common-law relationships, and local prejudices against sexual liaisons outside of marriage.[14]

But, as we have seen, a catalog of such ills may not be very interesting to someone concerned with the relationship apart from its local peculiarities—to someone concerned with the institution of monogamy and not with the fairness of the laws of Ontario. Needless to say, those who have defended monogamy as an institution have neither thought nor argued that the institution, no matter what its social environment and local forms, would rectify the social ills of the society or satisfy all the needs of the participants. At some times and under some conditions and for some individuals, marriage has no doubt contributed significantly to unhappiness.

But it is, after all, McMurtry's real aim to go beyond a criticism of the local conditions and the locally unique institution he has described. Indeed he seems to use this particular form of monogamy, complete with its sociogeographical and temporal context and restrictive principles, as a model on which to base his attacks on the institution as a whole. Thus, after having talked about "our marriage institutions," he suggests that *"the four principles of monogamous marriage"* (note the sudden generality) inhibit "the very effects they are said to promote."[15] Among those desirable effects are a closeness between the partners, a sanctuary from the pressures of outside society, and a loving context for child upbringing. And just how are these desired effects inhibited? Profound closeness, we are told, is "expropriated" and sanctuary from outside pressures is "prohibited" by "centralized official control of marriage."[16] But these, we respond, are certainly not problems with *monogamy*, or with a principle of "monogamous marriage." They are at most local conditions, the burden of which may be felt in marriage as elsewhere in the social structure. That is, on one hand, "centralized official control" is not necessary for marriage, but on the other hand such bureaucratic control *may* extend not only to marriage but also to one's job, residence, travel, education, and other aspects of life as well. The problem, then, is centralized official control and its effects, not marriage.

With a similar disdain for identifying clearly the object of his attack, McMurtry claims that the "number of adult sources of affection, interest, material support, and instruction for the young" is restricted by monogamy "in perhaps the most unilateral possible way consistent with offspring survival."[17] Now in the first place this is sheer hyperbole. Whether we look to the extended families of London's East End, to any number of preindustrial and tribal societies, to the Old South of Katherine Anne Porter, or to the Israeli kibbutz, there is, in general, no lack of sources of adult support for children in either the family itself or the community at large.[18] And the same is true to varying, though diminished, degrees even in a highly mobile industrial society. Furthermore, it is clear that what limits the sources of affection and support for children is not monogamy but social conditions and practices, including the type of housing, the cohesiveness of the extended family, the proximity and interest of friends and neighbors—that is, conditions that are largely extrinsic to marriage.

While listing the societal ills that are heaped at the doorstep of marriage, I might note that McMurtry also claims that there are economic disadvantages of monogamy, such as loss of "the security, range, and power of larger socioeconomic units" and loss of "the possibility of extradomestic freedom founded on more adult providers and upbringers." But here, once again, we have a criticism that presupposes a specific economic and social context for the marriage. These economic problems, if indeed they are problems at all, are not a fault especially of marriage or monogamy but a failure of the society and the individuals involved to form alliances that provide for these needs. After all, if the Israeli Kibbutz provides certain strengths that families collected into cities do not, it is not because the institution of monogamy exists in one place and not in the other. It is rather because we have failed to desire, or, perhaps, failed to combine our efforts in, cooperative ventures for the production of material needs, childcare, multifamily dwelling units, and so on—all of which are perfectly compatible with monogamous marriage.

Another class of criticisms McMurtry directs against monogamy is concerned with supposed psychological effects of the institution. We are told that monogamy "systematically promotes conjugal insecurity, jealousy, and alienation" and that it stimulates destructive aggression, apathy, frustration, dependence, lack of spontaneity, bad faith, sexual fantasizing, perversion, fetishism, prostitution, and pornography, and, presumably, that it does this to a greater extent than would other kinds of male-female relationships.[19] The obvious question here is whether and to what extent these psychological difficulties are (a) the effect of monogamy as opposed to other factors in the culture, such as the pressure to succeed in economic and social ways; (b) reducible by changes in the structure of marriage; and (c) less desirable than the psychological and social problems resulting from some other structure of male-female relationships.

So far as I am aware, McMurtry's charge amounts to little more than a bit of armchair speculation (neither more nor less supported than Fourier's analysis of passional man). McMurtry has made an empirically testable claim about the effects of marriage; it is one that most psychologists and sociologists writing on marriage do not affirm, not because they are apologists for the institution of marriage, but because they lack the requisite empirical evidence.[20] McMurtry's only indication of how he was led to these conclusions is a footnote in which we are told that cultures permitting extramarital sexuality have no reported consequences of jealousy. He is "led to speculate" that jealousy of a partner's extramarital sexual involvement is in proportion to the severity of cultural regulations against such involvements.[21] His speculations might better have led him to the conclusion that jealousy might be avoided by adherence to the principle "what's sauce for the goose is sauce for the gander." In any event, it is certain that such speculations do not begin to answer the crucial questions raised in a, b, and c, and that answers to these would be necessary before it would be reasonable to reject the institution of monogamy on grounds of the psychological harm that it does.

Finally, a third point in McMurtry's critique of monogamy is the claim that marriage is simply a form of private property in which the two partners own one another's sexual powers—marriage is ownership.[22] It would, I think, be worthwhile to briefly consider some of the similarities and differences between marriage, contracts, and ownership.

In the standard case of private property in which one owns a car, an umbrella, or a piece of land, ownership provides one with (1) the right to exclude others from access to or use of those items; (2) the right, should one so desire, to allow others access to or the use of those items; (3) the right to use those items as one sees fit, roughly to the point of not interfering with the rights of others; (4) the right to sell those items for other considerations—money, land, a car, and so on. In addition, it is also the case that (5) the items owned do not have an equal and reciprocal right to the owner. All of this, by the way, holds true in the paradigm case of ownership of human beings and their services—slavery.

By contrast, in the case of contracts one agrees to exchange services or goods with another legally recognized entity on a basis that both parties believe to be to their mutual advantage. The failure of one party to fulfill his part of his contract is in itself sufficient grounds for nonfulfillment by the other party and termination of the contract (or even restitution if that is called for). But the case is notably different if I own someone, say Jones, or his labor or services; for then there are no comparable rights or legally enforceable expectations by whatever (whomever) is owned. Now, just as the conventions of leasing and renting are different from owning, so too is contracting for a service different from owning it. *Thus it would be a gross logical error to argue that the structural similarities between these relations renders them identical.* But this is precisely what McMurtry does when he adduces the "systemic coherence" of marriage and ownership: "It would be remarkable if marriage in our society was not a relationship akin to private property. In our socioeconomic system we relate to virtually everything of value by individual ownership: that is, by the effective right to exclude others from the thing concerned."[23]

The thrust of my argument is that McMurtry has committed precisely the logical error discussed above; for marriage is yet another nonownership relation. It is not only that marriage fails to fulfill conditions of ownership but, contrary to the heart of McMurtry's analysis, marriage is not essentially "the maintenance by one man or woman of the effective right to exclude indefinitely all others from erotic access to the conjugal partner." That is, marriage in fact fails to fulfill even the *first* condition of ownership—the one that McMurtry cites as the "grounds of our marriage institution."[24]

To see that this is true we need only consider that each individual has, and after marriage retains, the sole right to enter into or refrain from sexual relations with others. It is not the right of one partner to prevent the other from engaging in sexual relationships with someone else. It is only the partner's right to ask for a termination of the marriage should this happen. Similarly, no one has the right by virtue of *marriage*, and independent of other social customs, to dispose of his partner's sexual powers as he might his private property. (One could not, for example, *sell* one's partner's sexual powers.) Thus, to attempt to assimilate marriage to ownership is surely a conceptual confusion.

If the marriage relationship is reducible to some other species of relationship at all, it is certainly more akin to what I have described as a contractual relationship than to an ownership relationship. That should not be surprising, for in this society marriage is, among other things, a kind of contract. (McMurtry himself notes that it is a unique kind of contract.[25]) I would not, however, want to suggest that marriage is essentially a contract or, indeed, that it is reducible to any other kind of relationship or institution. A contractual relationship is a legal relationship, and, while the marriage relationship may be a legal relationship in this culture, it can presumably exist in a prelegal society, or as a religious institution, or in quite different societies and under quite different social conditions. It is for this reason that I suggested earlier that the concept of marriage appears to be an irreducible one.

We can see from this investigation into some of the claims and criticisms to which the institution of monogamy has been subjected that many popular criticisms of it are in reality criticisms of social institutions, practices, and conditions with which it is in no way essentially related. Moreover, we have seen that any charges to be made on the basis of alleged psychological ills deriving from marriage require a substantial empirical basis that is not currently available. And finally, at least one interesting attempt to understand the real nature of marriage, namely, that it is "simply a form of private property," fails.

It may fairly be said that I have not provided much consolation for the wedded. But my task has merely been to show that a few of the arguments against monogamy are not as convincing as some may previously have thought. But nevertheless, while we may continue to nod assent to the assertion in *Twelfth Night* that we are "better well-hung than ill-wed," at least we no longer have any reason to deny the suggestion that we might be better off hanging together than hanging separately. And that may be some consolation.

NOTES

1. John McMurtry, "Monogamy: A Critique," herein, p. 169.

2. Monogamy contrasts with bigamy, trigamy, or any other form of polygamy. Each of these is a form of marriage in which there is marriage to more than one person at the *same time*. It is sometimes held that monogamy contrasts with digamy or deuterogamy, in which there is marriage to only one person at a time but to more than one person during a lifetime. However, in its broadest sense monogamy is compatible with digamy or deuterogamy. If we do not allow for more than one marriage during a lifetime, then we shall have to hold that we do not practice monogamy, and consequently that a critique or a defense of that institution is, from our point of view, merely academic.

3. Lloyd D. Easton and R. H. Guddat, eds., *Writings of the Young Marx on Philosophy and Society.* (Garden City, N.Y.: Doubleday, 1967), pp. 101-02. For a recent discussion of these ideas see Russell Jacoby, "The Politics of Subjectivity: Slogans of the American New Left," *New Left Review* 79 (May-June, 1973): 37-49. For an excellent discussion of the development of Marx's views on marriage and the family, including these quotations as well as central problems of the origins of male domination, I am indebted to an unpublished manuscript by Robert P. Neuman entitled "Karl Marx on Women, Marriage and the Family."

4. Easton and Guddat, *Writings*, p. 139.

5. Karl Marx, *Critique of Hegel's Philosophy of Right*, ed. J. O'Malley (Cambridge: The University Press, 1970), pp. xxxvii, 90.

6. Neuman notes that Marx was here taking up a "fundamental tenet of the 'critical utopian socialists'" and had not yet reached the point of calling for an end to private property.

7. Ibid.

8. Marx-Engels, *Werke*, 27:452. (Letter to P. V. Annenkev, Dec. 28, 1846).

9. Such as those in Marx's and Engels' *The Communist Manifesto* or *The German Ideology*.

10. Note McMurtry's talk of marriage as the "linchpin of our present social structure," p. 175. He too may be more concerned with an attack upon monogamy as a means of altering society in other ways rather than as an end in itself.

11. Charles Fourier, *Harmonian Man: Selected Writings of Charles Fourier*, ed. Mark Poster (Garden City, N.Y.: Doubleday, Anchor Books, 1971), p. 116-17.

12. But even in Fourier's case, the discovery that large communal groupings of the sort he advocates are more desirable than cities composed of families seems to be dependent upon particular economic circumstances. He says: "It is the only system adapted to the requirements of the passions; the only one by which industry can be rendered attractive ... if economy and profits can result only from large numbers and extensive combinations, God must have based his calculation on large associations; and our political theories which would base the accord of the passions on the smallest possible union, that of a single family, are utterly absurd" (p. 124).

13. McMurtry, "Monogamy," p. 167 and elsewhere. The four principles are detailed on pp. 167-69.

14. Ibid., pp. 167-69.

15. Ibid., p. 171.

16. Ibid., p. 170.

17. Ibid., p. 171.

18. See especially Michael Young and Peter Willmett, *Family and Kinship in East London* (London: Penguin, 1960). Also, "Is the Family Universal," Melford E. Spiro, in *American Anthropologist* 56 (1954): 839-46.

19. McMurtry, "Monogamy," pp. 171-72.

20. Even those (for example, psychologists) advocating social change, including a full range of possible marriage relationships, while claiming that conventional marriage and family life are responsible for possessiveness, jealousy, the prevailing neurotic climate, pervasive insecurity, and so on, offer no evidence. See, for example, Lawrence Casler, "Permissive Matrimony: Proposals for the Future," *The Humanist* (March/April 1974), p. 5. I am not arguing against complete freedom in these matters, but I see no reason to think changes in marriage a panacea for our emotional problems.

21. McMurtry, "Monogamy," note 10.

22. Ibid., pp. 172-73.

23. Ibid., p. 173.

24. Ibid.

25. Ibid., pp. 167-68.

Michael D. Bayles

Marriage, Love, and Procreation

The current era is one of that vulgar form of hedonism rejected by philosophical hedonists such as Epicurus and John Stuart Mill.[1] Apologists
thinly disguise the tawdriness of a hedonism of biological pleasures by
appeals to individual rights and autonomy. Far too frequently these
appeals merely mask a refusal to accept responsibility. This failure to accept personal responsibility is periodically atoned for by ritualistic and ill-
conceived attempts to help the poor and underprivileged people of the
world.

One of the central focuses of the current vulgar hedonism has been
sexual liberation. Premarital intercourse, gay liberation, no-fault divorce,
open marriage (read, "open adultery"), polygamy, and orgies all have their
advocates. About the only forms of sexual behavior yet to have strong advocates are pedophilia and bestiality. Any day now one may expect grade-
school children to assert their right to happiness through pedophilia and

animal lovers to argue that disapproval of bestiality is unfair to little lambs.

The result, especially in Western society, is an emphasis on sex that is out of all proportion to its significance for a eudaemonistic life—that is, a life worth living, including elements besides pleasure. The only ultimate test for the value of a life is whether at its end it is found to have been worth living. It is difficult to conceive of a person's thinking his life significant because it was a second-rate approximation to the sexual achievements of the notorious rabbit. However, many people seem to think such a life offers the highest ideal of a "truly human" existence, forgetting Aristotle's insight that reproduction is characteristic of all living things, not just humans.[2] Consequently, the institution of marriage has been attacked for hindering the achievement of this vulgar hedonistic ideal.

ATTACKS ON MARRIAGE

Not all attacks on the institution of marriage have been based solely on the vulgar hedonistic ideal. A more broad ranging, although no more plausible, attack has recently been made by John McMurtry. His attack is directed not against marriage per se but against that form of it found in Western society—monogamy. McMurtry does not merely find that monogamous marriage hinders the achievement of the vulgar hedonistic ideal. He also claims it is at least one of the causes of the following social ills: (1) Central official control of marriage "*necessarily* alienates the partners from full responsibility for and freedom in their relationship."[3] (2) Monogamy restricts the sources of adult affection and support available to children.[4] (3) It "systematically promotes conjugal insecurity, jealousy, and alienation. . . ."[5] (4) It "prevents the strengths of larger groupings."[6] (5) It stimulates aggression, apathy, frustration, lack of spontaneity, perversion, fetishism, prostitution, and pornography.[7] (6) It serves to maintain the status quo and capitalism.[8] (7) It supports the powerlessness of the individual family by keeping it small.[9] (8) By promoting many small families it creates a high demand for homes and consumer goods and services.[10] (9) It makes it necessary for many more males to sell their labor than would be necessary if monogamy were not practiced.[11] (10) By limiting opportunities for sexual satisfaction it channels unsatisfied desire into support for various institutions and interests.[12] (11) Finally, it promotes financial profit for lawyers, priests, and so forth, in marriage and divorce proceedings.[13] Such a catalog of evils omits only a few social problems such as political corruption and environmental deterioration, although even they are hinted at in numbers 8 and 11.

Many people have hoped that the simple-mindedness that attributes all or most or even many of society's ills to a single factor would disappear. At one time private ownership of the means of production was the *bête noir* of society.[14] Recently it has been replaced in that role by unlimited population growth.[15] Both of these beasts have been slain by the St. George of reasonableness.[16] McMurtry has called forth yet another single-factor beast. There is no reason to suppose this one to be any more powerful than its predecessors.

No attempt will be made in this essay to examine in detail McMurtry's criticisms of monogamous marriage. In general they are characterized by a lack of historical and sociological perspective. It is unclear whether he is attacking the ideal of monogamous marriage as it perhaps existed a hundred years ago or as it exists today. Yet this difference is crucial. A century ago divorce was not widely recognized or accepted; today that is not true. When divorce was not recognized, concubinage and prostitution were quite prevalent, as was simply abandoning one's family. Such practices certainly mitigated the effect of the strict social rules that McMurtry discusses. Also, he criticizes monogamy for limiting the access of children to adult affection and support, since they must rely upon their parents alone for care. But in the extended family, which existed until the urbanization of society, that limitation was considerably less common than it may be at present.

McMurtry seems to be unaware of the social realities of modern society. He emphasizes the law as it is written rather than the law in action. It is generally recognized that despite the wording of statutes, marriages can in practice now be dissolved by mutual consent.[17] Nor is adultery usually prosecuted in those states in which it is still a crime. Nor does McMurtry present any sociological evidence for the various effects that he claims monogamous marriage has. Sometimes the evidence may well be against him. For example, he claims that monogamy supports the high demand for homes. Yet, for a century in Ireland monogamy coincided with a low demand for new homes. Couples simply postponed marriage until the male inherited the home of his parents, and those who did not inherit often did not marry.[18]

Underlying McMurtry's view of monogamous marriage is the Kantian conception of the marriage contract. According to Kant, marriage "is the Union of two Persons of different sex for life-long reciprocal possession of their sexual faculties."[19] McMurtry takes the following principle to be the essential ground of monogamous marriage: "the maintenance by one man or woman of the effective right to exclude indefinitely all others from erotic access to the conjugal partner."[20] Since by "possession" Kant meant legal ownership and the consequent right to exclude others, these two views come to the same thing. They both view marriage as chiefly concerned with private ownership of the means to sexual gratification, thus combining capitalism with vulgar hedonism (although Kant was not a hedonist).

Such a view of marriage is pure nonsense. However, it has more plausibility in today's era of vulgar hedonism than it did in Kant's time. Historically, the official aims of marriage, according to the Catholic Church—which was the only church during the period of the establishment of monogamous marriage in Western society—were procreation and companionship. There was also a tendency to view it as a legitimate outlet for man's sinful nature.[21] It is this latter element that Kant and McMurtry have taken as the chief one.

In addition to the avowed purposes of marriage there were the actual social functions that it performed. The family unit was the basic social unit, not only for the education of children (that is, socialization, not formal schooling—which has only become widespread during the past century), but also for the production of necessities, including food and clothing, and for recreation. These historical functions of the extended-family unit based on monogamous marriage have been undermined by the development of industrial, urban society.[22] Consequently, the moral and legal status and functions of marriage require reexamination in the light of current social conditions.

Before undertaking such a reexamination it is necessary to distinguish between rules of marriage and attendant social rules. They are mixed together in the traditional social institution of monogamous marriage, but there is no necessity for this mix and it is probably unjustified. In particular one must distinguish between penal laws prohibiting various forms of sexual union—homosexual, premarital, adulterous—and private arranging laws granting legal recognition to the marital relationship.[23] Private arranging laws do not prescribe punishment for offenses; instead, they enable people to carry out their desires. People are not punished for improperly made marriages; instead, the marriages are invalid and unenforceable. Laws against fornication, prostitution, cohabitation, and homosexuality are almost always penal. Objections to them cannot be transferred directly to the marriage relationship. All of these penal laws could be abolished and monogamous marriage could still be retained.

It may be claimed that despite their nonpenal form, marriage laws do in fact penalize those who prefer other forms of relationship. If homosexual and polygamous relationships are not legally recognized as "marriages," then persons desiring these forms of relationship are being deprived of some degree of freedom. When considering freedom one must be clear about what one is or is not free to do. Consider, for example, the case of gambling. One must distinguish between laws that forbid gambling and the absence of laws that recognize gambling debts. The latter does not deprive people of the freedom to contract gambling debts; it simply does not allow the use of legal enforcement to collect them. Similarly, the absence of laws recognizing polygamous and homosexual marriages does not deprive people of the freedom to enter polygamous and homosexual unions. Instead, it merely fails to provide legal recourse to enforce the agreements of the parties to such unions. The absence of laws recognizing such marriages does not deprive people of a freedom they previously had, for they were never able to have such agreements legally enforced. Nor have people been deprived of a freedom they would have if there were no legal system, for in the absence of a legal system no agreements can be legally enforced. If there is a ground for complaint, then, it must be one of inequality—that one type of relationship is legally recognized but others are not. However, a charge of inequality is warranted only if there are no relevant reasonable grounds for distinguishing between relationships. To settle that issue one must be clear about the state's or society's interests in marriage.

The rest of this essay is concerned with the purposes or functions of the marriage relationship in which society has a legitimate interest. It is not possible here to set out and to justify the purposes for which governments may legislate. It is assumed that the state may act to facilitate citizens' engaging in activities that they find desirable and to protect the welfare and equality of all citizens, including future ones. Government has an especially strong responsibility for the welfare of children. Of course, these legitimate governmental or social interests and responsibilities must be balanced against other interests and values of citizens, including those of privacy and freedom from interference.

There is no attempt or intention to justify penal laws prohibiting forms of relationship other than monogamous marriage. Indeed, it is generally assumed that they ought not be prohibited and that more people will enter into them than has been the case. In such a context, monogamous marriage would become a more specialized form of relationship, entered into by a smaller proportion of the population than previously. Underlying this assumption are the general beliefs that many people are unqualified or unfit for a marital relationship and ought never to enter one and that many people marry for the wrong reasons. If true, these beliefs may explain why both marriage and divorce rates have been steadily rising in most Western countries during this century.[24]

PROMOTING INTERPERSONAL RELATIONSHIPS

Alienation from others and loss of community are perceived by many to be among the most serious ills of modern, mass society. In such a situation it seems unlikely that many would deny the need for intimate interpersonal relationships of affection. The importance of such relationships for a good or *eudaemonistic* life have been recognized by philosophers as diverse as Aristotle and G. E. Moore.[25] In considering such interpersonal relationships to be among the most valuable elements of a good life, one must distinguish between the value of a good and the strength of the desire for it. Many people have a stronger desire for life than for such interpersonal relationships, but they may still recognize such relationships as more valuable than mere life. Life itself is of little value, but it is a necessary condition for most other things of value.

Among the most valuable forms of interpersonal relationship are love, friendship, and trust. These relationships are limited with respect to the number of persons with whom one can have them. Classically, there has been a distinction between agapeic and erotic love. Agapeic love is the love of all mankind—general benevolence. The concept of erotic love is more limited. In today's world erotic love is apt to be confused with sexual desire and intercourse. But there can be and always has been sex without love and love without sex. Personal love is more restricted than either agapeic love or sexual desire. It implies a concern for another that is greater than that for most people. Hence, it cannot be had for an unlimited number of other people.[26] Similar distinctions must be drawn between friendship and acquaintance, trust of a political candidate and trust of a friend.

Such interpersonal relationships require intimacy. Intimacy involves a sharing of information about one another that is not shared with others. Moreover, it often involves seclusion from others—being in private where others cannot observe.[27] In some societies where physical privacy is not possible, psychological privacy—shutting out the awareness of the presence of others—substitutes. Consequently, these valuable interpersonal relationships require intimacy and usually physical privacy from others, and at the very least nonintrusion upon the relationship.

Moreover, these forms of interpersonal relationship require acts expressing the concern felt for the other person. In most societies acts of sexual intercourse have been such expressions of love and concern. It is not physically or psychologically necessary that sexual intercourse have this quasi-symbolic function, but it is a natural function of sexual intercourse. All that is here meant by "natural" is that in most societies sexual intercourse has this function, for which there is some psychological basis even though it is not contrary to scientific laws for it to be otherwise. Intercourse usually involves an element of giving of oneself, and one's sexual identity is frequently a central element of one's self-image. It is not, however, sexual intercourse that is intrinsically valuable but the feelings and attitudes, the underlying interpersonal relationship, that it expresses. Nonsexual acts also currently express such relationships, but sexual intercourse is still one of the most important ways of doing so. If sexual intercourse ceases to have this function in society, some other act will undoubtedly replace it in this function. Moreover, sexual intercourse will have lost much of its value.

If these interpersonal relationships of personal love and trust are of major value, it is reasonable for the state to seek to protect and foster them by according legal recognition to them in marriage. The specific forms of this recognition cannot be fully discussed. However, there is some basis for treating the partners to a marriage as one person. Historically, of course, the doctrine that the parties to a marriage are one person has supported the subjugation of women in all sorts of ways, for example, in their disability from owning property. But there is an underlying rationale for joint responsibility. Two people who, without a special reason such as taxes, keep separate accounts of income and expenditures do not have the love and trust of a couple who find such an accounting unnecessary. Moreover, in such a joint economic venture there is no point to allowing one party to sue the other. Only the advent of insurance, whereby neither spouse, but a third party, pays, makes such suits seem profitable. Another recognition of these relationships—albeit one not frequently invoked—is that one is not forced to testify against his or her spouse. More important is that neither party is encouraged to violate the trust and intimacy of the relationship, for example, by encouraging one to inform authorities about bedroom comments of his or her spouse. [28]

The character of these valuable forms of interpersonal relationship provides an argument against according marriages of definite duration legal recognition equal to that accorded those that are intentionally of indefinite duration. For it to be "intentionally of indefinite duration," neither partner may, when entering the marriage, intend it to be for a specific period of time, for example, five years, nor may the marriage contract specify such a period. The following argument is not to show that marriages for a definite duration should not be recognized, but merely to show that they should not have equal standing with those intentionally of indefinite duration. The basic reason for unequal recognition is that interpersonal relationships that are not intentionally of indefinite duration are less valuable than those that are.

Suppose one were to form a friendship with a colleague, but the two mutually agree to be friends for only three years, with an option to renew the friendship at that time. Such an agreement would indicate a misunderstanding of friendship. Such agreements make sense for what Aristotle called friendships of utility, but in the modern world these friendships are business partnerships. [29] While there is nothing wrong with business friendships, they do not have the intrinsic value of personal friendships. In becoming close personal friends with someone, one establishes a concern and trust that would be seriously weakened or destroyed by setting a time limit to the friendship. It is sometimes claimed that time limits may be set because people will only be together for a while. But one need not see a person every day or even every year to remain friends. However, extended separation usually brings about a withering away of the friendship.

Similarly, the personal relationship of love and trust in marriage is of lesser value if it is intentionally for only a definite period of time. Moreover, the entering into a relationship that is intentionally of indefinite duration and legally recognized symbolizes a strength of commitment not found in other types of relationships. While two unmarried people may claim that there is no definite limit to their mutual commitment, their commitment is always questionable. Entering into a marital relationship assures the commitment more than does a mere verbal avowal.

There are two common objections to this argument. First, it is sometimes said that there may be special reasons for making marriages of short, definite duration, for example, if one partner will only live in the area for a while. But a personal love that is not strong enough to overcome difficulties of moving to another area and possible sacrifices of employment is not as close and strong as a love that can. Many married couples make such compromises and sacrifices. Second, it is sometimes claimed that commitment is in fact stronger when not legally reinforced, when one does not need the law to support the relationship. However, this claim overlooks the fact that when a married couple's relationship rests substantially upon their legal obligations, their relationship has already begun to deteriorate. The strength of commitment is established by the willingness to enter into a legal relationship that cannot be broken simply, without any difficulties. A person who is not willing to undertake the risk of the legal involvement in divorce should he desire to terminate the relationship is probably unsure of his commitment. Moreover, the legal relationship provides security against a sudden and unexpected change in one's life—the breakup of the social aspects will take some time, giving one a chance to prepare for a new style of life. Even then the change is often very difficult.

Hence, if marriage is for the purpose of providing legal recognition of some of the most valuable interpersonal relationships, it should grant more protection and recognition to those intentionally of indefinite duration than to others. Such a conclusion does not imply that divorce should be impossible or exceedingly difficult. Friendships frequently do not last forever despite their not being intended for a limited period of time. The same may happen to a marital relationship. So while this argument supports not according legal recognition to relationships intended to be of definite duration equal to that accorded those intended to be of indefinite duration, it does not support restrictions on divorce in the latter case. Moreover, the average length of time of marriages has increased considerably since the seventeenth century. When a couple married then, one of them was likely to die within twenty years. With today's increased life expectancy, both parties may live close to fifty years after they marry.[30] Obviously, with such an increased possible length of marriage, there is a greater chance for marital breakdown and divorce. One may expect more divorces in marriages that have lasted twenty to twenty-five years simply because there are more such marriages. Nevertheless, such marriages are intentionally of indefinite duration—for life.

PROTECTING THE WELFARE OF CHILDREN

Another area of pervasive social interest that has historically centered in marriage concerns the procreation and raising of children. Society has an interest not only in the number of children born but their quality of life. This fact is in deep conflict with the current emphasis on the freedom of individuals to make reproductive decisions unfettered by social rules and restrictions. Moreover, it is an area in which social control has traditionally been weak. Child abuse is widespread, and efforts to prevent it are mediocre at best. There are few general legal qualifications or tests for becoming a parent. Yet parenthood is one of the most potentially dangerous relationships that one person can have with another. If one is a poor college teacher, then at worst a few students do not receive a bit of education they might have. But as a parent one potentially can ruin completely the lives of one's children. At the least, they may develop into psychological misfits incapable of leading responsible and rewarding lives.

Essentially, there are three areas of social interest and responsibility with respect to procreation and the raising of children. First, there is a social interest in the sheer number of children born. The current emphasis on population control makes this interest abundantly clear.[31] Second, there is a social interest in the potentialities of children. This area includes concern for genetic and congenital birth defects and abnormalities. Over 5 percent of all children born have a genetic defect. The possibility of genetic control of those who are born will soon take on major significance. Already, approximately sixty genetic diseases as well as almost all chromosomal abnormalities can be detected *in utero*, and adult carriers of about eighty genetic defects can be identified.[32] Given the possibility of genetic control, society can no longer risk having genetically disadvantaged children by leaving the decision of whether to have children to the unregulated judgment of individual couples. Some social regulations with respect to genetic screening and, perhaps, eugenic sterilization are needed. While potential parents have interests of privacy and freedom in reproductive decisions, the social interests in preventing the suffering and inequality of possibly defective children may outweigh them in certain types of cases.

Third, the care and development of those who are born is a social interest and responsibility. This interest has been recognized for some time in the form of children's homes and compulsory education. However, increasing knowledge about childhood development extends the area in which social interests and responsibility may be reasonably involved. To give an example at the most elementary level, the nutritional diet of children during their first three years is crucial for their future development. So also is their psychological support. The welfare of future generations is not a private but a social matter. It is a proper task of society, acting through its government, to ensure that the members of the next generation are not physical or psychological cripples due to the ignorance, negligence, or even indifference of parents.

Historically, society has attempted to control procreation through the institution of marriage. Society's means were primarily to stigmatize children born out of wedlock and to encourage the having of many children. It is now recognized that no useful purpose is served by stigmatizing children born out of wedlock as illegitimate. (However, some useful purpose may be served by not according children born out of wedlock all the rights of those born in wedlock, for example, inheritance without parental recognition.) The emphasis on having as many children as one can has also disappeared. It is not this historical concern with procreation that is misplaced in modern society but the forms that the concern has taken.

If society has the responsibility to protect the welfare of children, then some social regulation and control of human reproduction and development is justified. Such regulation and control need not be effected by penal laws. For example, social concern has traditionally been expressed in adoptions through regulations to ensure that those who adopt children are fit to care for them. That some regulations have been inappropriate and not reasonably related to the welfare of children is not in question. Rather, the point is that there has been regulation without penal laws, or at least without resorting primarily to penal laws. Nor can social regulation and control be solely by legislation. Legislation alone is usually ineffective; it must be supported by informal social rules and expectations.

Not only has modern biomedicine made sex possible without procreation; it has also made procreation possible without sex. The techniques of artificial insemination and fertilization, embryo transfer, ova donation, ectogenesis, and cloning now, or soon will, make it possible for people to reproduce without sexual intercourse.[33] Hence, not only may one have sex for pleasure, but one may reproduce for pleasure without sexual intercourse. Not only may people reproduce outside marriage; they are not even biologically required to have intercourse. Thus, sex and marriage may become dissociated from reproduction.

However, there are strong reasons for restricting procreation primarily to marriages of indefinite duration, which does not imply that such marriages should be restricted to procreation. Marriage has traditionally been the central social institution concerned with procreation. Consequently, if society is to exercise some control over procreation in the future, it would involve the least change in conditions to do so through marriage. Moreover, there is considerable evidence that the disruption of family life contributes to juvenile delinquency. Whether divorce or marital breakdown (with or without divorce) is a prime cause of such delinquency does not matter. The point is that the disruption of home life does seriously affect the development of children.[34] The chance of such disruption outside of a marriage that is intentionally of indefinite duration is higher than for that within. Moreover, there is some reason to believe that the presence of both mother and father is instrumental in the psychological development of children. In any case, the presence of two people rather than one provides the security that there will be someone to care for the children should one of the parents die. Generally, children are better off being with one parent than in a state orphanage, but better off still with both parents. Hence, for the welfare of children it seems best that procreation and child rearing primarily occur within the context of marriages intentionally of indefinite duration.

While society has a responsibility for the care and development of children, this general responsibility is best carried out if specific adults have obligations to care for specific children. In the past, the biological parent-child relation has reinforced the allocation of responsibility for specific children and has been a major factor in monogamy.[35] The separation of reproduction and sexual intercourse threatens disruption of this assignment. For example, if gestation occurs in an artificial womb in a laboratory, there may be no "parents," only a scientific research group. More realistically, if a woman has an embryo from ova and sperm donors transferred to her uterus, it is unclear who are the child's parents. However, if there is to be optimal care for children, specific adults must have obligations for specific children. It cannot be left to somebody in general, for then nobody in particular is likely to do it. "Let George do it" is too prevalent and careless an attitude to allow with regard to children.

McMurtry's contention that monogamy restricts the care for children is not well founded.[36] First, if there are no specific adults responsible for children, they may become "lost" in large groups and victims of the "it's not my job" syndrome. Second, monogamy per se does not cut children off from the support and care of others. One must distinguish the marital relationship from living arrangements. It is the isolated situation of the family that deprives children of such support. In many married-student housing complexes children have access to other adults. Even in general-residential neighborhoods with separate family housing units, such support is available if there is a sense of community in the neighborhood.

Given the social interests in and responsibility for the procreation and development of children, some more effective controls of parenthood appear desirable. If the primary locus of reproduction is to be within marriages of intentionally indefinite duration, then the easiest way to institute controls is to add requirements for people to enter such marriages. A few requirements such as blood tests are already generally prevalent. Alternatively, one might have a separate licensing procedure for procreation. Nonmarried couples and single people might also qualify for such licenses. Moreover, couples who want to marry but not have children would not have to meet requirements. However, the only requirements suggested below that might bar marriages are almost as important for those couples who do not have children as for those who do. If the requirements were tied to marriage they would be easier to administer. The only drawback is that unmarried people would not have to meet them. However, such requirements can and should be part of the medical practice of the "artificial" techniques of reproduction—artificial insemination and embryo transfer. And there are few if any effective methods, except generally accepted social rules, to control procreation outside of marriage.

One obvious requirement would be genetic screening. With modern medical techniques genetic problems do not imply that couples cannot become married, but they might be expected not to have children who are their genetic offspring. Artificial insemination and embryo transfer make it possible for almost everyone to have children, even though the children might not be genetically theirs. A general distinction between biological and social parenthood should be made, with legal emphasis on the latter.

More important, perhaps, is some general expectation of psychological fitness for family life and the raising of children. The difficulty with such an expectation is the absence of any clear criteria for fitness and reliable methods for determining who meets them. Perhaps, however, some formal instruction in family relations and child rearing would be appropriate. The Commission on Population Growth and the American Future has already called for an expansion of education for parenthood.[37] It is only a bit further to require some sort of minimal family education for marriage. Probably the easiest method for ensuring such education would be to make it a required subject in secondary schools. If that were done, few people would have difficulty meeting this requirement for marriage.

There should not be any financial or property qualifications for marriage.[38] Society's interest in and responsibility for the welfare of the population in general is such that governments should ensure an adequate standard of living for all persons. Were that to be done there would be no reason to impose any financial restrictions on marriage. Nonetheless, prospective parents should have more concern for their financial situation than is now frequently the case. The adequate care of children is an expensive task, financially as well as psychologically and temporally.

CONCLUSION

It may be objected that neither the argument from interpersonal relations nor that from the welfare of children specifically supports monogamous marriage. While loving relationships cannot extend to an indefinite number of people, they can extend to more than one other person. Also, a polygamous union may provide a reasonable environment for procreation. Hence, neither of the arguments supports monogamous marriage per se.

Logically, the objection is quite correct. But it is a misunderstanding of social philosophy to expect arguments showing that a certain arrangement is always best under all circumstances. The most that can be shown is that usually, or as a rule, one social arrangement is preferable to another. Practically, polygamous marriage patterns will probably never be prevalent.[39] For centuries they have been gradually disappearing throughout the world. If a disproportionate sex distribution of the population occurs in some areas or age groups (such as the elderly), then they may increase in significance. Unless that occurs, most people will probably continue to prefer marital monogamy.

More important, the burden of this paper has not been to defend the traditional ideal of marital union or even the current practice. Many of the traditional rules of marriage have been unjust, for example, the inequality between the sexes, both legally and in terms of social roles. Instead, it has been to defend social recognition of marriage of intentionally indefinite duration as a unique and socially valuable institution that society has interests in promoting and regulating. In particular, society has interests in and responsibility for promoting a certain form of valuable interpersonal relationship and protecting the welfare of children. Both of these purposes can be well served by monogamous marriage.

The image, then, is of a society with various forms of living together, but one in which marriage of intentionally indefinite duration would have a distinctive though lessened role as a special kind of socially and legally recognized relationship. There would not be laws prohibiting nonmarital forms of cohabitation. Divorce would be based on factual marital breakdown or mutual consent, with due regard for the welfare of children. Monogamous marriage would recognize a special form of personal relationship in which reproduction and child rearing primarily occur. Given the social interest in decreasing procreation, many people might marry but not have children, and others might not marry at all. Details of the legal marital relationship have not been specified, nor could they be in this brief essay except with respect to the main social interests. Questions of inheritance, legal residence and name, social-security benefits, and so on, have not been specified. Changes in laws with respect to many of these matters can be made without affecting the arguments for the value of, social responsibility for, and interests in marriage. Above all, it is an image in which sexual intercourse plays a much smaller role in the conception of marriage and the good life in general, a society in which vulgar hedonism has at least been replaced by a broader-based *eudaemonism*.

NOTES

1. Epicurus, "Letter to Menoeceus," in *The Stoic and Epicurean Philosophers*, ed. Whitney J. Oates (New York: Modern Library, 1957), p. 31. Epicurus even wrote, "Sexual intercourse has never done a man good, and he is lucky if it has not harmed him" (Fragment 8 in *The Stoic and Epicurean Philosophers*). John Stuart Mill, *Utilitarianism*, chap. 2, especially paragraphs 1-9.

2. *De Anima* 2. 4.

3. "Monogamy: A Critique," *The Monist* 56 (1972); reprinted herein, pp. 166-77. This quote appears on page 170 of this volume (italics added). Subsequent references to McMurtry's essay are to pages in this volume.

4. Ibid., p. 171.

5. Ibid.

6. Ibid.

7. Ibid., pp. 171-72.

8. Ibid., p. 173.

9. Ibid., p. 174.

10. Ibid.

11. Ibid.

12. Ibid., pp. 174-75.

13. Ibid., p. 175.

14. Karl Marx and Friedrich Engels, "Manifesto of the Communist Party," in *Basic Writings on Politics and Philosophy*, ed. Lewis S. Feuer (Garden City, N.Y.: Doubleday, Anchor Books, 1959), especially p. 24.

15. Paul R. Ehrlich, *The Population Bomb* (New York: Ballantine Books, 1968).

16. Even new Marxists perceive other sources of problems. See Milovan Djilas, *The New Class* (New York: Praeger, 1964); and, more generally, Richard T. De

George, *The New Marxism* (New York: Pegasus, 1968), chap. 2. The importance of population for pollution, with which it is most frequently connected, has been contested by Barry Commoner, *The Closing Circle* (New York: Knopf, 1971), pp. 133-35. Ehrlich now clearly recognizes that various causal factors are important, although he still disagrees with Commoner on the importance of population growth; see Paul R. Ehrlich et al., *Human Ecology* (San Francisco: W. H. Freeman and Company, 1973), chap. 7, esp. pp. 206, 213-15, 221.

17. Max Rheinstein, *Marriage Stability, Divorce, and the Law* (Chicago: University of Chicago Press, 1972), p. 251.

18. Edwin D. Driver, "Population Policies of State Governments in the United States: Some Preliminary Observations," *Villanova Law Review* 15 (1970): 846-47.

19. Immanuel Kant, *The Philosophy of Law*, trans. W. Hastie (Edinburgh: T. & T. Clark, 1887), p. 110.

20. McMurtry, "Monogamy," p. 172; italics in original omitted.

21. See John T. Noonan, Jr., *Contraception* (Cambridge, Mass.: Harvard University Press, 1966), pp. 312-14.

22. Keith G. McWalter, "Marriage as Contract: Towards a Functional Redefinition of the Marital Status," *Columbia Journal of Law and Social Problems* 9 (1973): 615.

23. Robert S. Summers, "The Technique Element of Law," *California Law Review* 59 (1971): 736-37, 741-45.

24. Burton M. Leiser, *Liberty, Justice and Morals* (New York: Macmillan Co., 1973), p. 126; R[oland] Pressat, *Population*, trans. Robert and Danielle Atkinson (Baltimore: Penguin Books, 1970), pp. 84, 86; U.S. Commission on Population Growth and the American Future, *Population and the American Future* (New York: Signet, New American Library, 1972), pp. 102-03.

25. Aristotle, *Nicomachean Ethics* 9. 9-12; George Edward Moore, *Principia Ethica* (Cambridge: At the University Press, 1903), pp. 188, 203-05.

26. It is thus misleading for McMurtry to write of monogamous marriage excluding "almost *countless* other possibilities of *intimate* union" with any number of persons (p. 168; my italics). On the limited nature of personal love or friendship see also Aristotle, *Nicomachean Ethics* 9. 10.

27. For a discussion of these relationships and the need for privacy, see Charles Fried, "Privacy," in *Law, Reason, and Justice*, ed. Graham Hughes (New York: New York University Press, 1969), pp. 45-69.

28. See the discussion (in another context) of such a case in Nazi Germany by H. L. A. Hart, "Positivism and the Separation of Law and Morals," *Harvard Law Review* 71 (1958): 618-20; and Lon L. Fuller, "Positivism and Fidelity to Law—A Reply to Professor Hart," *Harvard Law Review* 71 (1958): 652-55.

29. *Nicomachean Ethics* 8. 3. The vulgar hedonists treat marriage as a form of friendship for pleasure, but that is not the highest form of friendship.

30. Pressat, *Population*, p. 52.

31. For a more complete discussion see my "Limits to a Right to Procreate," in *Ethics and Population*, ed. Michael D. Bayles (Cambridge, Mass.: Schenkman Publishing Company, 1975).

32. Daniel Callahan, *The Tyranny of Survival* (New York: Macmillan Co., 1973), p. 219.

33. For a good general survey of these techniques and some suggestions for social controls, see George A. Hudock, "Gene Therapy and Genetic Engineering: Frankenstein Is Still a Myth, But It Should Be Reread Periodically," *Indiana Law Journal* 48 (1973): 533-58. Various ethical issues are discussed in Joseph Fletcher, *The Ethics of Genetic Control* (Garden City, N.Y.: Doubleday, Anchor Books, 1974). Successful human embryo implantation and growth to term after *in vitro* fertilization has been reported in Britain (see *Time*, July 29, 1974, pp. 58-59; and *Newsweek*, July 29, 1974, p. 70).

34. President's Commission on Law Enforcement and Administration of Justice, *The Challenge of Crime in a Free Society* (New York: Avon Books, 1968), pp. 184-89.

35. Daniel Callahan, "New Beginnings in Life: A Philosopher's Response," in *The New Genetics and the Future of Man*, ed. Michael P. Hamilton (Grand Rapids, Mich.: William B. Eerdmans Publishing Company, 1972), pp. 102-03.

36. "Monogamy," p. 171.

37. *Population and the American Future*, pp. 126-33, esp. 133.

38. For some suggested financial requirements as well as others, see Jack Parsons, *Population versus Liberty* (Buffalo, N.Y.: Prometheus Books, 1971), p. 349.

39. Even McMurtry appears to recognize this fact; see "Monogamy," p. 167.

Richard Wasserstrom

Is Adultery Immoral?

Many discussions of the enforcement of morality by the law take as illustrative of the problem under consideration the regulation of various types of sexual behavior by the criminal law. It was, for example, the Wolfenden Report's recommendations concerning homosexuality and prostitution that led Lord Devlin to compose his now famous lecture "The Enforcement of Morals." And that lecture in turn provoked important philosophical responses from H. L. A. Hart, Ronald Dworkin, and others.

Much, if not all, of the recent philosophical literature on the enforcement of morals appears to take for granted the immorality of the sexual behavior in question. The focus of discussion, at least, is on whether such things as homosexuality, prostitution, and adultery ought to be made ille-

This article is reprinted from Richard Wasserstrom, ed., *Today's Moral Problems* (New York: Macmillan Co., 1975), with the permission of the author.

gal even if they are immoral, and not on whether they are immoral.

I propose in this paper to consider the latter, more neglected topic, that of sexual morality, and to do so in the following fashion. I shall consider just one kind of behavior that is often taken to be a case of sexual immorality—adultery. I am interested in pursuing at least two questions. First, I want to explore the question of in what respects adulterous behavior falls within the domain of morality at all, for this surely is one of the puzzles one encounters when considering the topic of sexual morality. It is often hard to see on what grounds much of the behavior is deemed to be either moral or immoral, for example, private homosexual behavior between consenting adults. I have purposely selected adultery because it seems a more plausible candidate for moral assessment than many other kinds of sexual behavior.

The second question I want to examine is that of what is to be said about adultery if we are not especially concerned to stay within the area of its morality. I shall endeavor, in other words, to identify and to assess a number of the major arguments that might be advanced against adultery. I believe that they are the chief arguments that would be given in support of the view that adultery is immoral, but I think they are worth considering even if some of them turn out to be nonmoral arguments and considerations.

A number of the issues involved seem to me to be complicated and difficult. In a number of places I have at best indicated where further philosophical exploration is required, without having successfully conducted the exploration myself. This essay may very well be more useful as an illustration of how one might begin to think about the subject of sexual morality than as an elucidation of important truths about the topic.

Before I turn to the arguments themselves, there are two preliminary points that require some clarification. Throughout the paper I shall refer to the immorality of such things as breaking a promise, deceiving someone, and so on. In a very rough way I mean by this that there is something morally wrong in doing the action in question. I mean that the action is, in a strong sense of "prima facie," prima facie wrong or unjustified. I do not mean that it may never be right or justifiable to do the action—just that the fact that it is an action of this description always counts against the rightness of the action. I leave entirely open the question of what it is that makes actions of this kind immoral in this sense of "immoral."

The second preliminary point concerns what is meant or implied by the concept of adultery. I mean by "adultery" any case of extramarital sex, and I want to explore the arguments for and against extramarital sex, undertaken in a variety of morally relevant situations. Someone might claim that the concept of adultery is conceptually connected with the concept of immorality and that to characterize behavior as adulterous is already to characterize it as immoral or unjustified in the sense described above. There may be something to this. Hence the importance of making it clear that I want to discuss extramarital sexual relations. If they are always immoral, this is something that must be shown by argument. If the concept of adultery does in some sense entail or imply immorality, I want to ask whether that connection is a rationally based one. If not all cases of extramarital sex are immoral (again, in the sense described above), then the concept of adultery should either be weakened accordingly or restricted to those classes of extramarital sex for which the predication of immorality is warranted.

One argument for the immorality of adultery might go something like this: What makes adultery immoral is that it involves the breaking of a promise, and what makes adultery seriously wrong is that it involves the breaking of an important promise. For, so the argument might continue, one of the things the two parties promise each other when they get married is that they will abstain from sexual relationships with third parties. Because of this promise both spouses quite reasonably entertain the expectation that the other will behave in conformity with it. Hence, when one of them has sexual intercourse with a third party, he or she breaks that promise about sexual relationships that was made when the marriage was entered into and defeats the reasonable expectations of exclusivity entertained by the spouse.

In many cases the immorality involved in breaching the promise relating to extramarital sex may be a good deal more serious than that involved in the breach of other promises. This is so because adherence to this promise may be of much greater importance to them than is adherence to many of the other promises given or received by them in their lifetime. The breaking of this promise may be much more hurtful and painful than is typically the case.

Why is this so? To begin with, it may have been difficult for the non-adulterous spouse to have kept the promise. Hence that spouse may feel the unfairness of having restrained himself or herself in the absence of reciprocal restraint having been exercised by the adulterous spouse. In addition, the spouse may perceive the breaking of the promise as an indication of a kind of indifference on the part of the adulterous spouse. If you really cared about me and my feelings, the spouse might say, you would not have done this to me. And third, and related to the above, the spouse may see the act of sexual intercourse with another as a sign of affection for the other person and as an additional rejection of the nonadulterous spouse as the one who is loved by the adulterous spouse. It is not just that the adulterous spouse does not take the feelings of the nonadulterous spouse sufficiently into account; the adulterous spouse also indicates through the act of adultery affection for someone other than the nonadulterous spouse. I will return to these points later. For the present it is sufficient to note that a set of arguments can be developed in support of the proposition that certain kinds of adultery are wrong just because they involve the breach of a serious promise that, among other things, leads to the intentional infliction of substantial pain on one spouse by the other.

Another argument for the immorality of adultery focuses not on the existence of a promise of sexual exclusivity but on the connection between adultery and deception. According to this argument adultery involves deception. And because deception is wrong, so is adultery.

Although it is certainly not obviously so, I shall simply assume in this essay that deception is always immoral. Thus, the crucial issue for my purposes is the asserted connection between extramarital sex and deception. Is it plausible to maintain, as this argument does, that adultery always involves deception and is, on that basis, to be condemned?

The most obvious person upon whom deceptions might be practiced is the nonparticipating spouse; and the most obvious thing about which the nonparticipating spouse can be deceived is the existence of the adulterous act. One clear case of deception is that of lying. Instead of saying that the afternoon was spent in bed with A, the adulterous spouse asserts that it was spent in the library with B or on the golf course with C.

There can also be deception even when no lies are told. Suppose, for instance, that a person has sexual intercourse with someone other than his or her spouse and just does not tell the spouse about it. Is that deception? It may not be a case of lying if, for example, he or she is never asked by the spouse about the situation. Still, we might say, it is surely deceptive because of the promises that were exchanged at marriage. As we saw earlier, these promises provide a foundation for the reasonable belief that neither spouse will engage in sexual relationships with any other person. Hence the failure to bring the fact of extramarital sex to the attention of the other spouse deceives that spouse about the present state of the marital relationship.

Adultery, in other words, can involve both active and passive deception. An adulterous spouse may just keep silent or, as is often the case, the spouse may engage in an increasingly complex way of life devoted to the concealment of the facts from the nonparticipating spouse. Lies, half-truths, clandestine meetings, and the like may become a central feature of the adulterous spouse's existence. These are things that can and do happen, and when they do they make the case against adultery an easy one. Still, neither active nor passive deception is inevitably a feature of an extramarital relationship.

It is possible, though, that a more subtle but pervasive kind of deceptiveness is a feature of adultery. It comes about because of the connection in our culture between sexual intimacy and certain feelings of love and affection. The point can be made indirectly by seeing that one way in which we can in our culture mark off our close friends from our mere acquaintances is through the kinds of intimacies that we are prepared to share with them. I may, for instance, be willing to reveal my very private thoughts and emotions to my closest friends or to my wife but to no one else. My sharing of these intimate facts about myself is, from one perspective, a way of making a gift to those who mean the most to me. Revealing these things and sharing them with those who mean the most to me is one means by which I create, maintain, and confirm those interpersonal relationships that are of most importance to me.

In our culture, it might be claimed, sexual intimacy is one of the chief currencies through which gifts of this sort are exchanged. One way to tell someone—particularly someone of the opposite sex—that you have feelings of affection and love for them is by allowing them, or sharing with them, sexual behaviors that one does not share with others. This way of measuring affection was certainly very much a part of the culture in which I matured. It worked something like this: If you were a girl, you showed how much you liked a boy by the degree of sexual intimacy you would allow. If you liked him only a little you never did more than kiss—and even the kiss was not very passionate. If you liked him a lot and if your feeling was reciprocated, necking and, possibly, petting were permissible. If the attachment was still stronger and you thought it might even become a permanent relationship, the sexual activity was correspondingly more intense and intimate, although whether it led to sexual intercourse depended on whether the parties (particularly the girl) accepted fully the prohibition on nonmarital sex. The situation for the boys was related but not exactly the same. The assumption was that males did not naturally link sex with affection in the way in which females did. However, since women did link sex with affection, males had to take that fact into account. That is to say, because a woman would permit sexual intimacies only if she had feelings of affection for the male and only if those feelings were reciprocated, the male had to have and express those feelings too, before sexual intimacies of any sort would occur.

The result was that the importance of a correlation between sexual intimacy and feelings of love and affection was taught by the culture and assimilated by those growing up in the culture. The scale of possible positive feelings toward persons of the other sex ran from casual liking, at one end, to the love that was deemed essential to, and characteristic of, marriage, at the other. The scale of possible sexual behavior ran from brief, passionless kissing or hand-holding, at one end, to sexual intercourse, at the other. And the correlation between the two scales was quite precise. As a result, any act of sexual intimacy carried substantial meaning with it, and no act of sexual intimacy was simply a pleasurable set of bodily sensations. Many such acts were, of course, more pleasurable to the participants because they were a way of saying what their feelings were. And sometimes they were less pleasurable for the same reason. The point is, however, that sexual activity was much more than mere bodily enjoyment. It was not like eating a good meal, listening to good music, lying in the sun, or getting a pleasant back rub. It was behavior that meant a great deal concerning one's feelings for persons of the opposite sex in whom one was most interested and with whom one was most involved. It was among the most authoritative ways in which one could communicate to another the nature and degree of one's affection.

If this sketch is even roughly right, then several things become somewhat clearer. To begin with, a possible rationale for many of the rules of conventional sexual morality can be developed. If, for example, sexual intercourse is associated with the kind of affection and commitment to another that is regarded as characteristic of the marriage relationship, then it is natural that sexual intercourse should be thought properly to take place between persons who are married to each other. And if it is thought that this kind of affection and commitment is only to be found within the marriage relationship, then it is not surprising that sexual intercourse should only be thought to be proper within marriage.

Related to what has just been said is the idea that sexual intercourse ought to be restricted to those who are married to each other, as a means by which to confirm the very special feelings that the spouses have for each other. Because our culture teaches that sexual intercourse means that the strongest of all feelings for each other are shared by the lovers, it is natural that persons who are married to each other should be able to say this to each other in this way. Revealing and confirming verbally that these feelings are present is one thing that helps to sustain the relationship; engaging in sexual intercourse is another.

In addition, this account would help to provide a framework within which to make sense of the notion that some sex is better than other sex. As I indicated earlier, the fact that sexual intimacy can be meaningful in the sense described tends to make it also the case that sexual intercourse can sometimes be more enjoyable than at other times. On this view, sexual intercourse will typically be more enjoyable if strong feelings of affection are present than it will be if it is merely "mechanical." This is so in part because people enjoy being loved, especially by those whom they love. Just as we like to hear words of affection, so we like to receive affectionate behavior. And the meaning enhances the independently pleasurable behavior.

More to the point, an additional rationale for the prohibition on extramarital sex can now be developed. For given this way of viewing the sexual world, extramarital sex will almost always involve deception of a deeper sort. If the adulterous spouse does not in fact have the appropriate feelings of affection for the extramarital partner, then the adulterous spouse is deceiving that person about the presence of such feelings. If, on the other hand, the adulterous spouse does have the corresponding feelings for the extramarital partner but not toward the nonparticipating spouse, the adulterous spouse is very probably deceiving the nonparticipating spouse about the presence of such feelings toward that spouse. Indeed, it might be argued, whenever there is no longer love between the two persons who are married to each other, there is deception just because being married implies both to the participants and to the world that such a bond exists. Deception is inevitable, the argument might conclude, because the feelings of affection that ought to accompany any act of sexual intercourse can only be held toward one other person at any given time in one's life. And if this is so, then the adulterous spouse always deceives either the partner in adultery or the nonparticipating spouse about the existence of such feelings. Thus extramarital sex involves deception of this sort and is for that reason immoral even if no deception vis-à-vis the occurrence of the act of adultery takes place.

What might be said in response to the foregoing arguments? The first thing that might be said is that the account of the connection between sexual intimacy and feelings of affection is inaccurate—not in the sense that no one thinks of things that way but in the sense that there is substantially more divergence of opinion than the account suggests. For example, the view I have delineated may describe reasonably accurately the concepts of the sexual world in which I grew up, but it does not capture the sexual *Weltanschauung* of today's youth at all. Thus, whether or not adultery implies deception in respect to feelings depends very much on the persons who are involved and the way they look at the "meaning" of sexual intimacy.

Second, the argument leaves unanswered the question of whether it is desirable for sexual intimacy to carry the sorts of messages described above. For those persons for whom sex does have these implications there are special feelings and sensibilities that must be taken into account. But it is another question entirely whether any valuable end—moral or otherwise—is served by investing sexual behavior with such significance. That is something that must be shown and not just assumed. It might, for instance, be the case that substantially more good than harm would come from a kind of demystification of sexual behavior—one that would encourage the enjoyment of sex more for its own sake and one that would reject the centrality both of the association of sex with love and of love with only one other person.

I regard these as two of the more difficult unresolved issues that our culture faces today in respect of thinking sensibly about the attitudes toward sex and love that we should try to develop in ourselves and in our children.

Much of the contemporary literature that advocates sexual liberation of one sort or another embraces one or the other of two different views about the relationship between sex and love. One view holds that sex should be separated from love and affection. To be sure, sex is probably better when the partners genuinely like and enjoy being with each other. But sex is basically an intensive, exciting sensuous activity that can be enjoyed in a variety of suitable settings with a variety of suitable partners. The situation in respect to sexual pleasure is no different from that of the person who knows and appreciates fine food and who can have a satisfying meal in any number of good restaurants with any number of congenial companions. One question that must be settled here is whether sex can be thus demystified; another, more important, question is whether it would be desirable to do so. What might we gain and what might we lose if we all lived in a world in which an act of sexual intercourse was no more or less significant or enjoyable than having a delicious meal in a nice setting with a good friend? The answer to this question lies beyond the scope of this essay.

The second view of the relationship between sex and love seeks to drive the wedge in a different place. On this view it is not the link between sex and love that needs to be broken, but rather the connection between love and exclusivity. For a number of the reasons already given it is desirable, so this argument goes, that sexual intimacy continue to be reserved to and shared with only those for whom one has very great affection. The mistake lies in thinking that any "normal" adult will have those feelings toward only one other adult during his or her lifetime—or even at any time in his or her life. It is the concept of adult love, not ideas about sex, that needs demystification. What are thought to be both unrealistic and unfortunate are the notions of exclusivity and possessiveness that attach to the dominant conception of love between adults in our culture and others. Parents of four, five, six, or even ten children can certainly claim, and sometimes claim correctly, that they love all of their children, that they love them all equally, and that it is simply untrue to their feelings to insist that the numbers involved diminish either the quantity or the quality of their love. If this is readily understandable in the case of parents and children, there is no necessary reason why it is an impossible or undesirable ideal in the case of adults. To be sure, there is probably a limit to the number of intimate, "primary" relationships that any person can maintain at any given time without affecting the quality of the relationship. But one adult ought surely to be able to love two, three, or even six other adults at any one time without that love being different in kind or degree from that of the traditional, monogamous, lifetime marriage. And between the individuals in these relationships, whether within a marriage or without, sexual intimacy is fitting and good.

The issues raised by a position such as the one described above are also surely worth exploring in detail and with care. Is there something to be called "sexual love" that is different from parental love or the nonsexual love of close friends? Is there something about love in general that links it naturally and appropriately with feelings of exclusivity and possession? Or is there something about sexual love, whatever that may be, that makes these feelings especially fitting? Once again, the issues are conceptual, empirical, and normative all at once: What is love? How could it be different? Would it be a good thing or a bad thing if it were different?

Suppose, though, that having delineated these problems we were now to pass them by. Suppose, moreover, that we were to be persuaded of the possibility and the desirability of weakening substantially either the links between sex and love or the links between sexual love and exclusivity. Would it not then be the case that adultery could be free from all of the morally objectionable features described thus far? To be more specific, let us imagine that a husband and wife have what is today sometimes characterized as an "open marriage." Suppose, that is, that they have agreed in advance that extramarital sex is—under certain circumstances—acceptable behavior for each to engage in. Suppose that as a result there is no impulse to deceive each other about the occurrence or nature of any such relationships and that no deception in fact occurs. Suppose, too, that there is no deception in respect to the feelings involved between the adulterous spouse and the extramarital partner. And suppose, finally, that one or the other or both of the spouses then has sexual intercourse in circumstances consistent with these understandings. Under this description, so the argument might conclude, adultery is simply not immoral. At a minimum adultery cannot very plausibly be condemned either on grounds that it involves deception or on grounds that it requires the breaking of a promise.

At least two responses are worth considering. One calls attention to the connection between marriage and adultery; the other looks to more instrumental arguments for the immorality of adultery. Both deserve further exploration.

One way to deal with the case of the "open marriage" is to question whether the two persons involved are still properly to be described as being married to each other. Part of the meaning of what it is for two persons to be married to each other, so this argument would go, is to have committed oneself to have sexual relationships only with one's spouse. Of course, it would be added, we know that that commitment is not always honored. We know that persons who are married to each other often do commit adultery. But there is a difference between being willing to make a commitment to marital fidelity, even though one may fail to honor that commitment, and not making the commitment at all. Whatever the relationship may be between the two individuals in the case just described, the absence of any commitment to sexual exclusivity requires the conclusion that their relationship is not a marital one. For a commitment to sexual exclusivity is a necessary but not a sufficient condition for the existence of a marriage.

Although there may be something to this suggestion, it is too strong as stated to be acceptable. To begin with it is doubtful that there are many, if any, *necessary* conditions for marriage; but even if there are, a commitment to sexual exclusivity is not such a condition.

To see that this is so, consider what might be taken to be some of the essential characteristics of a marriage. We might be tempted to propose that the concept of marriage requires the following: a formal ceremony of some sort in which mutual obligations are undertaken between two persons of the opposite sex; the capacity on the part of the persons involved to have sexual intercourse with each other; the willingness to have sexual intercourse only with each other; and feelings of love and affection between the two persons. The problem is that we can imagine relationships that are clearly marital and yet lack one or more of these features. For example, in our own society it is possible for two persons to be married without going through a formal ceremony, as in the common-law marriages recognized in some jurisdictions. It is also possible for two persons to get married even though one or both lacks the capacity to engage in sexual intercourse. Thus, two very elderly persons who have neither the desire nor the ability to have intercourse can nonetheless get married, as can persons whose sexual organs have been injured so that intercourse is not possible. And we certainly know of marriages in which love was not present at the time of the marriage, as, for instance, in marriages of state and marriages of convenience.

Counterexamples not satisfying the condition relating to the abstention from extramarital sex are even more easily produced. We certainly know of societies and cultures in which polygamy and polyandry are practiced, and we have no difficulty in recognizing these relationships as cases of marriages. It might be objected, though, that these are not counterexamples because they are plural marriages rather than marriages in which sex is permitted with someone other than one of the persons to whom one is married. But we also know of societies in which it is permissible for married persons to have sexual relationships with persons to whom they are not married, for example, temple prostitutes, concubines, and homosexual lovers. And even if we knew of no such societies, the conceptual claim would still, I submit, not be well taken. For suppose all of the other indicia of marriage were present: suppose the two persons were of the opposite sex; suppose they had the capacity and desire to have intercourse with each other; suppose they participated in a formal ceremony in which they understood themselves voluntarily to be entering into a relationship with each other in which substantial mutual commitments were assumed. If all these conditions were satisfied we would not be in any doubt as to whether or not the two persons were married, even though they had not taken on a commitment of sexual exclusivity and even though they had expressly agreed that extramarital sexual intercourse was a permissible behavior for each to engage in.

A commitment to sexual exclusivity is neither a necessary nor a sufficient condition for the existence of a marriage. It does, nonetheless, have this much to do with the nature of marriage—like the other indicia enumerated above, its presence tends to establish the existence of a marriage. Thus, in the absence of a formal ceremony of any sort an explicit commitment to sexual exclusivity would count in favor of regarding the two persons as married. The conceptual role of the commitment to sexual exclusivity can, perhaps, be brought out through the following example. Suppose we found a tribe that had a practice in which all the other indicia of marriage were present but in which the two parties were *prohibited* even from having sexual intercourse with each other. Moreover, suppose that sexual intercourse with others was clearly permitted. In such a case we would, I think, reject the idea that the two persons were married to each other, and we would describe their relationship in other terms, for example, as some kind of formalized, special friendship relation—a kind of heterosexual "blood-brother" bond.

Compare that case with the following one. Again suppose that the tribe had a practice in which all of the other indicia of marriage were present, but instead of a prohibition on sexual intercourse between the persons in the relationship there was no rule at all. Sexual intercourse was permissible with the person with whom one had this ceremonial relationship, but it was no more or less permissible than with a number of other persons to whom one was not so related (for instance, all consenting adults of the opposite sex). While we might be in doubt as to whether we ought to describe the persons as married to each other, we would probably conclude that they were married and that they simply were members of a tribe whose views about sex were quite different from our own.

What all of this shows is that a *prohibition* on sexual intercourse between the two persons involved in a relationship is conceptually incompatible with the claim that the two of them are married. The *permissibility* of intramarital sex is a necessary part of the idea of marriage. But no such incompatibility follows simply from the added permissibility of extramarital sex.

These arguments do not, of course, exhaust the arguments for the prohibition on extramarital sexual relations. The remaining argument that I wish to consider is—as I indicated earlier—a more instrumental one. It seeks to justify the prohibition by virtue of the role that it plays in the development and maintenance of nuclear families. The argument, or set of arguments, might, I believe, go something like this:

Consider first a far-fetched nonsexual example. Suppose a society were organized so that after some suitable age—say 18, 19, or 20—persons were forbidden to eat anything but bread and water with anyone but their spouse. Persons might still choose in such a society not to get married. Good food just might not be very important to them because they have underdeveloped taste buds. Or good food might be bad for them because there is something wrong with their digestive system. Or good food might be important to them, but they might decide that the enjoyment of good food would get in the way of the attainment of other things that were more important. But most persons would, I think, be led to favor marriage in part because they preferred a richer, more varied diet to one of bread and water. And they might remain married because the family was the only legitimate setting within which good food was obtainable. If it is important to have society organized so that persons will both get married and stay married, such an arrangement would be well suited to the preservation of the family, and the prohibitions relating to food consumption could be understood as fulfilling that function.

It is obvious that one of the more powerful human desires is the desire for sexual gratification. The desire is a natural one, like hunger and thirst, in the sense that it need not be learned in order to be present within us and operative on us. But there is in addition much that we do learn about what the act of sexual intercourse is like. Once we experience sexual intercourse ourselves—and, in particular, once we experience orgasm—we discover that it is among the most intensive, short-term pleasures of the body.

Because this is so it is easy to see how the prohibition on extramarital sex helps to hold marriage together. At least during that period of life when the enjoyment of sexual intercourse is one of the desirable bodily pleasures, persons will wish to enjoy those pleasures. If one consequence of being married is that one is prohibited from having sexual intercourse with anyone but one's spouse, then the spouses in a marriage are in a position to provide an important source of pleasure for each other that is unavailable to them elsewhere in the society.

The point emerges still more clearly if this rule of sexual morality is seen as being of a piece with the other rules of sexual morality. When this prohibition is coupled, for example, with the prohibition on nonmarital sexual intercourse, we are presented with the inducement both to get married and to stay married. For if sexual intercourse is only legitimate within marriage, then persons seeking that gratification that is a feature of sexual intercourse are furnished explicit social directions for its attainment, namely, marriage.

Nor, to continue the argument, is it necessary to focus exclusively on the bodily enjoyment that is involved. Orgasm may be a significant part of what there is to sexual intercourse, but it is not the whole of it. We need only recall the earlier discussion of the meaning that sexual intimacy has in our own culture to begin to see some of the more intricate ways in which sexual exclusivity may be connected with the establishment and maintenance of marriage as the primary heterosexual love relationship. Adultery is wrong, in other words, because a prohibition on extramarital sex is a way to help maintain the institutions of marriage and the nuclear family.

I am frankly not sure what we are to say about an argument such as the preceding one. What I am convinced of is that, like the arguments discussed earlier, this one also reveals something of the difficulty and complexity of the issues that are involved. So what I want now to do in the final portion of this essay is to try to delineate with reasonable precision several of what I take to be the fundamental, unresolved issues.

The first is whether this last argument is an argument for the *immorality* of extramarital sexual intercourse. What does seem clear is that there are differences between this argument and the ones considered earlier. The earlier arguments condemned adulterous behavior because it was behavior that involved breaking a promise, taking unfair advantage of or deceiving another. To the degree to which the prohibition on extramarital sex can be supported by arguments that invoke considerations such as these, there is little question but that violations of the prohibition are properly regarded as immoral. And such a claim could be defended on one or both of two distinct grounds. The first is that action such as promise-breaking and deception are simply wrong. The second is that adultery involving promise-breaking or deception is wrong because it involves the straightforward infliction of harm on another human being—typically the nonadulterous spouse—who has a strong claim not to have that harm so inflicted.

The argument that connects the prohibition on extramarital sex with the maintenance and preservation of the institution of marriage is an argument for the instrumental value of the prohibition. To some degree this counts, I think, against regarding all violations of the prohibition as obvious cases of immorality. This is so partly because hypothetical imperatives are less clearly within the domain of morality than are categorical ones, and even more because instrumental prohibitions are within the domain of morality only if the end that they serve or the way that they serve it is itself within the domain of morality.

What this should help us see, I think, is the fact that the argument that connects the prohibition on adultery with the preservation of marriage is at best seriously incomplete. Before we ought to be convinced by it, we ought to have reasons for believing that marriage is a morally desirable and just social institution. And such reasons are not quite as easy to find or as obvious as it may seem. For the concept of marriage is, as we have seen, both a loosely structured and a complicated one. There may be all sorts of intimate, interpersonal relationships that will resemble but not be identical with the typical marriage relationship presupposed by the traditional sexual morality. There may be a number of distinguishable sexual and loving arrangements that can all legitimately claim to be called *marriages*. The prohibitions of the traditional sexual morality may be effective ways to maintain some marriages and ineffective ways to promote and preserve others. The prohibitions of the traditional sexual morality may make good psychological sense if certain psychological theories are true, and they may be purveyors of immense psychological mischief if other psychological theories are true. The prohibitions of traditional sexual morality may seem obviously correct if sexual intimacy carries the meaning that the dominant culture has often ascribed to it, and they may seem equally bizarre if sex is viewed through the perspective of the counterculture. Irrespective of whether instrumental arguments of this sort are properly deemed moral arguments, they ought not fully convince anyone until questions such as these are answered.

Frederick Elliston

In Defense of Promiscuity

The Western tradition has been remarkably conservative in its reflections on sexual morality.[1] Whether this conservatism is due to the fact that practically every major philosopher before Hegel was a bachelor male dedicated to the pursuit of some form of reason is a moot point on which I shall not speculate. Whatever the explanation, most philosophers have tended to formulate and resolve sexual issues in favor of the status quo. Perhaps because sexual promiscuity (the only type I shall consider) has usually been a practice widely at variance with prevalent norms, it has scarcely arisen as an issue at all—much less been criticized or defended. Today, however, sexual norms have changed—at least for an increasingly significant number of society's members. This change challenges the philosophers to question the assumptions on which the conventions that regulate our sex lives are based, much as recent political changes have provided the motive for a radical critique of social practices and institutions.[2]

My purpose here is to take up this challenge by offering a defense of promiscuity: first, I shall criticize current notions of promiscuity as inadequate and provide my own definition; second, I shall rebut some traditional arguments against promiscuity; and third, I shall defend it in terms of three sexual paradigms. I shall conclude with some reflections on the limits of my defense.

LINGUISTIC FORAYS

What is meant by "promiscuity"? It may be that the word has no descriptive content, but only emotive and/or hortatory force. On this view, to condemn a practice or person as promiscuous is simply to express feelings of disapproval, or to issue a prohibitive "Stop!" This position attempts to resolve the issue of meaning by limiting "promiscuity" to its emotional or prescriptive force.[3] Even this restriction, though, does not eliminate all of the problems. For not all people oppose promiscuity, and hence the intended overtones are not always negative. And this position leaves an important question unanswered: To what kinds of persons or actions does the term apply? Only when this question has been answered are we in a position to ask how we should feel about, act toward, or react to promiscuous people or behavior.

The *Oxford English Dictionary* defines "promiscuous" as: "without distinction, discrimination or order." *Webster's New Twentieth Century Dictionary* adds: "engaging in sexual intercourse indiscriminately or with many persons." The root notion operative in these definitions is *indiscriminate*, sometimes signified quantitatively, according to *Webster's*.

But this definition is too broad and begs the question at hand. For the promiscuous person clearly does draw *some* distinctions: typically he or she does not derive sexual satisfaction from a lover's shoe or copulate with a dead body or a sibling. In such cases more precise terminology is applied —fetishism, necrophilia, or incest. Even a promiscuous person usually discriminates between things and persons, between living people and dead people, between people who are members of the family and those who are not. Since some distinctions are operative, the suggestion that a promiscuous person is *completely indiscriminate* is too strong.

Similar difficulties arise with *Webster's* numerical criterion: How many liaisons must a person engage in before he or she is promiscuous? Clearly more than one is required; anyone who has made love to only one person cannot (logically) be labeled "promiscuous." But is two enough? Perhaps a person who carries on two affairs would be called "promiscuous." But imagine someone who married at twenty and who remarried at forty, two years after his wife died. Clearly, under these conditions he is not promiscuous. If two is not enough, then increase the number to three and repeat the scenario: married at twenty, forty, and sixty, two years after each wife died. This twice-widowed "Romeo" satisfies *Webster's* numerical criterion, for he has engaged in sex with many (that is, three) people; and yet he is clearly not promiscuous. As more marriages are added it still remains uncertain at what point a person becomes promiscuous. And even if a clear line could be drawn, the question would immediately arise: Why draw it there, for what is the criterion for assessing the number of liaisons that suffice to justify the judgment "promiscuous"? This is a further legitimate question raised by *Webster's* definition but left unanswered.

Of course these examples deal with sequential liaisons, which may be more problematic than their simultaneous counterparts. But I think the basic problem remains: Is a person who carries on two serious loving affairs that endure for a lifetime promiscuous? I think not. Then again, if two are not enough, how many are required and on what grounds?

By these two counterattacks I am suggesting that it is *false* that a promiscuous person is indiscriminate and *facile* to assess promiscuity numerically. But what is it, then, that invites this judgment? More likely the condemnation arises not because such people do not discriminate *at all,* but because they fail to discriminate *according to the prevalent sexual code.* Promiscuous behavior challenges our sexual conventions, thereby giving this label its emotive force and prescriptive overtones.[4]

More precisely, promiscuity violates a very special principle that regulates our erotic life: "Sexual relations shall be exclusively heterosexual and . . no sexual activity shall take place outside monogamous unions which are, intentionally at least, life-long."[5] It is this "Western norm," as Ronald Atkinson terms it, that prescribes the *distinctions* to be drawn, the *discriminations* to be made, and the *order* to be upheld in our sex lives, to which the definition in the *Oxford English Dictionary* alludes.

But to say that promiscuity violates the Western norm is still too broad, for so does coprophilia. Though many people use the term in this vague sense, a more precise definition is needed.

Promiscuity is sometimes identified with "free love." This persuasive definition (or redefinition) may induce some to accept this sexual pattern because freedom, like motherhood, is a good everyone is supposed to espouse. But what exactly is the sexual freedom in question? If it means freedom from *all* sexual prohibitions (including, for example, those against perversions), then this rephrasing is again too broad. And if it means freedom from just the Western norm (which would allow perverted sex within marriage), then it is no improvement. Moreover "free love" is a misleading expression: like everything else, sex has its price—assessed in terms of time, effort, emotional tensions, and a trade off of other benefits and burdens.

Promiscuity may be identified with recreational sex—intercourse just for the fun of it. But this definition is disquieting because of what might be hidden under the adverb "just"; and the term "fun" would align the defenders of promiscuity with that "vulgar hedonism" that some may want to reject in favor of a broader conception of the good life. Though when it harms no one promiscuity may be defensible simply on the grounds that it provides pleasure, this justification should not be built into the definition. A more neutral definition is preferable in order to avoid this commitment at the outset and thereby leave open the question of its justification.

Neither the definitions of the *Oxford English Dictionary* nor *Webster's New Twentieth Century Dictionary*, nor any of the current philosophic or popular notions is satisfactory. In view of the failure of these linguistic forays to uncover a viable definition I shall offer my own. In so doing I cross a thin but significant boundary between linguistic analysis and linguistic revision. And conceding Wittgenstein's insight that language is a form of life, the dispute over the definition of promiscuity cannot be regarded as merely semantic.

With these caveats (or concessions), I shall offer the following definition, or redefinition: "promiscuity" means sex with a series of other adults, not directly related through marriage, with no commitments. Let me explain each component in turn.

First, promiscuity demands *copulation*—its *telos* is sexual intercourse. Someone who engages in the rituals of seduction without this goal is perhaps a flirt or a "tease"—but is not promiscuous. Of course not every seduction succeeds. But at least the intention to consummate the relation must be present on all occasions and realized on some. Whether the sex is "straight" or perverted is irrelevant, for these are two different phenomena. One can be perverted and not promiscuous, or promiscuous and not perverted: a lifelong incestuous relation renders a person perverted but not promiscuous; and many promiscuous liaisons accord with the paradigm of natural sex—"the two-minute emissionary missionary male-superior ejaculation service."[6]

Second, *repetition* is essential—the pursuit of a new partner must recur. Promiscuity on only one occasion is logically impossible. If someone is remarkably casual about his or her one affair, he or she may be labeled "superficial" or "unfeeling," but cannot be called promiscuous. Different partners on several occasions must be sought. The *number* of affairs per se does not suffice to delineate promiscuity (the mistake of *Webster's* definition); plurality is a necessary but not a sufficient condition of promiscuity.

Third, both partners must be *adults*. If one partner is a child, then their behavior is pedophilia. If the child is a son or daughter, it is incest. In neither case is it promiscuity. Adulthood cannot be fixed chronologically; it signifies a degree of maturity some teen-agers have and some elderly people lack. The other adult need not be of the opposite sex. Homosexuals and lesbians per se are not necessarily promiscuous. Some make significant personal sacrifices to maintain their relationship; though their behavior violates the Western norm, it is not promiscuous, because of the commitment their sacrifices signify.

Fourth, the couple cannot be directly related through *marriage*. It is logically impossible for husband and wife to engage in promiscuity with one another, though of course their sex play may sometimes bear a "family resemblance" to it. Similarly, sex between a brother and sister, even when they are adults, is a different phenomenon. It is possible to be promiscuous with distant cousins to whom one is not *directly* related through marriage; different societies draw the lines for incest in different ways.[7]

Finally and most decisively, promiscuity is *noncommital* sex. It defies the traditional connection between sex and marriage—not just as a social institution, but as a symbol of a serious, loving, and intentionally lifelong relation. Promiscuity asserts a freedom from the obligation within or without marriage to "love, honor, and obey" and a freedom to engage in sex with any peer who agrees. These refusals to issue promissory notes for affection and support throughout an indefinite future and to issue a guarantee of sexual exclusivity are promiscuity's most significant departures from the traditional sexual norm.

Is such behavior defensible? I shall now turn to some familiar arguments against it.

REBUTTALS AND REJOINDERS

Several arguments can be offered in defense of the Western norm and hence in opposition to promiscuity. As I shall try to demonstrate in my rejoinders, none are sound.

1. *The Western Norm and Technology.* At one time a strong argument might have been made in defense of the Western norm by invoking the causal connection between sex and reproduction: unless the natural processes are interrupted, intercourse leads to procreation; for the sake of children, on whom society's future depends, promiscuity is rightly prohibited in order to confine sex to marriage, as that secure and loving context within which children can best be raised. As stated, this argument relies on two claims, the first factual and the second normative.

The first premise has been falsified by technology: the advances of medicine have made available reliable birth-control devices and reasonably safe techniques for sterilization and abortion, thereby making sex possible without the risk of conception or birth. Second, the absolute value of the nuclear family as the *only* context for child rearing is at least problematic: experiments in communal living and the increasing number of single parents provide some evidence that the needs of the child can be met either through a plurality of parent figures or through just one individual. Moreover, even granting the risk of pregnancy, despite precautions, and the value of the nuclear family, despite alternatives, the prohibitions against promiscuity would not follow. First, pregnancies can be terminated. With the exception of the Roman Catholic Church, many concede the legitimacy of abortion, at least during the first trimester. Second, even if this option is disregarded, it should be emphasized that promiscuity is *logically* compatible with *some* commitments to one's partner in the event of pregnancy and to the child in the event of its birth. Promiscuity does not preclude such contingent agreements; it rules out only emotional and sexual commitments as a precondition of sex—the promise to love the other exclusively and to share a life completely.

This rejoinder asserts that available technology should be used as a safeguard against undesirable consequences. But "can" does not always entail "ought": not everything science is capable of doing should be done. Some, notably Roman Catholics, have argued strongly against the use of such means.

2. *The Inseparability Premise and Promiscuity.* The Roman Catholic

position is that the sex act [8] has two inseparable functions: to foster the physical, emotional, and spiritual union of man and woman, and to reproduce the species. If this claim were true, then the use of birth-control devices or sterilization and abortion techniques would be prohibited. Promiscuity would then become more hazardous since without contraceptives the risk of pregnancy would be much greater; and it would become less frequent since only *coitus interruptus* and the rhythm method could be practiced to avoid conception. Of course abstinence and masturbation would be alternatives; but to practice them is to cease to be promiscuous.

The most recent defense of this inseparability premise is found in Pope Paul VI's *Humanae Vitae*: to violate the inseparability of the unitive and procreative aspect of sex is "to contradict the nature of both man and woman and of their most intimate relationship, and therefore it is to contradict also the plan of God and His will."[9]

Carl Cohen contends that this inseparability premise is false.[10] First, it has no basis in scripture or natural law, but rests only on a fallacious *argumentum ad verecundiam*. Second, the entailed prohibition against birth control would cause overpopulation and hunger. Third, the fear of pregnancy and the ensuing inhibitions thwart the conjugal love that the Church promulgates. Fourth, the assumption that all sexual processes must be completed is erroneous, for we recognize acts with erotic overtones that rightly remain unconsummated (for example, a father's love for his daughter). Fifth, the integrity of the spiritual and natural is frequently denied without transgressing a divine (or moral) command—for example, eating for pleasure rather than nourishment. And finally, if the Church sanctions drugs to promote physical health, it should permit drugs (for example, oral contraceptives) to promote sexual health.

Though Cohen's six points may not persuade all Catholics,[11] they do provide an impressive list of reasons for legitimizing birth control. Though admittedly his purpose is to defend their use within marriage, this limitation is not demanded by his logic. They serve to justify the use of the technology that severs the causal tie on which the earlier rebuttal of promiscuity depended.

3. *Promiscuity as a Threat to Monogamy*. Like adultery, promiscuity may be judged immoral on the grounds that it endangers one of our society's central and sacred institutions—monogamous marriage:[12] allowing people to achieve sexual gratification while escaping long-term commitments undermines this basic institution in a way that threatens the stability of our society; in self-defense, society rightly imposes social sanc-

tions against the threatening promiscuous behavior.

This argument rests on two assumptions: first, that promiscuity has adverse effects on monogamy; and second, that monogamy is socially superior to the alternatives.

The first assumption is a questionable causal claim. For despite the recent weakening of sexual taboos, marriage continues to be a popular practice. Even conceding the high divorce rate does not weaken this claim, for many who are divorced remarry—thereby testifying to the value they accord this institution. Consequently, the so-called new morality is not clearly harming marriage. Indeed, two alternative hypotheses about the causal relation between promiscuity and monogamy are equally plausible: by providing for a broader range of sex partners from which to select a spouse promiscuity increases the probability of sexual compatibility within marriage, and hence the probability of a more "successful" marriage (at least according to this one criterion of success—the satisfaction of one need); and by eliminating the need to marry *merely* for sexual gratification (and hence to disregard those other factors that contribute to successful marriages, such as respect, considerateness, shared values, love, and compassion), promiscuity again increases the likelihood of a successful marriage. Perhaps the trouble with premarital unions, trial marriage, and open marriage is that they have not been tried, for the strong presumption that monogamy is the only way to institutionalize our sex life works against such experiments. Freeing sex of the monopoly of marriage could provide for new institutions that might satisfy more effectively the emotional and physical needs of society's members and offer greater scope for the exercise of personal freedom and initiative in creating new lifestyles. Though society once had the right to insist that its members have a "license to procreate," to use Michael Bayles's expression, with the development of new contraceptives it no longer has the right to insist on a license to copulate. Abolishing the demand for such a license by permitting promiscuity may ease the unnecessary and spurious pressures on monogamy, so as to promote rather than prevent healthy changes within this institution.

4. *Lying, Deceiving, and Exploiting.* According to the popular prototype, promiscuous people are unfaithful and unreliable: they break promises, say things that are not true, and use others for their own sexual gratification. If this prototype were true, promiscuity would indeed be wrong, because it would violate familiar moral rules: people are supposed to keep their promises, tell the truth, and not deceive or exploit others. But does promiscuity *necessarily* involve these forms of immorality?

At one time these subterfuges may have been necessary in order to obtain sex and yet avoid commitments. To circumvent the Western norm, which was justified when copulation entailed procreation, those who wanted *only* the "joys of sex" were forced to tease, tempt, and manipulate. Under these circumstances promiscuity is wrong—*not* because it is promiscuity, but because it violates well-established ethical principles. The moral fault lies not in noncommittal sex but in the lies, deceptions, and exploitation to which some *happen* to have recourse in order to have intercourse. Such immoral behavior is only contingently associated with promiscuity; logically, rather than empirically, it is not necessary. In some groups or societies openly promiscuous behavior is tolerated, if not encouraged. When the threat of pregnancy is minimized, sex for its own sake becomes possible, enjoyable, and desirable—thereby making many of the earlier reasons for lying, deceiving, and exploiting invalid. That promiscuity must involve immoral behavior then becomes an anachronism, an empirical claim that is no longer true. Promiscuity per se or prima facie is not wrong. At most, it is the immoral things promiscuous people sometimes happen to do that are wrong.

This defense is complicated by the fact that a double standard is operative within large segments of society: men are allowed to "sow their wild oats," whereas women are denigrated as "loose" or "fallen" for the same behavior. Though this sexual inequality may once have served to protect women who had more to lose through such "sins" (for it is women who become pregnant, and not men), now it discriminates against them. Because of this double standard, promiscuity is to the advantage of males and to the disadvantage of females. Consequently it becomes exploitive in a more subtle fashion: men receive sexual gratification; women receive social condemnation.

This argument invites the initial rejoinder that it is not promiscuity that is wrong, but the double standard. In this case it is not promiscuity that we should abandon, but the double standard that places promiscuous women at a disadvantage in comparison to promiscuous men. However, this response may be too facile, too theoretical in its disregard for the reality of the social inequality of the sexes. Yet, even conceding the inadequacy of this initial rejoinder, this argument against promiscuity on the grounds that it exploits women would not apply to all cases: women immune or indifferent to social reprobation and members of groups without a double standard could still be promiscuous and yet not necessarily exploit others or be exploited by them. Since promiscuity cannot be shown to be wrong in all cases, the charge that it necessarily violates generally accepted moral principles is false.

5. *Personal Emotional Security and Growth*. Peter Bertocci argues against premarital sex, and by implication against promiscuity, on the grounds that it threatens "personal emotional security."[13] He contends that the demand for sex outside marriage exhibits a lack of self-discipline in people who cannot control their desires, and a failure to show respect and consideration for those on whom the demand is placed. Such undisciplined and inconsiderate behavior places needless strain on the relationship, threatening to destroy whatever values it embodies.

Is it true that a promiscuous person is completely lacking in self-discipline? The ritual of seduction frequently has its own carefully observed logic in the selection of a suitable consort, the finesse of the "first approach," and the rhythms of attracting and repulsing, until the ceremony reaches its *telos*.[14] What Bertocci perceives as incoherent or irrational behavior is really a self-conscious refusal to be directed by the Western norm. But promiscuous people should not be faulted for failing to regulate their actions according to a principle they reject.

Does promiscuity entail inconsiderateness? The rejoinder here parallels the earlier refutation of the charge that promiscuity is necessarily exploitive. The fact that some promiscuous people are rude, brusque, or selfish does not establish this logical tie, any more than the fact that some doctors collect stamps establishes a logical tie between medicine and philately. Only if respect is defined in terms of the Western norm is promiscuity necessarily disrespectful. Though such a definition is possible, it would beg the question at hand, which must remain empirical. Acknowledging the other's freedom to engage or not engage in noncommittal sex demonstrates some degree of respect. And at each subsequent stage of the battle of the sexes, its dialectical impetus arises through the joint effort to preserve the other's freedom.[15] The reciprocity of initiatives whereby each person asserts his or her selfhood, presided over by moral rules that embody recognition for "man as an end in himself" (to use Kant's somewhat chauvinistic phrase), provides further testimony for respect.

Does promiscuity threaten what is valuable in the relation? Of course the answer depends in part on what is considered valuable; pleasure, freedom, and respect certainly *need not* be endangered. Bertocci believes that the emotional tensions and guilt feelings that arise from violating the taboos against nonmarital sex will corrode the relation. But this harm can alternatively be eliminated by abolishing the taboos instead, so that promiscuity would no longer count as an infraction and hence no longer generate the strain that it now does. Since the traditional supports for these taboos have collapsed through an advancing technology, abolishing the Western norm is the more rational solution.

It is not promiscuity that is bad, but the arguments that purport to rebut it. These rejoinders to those arguments, though, do not prove that promiscuity itself is morally good, for I have not considered all possible arguments against it. And even if I had, the conclusion would not follow logically: promiscuity could still be bad although no one has formulated a good argument to prove it.

Perhaps promiscuity is neither good nor bad in any moral sense, but purely a matter of individual taste. To categorize it as an aesthetic rather than ethical issue concedes its normative status, but removes it from the sphere of other-regarding virtues. But even granting this move, some critical issues would remain: Is promiscuity in good taste or bad taste, and how does one decide?

Alternatively, promiscuity might be dismissed as neither a moral nor an aesthetic issue but a prudential one—a question of what is to the advantage of the agent within the sphere of actions that affect only him or her. This approach too leaves critical issues unresolved: Is promiscuity to my advantage or disadvantage, and how do I decide? Moreover this reduction of the normative to the prudential seems to disregard the fact that it takes two people (minimally) to be promiscuous—that is, others are involved.

Such attempts to categorize promiscuity presuppose a clarity and consensus on the nature of good taste and personal advantage that is altogether lacking in the literature. So I shall eschew these ways of demonstrating that promiscuity is positively a good thing in favor of a less traditional defense.

PARADIGMS AND ARCHETYPES

Development of a satisfactory sexual philosophy is hindered in part by lack of knowledge: Just what are the contingent ties between sexual intercourse, love, marriage, and the things or activities we find valuable? This difficulty is further compounded by linguistic confusions: the language at our disposal is notoriously vague and radically ambiguous. Moreover these two shortcomings are aggravated by a third: the absence of accepted paradigms for conceptualizing our sex life and of corresponding archetypes to give substance to our ideals. I shall now turn to three descriptive and normative models for understanding and directing sexual activities. In each case, I shall argue, promiscuity plays a legitimate role.

1. *A Classical Liberal Defense.* According to John Stuart Mill's principle of liberty, "the sole end for which mankind are warranted, individually or collectively, in interfering with the liberty of action of any of their number is self-protection. That the only purpose for which power can be rightfully exercised over any member of a civilized community, against his will, is to prevent harm to others. His own good, either physical or moral, is not a sufficient warrant."[16]

Promiscuity falls within this domain of individual liberty provided those who engage in it satisfy two conditions: they must observe some traditional moral rules, and they must exercise extreme care to avoid unwanted births. The conventional prohibitions against lying, deceit, and exploitation serve to prevent harm to others—most immediately to the person exploited or deceived and less immediately, but no less importantly, to others indirectly affected. The second proviso is designed to avoid illegitimacy, abortion, adoption, and forced marriage—not to mention the social stigma of an unwanted pregnancy, unmarried motherhood, or bastardy. Assuming then that promiscuity (as defined earlier) satisfies these two negative conditions, what can be said in its defense?

For at least some of the people some of the time sex is fun. Whatever else may be true of it, at the barest level sex remains an intensely pleasing physical activity. Like the satisfaction of an appetite (such as eating) or the release of tension (such as a good drive in golf), sex is physically enjoyable. Midst the mystification of sex it should not be forgotten that sex is and continues to be sensual; the erotic appeal of another engages all of our senses in a way equaled by few (if any) other physical activities. One paradigm that must be acknowledged by all is that sex is a type of bodily interaction that can be intensely pleasing. Granted the two earlier provisos, sex is good for this reason, if no other.

This defense does not entail that pleasure alone is good. The underlying hedonism is not "vulgar," to use Michael Bayles's term, for no attempt need be made to reduce sex merely to a sensation of pleasure.[17] A variety of things good in themselves can be acknowledged while still insisting that pleasure as "the joy of sex" is one of them. Insofar as promiscuity maximizes the pleasures that can be derived from sex, it is good; and insofar as the prohibition against promiscuity is a limitation on the pleasures to be derived from sex, it is unwarranted—in a word, "bad."

Despite his insistence that pleasure and pleasure alone is good in itself,[18] Mill himself gives evidence that he is not a vulgar hedonist. In defending his principle of liberty he suggests that happiness is not so much a sensation of pleasure as the full development of an individual's "higher faculties." Quoting Wilhelm von Humbolt with enthusiastic agreement, Mill asserts that the end of man is "the highest and most harmonious development of his powers to a complete and consistent whole."[19] This remark suggests a second defense of promiscuity within classical liberalism: the freedom to be promiscuous can contribute to the full growth of the human personality.

In many areas, such as clothing, vocation, and recreation, the need for experimentation and diversity is recognized and conceded. Mill defends his principle of liberty, not just in the intellectual arena by arguing for freedom of thought and discussion, but in the practical domain with his insistence on the individual's right to form and carry out his own "plan of life."[20] The lack of commitment that characterizes promiscuity is a freedom to explore patterns of sexual behavior at variance with the tradition. This exploration can engage one's "higher faculties" of reason, judgment, and good taste.[21] Promiscuity opens up to each person a broader range of sex partners and practices.

From the standpoint of classical liberalism, then, promiscuity may increase the pleasures of individuals, enhance the cultivation of their higher faculties (happiness in the eudaemonian sense) and enrich society with the ensuing institution.

2. *Sex as Body Language.* The sexual paradigm operative in the liberal defense of promiscuity has its limitations. For though sex is admittedly a form of bodily interaction that leads to pleasure, it is clearly more than that in some sense. In his papers "Sexual Paradigms" and "Sex and Perversion,"[22] Robert Solomon suggests what this "more" might be: As body language, sex has "meaning" that goes beyond its physical dimensions.

Just as words are more than marks and sounds, sex is more than thrusts and moans, caresses and sighs. Just as verbal language has a dimension of meaning beyond phonemes and morphemes,[23] so body language has a significance beyond the intertwining of two bodies. The sentences and words of verbal languages have their analogues in the gestures and particular movements of body language. As in all language, these latter are subject to rules that demarcate well-formed formulae. Body language has its own semantics and syntax.

This type of language can serve to express feelings, to state intentions, and to issue commands or invitations. An embrace can express genuine affection. A nod toward the bedroom door conjures up a familiar series of events. A sly glance may frequently initiate the rituals of seduction. Of course not all body language is sexual. Canadian Prime Minister Pierre Trudeau's infamous shrug communicates political indifference.[24] A policeman's hand signal issues a legal command. And holding open an elevator door is an invitation to enter something far more prosaic than what a coy smile offers. Meaning here as elsewhere depends on context. What imparts sexual significance to body language is the kind of possibility intimated—namely, intercourse, or some incomplete moment in the dialectical movement toward it.

Promiscuity has instrumental value in that it can facilitate the mastery of one kind of body language. To be in command of a language is to possess an extensive vocabulary, clear diction, and rhetorical devices for conveying meaning. These verbal skills are acquired through social interaction. Sexual body language is learned through sexual interaction.

Sexual experiences enable an individual to develop a repertoire of gestures for communicating desire and affection and of decisive movements that clearly state intentions of love or amusement. People can be moved not only by the things we *say* but by the things we *do*—with them, for them, or to them. Desire and satisfaction can be communicated not only through verbal exchanges such as "please" and "thank you," but through a lingering look and an appreciative caress. To a shattered ego a physical embrace may express far more reassurance than its verbal counterparts, and a kiss may convey desire more eloquently than pleas or poems. The subjectivity of another, their autonomy and individuality, is confirmed in the dialectics of sex: in the reversals of their roles as the initiator and the intiated, the aggressor and the pursued, the lover and the loved, each can experience his or her own incarnate freedom and acknowledge that of the other. Like verbal etiquette, the sexual rituals of flirtation and seduction are subject to rules that prohibit interruption while another is "speaking," that prescribe that each be allowed to participate fully in the conversation, and that exclude insults, attacks, and abuses. The observance of this etiquette is an acknowledgment of the selfhood of the other. The acquisition of it is one of the opportunities promiscuity provides.

Strict adherence to the Western norm places our sex lives in a straightjacket that curtails body language to "I love you," the *only* message to be delivered, to just *one* person, with *fixed* diction and intonation—until the disillusioned pair have become bored by the repetition.

Sex and eating are frequently compared, since both are appetites whose satisfaction is socially regulated. Consider a society where the following etiquette is operative. Each man is allowed to dine with only one woman. Before their first meal begins, each receives a solemn injunction: "Thou shalt dine with none other, so long as you both shall live." Their partnership is exclusive; no one may be invited to the meal ("three is a crowd"). Only the utensils already provided and accepted by others may be used; bringing a new gadget to the meal is an innovation attempted by many, though (curiously) condemned by all. Throughout the remaining meals the menu is fixed on the grounds that meat and potatoes are the most nourishing foods. The ways in which these meals are prepared and consumed is subject to strict regulation: one is not supposed to touch the food with one's hands; everyone must keep an upright position (it is considered an insult, for one to stand while the other lies). Interaction is drastically curtailed: one is not allowed to exchange dishes; one must feed only oneself (for a man to place his spoon in his partner's mouth is a mortal sin). These rules prescribe that each person gratify his own appetite, but in the company of a select other (to eat alone is forbidden, though many do).[25] During the meal a typical conversation consists of compliments—how good the meal is and how agreeable the company—regardless of their truthfulness.

If food and sex were only the satisfaction of appetites, these restrictions might be defensible—though the prohibitions against some changes would still be contentious. However, some innovations, at least for some people, not only could enhance the efficiency of such practices, but could add to their *meaning* as well. To "dine" with several different people can make eating not only more pleasant, but more enlightening too. To vary the "menu" is a safeguard against boredom that not only expands the topic of conversation, but also has nutritional value. To invite a guest similarly intensifies the conversation, which need not dissolve into monologues if considerateness is shown by all.[26] People should be allowed to get their fingers sticky (sex is wet) and to eat alone (masturbation makes neither your eyesight grow dim nor your hair fall out). Sometimes it may be more convenient to eat standing up or lying down: the exceptions of one society may elsewhere be the rule. More interaction can make the experience more significant; for example, switching dishes when the desires are different (to the dismay of many, they frequently only *look* different) provides variety that, after all, is still "the spice of life." If the food is not well-cooked and the company is no longer mutually attractive, admit these shortcomings; such honesty may lead to better meals. Only recently have the stereotypes that determined who issued the invitations, and who prepared the meal and did the serving, begun to dissolve. Exchanging traditional sex roles by allowing the woman to show greater initiative (if not aggression) can enhance mutual understanding and respect by dramatizing what it is to be in the other person's place.

Loosening the restrictions of the Western norm in these ways is tantamount to permitting, if not promulgating, promiscuity. The ensuing changes promise to make our sex lives not only physically more satisfying, but also more meaningful. This second defense of promiscuity has expanded the model of sexual behavior from mere bodily interaction for pleasure to a form of corporeal dialogue. With the third defense, to be offered next, these models are expanded further, to envelop man in the totality of his concrete existence.

3. *Authentic Sexuality: An Existential Defense of Promiscuity.* Heidegger's insistence that Being-with (*Mitsein*) is an essential structure of existence correctly stresses that the human personality is always situated within a social matrix.[27] My world includes others to whom I relate in various modes of solicitude. To this Heideggerian insight Merleau-Ponty adds that sexuality is an irreducible dimension of the being of the self as body subject: the erotic contours of the world reflect my incarnate being as sexual within that *gestalt* that is my existence taken as a whole.[28] Conjoining these two insights yields *eros* as a dimension of all modalities of social existence.

Among the three basic ways to be with others—against them, for them, or indifferently passing them by—Heidegger distinguishes two positive modes of "solicitude" (*Fürsorge*): to leap-in (*einspringen*) is to perform some task for another; to leap-ahead (*vorausspringen*) is to prepare another for their genuine or authentic (*eigentlich*) possibilities.[29] This authenticity stands in contrast to the inauthenticity of everyday life, which is lived under the domination of the "they-self" (*das Man*) and distinguished by a lack of distinction in public, anonymous ways of thinking and acting.[30]

This everyday immersion in the commonplace, with its uncritical assimilation of the traditional, is disrupted by the call of conscience,[31] which summons the self (*Dasein*) to the recognition and acceptance of its finitude, or what Heidegger somewhat misleadingly calls "guilt."[32] My choices (*Existenz*) are finite: in pursuing one path I must forego its alternatives. My power over the world into which I am thrown (*geworfen*) is finite: some aspects of my situation remain forever beyond my control. And finally, my genuine existence, even when attained, is bounded by inauthenticity: the accommodating and tranquilizing ruses of the mediocre (*durchschnittlich*), leveled-down public life constantly tempt me to abandon personal initiative and responsibility. [33] This finitude is also temporal: my death is the ever-present possibility of my no longer having a world in which to reside, an eventuality certain to overcome me, though the moment always remains indefinite.[34] Authenticity (*Eigentlichkeit*) arises as a resolve (*Entschluss*) to remain open (*Erschliessen*) to this finitude—to be responsive to the summons to guilt and to anticipate (*vorlaufen*) death.[35] In their everyday lives, and indeed throughout a philosophical tradition, people have closed themselves off (a kind of ontological untruth for Heidegger[36]) from guilt and death, hence from that reality that they are and from that totality of entities (*Ganzheit des Seienden*) to which they are inextricably bound.

Authentic sexuality—admittedly a rather un-Heideggerian conjunction—requires a similar openness to others. Commitments are chains that bind us to some and exclude us from others, blinders that narrow down the field of social praxis to a privileged one (monogamy) or few (friendship). To elicit the many facets of the human personality requires a dynamic network of social interaction. Full sexual growth similarly requires a receptivity to the many erotic dimensions of social existence. Promiscuity provides this openness through its freedom from emotional and sexual commitments.

In the Western tradition love has been mistakenly treated as exclusive because it is erroneously thought of as possessive (compare, to "have" a woman), or that in which I have invested my will, in Hegelian terms.[37] But another person (*Mitdaseiende*) is neither a tool (*Zuhandene*) to be appropriated to my ends, nor a mere object of cognition (*Vorhandene*) to be explored. Rather, others are entities like me, with whom I share a world. Consequently love should be construed in Heideggerian terms as a leaping-ahead that affirms another's genuinely human possibilities, or in R. D. Laing's terms, as the confirmation of that which is true and good in another.[38]

The tradition has reversed the relation between sex and love—for reasons that once applied but, as previously pointed out, that are now anachronistic. The nakedness of sexual intercourse is not only physical, but psychological and emotional too: by laying bare not just our bodies, but our thoughts and feelings, two people can achieve a privileged moment from which they may *then* decide what kinds of commitments subsequently to make to one another. Promiscuity prepares for this moment through its "lack of commitment." To insist on an emotional involvement that closes off the future as a condition of this sexual self-revelation to others is, ironically, to frustrate the growth of the very love that such commitments are intended to cultivate. And to insist that this commitment as love can be made to only one other person is to succumb to the ontological fallacy of confusing people with things.

With its freedom from emotional and sexual restrictions promiscuity can play an important role in the achievement of authentic sexuality. This negative freedom-from is a positive freedom-for a genuinely human mode of social and sexual interaction.

CONCLUDING UNSCIENTIFIC POSTSCRIPT

My remarks might suggest that I believe promiscuity is *always* right. But this conclusion overstates my position. The claim I have sought to defend is more modest: for some of the people some of the time promiscuity is a good thing. Such behavior is curtailed by moral obligations to tell the truth, to be honest, and to respect others. It is also limited in time: for some, on occasion, promiscuity may not yet, or no longer, be good. To put my defense in perspective I shall conclude with a nod to Kierkegaard.

Kierkegaard's refutation of the Don Juan complex locates promiscuity as one stage on life's way.[39] Aping the Hegelian dialectic, of which he is both master and critic, he notes that the cause of its ultimate demise is boredom: despite the novelty achieved through the rotation method (varying the fields on which one's "seed" is sown), the full pursuit of the life of the senses ultimately succumbs to a cycle of sameness from which it can be rescued only by advancing to a higher mode of existence—the principled life of the ethical stage.[40]

Applied to the preceding sexual paradigms, Kierkegaard's insight suggests three corresponding resolutions of promiscuity. First, the good sex life cannot be achieved through physical gratification alone. The moral commitment represented by the Western norm is an attempt to achieve the advance Kierkegaard extols: wedded love regulated by reason seeks to overcome and yet to preserve (*aufheben*) the fleeting pleasures of the body. To deny this dialectical movement is to deny one's full humanity, to be arrested at a lower level of existence. Second, it may be noted that what the dialogue carried on through the body achieves in breadth it may lose in depth: having talked with many, we may discover that our most meaningful dialogue can be carried on with one. The commitment to this one person becomes, henceforth, a "natural" way to safeguard and foster this corporeal dialogue. The prohibitions against multiple dialogues were overthrown at the earlier stage so that this one person might be found and now they serve only as superfluous restrictions that need not be enforced to be observed. Finally, the openness of authentic sexuality may likewise achieve a moment at which a full commitment to a single other is its natural fruition; through its own catharsis the promiscuous life may discover a completion in Buber's I-Thou relation.[41] On such occasions promiscuity ceases to be of value in the sexual life of the individual. Indeed, from this point on not to abandon it would be as wrong as the prohibitions against it were at the earlier stage.

From this temporal perspective promiscuity has definite but limited value in the movement toward a sexual ideal. Michael Bayles is correct in his insistence that the intentionally lifelong relationship is intrinsically more valuable, but wrong in his (implicit) suggestion that intentionally temporary relations are of no value.[42] The principled life represented by the traditional commitment "to love, honor, and obey" signifies a higher mode of existence that partially transcends the vicissitudes of time. Whether this ideal is expressed in Platonic terms, as the longing for a love that is eternal,[43] or in Buber's terms, as a full awareness of the other in their unity, totality, and uniqueness, it must be wrung from man's historical existence. The value of promiscuity is located in the pursuit of just such ideals.

NOTES

1. I am grateful to Professors Willard Enteman and Jan Ludwig for suggestions and criticisms that helped to rescue this paper from some of its more egregious errors and confusions.

2. See, for example, Robert Paul Wolff's *In Defense of Anarchism* (New York: Harper & Row, 1970). Though I shall not pursue the parallels between political and sexual life, I believe anarchy represents a moment in Wolff's account of political obligation analogous to the promiscuous moment in sexual morality: each is marked by a radical freedom that serves as the transcendental ground for subsequent commitments and obligations.

3. This thesis was advanced by A. J. Ayer in *Language, Truth and Logic* (New

York: Dover, 1946), chap. 6, in order to account for the nonscientific (that is, non-descriptive) character of moral discourse. See C. L. Stevenson, *Ethics and Language* (New Haven: Yale University Press, 1944) and R. M. Hare, *The Language of Morals* (London: Oxford University Press, 1952) for subsequent refinements of this thesis.

4. What is true of promiscuity is also true of perversion: violations of the operative code tend to make our adrenalin flow. For one explanation of this emotional reaction to unnatural sexual acts see Michael Slote, "Inapplicable Concepts and Sexual Perversion," herein, pp. 261-67.

5. Ronald Atkinson, *Sexual Morality* (London: Hutchinson, 1965), p. 45.

6. See Robert Solomon, "Sex and Perversion," herein, p. 271.

7. The boundaries of incest vary from society to society and, indeed, between groups within society. Freud sought to account for these differences in the incest taboo in terms of myth, Darwinism, and anthropology. See *Totem and Taboo* (New York: New Republic, 1931), pp. 249 ff. Some have tried to show it is instinctive (see Robert H. Lowrie, *Primitive Society* [New York: Liveright, 1920]). Others explain the prohibition as a safeguard against biological degeneration due to inbreeding (see Lewis H. Morgan, *Ancient Society* [New York, 1877] pp. 69, 378, 424), or as a way of expanding and hence protecting the tribe (E. B. Tylor, "On a Method of Investigating the Development of Institutions; Applied to Laws of Marriage & Descent," *Journal of the Anthropological Institute* 18 [1888]: 245-69), or as a consequence of the prohibition against shedding the blood of one's own totemic group (Émile Durkheim, "La prohibition de l'incest et ses origins," *L'Anee Sociologique* 1 [1898]: 1-70). For a more recent treatment see S. Kirson Weinberg, *Incest Behavior* (New York: Citadel, 1955).

8. To refer to this as the "conjugal act," as the Roman Catholic Church does, is to beg the question of sex outside marriage. This restriction has a long and venerable tradition within Roman Catholicism, beginning with St. Paul's warning that it is better to marry than to burn in hell. See the following: Augustine, *De Genesi ad Litteram*, Book IX, cap. 7, n. 12; Thomas Aquinas, *On the Truth of the Catholic Faith*, Book 3, parts 1 and 2; Pope Leo XIII, *Rerum Novarum* (1891); and Pope Pius XI, *Casti Connubii* (1930).

9. Pope Paul VI, *Humanae Vitae*, "Faithfulness to God's Design," reprinted herein, pp. 131-49.

10. Carl Cohen, "Sex, Birth Control, and Human Life," *Ethics* 79 (1969): 251-62; reprinted herein, pp. 150-65.

11. See, for example, E. D. Watt, "Professor Cohen's Encyclical," *Ethics* 80 (1970): 218-21.

12. Richard Wasserstrom considers this point in his article "Is Adultery Immoral?" herein, pp. 207-21.

13. See Peter Bertocci, *The Human Venture in Sex, Love and Marriage* (New York: Associated Press, 1949), chap. 2, and his *Sex, Love and the Person* (New York: Sheed & Ward, 1967).

14. For an entertaining description of this ritual see Soren Kierkegaard, *Diary of a Seducer*, trans. K. Fick (Ithaca, N.Y.: The Dragon Press, 1935).

15. In *Being and Nothingness* (Part 3, chap. 3) Sartre transmutes the celebrated

Hegelian dialectical battle for prestige between the master and slave of *The Phenomenology of Mind* (pp. 228-40) into the notorious battle of the sexes. The intervening link between Sartre and Hegel is Alexander Kojève; see his *Introduction to the Reading of Hegel,* trans. J. H. Nichols (New York: Basic Books, 1969), pp. 31-70.

16. *The Essential Works of John Stuart Mill,* ed. Max Lerner (New York: Bantam, 1961), p. 263.

17. See Michael Bayles, "Marriage, Love, and Procreation," herein, pp. 190-206.

18. Mill, *The Essential Works,* pp. 193ff.

19. Ibid., p. 306.

20. Ibid., p. 307. Mill's insistence on the freedom to create one's own mode of life and his emphasis on individuality and the cultivation of human faculties align him with the existential tradition of Sartre ("condemned to be free"; "fundamental project") and Heidegger (*Seinkönnen*—"potentiality for Being") more than Mill's interpreters have yet recognized. I quoted Wilhelm von Humbolt earlier because he (and Aristotle) may provide the historical link.

21. Mill, *The Essential Works,* p. 323.

22. R. C. Solomon, "Sexual Paradigms," *Journal of Philosophy* 71 (1974): 336-45; and "Sex and Perversion."

23. Max Black, *The Labyrinth of Language* (New York: Praeger, 1968), chap. 2, provides one explanation of this terminology.

24. Those less familiar with the gallic (and galling) tendencies of Canadian politics should consult Walter Stewart, *Shrug: Trudeau in Power* (New York: Outerbridge, 1971).

25. Lest the analogy seem far-fetched by this point, it is worth recalling that Kant was one respected moral philosopher who regarded sex as mutual masturbation, salvaged only by the sanctity of matrimony. See Immanuel Kant, *Lectures on Ethics,* trans. Louis Infield (London: Methuen, 1930), pp. 162-71.

26. The conclusion that group sex is necessarily dissatisfying may be a faulty inference from the failures of its unskilled practitioners who have not yet mastered the complexities of multi-person corporeal conversations.

27. See Martin Heidegger, *Being and Time,* trans. J. Macquarrie and E. Robinson (New York: Harper & Row, 1962), sec. 27.

28. Maurice Merleau-Ponty, *The Phenomenology of Perception,* trans. Colin Smith (New York: Humanities Press, 1962), Part 1, chap. 6.

29. *Being and Time,* sec. 26. R. Weber, in "A Critique of Heidegger's Concept of 'Solicitude,'" *New Scholasticism* 42 (1965): 537-60, misinterprets mineness (*Jemeinigkeit*) and the nonrelational character of death, thereby generating her spurious paradoxes. For a more faithful but less direct account see J. Macquarrie's excellent book *Existentialism* (Baltimore: Penguin, 1973), chap. 5, "Existence and Others."

30. *Being and Time,* sec. 27. For an explication of inauthenticity see Ernest H. Freund, "Man's Fall in Martin Heidegger's Philosophy," *The Journal of Religion* 24 (1944): 180-87.

31. *Being and Time,* secs. 54-57.

32. Ibid., sec. 58. On Heidegger's existential notion of guilt see Michael Gelven, *Winter Friendship and Guilt* (New York: Harper & Row, 1972); D. V. Morano,

Existential Guilt: A Phenomenological Study (Assen, The Netherlands: Van Gorcum, 1973); C. O. Schrag, *Existence and Freedom* (Evanston, Ill.: Northwestern University Press, 1961), chap. 6.

33. *Being and Time*, secs. 25-27, 35-38.

34. Ibid., division C, chap. 1.

35. On Heidegger's existential notion of death see J. G. Gray, "Martin Heidegger: On Anticipating my own Death," *Personalist* 46 (1965): 439-58; R. Hinners, "Death as Possibility," *Continuum* 5 (1967): 470-82; and B. E. O'Mahoney, "Martin Heidegger's Existential of Death," *Philosophical Studies* (Ireland) 18 (1969): 58-75.

36. Heidegger explicates his ontological notion of truth and relates this to the epistemological concepts in section 44 of *Being and Time* and in his essay "On the Essence of Truth," in *Being and Existence*, ed. W. Brock (Chicago: Gateway, 1949). This central concept has attracted much discussion. Ernst Tugendhat's *Der Wahrheitsbegriff bei Husserl und Heidegger* (Berlin: W. de Gruyter, 1970) is perhaps the most noteworthy.

37. G. W. F. Hegel, *The Philosophy of Right*, trans. T. M. Knox (London: Oxford University Press, 1942), pp. 40-56.

38. R. D. Laing, *Self and Others* (Baltimore: Penguin, 1971), chap. 7.

39. See Soren Kierkegaard, "The Rotation Method" (reprinted from *Either/Or*), in *A Kierkegaard Anthology*, ed. R. Bretall (New York: Modern Library, 1946), pp. 21-32.

40. In his recourse to the rational to overcome the sensual (or the "aesthetic," as Kierkegaard somewhat misleadingly terms it), Kierkegaard's solution to the morality of sex resembles Kant's (see note 23).

41. I have not tried to develop a notion of authentic sexuality on the model of Buber's I-Thou, though such an interpretation could be provided, because what I find lacking in Buber but present in Heidegger is a fuller recognition of the historicity of such ideals. For a Buberian interpretation of sexuality see M. Friedman, "Sex in Sartre and Buber," in *Sexuality and Identity*, ed. H. Ruitenbeek (New York: Bantam, 1970), pp. 84-99.

42. See p. 197. Though Bayles does not quite say they are of no value whatsoever, he believes that they are not sufficiently valuable to warrant legal protection.

43. See D. P. Verene, "Sexual Love and Moral Experience," herein, pp. 105-15; and his *Sexual Love and Western Morality* (New York: Harper & Row, 1972), pp. 10-47.

THE LOGIC OF DEVIATION

Thomas Nagel

Sexual Perversion

There is something to be learned about sex from the fact that we possess a concept of sexual perversion. I wish to examine the concept, defending it against the charge of unintelligibility and trying to say exactly what about human sexuality qualifies it to admit of perversions. But let me make some preliminary comments about the problem before embarking on its solution.

Some people do not believe that the notion of sexual perversion makes sense, and even those who do, disagree over its application. Nevertheless, I think it will be widely conceded that if the concept is viable at all, it must meet certain general conditions. First, if there are any sexual perversions, they will have to be sexual desires or practices that can be

This article is reprinted from the *Journal of Philosophy* 66, no. 1 (January 16, 1969), with the permission of the publisher and author.

plausibly described as in some sense unnatural, though the explanation of this natural/unnatural distinction is, of course, the main problem. Second, certain practices, such as shoe fetishism, bestiality, and sadism will be perversions if anything is; other practices, such as unadorned sexual intercourse, will not be; and about still others there is controversy. Third, if there are perversions, they will be unnatural sexual *inclinations* rather than merely unnatural practices adopted not from inclination but for other reasons. I realize that this is at variance with the view, maintained by some Roman Catholics, that contraception is a sexual perversion. But although contraception may qualify as a deliberate perversion of the sexual and reproductive functions, it cannot be significantly described as a *sexual* perversion. A sexual perversion must reveal itself in conduct that expresses an unnatural *sexual* preference. And although there might be a form of fetishism focused on the employment of contraceptive devices, that is not the usual explanation for their use.

I wish to declare at the outset my belief that the connection between sex and reproduction has no bearing on sexual perversion. The latter is a concept of psychological, not physiological interest, and it is a concept that we do not apply to the lower animals, let alone to plants, all of which have reproductive functions that can go astray in various ways (think, for example, of seedless oranges). Insofar as we are prepared to regard higher animals as perverted, it is because of their psychological, not their anatomical similarity to humans. Furthermore, we do not regard as a perversion every deviation from the reproductive function of sex in humans: sterility, miscarriage, contraception, abortion.

Another matter that I believe has no bearing on the concept of sexual perversion is social disapprobation or custom. Anyone inclined to think that in each society the perversions are those sexual practices of which the community disapproves should consider all of the societies that have frowned upon adultery and fornication. These have not been regarded as unnatural practices, but have been thought objectionable in other ways. What is regarded as unnatural admittedly varies from culture to culture, but the classification is not a pure expression of disapproval or distaste. In fact it is often regarded as a *ground* for disapproval, and that suggests that the classification has an independent content.

I am going to attempt a psychological account of sexual perversion, which will depend on a specific psychological theory of sexual desire and human sexual interactions. To approach this solution I wish first to consider a contrary position, one that provides a basis for skepticism about the existence of any sexual perversions at all, and perhaps about the very significance of the term. The skeptical argument runs as follows:

Sexual desire is simply one of the appetites, like hunger and thirst. As such it may have various objects, some more common than others perhaps, but none in any sense "natural." An appetite is identified as sexual by means of the organs and erogenous zones in which its satisfaction can be to some extent localized, and the special sensory pleasures that form the core of that satisfaction. This enables us to recognize widely divergent goals, activities, and desires as sexual, since it is conceivable in principle that anything should produce sexual pleasure and that a nondeliberate, sexually charged desire for it should arise (as a result of conditioning, if nothing else). We may fail to empathize with some of these desires, and some of them, like sadism, may be objectionable on extraneous grounds, but once we have observed that they meet the criteria for being sexual, there is nothing more to be said on *that* score. Either they are sexual or they are not: sexuality does not admit of imperfection, or perversion, or any other such qualification—it is not that sort of affection.

This is probably the received radical position. It suggests that the cost of defending a psychological account may be to deny that sexual desire is an appetite. But insofar as that line of defense is plausible, it should make us suspicious of the simple picture of appetites on which the skepticism depends. Perhaps the standard appetites, like hunger, cannot be classed as pure appetites in that sense either, at least in their human versions.

Let us approach the matter by asking whether we can imagine anything that would qualify as a gastronomical perversion. Hunger and eating are importantly like sex in that they serve a biological function and also play a significant role in our inner lives. It is noteworthy that there is little temptation to describe as perverted an appetite for substances that are not nourishing. We should probably not consider someone's appetites as perverted if he liked to eat paper, sand, wood, or cotton. Those are merely rather odd and very unhealthy tastes: they lack the psychological complexity that we expect of perversions. (Coprophilia, being already a sexual perversion, may be disregarded.) If, on the other hand, someone liked to eat cookbooks or magazines with pictures of food in them, and preferred these to ordinary food—or if when hungry he sought satisfaction by fondling a napkin or ashtray from his favorite restaurant—then the concept of perversion might seem appropriate (in fact it would be natural to describe this as a case of gastronomical fetishism). It would be natural to describe as gastronomically perverted someone who could eat only by having food forced down his throat through a funnel, or only if the meal were a living animal. What helps in such cases is the peculiarity of the desire itself, rather than the inappropriateness of its object to the biological function that the desire serves. Even an appetite, it would seem, can have perversions if in addition to its biological function it has a significant psychological structure.

In the case of hunger, psychological complexity is provided by the activities that give it expression. Hunger is not merely a disturbing sensation that can be quelled by eating; it is an attitude toward edible portions of the external world, a desire to relate to them in rather special ways. The method of ingestion—chewing, savoring, swallowing, appreciating the texture and smell—is an important component of the relation, as is the passivity and controllability of the food (the only animals we eat live are helpless mollusks). Our relation to food depends also on our size: we do not live upon it or burrow into it like aphids or worms. Some of these features are more central than others, but any adequate phenomenology of eating would have to treat it as a relation to the external world and a way of appropriating bits of that world, with characteristic affection. Displacements or serious restrictions of the desire to eat could then be described as perversions, if they undermined the direct relation between man and food that is the natural expression of hunger. This explains why it is easy to imagine gastronomical fetishism, voyeurism, exhibitionism, or even gastronomical sadism and masochism. Indeed, some of these perversions are fairly common.

If we can imagine perversions of an appetite like hunger, it should be possible to make sense of the concept of sexual perversion. I do not wish to imply that sexual desire is an appetite—only that being an appetite is no bar to admitting of perversions. Like hunger, sexual desire has as its characteristic object a certain relation with something in the external world; only in this case it is usually a person rather than an omelet, and the relation is considerably more complicated. This added complication allows scope for correspondingly complicated perversions.

The fact that sexual desire is a feeling about other persons may tempt us to take a pious view of its psychological content. There are those who believe that sexual desire is properly the expression of some other attitude, like love, and that when it occurs by itself it is incomplete and unhealthy—

or at any rate subhuman. (The extreme Platonic version of such a view is that sexual practices are all vain attempts to express something they cannot in principle achieve: this makes them all perversions, in a sense.) I do not believe that any such view is correct. Sexual desire is complicated enough without having to be linked to anything else as a condition for phenomenological analysis. It cannot be denied that sex may serve various functions—economic, social, altruistic—but it also has its own content as a relation between persons, and it is only by analyzing that relation that we can understand the conditions of sexual perversion.

It is very important that the object of sexual attraction is a particular individual, who transcends the properties that make him attractive. When different persons are attracted to a single person for different reasons—eyes, hair, figure, laugh, intelligence—we feel that the object of their desire is nevertheless the same, namely, that person. There is even an inclination to feel that this is so if the lovers have different sexual aims, if they include both men and women, for example. Different specific attractive characteristics seem to provide enabling conditions for the operation of a single basic feeling, and the different aims all provide expressions of it. We approach the sexual attitude toward the person through the features that we find attractive, but these features are not the objects of that attitude.

This is very different from the case of an omelet. Various people may desire it for different reasons, one for its fluffiness, another for its mushrooms, another for its unique combination of aroma and visual aspect; yet we do not enshrine the transcendental omelet as the true common object of their affections. Instead we might say that several desires have accidentally converged on the same object: any omelet with the crucial characteristics would do as well. It is not similarly true that any person with the same flesh distribution and way of smoking can be substituted as object for a particular sexual desire that has been elicited by those characteristics. It may be that they will arouse attraction whenever they recur, but it will be a new sexual attraction with a new particular object, not merely a transfer of the old desire to someone else. (I believe this is true even in cases where the new object is unconsciously identified with a former one.)

The importance of this point will emerge when we see how complex a psychological interchange constitutes the natural development of sexual attraction. This would be incomprehensible if its object were not a particular person, but rather a person of a certain *kind*. Attraction is only the beginning, and fulfillment does not consist merely of behavior and contact expressing this attraction, but involves much more.

The best discussion of these matters that I have seen is in part three of Sartre's *Being and Nothingness*.[1] Since it has influenced my own views, I shall say a few things about it now. Sartre's treatment of sexual desire and of love, hate, sadism, masochism, and further attitudes toward others, depends on a general theory of consciousness and the body that we can neither expound nor assume here. He does not discuss perversion, partly because he regards sexual desire as one form of the perpetual attempt of an embodied consciousness to come to terms with the existence of others, an attempt that is as doomed to fail in this form as it is in any of the others, which include sadism and masochism (if not certain of the more impersonal deviations) as well as several nonsexual attitudes. According to Sartre, all attempts to incorporate the other into my world as another subject, that is, to apprehend him as at once an object for me and a subject for whom I am an object, are unstable and doomed to collapse into one or the other of the two aspects. Either I reduce him entirely to an object, in which case his subjectivity escapes the possession or appropriation I can extend to that object; or I become merely an object for him, in which case I am no longer in a position to appropriate his subjectivity. Moreover, neither of these aspects is stable: each is continually in danger of giving way to the other. This has the consequence that there can be no such thing as a *successful* sexual relation, since the deep aim of sexual desire cannot in principle be accomplished. It seems likely, therefore, that this view will not permit a basic distinction between successful, or complete, and unsuccessful, or incomplete, sex and therefore cannot admit the concept of perversion.

I do not adopt this aspect of the theory, nor many of its metaphysical underpinnings. What interests me is Sartre's picture of the attempt. He says that the type of possession that is the object of sexual desire is carried out by "a double reciprocal incarnation" and that this is accomplished, typically in the form of a caress, in the following way: "I make myself flesh in order to impel the Other to realize *for-herself* and *for me* her own flesh, and my caresses cause my flesh to be born for me in so far as it is for the Other *flesh causing her to be born as flesh.*"[2] The incarnation in question is described variously as a clogging or troubling of consciousness, which is inundated by the flesh in which it is embodied.

The view I am going to suggest—I hope in less obscure language—is related to Sartre's, but differs in allowing sexuality to achieve its goal on occasion and thus in providing the concept of perversion with a foothold.

Sexual desire involves a kind of perception, but not merely a single perception of its object, for in the paradigm case of mutual desire there is a complex system of superimposed mutual perceptions—not only perceptions of the sexual object, but perceptions of oneself. Moreover, sexual awareness of another involves considerable self-awareness to begin with—more than is involved in ordinary sensory perception. The experience is felt as an assault on oneself by the view (or touch, or whatever) of the sexual object.

Let us consider a case in which the elements can be separated. For clarity we will restrict ourselves initially to the somewhat artificial case of desire at a distance. Suppose a man and a woman, whom we may call Romeo and Juliet, are at opposite ends of a cocktail lounge with many mirrors on its walls, permitting unobserved observation and even mutual unobserved observation. Each of them is sipping a martini and studying other people in the mirrors. At some point Romeo notices Juliet. He is moved, somehow, by the softness of her hair and the diffidence with which she sips her martini, and this arouses him sexually. Let us say that X *senses* Y whenever X regards Y with sexual desire. (Y need not be a person, and X's apprehension of Y can be visual, tactile, olfactory, and so on, or purely imaginary. In the present example we shall concentrate on vision.) So Romeo senses Juliet, rather than merely noticing her. At this stage he is aroused by an unaroused object; so he is more in the sexual grip of his body than she of hers.

Let us suppose, however, that Juliet now senses Romeo in another mirror on the opposite wall, though neither of them yet knows that he is seen by the other (the mirror angles provide three-quarter views). Romeo then begins to notice in Juliet the subtle signs of sexual arousal: heavy-lidded stare, dilating pupils, a faint flush. This of course renders her much more bodily, and he not only notices but senses this as well. His arousal is nevertheless still solitary. But now, cleverly calculating the line of her stare without actually looking her in the eyes, he realizes that it is directed at him through the mirror on the opposite wall. That is, he notices, and moreover senses, Juliet sensing him. This is definitely a new development, for it gives him a sense of embodiment, not only through his own reactions, but also through the eyes and reactions of another. Moreover, it is separable from the initial sensing of Juliet, for sexual arousal might begin with a person's sensing that he is sensed and being assailed by the perception of the other person's desire rather than merely by the perception of the person.

But there is a further step. Let us suppose that Juliet, who is a little slower than Romeo, now senses that he senses her. This puts Romeo in a position to notice, and be aroused by, her arousal at being sensed by him. He senses that she senses that he senses her. This is still another level of arousal, for he becomes conscious of his sexuality through his awareness of its effect on her and of her awareness that this effect is due to him. Once she takes the same step and senses that he senses her sensing him, it becomes difficult to state, let alone imagine, further iterations, though they may be logically distinct. If both are alone, they will presumably turn to look at each other directly, and the proceedings will continue on another plane. Physical contact and intercourse are perfectly natural extensions of this complicated visual exchange, and mutual touch can involve all the complexities of awareness present in the visual case, but with a far greater range of subtlety and acuteness.

Ordinarily, of course, things happen in a less orderly fashion—sometimes in a great rush—but I believe that some version of this overlapping system of distinct sexual perceptions and interactions is the basic framework of any full-fledged sexual relation and that relations involving only part of the complex are significantly incomplete. The account is only schematic, as it must be to achieve generality. Every real sexual act will be psychologically far more specific and detailed, in ways that depend not only on the physical techniques employed and on anatomical details but also on countless features of the participants' conceptions of themselves and of each other, which become embodied in the act. (It is a familiar enough fact, for example, that people often take their social roles and the social roles of their partners to bed with them.)

The general schema is important, however, and the proliferation of levels of mutual awareness it involves is an example of a type of complexity that typifies human interactions. Consider aggression, for example. If I am angry with someone, I want to make him feel it, either to produce self-reproach by getting him to see himself through the eyes of my anger and to dislike what he sees, or to produce reciprocal anger or fear by getting him to perceive my anger as a threat or attack. What I want will depend on the details of my anger, but in either case it will involve a desire that the object of that anger be aroused. This accomplishment constitutes the fulfillment of my emotion through domination of the object's feelings.

Another example of such reflexive mutual recognition is to be found in the phenomenon of meaning, which appears to involve an intention to produce a belief or other effect in another by bringing about his recognition of one's intention to produce that effect. (That result is due to H. P. Grice,[3] whose position I shall not attempt to reproduce in detail.) Sex has a related structure: it involves a desire that one's partner be aroused by the recognition of one's desire that he or she be aroused.

It is not easy to define the basic types of awareness and arousal of which these complexes are composed, and that remains a lacuna in this discussion. I believe that the object of awareness is the same in one's own case as it is in one's sexual awareness of another, although the two awarenesses will not be the same, the difference being as great as that between feeling angry and experiencing the anger of another. All stages of sexual perception are varieties of identification of a person with his body. What is perceived is one's own or another's *subjection* to or *immersion* in his body, a phenomenon that has been recognized with loathing by St. Paul and St. Augustine, both of whom regarded "the law of sin which is in my members" as a grave threat to the dominion of the holy will.[4] In sexual desire and its expression the blending of involuntary response with deliberate control is extremely important. For Augustine, the revolution launched against him by his body is symbolized by erection and the other involuntary physical components of arousal. Sartre too stresses the fact that the penis is not a prehensile organ. But mere involuntariness characterizes other bodily processes as well. In sexual desire the involuntary responses are combined with submission to spontaneous impulses: not only one's pulse and secretions but one's actions are taken over by the body; ideally, deliberate control is needed only to guide the expression of those impulses. This is to some extent also true of an appetite like hunger, but the takeover there is more localized, less pervasive, less extreme. One's whole body does not become saturated with hunger as it can with desire. But the most characteristic feature of a specifically sexual immersion in the body is its ability to fit into the complex of mutual perceptions that we have described. Hunger leads to spontaneous interactions with food; sexual desire leads to spontaneous interactions with other persons, whose bodies are asserting their sovereignty in the same way, producing involuntary reactions and spontaneous impulses in *them*. These reactions are perceived, and the perception of them is perceived, and that perception is in turn perceived; at each step the domination of the person by his body is reinforced, and the sexual partner becomes more possessible by physical contact, penetration, and envelopment.

Desire is therefore not merely the perception of a preexisting embodiment that in turn enhances the original subject's sense of himself. This explains why it is important that the partner be aroused, and not merely aroused, but aroused by the awareness of one's desire. It also explains the sense in which desire has unity and possession as its object: physical possession must eventuate in creation of the sexual object in the image of one's desire, and not merely in the object's recognition of that desire or in his or her own private arousal. (This may reveal a male bias. I shall say something about that later.)

To return, finally, to the topic of perversion: I believe that various familiar deviations constitute truncated or incomplete versions of the complete configuration and may therefore be regarded as perversions of the central impulse.

In particular, narcissistic practices and intercourse with animals, infants, and inanimate objects seem to be stuck at some primitive version of the first stage. If the object is not alive, the experience is reduced entirely to an awareness of one's own sexual embodiment. Small children and animals permit awareness of the embodiment of the other, but present obstacles to reciprocity, to the recognition by the sexual object of the subject's desire as the source of his (the object's) sexual self-awareness.

Sadism concentrates on the evocation of passive self-awareness in others, but the sadist's engagement is itself active and requires a retention of deliberate control that impedes awareness of himself as a bodily subject of passion in the required sense. The victim must recognize him as the source of his own sexual passivity, but only as the active source. De Sade claimed that the object of sexual desire was to evoke involuntary responses from one's partner, especially audible ones. The infliction of pain is no doubt the most efficient way to accomplish this, but it requires a certain abrogation of one's own exposed spontaneity. All this, incidentally, helps to explain why it is tempting to regard as sadistic an excessive preoccupation with sexual technique, which does not permit one to abandon the role of agent at any stage of the sexual act. Ideally one should be able to surmount one's technique at some point.

A masochist on the other hand imposes the same disability on his partner as the sadist imposes on himself. The masochist cannot find a satisfactory embodiment as the object of another's sexual desire but only as the object of his control. He is passive not in relation to his partner's passion but in relation to his nonpassive agency. In addition, the subjection to one's body characteristic of pain and physical restraints is of a very different kind from that of sexual excitement: pain causes people to contract rather than dissolve.

Both of these disorders have to do with the second stage, which involves the awareness of oneself as an object of desire. In straightforward sadism and masochism other attentions are substituted for desire as a source of the object's self-awareness. But it is also possible for nothing of that sort to be substituted, as in the case of a masochist who is satisfied with self-inflicted pain or of a sadist who does not insist on playing a role in the suffering that arouses him. Greater difficulties of classification are presented by three other categories of sexual activity: elaborations of the sexual act, intercourse of more than two persons, and homosexuality.

If we apply our model to the various forms that may be taken by two-party heterosexual intercourse, none of them seem clearly to qualify as perversions. Hardly anyone can be found these days to inveigh against oral-genital contact, and the merits of buggery are urged by such respectable figures as D. H. Lawrence and Norman Mailer. There may be something vaguely sadistic about the latter technique (in Mailer's writings it seems to be a method of introducing an element of rape), but it is not obvious that this has to be so. In general, it would appear that any bodily contact between a man and a woman that gives them sexual pleasure is a possible vehicle for the system of multilevel interpersonal awareness that I have claimed is the basic psychological content of sexual interaction. Thus a liberal platitude about sex is upheld.

About multiple combinations the least that can be said is that they are bound to be complicated. If one considers how difficult it is to carry on two conversations simultaneously, one may appreciate the problems of multiple simultaneous interpersonal perception that can arise in even a small-scale orgy. It may be inevitable that some of the component relations should degenerate into mutual epidermal stimulation by participants otherwise isolated from each other. There may also be a tendency toward voyeurism and exhibitionism, both of which are incomplete relations. The exhibitionist wishes to display his desire without needing to be desired in return; he may even fear the sexual attentions of others. A voyeur, on the other hand, need not require any recognition at all by his object, certainly not a recognition of the voyeur's arousal.

It is not clear whether homosexuality is a perversion if that is measured by the standard of the described configuration, but it seems unlikely. For such a classification would have to depend on the possibility of extracting from the system a distinction between male and female sexuality; and much that has been said so far applies equally to men and women. Moreover, it would have to be maintained that there was a natural tie between the type of sexuality and the sex of the body and that two sexualities of the same type could not interact properly.

Certainly there is much support for an aggressive-passive distinction between male and female sexuality. In our culture the male's arousal tends to initiate the perceptual exchange; he usually makes the sexual approach, largely controls the course of the act, and of course penetrates whereas the woman receives. When two men or two women engage in intercourse they cannot both adhere to these sexual roles. The question is how essential the roles are to an adequate sexual relation. One relevant observation is that a good deal of deviation from these roles occurs in heterosexual intercourse. Women can be sexually aggressive and men passive, and temporary reversals of role are not uncommon in heterosexual exchanges of reasonable length. If such conditions are set aside, it may be urged that there is something irreducibly perverted in attraction to a body anatomically like one's own. But alarming as some people in our culture may find such attraction, it remains psychologically unilluminating to class it as perverted. Certainly if homosexuality is a perversion, it is so in a very different sense from that in which shoe-fetishism is a perversion, for some version of the full range of interpersonal perceptions seems perfectly possible between two persons of the same sex.

In any case, even if the proposed model is correct, it remains implausible to describe as perverted every deviation from it. For example, if the partners in heterosexual intercourse indulge in private heterosexual fantasies, that obscures the recognition of the real partner and so, on the theory, constitutes a defective sexual relation. It is not, however, generally regarded as a perversion. Such examples suggest that a simple dichotomy between perverted and unperverted sex is too crude to organize the phenomena adequately.

I shall close with some remarks about the relation of perversion to good, bad, and morality. The concept of perversion can hardly fail to be evaluative in some sense, for it appears to involve the notion of an ideal or at least adequate sexuality that the perversions in some way fail to achieve. So, if the concept is viable, the judgment that a person or practice or desire is perverted will constitute a sexual evaluation, implying that better sex, or a better specimen of sex, is possible. This in itself is a very weak claim since the evaluation might be in a dimension that is of little interest to us. (Though, if my account is correct, that will not be true.)

Whether it is a moral evaluation, however, is another question entirely, one whose answer would require more understanding of both morality and perversion than can be deployed here. Moral evaluation of acts and of persons is a rather special and very complicated matter and by no means are all of our evaluations of persons and their activities moral evaluations. We make judgments about people's beauty or health or intelligence that are evaluative without being moral. Assessments of their sexuality may be similar in that respect.

Furthermore, moral issues aside, it is not clear that unperverted sex is necessarily *preferable* to the perversions. It may be that sex that receives the highest marks for perfection *as sex* is less enjoyable than certain perversions, and if enjoyment is considered very important, that might outweigh considerations of sexual perfection in determining rational preference.

That raises the question of the relation between the evaluative content of judgments of perversion and the rather common *general* distinction between good and bad sex. The latter distinction is usually confined to sexual acts, and it would seem, within limits, to cut across the other: even someone who believed, for example, that homosexuality was a perversion could admit a distinction between better and worse homosexual sex, and might even allow that good homosexual sex could be better *sex* than not very good unperverted sex. If this is correct, it supports the position—if judgments of perversion are viable at all—that they represent only one aspect of the possible evaluation of sex, even *qua sex*. Moreover it is not the only important aspect: certainly sexual deficiencies that evidently do not constitute perversions can be the object of great concern.

Finally, even if perverted sex is to that extent not so good as it might be, bad sex is generally better than none at all. This should not be controversial: it seems to hold for other important matters, like food, music, literature, and society. In the end, one must choose from among the available alternatives, whether their availability depends on the environment or on one's own constitution. And the alternatives have to be fairly grim before it becomes rational to opt for nothing.

NOTES

1. Trans. Hazel E. Barnes (New York: Philosophical Library, 1956).
2. Ibid., p. 391. Sartre's italics.
3. "Meaning," *Philosophical Review* 66, no. 3 (July 1957): 377-88.
4. See Romans 7:23, and the *Confessions*, Book 8, v.

Michael Slote

Inapplicable Concepts and Sexual Perversion

In this essay I shall argue that the ordinary concept of unnatural or perverted behavior (or acts) is inapplicable in principle, and I shall attempt to
explain something of the nature of this inapplicability.[1]

    Philosophers have long been perplexed about what is meant by
calling an act or behavior unnatural. And, indeed, many have thought that
the notion was self-contradictory, ill defined, or strictly emotive. In calling
an act unnatural we are not, for example, simply saying that it is wrong or
heinous. The crimes of the Mafia are not, typically, unnatural. Usually it is
"deviant" sexual or sexually related behavior that is called unnatural.
Thus homosexuality or fetishism is sometimes thought to be a kind of unnatural behavior. However, it is difficult to say what constitutes this unnaturalness.[2] In calling the behavior of a homosexual unnatural, people
are not, it seems, just saying that it is rare or atypical sexual behavior,[3] or
that it is wrong sexual behavior. Certain feats of sexual prowess or endur-
ance are atypical and rare but hardly unnatural, at least to the ordinary

261

way of thinking. And most people who consider adultery or fornication wrong would never consider them to be unnatural.

Nor is unnaturalness a particularly religious concept that consists in the idea of transgression against the natural order of sexual morality instituted by God. Believing Christians may find incest and homosexuality unnatural, but they do not, for example, consider adultery or fornication unnatural—even though they presumably believe that such behavior transgresses divinely instituted sexual standards. Nor should we be led into the swamps of teleology to claim that unnatural sexual acts are to be thought of as being those that go against the purpose of sex. For it is difficult, even in theological terms, to make much sense of the idea that sex has a purpose, and that idea may well be conceptually and/or morally confused. And even if there is a purpose to sex and that purpose is procreation, it will be hard for a teleological theory to explain how anyone could think that oral-genital sex, as part of the buildup to coitus, was any more unnatural than kissing, as part of that buildup. Finally, it would seem that unnaturalness does not consist in incomprehensibility or ununderstandableness, in any straightforward way. It is true that we often use the phrase "naturally enough" as a rough synonym for "understandably enough." But there seems to be no such intersubstitutability between "unnaturally" and "ununderstandably" (or "incomprehensibly"). Furthermore it is hard to see how talk of ununderstandable acts can be pejorative in the way and to the degree that talk about unnatural acts is; so we shall have to look elsewhere for an adequate account of the concept of unnatural acts or behavior.

My own view is that there may well be no applicable concept of an unnatural act or of unnatural behavior. To say that an act is unnatural is to say, in effect, that it is outside of nature or our world. And such a claim cannot in principle be true. However, I am by no means saying that the concept of unnatural acts or behavior is inapplicable because of the failure above and elsewhere to analyze that concept. The claim here of inapplicability is justified only as part of a theory that helps to explain, or fits in well with, certain important data, among which are the facts that the words "unnatural act" and "unnatural behavior" express horror and that people who are knowledgeable and not fearful about certain behavior are reluctant to call such behavior unnatural.

The acts we call unnatural horrify us, but why should that make us put such acts outside our world—beyond the pale, as it were? Idiots are rather horrifying too, but they are not called unnatural. Let me suggest that the difference here is that the kinds of acts people call unnatural are those that most people have some impulse toward that they cannot or will not admit to having. If we are to believe depth psychology, most of us have inside us at some (unconscious) level desires for incest, homosexuality, and even one or another form of fetishism. But these are the kinds of impulses people almost never, without undergoing therapy, admit to having. The behavior of idiots is perhaps horrifying and frightening. But it does not threaten from within; it is not tied to any inner impulse that we will not admit to having.

The idea, then, is that sexual behavior for which we ourselves have repressed inner impulses is what comes to be called "unnatural." By calling it "unnatural" we think of it as banished to a world other than ours, and this helps to reassure us that the impulse toward such behavior is not *in us*. There is typically no such need for reassurance about idiocy. There is no need to keep repressed and disarmed the thought that we have elements of idiocy within, for there is no (literal) idiocy in most of us and most of us are aware of that fact. And much the same is true for adultery or fornication. We do not call such behavior "unnatural." And part of the reason is that inner impulses toward such behavior somehow do not threaten our ease and self-image in the way that, for example, inner impulses toward incest do. Most people who think there is something wrong with adultery are still willing to admit (to themselves) that they have some desires or wishes in that direction. Such desires are not repressed or unconscious. But desires for incest and homosexuality typically are repressed, unconscious, and so threatening that drastic means will, if necessary, be used to keep those desires unconscious and prevent us from recognizing their presence within us. The use of inapplicable descriptions is certainly drastic enough. But on any psychoanalytical or depth-psychological account of such matters, a person's claim that certain behavior is unnatural will at most be the expression of a necessarily false *unconscious* or *subconscious* belief that the behavior is not in the (natural) world with him, and he will not consciously realize the inapplicability of his description. But such a "drastic," unconscious belief is one very effective means by which a person can and does defuse the thought (and allay the fear) that such behavior is something he really desires deep down. Thus in saying that certain behavior is unnatural we give ourselves the "message" that certain behavioral tendencies are not in the (natural) world with us, and so not in us. And this helps to repress or keep repressed those very tendencies.[4]

Of course, I have not said much about why there is any need in the first place to repress desires for incest, homosexuality, and the like. But it should be clear that I believe that this has something to do with the fact that such desires exist in most people but are incompatible with some of the most important or urgent demands of family and society—for example, harmony and uncompetitiveness within the family and the long-run continuation of society as a whole. In much of what I have been saying, I have presupposed the truth of certain depth-psychological or psychoanalytical assumptions or theories. And this may make much of what I have said suspect to some people. But I think there is enough value or interest in various depth-psychological theories to make it worthwhile for us to use them to cast light on the problems we have been discussing, or at least to point up new directions in which further thought and exploration should be undertaken. And in any case, I think that the most important parts of the psychological argumentation we have used can be made independent of any particular abstruse psychological theory and based simply on commonsense insight about human nature.

It is one of the chief merits of our "inapplicability" theory of unnaturalness that it enables us to explain why psychologically educated people are less willing to speak of unnatual behavior than most people are. Such people are—for better or worse—usually willing to concede the existence of impulses toward incest, homosexuality, and so on, in themselves. So they have less fear of those impulses and of admitting their existence than do most people, and thus have less need for the above-described mechanism of keeping those impulses defused and repressed by thinking of them—of necessity incorrectly—as not within their (natural) world.

I have argued, then, that the concept of unnatural behavior involves the idea of behavior that is not in nature (with us); and I have said something about the possible psychology of the way such a concept might come to be applied in ignorance of its inapplicability. Without a plausible psychological theory of this kind, our claim that the notion of unnatural behavior is inapplicable to the actual (nonfiction) world would be at least somewhat problematic, since any reasonable principle of charity would have us, other things being equal, assume that people do not generally talk and think in ways that could not conceivably be correct. I hope, then, that the total philosophical-cum-psychological view offered here gives us reason to believe that the notion of an unnatural act or of unnatural behavior is inapplicable in principle.

Let us turn now to the notion of sexual perversion. Many enlightened or rationalistic people have felt that the concept of perversion is illegitimate and inapplicable—an irrational holdover from the heyday of religious intolerance and unscientific thinking. Some philosophers have disagreed. Thomas Nagel, for example, has offered in his paper "Sexual Perversion" a model of human sexuality: (roughly speaking) nonperverted sexual activity involves two people (creatures) being attracted to and by each other and being further aroused by the perception of each other's arousal. Deviation from this standard or model is presumably to count as perverted or unnatural. Nagel's model, which derives from certain ideas of Sartre's in *Being and Nothingness*, is certainly interesting in and of itself, and it may well set a standard for what is to count as ideal sex. But it does not seem to set a standard for what is to count as nonperverted sex. On Nagel's account, two people (or animals?) who engage in a sexual act in such an unsubtle, in-heat way as not to be aroused by each other's arousal are not engaging in fully unperverted sexual activity. This claim seems to be out of touch with our ordinary use of "perversion" and with any technical use of the term that I am aware of. I think a good deal more argument is needed if Nagel wants to show that deviations from his model count as sexually perverted rather than merely as nonideal—or as Sara Ruddick has suggested, incomplete.[5] Indeed, late in his paper even Nagel seems willing to make some concessions about the adequacy of his model to capturing the notion of sexual (non)perversion.[6]

Of course the terms "perverted" and "perversion" occur in psychiatric and psychoanalytic writings. But if those terms express a valid applicable concept in such contexts, that is only because they are used there in a technical way and not in their ordinary sense. In their ordinary sense the terms "perverted" and "perversion" express horror or fear. They do so because the ordinary concept of perverted behavior or of perversion involves the notion of unnatural behavior, and we have already seen how the notion of unnaturalness may be used to express and yet also to allay horror or fear. Technical psychiatric or psychoanalytic usage of "perverted" and "perversion" does not express horror, and that is because such usage does not involve the idea of unnaturalness. Psychiatrists and psychoanalysts presumably understand and are unafraid of "perverted behavior" more than most people; so if our above views are correct, they have less motive or need to call such behavior unnatural than most other people. And what also supports the idea that technical usage of "perverted" and "perversion" does not involve the concept of unnaturalness is the fact that those professionals who speak of perversions never seem to speak of unnatural behavior in any technical or nontechnical sense. I think, then, that technical usage of "perverted" and "perversion" does not express horror the way ordinary usage of those terms does. Of course we have not specified the actual content of the (or of *a*) technical psychiatric concept of perversion, and this would be difficult to do. But whatever its full delineation, such a technical notion presumably involves at least the idea of deviation from some favored, explanatorily rich, ideal-typic causal model of the development of human sexual motivation.

The ordinary notion of perversion seems to involve the idea of unnaturalness. It would appear that perverted sexual behavior is by definition unnatural sexual behavior; and since the latter notion is inapplicable, so is the former. Thus when we call certain behavior "perverted" in the ordinary sense we express and counteract our own impulses and fears in much the same way that we do when we call behavior "unnatural."

Even Nagel is willing to admit that perversion entails unnaturalness. But he seeks to salvage the applicability of the idea of perversion, while admitting there is a case against its applicability, by use of the behavioral-motivation interaction model mentioned earlier. Yet if his model does not capture the idea of sexual (non)perversion but only of some perhaps related sexual ideal, then we may have to take seriously the thought that the whole ordinary notion of sexual perversion is illegitimate. And the theory presented here is an attempt to justify such a claim of illegitimacy and show how such an illegitimate concept could possibly exist, take hold, and flourish—at least among the psychologically uninformed. Our theory may, moreover, have a bearing on the moral validity and conscionability of various current punitive laws relating to "perverted behavior." If nothing really is perverted in the nontechnical sense used by legislators, and if those laws in some way stem from the repression of feared impulses toward such "perverted behavior" on the part of the legislators or the general public, then it should be possible to argue that at least some such laws simply should not exist.

I would not, however, like to leave the impression that I subscribe uncritically to the assumption that only sexually related behavior can be called perverted, given the ordinary usage of the term. Some people might consider cannibalism perverted (and Nagel himself describes a case of what might be thought by some people to count as an eating perversion). But however loosely the ordinary notion of perverted behavior relates to the sexual realm, it still conveys the idea of unnaturalness and is inapplicable for that reason. Thus if we call cannibalism perverted, we may well do so in the service of the repression of our own cannibalistic impulses and our fear of them. For these primitive impulses to devour and incorporate exist at a deep or unconscious level in most people, according to much of depth-psychological or psychoanalytic theory.

In the light of what I have said about the inapplicability of the notions of an unnatural act and of perverted behavior, I think it might be profitable for the philosophers to look for other instances and perhaps other kinds of inapplicable concepts. I am inclined to think, for example, that the concept of a monster is the concept of a frightening creature that is (in some appropriate sense) unnatural, and thus that that concept is inapplicable to nonfiction reality—educated people do not think of dinosaurs as monsters. And I believe that the psychology of the use of "monster" could be shown to be quite similar to that of the use of "perverted behavior." Other concepts that I think might, upon further examination, prove to be inapplicable include "uncanny," "eerie," "freak," and "obscene." And since psychology has an important role to play in theories that claim that one or another concept is inapplicable in principle (to the real, nonfiction world), I imagine that there remains a great deal for philosophy and psychology to do together in investigating the variety and etiology of these and other possibly inapplicable concepts.

NOTES

1. I am indebted to Thomas Nagel, Saul Kripke, George Boolos, Donald Davidson, and David Levin for helpful comments on this paper, which is an extract from a longer paper in which the inapplicability of the concept "monster" and the inapplicability of the concept "perverted behavior" are argued for in quite similar (and hence mutually reinforcing) ways.

2. Some of these points are made by Thomas Nagel in "Sexual Perversion," *The Journal of Philosophy* 66, no. 1 (January 16, 1969): 5-17; reprinted herein, pp. 247-60.

3. The idea that unnaturalness consists in atypicality or unusualness is suggested by Stendhal in *On Love* (Garden City, N.Y.: Doubleday, 1947), p. 97.

4. For classic psychoanalytic use of the idea that unconscious beliefs can help repress certain fears, see, for example, Freud's "Splitting of the Ego in the Defensive Process," in his *Collected Papers*, vol. 5 (London: Hogarth Press, 1956), pp. 372-75; O. Fenichel's *The Psychoanalytic Theory of Neurosis* (New York: Norton, 1945), pp. 474-84; and also Fenichel's *Outline of Clinical Psychoanalysis* (New York: Norton, 1934), esp. pp. 13, 40, 52, 63, 260ff, 275f.

5. See her "On Morality," in J. Rachels, ed., *Moral Problems* (New York: Harper & Row, 1971), pp. 84-105.

6. Another problem with Nagel's model is that it leaves unexplained why so many people think of homosexuality as a perversion.

Robert Solomon

Sex and Perversion

Sexuality is often said to be one of the appetites, like thirst and hunger—an instinctual drive, the animal lust that invades the ego from the sub-conscious "it" and that is without logic, morality, scruples, and often with-out taste. But if sexuality were merely an appetite, it would be inexplicable that our lives should be so complicated, so threatened, so secretive and repressed, so ritualized and obsessed by a desire that has so little survival value and such dangers. Like the appetites, sexuality admits of failures of both deficiency and excess, although it is understandably only the former that is common cause for grievance. Sexuality also admits of infinite variations for the sake of sociability, elegance, taste, and diversion, once its most primitive demands have been met, and here again it resembles thirst and hunger. But sexuality, at least in this and many other societies, is thought to have a dimension that hunger and thirst surely lack, a moral and interpersonal dimension that is essential to our very conception of

sexuality. This is nowhere more evident than in the notion of "sexual perversion," for which there are no plausible analogues in the appetitive
realms of food and drink.[1]

PERVERSION

"Perversion" is an insidious concept. It presents itself as a straightforward descriptive term, but carries with it an undeniable connotation of
moral censure. To describe a person or an activity as perverse is not yet a
full-blown moral condemnation, for it need not entail that one *ought* not
to indulge in such activities. Yet such censure may be more offensive than
open moral condemnation, for it suggests that the person in question is
"sick" or an inferior human being or that the activity is depraved. Freud,
for example, while resisting all moral evaluation of perversions, does not
hesitate to characterize them as matters of "arrested development." Similarly, moralists find an easy refuge in such apparently descriptive and
quasi-moral categories, for it provides them with an arsenal of weapons for
self-righteous abuse of others that is made all the more effective by its
ability to disavow moral intent and to draw on the researches of science.
Accordingly, I want to begin by noticing how the very idea of "sexual
perversion" forces many of our attitudes about ourselves and our
relationships with other people to the defensive, and, in so doing, places
what we might call "straight sex" above criticism by making it the criterion by which other sexual activities are judged. What I should like to
argue, perhaps perversely, is that the very idea of "sexual perversion" is
itself perverse.

It is worth insisting from the outset that perversion has nothing to do
with statistics. Perversions cannot be identified or condemned just because
they happen to be activities that are engaged in by a small number of
people. But neither, then, can these same activities be defended on
statistical grounds. Kinsey's early figures, which suggest that 95 percent of
American adult males engage in "perverse" activities, prove nothing. Nor
does the current popularity of pornographic movies and the consequent
porno-business boom constitute a case for the defense or redefinition of
sexual perversion. It is a symptom of our logical incontinence that we so
typically appeal to statistics to defend our personal prejudices, when we
would reject the same appeal were the figures turned against us. The same
sexual activities that were once defined and attacked on the basis of their
infrequency are now typically defended by appeal to the large number of

"respectable" middle-class couples who enjoy them. But the fact that thousands of middle-aged, middle-class New Yorkers paid five dollars each to watch the swallowing of the giant genitalia in *Deep Throat* does not constitute a statistical or an economic defense of fellatio, or voyeurism, or pornography. But, insofar as perversion is a quasi-moral concept, the defensive traditionalists are in the right; the topic of perversion is not subject to argument by numbers. It could be, in fact, that "straight sex," once we get straight about sex, could itself be a "perversion" of sexuality.

"Sexual perversion" indicates deviation from a norm, but not from a statistical norm. Perversion is an *abuse* of an established function, a corruption, not simply a diversion or a deviation. Sexuality, like all human activities, serves some natural purpose, some end that we can recognize as a reason for putting up with considerable anxiety and aggravation in a lifelong rabbit-race that only occasionally meets our expectations and is too infrequently satisfied at all for most people. It is the *importance* of sexuality in our lives that cries out for explanation, and such explanations are typically in terms of the fact that sexuality is a "natural" activity, that it is an instinct, part of our animal nature, a biological need, and so on. Accordingly, the idea of sexual perversion is derivative of this idea of natural purpose, and perverse activities are those that deviate from this purpose taken as a norm. Sexual perversion is acting at cross-purposes with nature. But then, what is "natural sex"?

It is fair enough to try to provide an account of "natural sex" by an appeal to "nature." And sex does serve an obvious biological function, that of reproduction (or, moving from the biological to the pious, "procreation"). As such, not only human adults but animals of most kinds and many plants engage in sexual activity or, at least, are "sexual beings" in a familiar technical sense. Natural sex, accordingly, is that which aims at reproduction (although there is a serious ambiguity here of whether it is nature that aims or rather those engaged in sexual activity who aim at reproduction).

I take it to be beyond argument that human sexuality is more than this. In fact, one might argue that most human sexual activity not only is not aimed at reproduction but is practiced *in spite of* the threat of reproducing. (This is true even of those who would argue that contraception and abortion are wrong.) This pervasive interest in nonreproductive sexuality is not a matter of widespread sexual perversion, although doubtless there are still those who would argue so. Rather it is due to the very nature of sexuality itself. Arguments to the contrary, whether derived from personal neuroses or high-level theological doctrines (or both), exemplify a profound disregard for the realities of human life, and reality is all that interests us here. Our starting point will be that human sexuality has its own "natural purposes," its own "nature," apart from any *further* purposes attributed to our creator, and apart from any biological function of increasing the numbers of an already too numerous natural kind.

NATURAL SEX

What is "natural sex"? It seems reasonable to look to nature for an account, but it is clear from the history of the philosophical concept of "nature" that this is not what has been intended. The concept of "nature" is our inheritance from Aristotle and then from the Enlightenment, and as such it betrays the familiar sophistries of those pervasive forms of Western thinking. When the philosophes of eighteenth-century France and their counterparts in England and America appealed to "nature," it was rarely biological nature that they had in mind. Rather, "nature" served as a particularly solid and incontrovertible court of appeal, beyond the reach of the dogmas and practices of particular traditional and typically outdated societies. However, "nature" is not the natural world, but man's "natural reason." "Nature" is what is rational, not what is biological, and has a decided moral edge. When philosophers sought a "natural religion" or "natural justice," for example, they were not appealing to a "return to nature," to nature worship or animal faith, nor to the "law of the jungle." They were appealing to *reason*, to rational faith and rational law. And so, too, "natural sex," as part of this tradition, is not a call for bestiality or rear-entry intercourse, but to "rational sex." Thus we should not be surprised that most talk of "natural sex" carries with it a decided moral overtone. And, since sex is generally considered to be a paradigm of *ir*rational human activity, we should not be surprised that "rational sex" tends to emerge as *minimal* sex.

Even after sexuality has been severed from its reproductive consequences, the obsession with quick, efficient heterosexual intercourse—the two-minute emissionary missionary male-superior ejaculation service[2] —remains. Even with the traditional biological and theological arguments defused, the conclusion—the equation of male-evacuation lust with sexuality—persists.[3] Whenever the appeal to "natural sexuality" arises, it is necessary to balance the account by reference to the perverse wisdom of the notorious Marquis de Sade, who was a genius at twisting "arguments from design" to justify his own tastes. He argued and profusely illustrated the proposition that any possible human sensuous activity, whether buggery or impassioned murder, could not help but be "natural." Against the horror of the pious concerning the "wasting of seed," in Onanism and masturbation, de Sade wryly comments that nature herself seems to have arranged generously for such "spillage." Against the "natural design" arguments for genital intercourse, de Sade argues with vengeance—turning the Enlightenment against itself—that the relative sizes of the various apertures and protrusions of the human body could only have been so fittingly designed in order to be employed accordingly. If "nature" is to be the standard, argues de Sade, we can find much in nature that is cruel and destructive, surprisingly little that is truly creative; and so cruelty and rape are at least as "natural" as reproductive intercourse. Of course there is a second thread of argument that pervades de Sade's thesis—that this indifference of the universe and nature is an outrage to us. Much as Camus was to argue a similar thesis above the belt more recently, de Sade argues that Nature's indifference to waste and cruelty is a cause for contemptuous assault and scorn on our part. But if the arguments seem at odds with each other, the upshot is the same—any act humanly possible is as natural, or as unnatural, as any other.

FREUD'S REINTERPRETATION OF SEXUALITY

The breakdown of this "rational" and quasi-moral, pious view of sex owes much to Sigmund Freud, the single most important theoretician in the modern fight for sexual liberation.[4] It was Freud, primarily in his "Three Contributions to the Theory of Sex," who changed our conception of sexuality from reproduction to sex-for-its-own-sake, to personal satisfaction. (Although it is necessary to stress that Freud took the new concept, as well as the old one, to be a *biological*, and thereby a "natural," conception.) It was Freud who argued that sexual activity is aimed at release of tension or "discharge" (which he called, misleadingly, "pleasure") and as such aims at no further goals. So conceived, the paradigm sexual activity might be thought of not in terms of heterosexual intercourse but in terms of scratching an itch. Of course the activity that releases tension also serves to increase the tension to be released (the greater the "pleasure"). So conceived, genital sex is but a single possibility for sexual activity, based on the *contingency* that the genitals of an adult generally provide the most prominent erogenous zone; that is, it itches or can be made to itch more than any other place on the body and thus feels better when appropriately scratched. Freud's theory, although based on painstaking empirical observations, clearly marks a conceptual or philosophical revolution as well as a scientific one. According to this conception of sex, heterosexual intercourse loses both its logically and its biologically privileged position in the repertoire of human sexual response. It is no longer *logically* privileged because sex is now conceived in terms of discharge (or "pleasure"), and it is at most a contingent fact (and probably not even that) that most people gain the greatest release of tension (or "pleasure") from intercourse alone. It is no longer biologically privileged because sex as sex is no longer conceived in terms of the further purposes it serves but rather in its own terms. It should be noted that sexuality, so conceived, is no longer "an aspect of," but is the contrary of, reproductive sex: it is defined as an activity that, as sex, has no further aims. Accordingly, intercourse with the explicit intention to conceive children is no longer pure sex, but sex plus something else.

We might also make note of the fact that sexuality, so conceived, can be used to serve other, ulterior purposes as well. In fact sex aimed at reproduction is probably the least frequent, and also philosophically the least interesting, of the varieties of "impure sex," that is, sexuality not for its own sake, sex for pleasure. People use sex as an expression of power, or as an expression of impotence (the one often parading as the other), as a way of going to sleep, as a way of getting even, as a way of getting ahead in careers, as a way of distracting themselves, as a way of demeaning themselves, and so on. On Freud's account, these various extrasexual aims, however commonly they might be conjoined with sexual desire and activity, are not themselves sexual, and sexuality is not to be identified with any of them. Once sexuality is so conceived, the road is opened to a new interpretation of its extent and domain. Under the old pious and puritanical conception, sex was for strictly ulterior purposes, and pleasure was at most a by-product: excess pleasure was condemnable as "unnatural." And under the old conception, sexual activity was limited to being a means to an end. Its paradigm accordingly was male "evacuation lust" (coupled with female submissiveness). A sexual perversion, then, was any alteration in this basic function, even prolongation beyond the minimum requisite time for ejaculation of the male, any alteration in position, and needless to say, any attempt or desire on the part of either for equal enjoyment on the part of the female. It is with Freud that this horror story loses its grounds, for sex as release of tension or "pleasure" or "satisfaction" is not related to any particular social or sexual roles, nor aimed at serving any function beyond the release of tension (which, Freud also realizes, is intentionally created for the sake of releasing it), and so the old restrictions melt away. Sexual release need not be through intercourse alone, nor need it even involve intercourse; it need not be heterosexual, nor need it even involve more than a single person. Here is the "Copernican revolution" of our sexual liberation. It always strikes me as unfair, if not insulting or embarrassing, that Freud is so often dismissed for his sexual conservatism and blamed for enforcing the attitudes that have encouraged male repression and female oppression. But Freud is the revolutionary who, like most revolutionaries, was unable to free himself of the old prejudices, now seen as weaknesses, that he was instrumental in overcoming. Without Freud, the questions that now appear as accusations against him could not even be asked. It is with him that former "sexual perversions," including enjoyment, can now claim legitimacy as full-blooded, "natural" sexual activities.[5]

It is well known how Freud extended the scope of sexuality far beyond its traditional limitations. From his account of sexuality as "release of tension," we can easily see how he did this, and how it became possible for him to account for the rich empirical findings of child psychology with his revised and expanded notion of sexuality. As release of tension, oral and anal sexuality are literally sexual although they need not involve any use or association with the genitals or with reproductive functions. Oral sexuality, for example, is sexuality because appropriate stimulation of the lips, tongue, and mucous membranes of the mouth is "satisfying." Yet oral sexuality may be distinguished from other forms of oral satisfaction, notably eating and drinking, by the fact that it appears as an end in itself (even if, as Freud insists, the erogenous functions of the mouth may be consequent to associations with the satisfactions of eating). In other words, oral sexuality, like genital sexuality, must be (on Freud's account) satisfaction of an autonomous sort, not satisfaction of anything else. Yet, again, this is not to say that it cannot be used to achieve some further goal, nor is it to say that sexual satisfaction cannot accompany some other satisfaction. Eating might be conceived as a sexual activity, but not as a pure sexual activity, such as, for example, thumb-sucking or pipe-smoking. Again, the new conception of sexuality is release of pleasure for its own sake. It follows that any part of the human body has an equal biological and logical claim as an "erogenous zone" and that any human activity has an equal claim as a "sexual activity."

Freud's own account of sexuality becomes inconsistent precisely at the moment he abandons this radical conclusion and returns to the primacy of evacuation lust, supported by questionable genetic arguments that suggest that all the sexual perversions, although admittedly "normal," are cases of regression and "arrested development." But Freud's own reconception of sexuality undermines both evacuation lust and his quasi-moral conception of the maturity of pleasures. There is no a priori or scientific way to determine the maturity or preferability of one erogenous zone or activity over another. (Again, statistics and even universal practices have no weight here.) Evacuation lust and heterosexual intercourse might themselves be conceived as an early stage in sexual development at which the bourgeosie of turn-of-the-century Vienna had become fixated.

It is clear that Freud's account of sexuality and sexual perversion is inadequate as it stands, as well as inconsistent. If there were no limitation whatever on the scope of sexual activities, then every motivated human activity, insofar as it released tension or gave pleasure, would count as sexual. But this "pansexualism" is clearly nonsense. Freud himself continually repudiated it, even if his own position seemed to commit him to it nevertheless. Pansexualism has been best described by John Barth:

> The dance of sex: If one had no other reason for choosing to subscribe to Freud, what could be more charming than to believe that the whole vaudeville of the world, the entire dizzy circus of history, is but a fancy mating dance? That dictators burn Jews and businessmen vote Republican, that helmsmen steer ships and ladies play bridge, that girls study grammar and boys engineering all at behest of the Absolute Genital? When the synthesizing mood is upon one, what is more soothing than to assert that this one simple yen of humankind, poor little coitus, alone gives rise to cities and monasteries, paragraphs and poems, foot races and battle tactics, metaphysics and hydroponics, trade unions and universities? Who would not delight in telling some extragalactic tourist, "On our planet, sir, males and females copulate. Moreover, they enjoy copulating. But for various reasons they cannot do this whenever, wherever, and with whomever they choose. Hence all this running around that you observe. Hence the world"? A therapeutic notion! [6]

But even if any activity *might* be a sexual activity in an appropriate (that is, a sexual) context, it is surely false that every motivated human activity *is* in fact sexual. If sexuality were merely release of tension for its own sake, the paradigm of sexuality would remain, as I suggested, the scratching of an itch, and if that itch happened to involve the genitals, sexuality would take as its paradigm masturbation. But this concept of sexuality, which agrees with the traditional conceptions in accepting as its paradigm the sexual "union" of two people, surely is not our concept. And, given Freud's account, the appropriate question is why we bother, given the enormous amount of effort and the continuous threats to our egos and our health, to attempt to engage in sex mutually instead of in solitude and in the safety and convenience of our own rooms. On this account it would seem that our sexual paradigm ought to be masturbation, and sexual release with other people an unnecessary complication. And before he backslides into heterosexual evacuation lust, Freud appears to hold just this view, insofar as sexual release to bodily tension remains for him the "primary process." But clearly our sexual paradigms are to be found elsewhere, in our attraction for and enjoyment of other people, in what Freud calls the "secondary processes." According to Freud it is not just the body that seeks release, but the "psychic apparatus," and the tension from which it suffers is not due to "inner" tensions alone, but to relations and identifications with sexual "objects," that is, other people.[7]

In insisting that the paradigm of sexuality involves a relationship with other people, let me quickly point out that this is as far as can be from the pious linkage of sex and love. One may love another person with whom he or she is sexually involved, but there are any number of attitudes he or she might take toward the person to whom he or she is sexually attracted, among which, unfortunately, hate, fear, resentment, anger, jealousy, insecurity, mastery, and competition are probably far more common and more powerful than the rare and delicate threads of love and respect.

Freud's revolutionary breakthrough, though incomplete, was also too radical. In focusing our attention on the autonomous tension-releasing function of sexuality he freed sexuality from its former religious and moral restrictions, but at the expense of completely cutting it off from all other human activities. This new-found autonomy of sexuality, the source of our sexual freedom, has now become our main sexual problem. As more of us enjoy more sexual activity, sex itself has become less satisfying and more "meaningless." We now have to see once again that sexual tension and its release is not the whole of sex, nor even its major aspect. Rather it is Freud's "secondary" aspect of sexuality, the "psychical" aspect, that explains its nature and its overwhelming importance in our affairs. For sex is primarily for us a way of relating to other people and only secondarily and in a primitive way a matter of release of "sexual tension."

The belief that sexuality is primarily a matter of enjoyment has become commonplace since Freud; in fact it is often suggested that sexual activity is the closest we can come to "pure pleasure." But this emphasis on pleasure, like Freud's stress on release of tension (these were equivalent for him), fails to explain the enormous stress we put on these activities. (Man is basically *not* a pleasure-seeking animal.) It fails to explain why sex for us is *essentially* with other people, why our own enjoyment in sex is so bound up with the pleasure of someone else. Aristotle, in his attack on the hedonists of his day, insisted that pleasure was not an activity itself but rather an accompaniment of gratifying activity. In sex, we are not satisfied by our enjoyment, but rather we enjoy ourselves because we are satisfied. But then, once again, what is the activity that we satisfy in sexuality?

The problem still with us is the predominantly male paradigm of "evacuation lust," once rationalized as the "natural" means to reproduction, now justified by appeal to the "natural" enjoyment it involves. Sexuality typically involves discharge of tension (both physical and psychological), but Freud's "primary process" is not the essence of sexuality, and evacuation lust is not its paradigm. One might say that evacuation lust plays a role in sex similar to swallowing in wine tasting. It is typically the "end" of the activity, but surely neither its goal nor its essence (it is even frowned upon in professional circles). I take our obsession with evacuation lust, in the post-Freudian as well as pre-Freudian mentality, to be a symptom of our sensual and aesthetic deprivation, like the lusty and excessive need of a "wino" who swallows without tasting a glass of delicate white Burgundy. If there is a category of sexual perversion, of abusive and demeaning sex, what often passes for "normal" or "straight" sex surely deserves a place on the list. And what is essential to sex will remain hidden from us so long as we remain fixated on the wonders of the genital orgasm.

One might suggest that what properly characterizes sexuality is not the narrow conception of pleasure entailed by the evacuation-lust model but rather the broader conception of pleasure as sensuousness. And, of course, this would be reasonable enough. It reinstates Freud's important demand that sexuality may involve any part of or the whole body, as well as the genitals. And sexuality, whatever else it may be, is surely a bodily conception. (One may be forced to stretch this demand slightly to include purely verbal or visual sexual activities—for example: telephone sex, anonymous or not; and pornography, where the body is only referred to or represented rather than actually touched. But I think it is somewhat of a tautology that no desire or activity can be sexual if it does not involve the body as a center of focus. I take it that this is what Sartre intends by his awkward phrase, "incarnation of oneself as flesh.") Which parts of the body are paradigmatically sexual varies considerably, of course, from society to society, and so do the roles of the various nontactile senses in sexual activities. In our society female breasts have acquired a somewhat bizarrely exaggerated sexual role; the sense of smell, a mysteriously diminished and even taboo sexual sense. Because of this variation it is not easy to distinguish those bodily activities that are essentially sexual from those that are not. Wrestling and dancing, acrobatics and athletics, for example, involve considerable bodily contact; yet we would not want to say that they are in every instance sexual. Teen-age petting and dancing may differ from these other activities only in minute details, yet be clearly sexual. And the wrestling scene from *Women in Love*, for example, is surely more than "symbolically" sexual. A furtive glance across the room may be highly sexual in spite of the fact that it involves the most minute movements. We may agree without controversy that sexuality is essentially physical. Yet bodily focus is not sufficient to distinguish sexuality. What else would be sufficient?

An additional component of sexuality, also to be found in Freud, is tension and the expectation of its release. "Arousal," on this account,[8] is not merely a preliminary to sexuality but part of its essence. (Even boring sex is exciting, insofar as it is sex at all.) The fact that excitement is essential to sexuality explains how it is that many people find danger "highly sexual" and why many sexual relations can be improved if they are made a bit more daring or dangerous (short of terror, which understandably kills sexual enthusiasm). The same equation allows us to understand the confused medley of reactions we find to cinematic violence. It also allows us to understand one of the apparent anomalies of our sexual behavior, the fact that our most satisfying sexual encounters are often with strangers, where there are strong elements of tension—fear, insecurity, guilt, anticipation. Conversely, sex may be least satisfying with those whom we love and know well and whose habits and reactions are extremely well known to us. It ought to strike us as odd that we can be upsettingly attracted to a stranger who is not particularly attractive, who shares little in common with us, and who presents us with an evident set of personal and perhaps moral and medical threats. At the same time, married couples who find each other most attractive, compatible, nonthreatening, and comfortable often find intercourse more of a routine or a repetitive ritual, or as evacuation lust, to be completed efficiently and without fanfare, or perhaps as a battleground, with only a minimum of sexual desire or excitement.

But tension, arousal, and excitement, together with bodily sensuality, still add up to something much less than sexuality. Enthusiastic acrobatics or dancing is still less than sexual, and a gentle touch on a finger or cheek cannot be understood simply in the above terms. Moreover, the concepts of "tension," "arousal," and "excitement" tell us far less than they might at first appear to. We might think that such tension is uniquely sexual, but it is not. Arousal is arousal, whether it is found in reactions of fear, anger, hatred, anxiety, love, or desire. As far as excitement itself is concerned, making love, dancing, a cold shower, a Librium, a fistfight, or a two-mile jog might be equally effective. What makes tension, arousal, and excitement sexual is the nature of its object, what the tension is *about*. And it is not mere sensuality that is aroused, and it is not merely a human body (one's own or someone else's) that excites us. But to understand this "something more" that is essential to sexuality we shall have to leave the safe and well-explored confines of sensuousness and the variety of bodily activities and modes of coupling. We need a new theory in which sensuality and bodily activities and excitement might be mentioned in passing, but only as "but of course. . . ."

SEX AS LANGUAGE

Sexuality is primarily a means of communicating with other people, a way of talking to them, of expressing our feelings about ourselves and them. It is essentially a language, a body language, in which one can express gentleness and affection, anger and resentment, superiority and dependence far more succinctly than would be possible verbally, where expressions are unavoidably abstract and often clumsy. If sexuality is a means of communication, it is not surprising that it is *essentially* an activity performed with other people. And, if it is our best means to express what are often our dominant and difficult-to-verbalize feelings and relationships, it is not surprising that sexuality is one of the most powerful forces in our lives.

It is also evident, though not obvious, that any bodily contact and any human activity, including genital contact and the physical activity of intercourse, both might and might not be sexual. (It is difficult, but not impossible, for gentle genital contact and intercourse not to be sexual, just as it is difficult, as Wittgenstein said, to say "It is cold" in English and not mean by that that it is cold. But in a suitable context, for example, speaking in code, one might mean almost anything by "It is cold." Similarly, in suitably asexual contexts, for example, on a movie set or in a Masters and Johnson experiment, genital contact and intercourse may not be sexual, for then they would not be plausible instances of body language.)

There are other body languages, of course, and most of them can be more or less distinguished from sexual body language. Aggression, for example, while often sharing a body vocabulary with sexuality, is surely distinct. Fear is also expressed in body language, sharing some of its vocabulary with sexuality, but its bodily expression is not sexual as such. Defense, insecurity, domination, and self-confidence, and any number of various desires (including particular sensuous pleasures) are also expressed in body language. Sex is basically a nonverbal language that takes bodily movements, postures, and sensations as its form, whatever content it expresses. Now, in a sense there is but one body language, since we have but one body; but there can be different body languages, much as there are different verbal languages, in different societies. Edgar Rice Burroughs imagines a people who laugh to express sadness and cry to express amusement. More within reality, Chinese open their eyes to express anger, whereas we narrow them; so we can imagine, and find, peoples whose sexual expressions vary considerably from ours. Body languages must be publicly learned and will vary between different groups, although there are obviously biological restrictions that supply the depth grammar of all human body languages. Not all body language is sexual, and not all people need have a sexual language. (There are societies in which intercourse serves a purely reproductive or ritualistic function, or even a la Freud, the pure function of providing pleasure. Such a society, however, ours is not.

The basic vocabulary of body language is the gesture, which might be an activity but is usually an expression or a stance. The gesture is the bodily equivalent of a sentence. Particular movements (for example, the lifting of an arm) and touches have meaning only as part of a gesture.[9] Body languages, like verbal languages, are born and grow in a societal context, as means of communication. They are, to use J. L. Austin's term, "performances" (the notion of "constative" or "descriptive" makes only minimal sense here), and they are learned and have meaning only in context. Of course, once one learns the body language, one can employ it, so to speak, alone. But in body language, as in verbal language, there can be no strictly private language. (Autoeroticism, far from being our sexual paradigm, is at best considered a borderline case.) Having learned the body language, one who travels for the sake of "adventure" to a paradisical island or to a radically different society will be grossly misunderstood. Or one can conscientiously, as does a dancer, learn new expressions and new forms of expressive elegance. But one first needs a language to vary, a given language in order to learn another. Body language, again like verbal language, is the realization of a capacity that is not equally shared by everyone. Some people are inarticulate, even retarded, others brilliant and creative. Sexual "losers" are often people who suffer more from bodily inarticulateness than verbal inability, and impotence is more often a matter of aphasia than physical damage. There are those whose body language is forceful without being either articulate or graceful. And there are those who, perhaps forceful, perhaps not, are elegant and even creative in their use of body language. An athlete might be forceful, but not articulate, and in spite of his skills of physical enunciation and projection and his large bodily vocabulary, have nothing to say. A dancer might be highly elegant, but ultimately be a solipsist. Most people, needless to say, here as in speech, know only those features of the language that are most common, most easily articulated, least committal, and least personal. Some people, including dancers by profession, articulate their body language with such perfection that every gesture is an exact and perfect expression.

Whatever else sexuality might be and for whatever purposes it might be used or abused, it is first of all language. When spoken it tends to result in pregnancy, in scandal, in jealousy and divorce (the "perlocutionary" effects of language, in Austin's terminology). It is a language that, like verbal language, but sometimes more effectively, can be used to manipulate people, to offend and to ingratiate oneself with them. It can be enjoyable, not just on account of its phonetics, which are neither enjoyable nor meaningful in themselves, but because of *what* is said. One enjoys not just the tender caress but the message it carries; and one welcomes a painful thrust or bite not because of masochism but because of the meaning, in context, that it conveys. Most sexologists, one might add, commit the McLuhanesque fallacy of confusing the medium with the message.

Sexuality, while having a certain structure that confines it, can take any number of forms. It is a language we first learn on the borderlines of sex, in shaking hands, standing with our hands on our hips, letting a cigarette droop from our lips in Junior High School, scratching our forehead or our thighs in public, looking at each other, kissing, smiling, walking, and eventually, petting and making love. Like dancing, sexuality is an extension and fine development of everyday movements, capable of open-ended refinement and individual variation, as poetry of the body. But

where dancing takes its audience to be anonymous and its message impersonal, sexuality is always personal and deeply revealing. One might argue
that sexuality is much less refined, much less self-consciously an "art"
than dancing; but this, I would counter, is a mark of our general vulgarity
and lack of self-consciousness in all things important. Nothing can or
ought to be more human an art form than intimate communication.

We can now see what is wrong with "pansexualism," the idea that all
human activities are sexual. Not all human activities are linguistic activities, for not all activities are intended to communicate or express either desire or interpersonal feelings. Athletic activity, acrobatics, and much
dancing, for example, may be concerned with the precise performance of
the body, but those activities themselves are not intended to communicate
or express personal desire or feelings. And of course there are many
activities that are communicative and expressive that are not essentially
sexual, for example, writing poetry or philosophy, signaling a right-hand
turn, or sending a telegram. But any human activity *can* be sexual insofar
as it involves the use of the body as an expression of interpersonal desire.
(Stances and postures need not involve touching. Consider, for example, a
"provocative" appearance.) But unlike verbal language, body language is
not well adapted to addressing large audiences and consequently can only
appear vulgar when removed from a more intimate setting. Similarly, sex,
as language, is predominantly reciprocal. And that is why mutual touch
and intercourse must remain our paradigm.

SEXUAL PERVERSION REINTERPRETED

If sexuality is a form of language that can be used to express almost anything, it follows that the use of sexuality admits of any number of creative as well as forced variations. As a language it also admits of breaches in
comprehension, and it is here that we can locate what little is left of our
conception of "sexual perversion." It should now be clear that this is not a
moral term but more a logical category, a breach of comprehensibility.
Accordingly, it would be advisable to drop the notion of perversion altogether and content ourselves with "sexual incompatibility" or "sexual
misunderstanding." It is not always easy to distinguish abuses of the
language from abuses expressed by the language, or to separate nonsense
from sophistry, sexual fanaticism from sexual "politics." It is not always
clear what is to count as a literal expression, a metaphorical usage, an
imaginative expression, a pun, a solecism, or a bad joke. And so what

might be taken as incomprehensibility and perversion by a sexual conservative would be taken as poetry or pun by someone else. Perversion, then, is a communication breakdown; it may have general guidelines but ultimately rests in the context of the bodily mutual understanding of the people involved. Quite the contrary of a moral or quasi-moral category, "sexual incompatibility" is strictly relativized, within the language, to the particular people involved.

If sexuality is essentially a language, it follows that masturbation, while not a perversion, is a deviation and not, as Freud thought, the primary case. Masturbation is essentially speaking to oneself. But not only children, lunatics, and hermits speak to themselves; so do poets and philosophers. And so masturbation might, in different contexts, count as wholly different extensions of language. With Freud, we would have to distinguish masturbation as autoeroticism from masturbation as narcissism—the first being more like muttering to oneself, the latter more like self-praise; the first being innocent and childlike, the latter potentially either pathetic or selfish and self-indulgent. Masturbation is not "self-abuse," as we were once taught, but it is, in an important sense, self-denial. It represents an inability or a refusal to say what one wants to say, going through the effort of expression without an audience, like writing to someone and then putting the letter in a drawer. If sexuality is a language, then it is primarily communicative. Autoeroticism, therefore, along with Freud's primary processes, is not primary at all, but conceptually secondary or derivative, similar to a young child's early attempts at langauge, which can be interpreted as phonemes only within the context of the language his parents already speak. But any langauge, once learned, can be spoken privately. Masturbation is this secondary, private use of sexual language—minimal rather than primary, the Archimedean standpoint of sex, essential as an ultimate retreat, but empty and without content. Masturbation is the sexual equivalent of a Cartesian soliloquy.

It is clear that between two people almost any activity *can* be fully sexual when it is an attempt to communicate mutual feelings through bodily gestures, touches, and movements. But this requires serious qualification. Expressions of domination and dependence are among the most primitive vocabulary items in our body language. But these may go beyond mere expressions and gestures to become a kind of "acting out"; and there is a difference, if only of degree, between gestures and full-blooded actions. When expressions of domination and dependence turn into actions, they become sadism and masochism, respectively. If these feelings are not complementary, they can only be interpreted as a communication breakdown, as sexual incompatibility. When sadistic actions are not expected, they are to sexuality as real bullets in a supposedly prop gun are to the stage. Again, the possible extension of sexual language depends mutually upon the participants. The subtlety and explicitness of a language depends upon the perceptivity of the conversationalists. For the articulate and the quick, sadism and masochism may consist of an apparently minor change in sexual positions, a slight but degrading change of posture that is ample expression of mutually negative or hostile feelings or of complementary dominance and submission. For the more dense or uninitiated, such expression may require outright infliction of pain or discomfort, a painful pinch or punch. In many cases we might want to say that, as Billy Budd was inarticulate, and violent as a result, sadism and masochism may be matters of inarticulateness and lack of interpersonal perception as well as products of the hostile feelings to be expressed.

There is no reason, apart from traditional squeamishness, to suppose that the employment of parts of the body other than the genitals in sexuality is perverse or need result in a breakdown of communication. Not only are these not perversions in themselves, but it may well be that those who would call them perversions are somewhat perverse themselves. The cry of perversion with regard to body language is very much like that of censorship with regard to the written word. To judge something tasteless is often itself a sign of bad taste, as in the case of the judges who banned *Ulysses* or *Lady Chatterley's Lover*. They did not prove abuses of language by the authors they condemned but rather, by attempting to castrate the language and expel some of its finest moments, displayed themselves as illiterates. Similarly, sexuality conceived as a language of intimacy and feeling that calls for ever new variation and inventiveness has as its worst violators those who, unimaginative and illiterate themselves, attempt to force others to accept their limited and impoverished vocabulary. But it might also be admitted, though it rarely is, that the common sexual variations are not for the sake of variety and pleasure alone. Oral sex and anal sex, for example, carry unavoidable expressions of domination and subservience, though these surely need not be considered degrading (as they are treated in some of Norman Mailer's writings) and may be exceptionally expressive of tenderness and trust.

Vulgarity, in this as in any art form, can be a charm in small doses but an offense when overdone. It is because sex is a language that demands subtlety and artfulness that over-frankness and vulgarity are, if not perversions, at least gross abuses of the language, as very bad poetry might still be considered poetry. This explains, for example, why overt propositions and subway exhibitionism are generally offensive, which is a mystery if one considers sex, as most people do, one of the "appetites." There are, for example, no acceptable sexual expressions that are parallel to the straightforward expression of hunger in "Let's eat" or "When is dinner?" or "Dinner is ready." Eating, of course, can be much more than the satisfaction of hunger; it can become an elegant social (and thereby also, sometimes, sexual) activity as well. But sexuality, far from being the "animal" instinct in us, appears only in those human activities where considerable refinement is possible. Sexuality permits of vulgarity only because it is itself a matter of refinement. It is therefore not at all one of those physiological functions that well-meaning sexual pedants often describe. Thus blatant sexual propositions and subway exhibitionism are offensive, not because they deviate from some "normal sexual aim" (the former, at least, being an unusually direct approach to the "normal sexual aim"), but because they are vulgar, the equivalent of an antipoetry poet who writes an entire poem consisting of a single vulgar word, or a comedian who, unable to handle condensation and understatement, has to spell out his obscene jokes explicitly. Similarly, sexuality lies in subtlety. There is sometimes nothing less appealing or satisfying, even when one is in a fully sexual mood, than a too-straightforward sexual encounter, "unadorned" by preliminary conversation—both verbal and bodily.

To other so-called perversions the same considerations apply, and the degree of the breakdown in communication is not always clear. Sexual activities themselves are not perverted; people are perverted. Fetishism in general might be a product of stupidity, poor vocabulary, or fear of communicating, but it might be extreme ingenuity in the face of an impoverished sexual field. A voyeur might be someone with nothing to say, but the voyeur might count as a good listener in those cases in which he makes himself known. Sexual *in*versions, as Freud calls them, are not deviations of *sex* (according to the theory developed here, homosexuality is not such an inversion), but relations with children or animals would be like carrying on an adult conversation with a child who does not have the vocabulary to understand or a dog who nods dumb agreement to every proposal. Multiple sexual encounters are surely not in themselves perversions; quite the contrary, languages are not designated for exclusive two-party use. But it is clear that such multiple relationships, like trying to hold several conversations at once or working on several books at the same time, can be

distracting, confusing, and ultimately disastrous. There is some difference
—but only in manageability—between Don Juanism, or serial multiplicity,
on one hand, and group sex, on the other. In the first case one risks carrying over from one conversation gestures that are appropriate to another,
but such relationships offer the compensation and reward of being always
fresh and novel, without the immediate danger of falling into the bodily
equivalent of a Harold Pinter conversational rut. (Here, too, we can appreciate the attractiveness of strangers over those whom we already know
well.) Group sex, on the other hand, makes the matter of gesture and
response immensely complicated, and while it creates the serious danger
of simultaneous incoherent polylogues, it offers the rare possibility of linguistic forms unavailable with fewer voices, much as a larger group of
musicians, after protracted training, can create movements impossible for
smaller groups and soloists. Therefore, whether or not Don Juanism and
group sex are satisfying depends, as before, not on the nature of the
activity but on the skill and performance of the participants.

There is, however, still room for a concept of sexual perversion. It
does not involve any deviation of "sexual aim or object," as Freud insisted,
nor does it involve any special deviation in sexual activity, peculiar parts of
the body, special techniques, or personality quirks. As a language, sex has
at least one possible perversion: the nonverbal equivalent of lying, or *insincerity*. And, as an art, sex has a possible perversion in *vulgarity*. Given the
conception of sexuality as the art of body language that I have defended,
we are forced to see the brutal perverseness of our conception of sexuality,
in which insincerity and vulgarity, artificial sexual "roles" and "how-to"
technology still play such an essential and generally accepted part.

NOTES

1. Thomas Nagel, in "Sexual Perversion," *The Journal of Philosophy* 66 (January 16, 1969), reprinted herein, pp. 247-60, suggests some such analogues, for example, smearing an omelet on one's face. But however rude, vulgar, or humorous
such a performance might be, it surely does not display the moral repugnance that
sadism and pederasty are commonly agreed to have.

2. Cf. John Barth, *Giles Goat-Boy* (New York: Fawcett World Library, 1974),
p. 235: "there is no term for 'service' that is not obscene, clinical, legalistic,
ironic, euphemistic, or periphrastic." For the sake of brevity, I will henceforth
refer to this obsession, borrowing a term from a poem by D. H. Lawrence, as
"evacuation lust." From "Sex and Trust," in *Collected Poetry*, vol. 2, p. 197.

3. What makes many of Norman Mailer's literary sexual exploits so offensive is not an excessive sense of perversity so much as an enduring and brutally unsubtle obsession with biology and male-dominated traditional "evacuation lust." See, for example, *An American Dream*, chap. 1.

4. Scientifically, Freud owed much to his predecessors, Krafft-Ebing and Havelock Ellis, among others. But it was Freud who used these findings so dramatically, not only to increase our knowledge but to change our very conception of sexuality.

5. Freud lays the groundwork for the argument that any sexual activity is "natural," but he is still caught in Enlightment and Victorian morality. It must be admitted that Freud's notion of "discharge" bears too strong a resemblance to a male perspective of sexuality. He does fall into embarrassing lapses in commenting on "the cultural stunting and . . . the conventional reticence and insincerity of women," and there are telling metaphors ("piercing the tunnel from both sides") that betray a defensive male posture. Regarding intercourse, he is still caught in the paradigm of "evacuation lust," and considers as perversions "anatomical transgressions of the bodily regions destined for sexual union or a lingering at the intermediary relations to the sexual object which should normally be rapidly passed, on the way to the definite sexual aim." With regard to his own revolutionary thought Freud must be considered something of a frightened reactionary. But we should give full weight to Lou Andreas-Salome's comment in her *Freud Journal*: ". . . confronted by a human being who impresses us as great should we not be moved rather than chilled by the knowledge that he might have attained his greatness only through his frailties" (p. 163).

6. *End of the Road* (Garden City, N.Y.: Doubleday, 1967), p. 93.

7. Of course, fetishists are attracted primarily to people parts, rather than to people as such. But a moment's reflection is sufficient to realize that fetishists are attracted to people parts—a breast, a calf, or even a shoe—just because they are in fact parts of people to whom they are attracted. Of course, there may be persons who are in fact attracted to people parts that are detached, but we would not consider them fetishists or perverts, but rather ghouls.

8. Nagel takes such "arousal" as central to his analysis, too.

9. Cf. Gottlob Frege on words and sentences in, for example, "On Sense and Nominatum," in *Readings in Philosophical Analysis*, ed. Herbert Feigl and Wilfred Sellars (New York: Appleton-Century-Crofts, 1949), pp. 85-102.

Joseph Margolis

The Question of Homosexuality

The psychiatric discussion of homosexuality is at the present time pretty
much in a shambles. The reasons happen to be largely conceptual, and
expose, more effectively than any mere polemic, the extent to which our
moral prejudices masquerade as medicine. Needless to say, the earnest
quackery focused on one putative medical category is bound to manifest
itself in others.

Early in December 1973 the board of trustees of the American Psychiatric Association voted to discontinue listing "homosexuality per se" as
a "psychiatric disorder," defining it instead as a "sexual orientation disturbance."[1] The board did not by its action alter the classification of
homosexuality in the American Psychiatric Association's *Diagnostic and
Statistical Manual of Mental Disorders (DSM-2)*.[2] There it is classified as
a distinct mental disorder. It has been so classified by the profession for
about one hundred years. The second edition of the manual introduced a
good number of diagnostic changes in the original 1952 publication

(*DSM-1*), but none affect the declassification of sexual disorders,[3] in spite of the fact that other professional bodies have been actively advocating the removal of homosexuality as an illness for some time—notably, the National Association for Mental Health and the Group for the Advancement of Psychiatry.[4] Furthermore, the nomenclature of the manual is intended to adhere as closely as possible to the classification provided in the World Health Organization's *International Classification of Diseases* (*ICD*).[5] This, in effect, means that the manual's use of the terms "disorder," "mental disorders," and "nonpsychotic mental disorders" is intended to designate medically significant syndromes properly falling under the *ICD*'s generic classification of disease (though not all the categories there provided designate diseases). In fact, the manual adheres to the *ICD-8*'s diagnostic code numbers, with certain designated exceptions; and the efforts of Dr. Henry Brill, who was active in the preparation of *DSM-2*, seem to have influenced as well the final form of *ICD-8*, with regard to the classification of mental disorders.[6]

The relevant *DSM* category 302, headed "sexual deviations," includes the following: homosexuality (302.0); fetishism (302.1); pedophilia (302.2); transvestitism (302.3); exhibitionism (302.4); voyeurism (302.5); sadism (302.6); masochism (302.7); other sexual deviation (302.8); and unspecified sexual deviation (302.9).[7] Voyeurism, sadism, and masochism are categories added to *ICD-8* "for use in the United States only"; that is to say, the restriction represents a lack of international agreement on their classification as mental disorders. Unspecified sexual deviation is, apparently, an *ICD-8* category, "to be avoided in the United States or used by record librarians only."[8] The entire category 302 is listed, together with personality disorders, alcoholism, and drug dependence, as "personality disorders and certain other non-psychotic mental disorders"; they were, apparently, linked as personality disorders in *DSM-1*. The subcategories are not described in the manual; the only description rendered is as follows:

> This category is for individuals whose sexual interests are directed primarily toward other than people of the opposite sex, toward sexual acts not usually associated with coitus, or toward coitus performed under bizarre circumstances as in necrophilia, pedophilia, sexual sadism, and fetishism. Even though many find their practices distasteful, they remain unable to substitute normal sexual behavior for them. This diagnosis is not appropriate for individuals who perform deviant sexual acts because normal sexual objects are not available to them.

Needless to say, the description is extremely slim, loose, unsystematic, and tendentious.

Prominent in the American Psychiatric Association's recent reversal regarding the classification of homosexuality was Dr. Robert L. Spitzer, who seems to have played an important role both in the preparation of *DSM-2* and in the APA's reasoned reversal (Spitzer served as head of the APA Task Force on Nomenclature and Statistics). Defending that action, Spitzer held that: "By removing homosexuality from the nomenclature we are not saying it is abnormal but we are not saying it is normal. And I also believe that normal and abnormal are, strictly speaking, not psychiatric terms."[9] The obvious difficulty that Spitzer's remark exposes is this: If "normal" and "abnormal" are not technical psychiatric terms, how can any mental disorder—in particular those classified together with sexual deviations—be properly so designated? And if "normal" and "abnormal" do designate objectively determined psychiatric distinctions, how are they actually to be discerned? On what grounds was homosexuality formerly classified as a mental disorder, as a form of sexual deviation, as not normal, and on what grounds is it now to be removed from the nomenclature? Clearly, the attempt of the APA to accommodate prevailing changes in personal convictions threatens to undermine the entire foundation of the manual. Spitzer apparently has admitted the pressure of the gay-liberation movement, but insists that the new category is psychiatrically sound.[10]

There seems to be considerable uncertainty in psychiatric circles as to whether so-called sexual deviations are, as disorders, to be classified as illnesses. The manual clearly subsumes mental diseases under mental disorders—"disease" regularly signifies a well-articulated syndrome in which physical causes are decisive; the reliable application of the term trails off as the etiology is linked, as in schizophrenia, to thought and mood disorders. The term "illness" never occurs in the manual except in certain titles of disorders—the varieties of so-called manic-depressive illness, for instance, where there is some reason to think the term "disease" is resisted, even though the syndromes are highly articulated, precisely because physical causes cannot be reliably assigned.[11]

On the other hand, "disorder" is nowhere defined in the manual and occurs in the major disease categories of *ICD-8* only in the major heading "mental disorders" (which corresponds, broadly, to the distinction of the *DSM*. In the *ICD-8*, clearly, "disease" does not actually cover all so-called "major disease categories," since other categories include "neoplasms," "complications" (as of pregnancy, childbirth, and the puerperium), "congenital anomalies," "certain causes of perinatal morbidity and mortality" (which may or may not include diseases), "symptoms and ill-defined conditions" (which may or may not include diseases), "accidents, poisonings, and violence." Nevertheless, nearly all informal discussions of mental disorders—whether by psychiatrists or others—tend to treat well-articulated disorders, particularly those in the manual, as illnesses. "Illness" seems to serve either as a substitute for "disease," wherever the etiology is not known to be definitely physical or is taken to be primarily concerned with affective processes or processes of mood or thought, or as a general term signifying a clinically significant departure from norms of health, whether or not the etiology is clear.

In an instructive exchange between Dr. Spitzer and Dr. Irving Bieber (professor of clinical psychiatry, New York Medical College) published by the *New York Times*,[12] the term "disease" never occurs, and Spitzer and Bieber do not use "disorder" and "illness" in the same sense: Spitzer (expressing the intentions of the APA) appears to regard "mental disorder" and "mental illness" as synonymous; and Bieber expressly wishes to use these terms as nonequivalent. The upshot is that Spitzer, claiming that it "does not meet the criteria for psychiatric disorder," denies that homosexuality is a mental illness; and Bieber, agreeing that it is not a mental illness, nevertheless regards it as a "psychiatric disorder." Usefully, Bieber also observes that voyeurism, fetishism, asexuality (celibacy), and frigidity are not, on his view, psychiatric illnesses; futhermore, he claims, they are not mental disorders, even if they appear (as do voyeurism and fetishism, for instance) in the *DSM*.

The difference between Spitzer and Bieber bears quite decisively on the medical controversy about homosexuality (and other sexual deviations). For Bieber expressly says the following:

> I say homosexuality is a psychiatric injury to function and belongs in any psychiatric manual. Now that doesn't mean I consider it an illness any more than I consider frigidity an illness. As long as something like frigidity will be in the manual, disorders of sexual functioning and homosexuality belong there. And to differentiate two types, to take what is really the most injured homosexual and say he shouldn't be in the *DSM*, and that the least injured, the one who has the potential left for restoring his heterosexuality, should be diagnosed as a sexual orientation disorder, to me seems wild.[13]

The point is fairly made, because Spitzer says:

> If homosexuality does not meet the criteria for psychiatric disorder, what is it? Descriptively, we can say that it is one form of sexual behavior. However, in no longer considering it a psychiatric disorder, we are not saying that it is normal or that it is as valuable as heterosexuality. We must recognize that for those homosexuals who are troubled, or dissatisfied with their homosexual feelings, that we are then dealing with a psychiatric disorder because we then have subjective distress.[14]

What the disagreement comes to is this: Bieber regards homosexuality as a psychiatric disorder (but not an illness) because it is an "injury to function," that is, to natural or normal function; and Spitzer admits that homosexuality may produce "subjective distress" in terms of the functioning preferred by those who happen to be homosexually inclined, although "normal" and "abnormal" are not psychiatric distinctions. Bieber holds heterosexual functioning to be injured by homosexuality: "in all homosexuals," he says, "there has been a disturbance of normal heterosexual development" (though he does *not* claim that such a disturbance is always behaviorally manifested or even felt as "subjective distress"—on the contrary, he seems to regard the "satisfied" homosexual as even more disturbed than the homosexual upset with his own condition). But though Spitzer resists the view that homosexuality is an injury (in a sense analogous to that in which the crippled are injured), he admits that it may contribute to psychiatric disorders. He faces, therefore, two sorts of difficulty. First, he offers no criterion for determining what is and what is not a psychiatric disorder—to which homosexuality could contribute (he has, it will be remembered, denied that psychiatric distinctions depend on the normal and abnormal). Second, he (and the board of trustees of the American Psychiatric Association) is disinclined to treat homosexuality and heterosexuality as fully equal and acceptable alternatives on any relevant psychiatric scale (after all, he and they construe homosexuality as a "sexual orientation disturbance"—though only for those homosexuals actually in conflict about their sexual orientation, only for those who may wish to change it or learn to live with it better).

So there is an obvious lacuna in the new APA ruling. Why did not the recommendation of Spitzer's committee consider *heterosexuality* as a "sexual orientation disturbance"—though *only*, of course, for those heterosexuals actually in conflict about their sexual orientation, only for those who wish to change it or learn to live with it better? It is obvious that the APA considers heterosexuality preferable in some (suppressed) psychiatrically significant way. Spitzer himself favorably cites Freud's remark, in a letter, in 1955, to the effect that homosexuality "cannot be classified as an illness. We consider it to be a variation of the sexual function produced by a certain arrest of sexual development."[15] Freud's view, however, for good or bad, squarely rests on a model of sexual normality; but Spitzer (and presumably the APA) has rejected this view in construing homosexuality as a disturbance *in terms of the "subjective distress" of particular homosexuals.* "Subjective distress" argues that homosexuality and heterosexuality should be treated symmetrically; but in that case there would be no sense—as Bieber quite rightly points out—in including homosexuality as a distinct category of mental disorder (or at least in including it without adding a complementary category regarding heterosexuality). Beyond this it should be noted that the classification "sexual orientation disturbance" designates a novel category not hitherto employed, explicated solely in terms of subjective distress. Consequently it is a parasitic category of a peculiar sort: it characterizes homosexuality (a form of "sexual orientation") as a "disturbance" if and only if it is causally responsible for some form of regularized "subjective distress" or "generalized impairment in social effectiveness or functioning"! But of course *any orientation* can and does so function for some population. There is only one possible explanation for the new category: it is premised on an at least attenuated commitment to Freudian notions of sexual normality, but formulated in terms of an official refusal to designate heterosexuality and homosexuality, as such, as normatively ordered psychiatric preferences.

Bieber's view is more orthodox and more plausible, in terms of the *DSM-2.* But it is also more directly vulnerable in just those terms in which Spitzer's committee was responding to newer social tendencies: an enormous number of homosexuals seek no clinical help for their homosexual "condition," are as comfortable and as "functional" socially as the ordinary run of heterosexuals, and view their own therapeutic problems as etiologically neutral to their "sexual orientation." Bieber's thesis that homosexuality *as such* is an injury to (heterosexual) function—more clinically poignant in the instance of a satisfied homosexual than in the instance of a troubled one (a sort of "crippling")—cannot possibly be understood except in terms of a general Freudian model, no matter how attenuated or modified.

But in that connection, it is extremely interesting that neither Bieber nor Spitzer ever considers the widespread phenomenon of bisexuality.

Clinical psychologists not already committed to a Freudian model and attentive to actual consultations report that bisexual practice is a distinct phenomenon, that so-called homosexuals are very often bisexual, that bisexuality exhibits an extremely wide range of alternative forms of sexual "orientation," including, prominently, the rejection of fixed sexual roles. Futher, bisexuality need not and characteristically does not entail an "injury" to heterosexual functioning, regardless of whether such functioning is viewed as normal and natural on any manageable scale whatsoever. [16] Bisexuals tend to be classified as homosexuals rather in the same spirit in which racially mixed people in the United States are classified as blacks. In any case, Bieber's thesis forces us to consider the notion of normal or natural (sexual) functioning. For one thing, bisexuality does not (by definition) interfere with heterosexual functioning—and yet, undoubtedly, it would be regarded as a form of sexual deviation (perhaps even a more alarming form than homosexuality), might even be thought to "cripple" or "injure" heterosexuality (which apparently must be exclusive, on the orthodox view), and might well be expected to produce a significant amount of "subjective distress" (even in the absence of confirming evidence). Further, it is by no means clear how to defend any exclusive norm of nondeviant sexual functioning on psychiatric or scientific grounds without resting one's case on shifting views of social preference and tolerance—which undercuts the presumption of the therapeutic community.

Broadly speaking, homosexuality (and other forms of so-called sexual deviation) is viewed pejoratively in one of three distinct ways—either it is said to be a form of illness, or a form of criminal behavior, or a behavioral perversion. [17] There are systematic difficulties with each strategy, but they are, it should be noted, dialectically linked with one another. A full analysis of each category would take us too far afield. [18] Let it suffice to acknowledge that crime and illness represent institutionalizations, along somewhat different lines, of the dominant prudential interests of given societies. We have already noted the conceptual embarrassment to psychiatry of construing homosexuality as a form of illness: to speak of illness presupposes norms of bodily and mental and emotional functioning that can be independently validated. But however reasonable it may be to postulate certain syndromes as disorders—assuming the most limited and nontendentious level of functioning relative to prudential objectives, for instance, preserving life, minimizing pain, maintaining the movement of limbs, and the like—it can hardly be denied (on the empirical evidence) that homosexuality per se cannot be characterized as interfering with such prudential objectives. It is fair to say that to classify homosexuality as an illness or disorder as such is effectively to intrude moral or moral-like preferences in the guise of medicine.[19]

Rather little needs to be said about the complaint that homosexuality is a criminal activity. First of all, the complaint is likely to depend on contingent and irrelevant considerations—for example, that a particular episode (otherwise not so classifiable) was not an act between consenting adults; in the same spirit, and equally irrelevantly, voyeurism might be construed as an invasion of privacy. Secondly, there is a strong movement to decriminalize homosexuality precisely on the grounds that it forms one of those anomalous "crimes without victims," *unless* one supposes (analogously with the practice of medicine) that homosexuality violates in some sense certain inalienable prudential or overriding goods proper to human life itself—*regardless* of the apparent preferences of otherwise competent adults. Crime entails harm or the threat of harm to another. This is why, assuming the prevailing prudential concerns of given communities (for instance, preserving life, avoiding maiming and bodily injury, securing property, and the like), it is relatively easy to specify crimes without invoking norms of personal development or morally tendentious values of just that sort—with the important exceptions of political crimes and so-called crimes without victims. But crimes against the self are impossible to detail without reference to some conception of the normatively moral development of human beings. This is not to say that criminal law is independent of the moral preferences of particular societies—that is impossible.[20] It is to say only that criminal law may be relatively free from an explicit dependence on "public morality," publicly approved standards of personal conduct that cannot be said to impinge, except tendentiously, on the minimal prudential interests of the community.[21] Hence, arguments against construing homosexuality as an illness may be readily complemented, and with at least as much force, by arguments against construing it as a criminal activity.

There remains the question of perversion. To construe homosexuality as a perversion is to construe it as a sexual deviation—not primarily of a statistical sort—that fails in some significant respect to conform with "appropriate" norms of sexual behavior and desire. Emphasis should be placed on the deliberate vagueness of the qualification "appropriate." The appropriate norms might be said to be medical or legal—in which case the provisions already considered would be called into play. On that interpretation the category of perversion is directly linked to the prevailing prudential interests of a society, and constraints are plausibly justified in terms of therapeutic and criminal considerations. "Functional" norms, however, may be elaborated along different lines. For instance, prudential values of a sort larger than the merely medical or legal may be claimed to be affected: homosexuality and other so-called sexual perversions may be said to threaten the survival of a people in deflecting sexual practice away from the reproductive function. Or, moral values, which prudential values serve merely instrumentally, may be claimed to be affected: homosexuality and other so-called perversions may be said to threaten the correct obligations and the like that bind human beings in their most intimate personal relations by attracting them appetitively into incompatible practices. Or, values regarding personal development and personal relationships that are neither clearly moral nor prudential—possibly, in some serious sense, aesthetic values regarding the quality of life—may be claimed to be affected: homosexuality and other so-called perversions may be said to threaten the "richness" or "fullness" or "style" or "quality" of life by diverting our tastes into narrower, more restricted, or less than fully "human" options. It is plain that condemnatory strategies of all these sorts have actually been pursued—some elaborated in functional terms, some not.

There are large difficulties confronting any claims about discovering the natural or normal functions or relations proper to human beings. There is no point in detailing these difficulties here.[22] It is enough to note that they are all related to the fact that, biologically, human beings may be classified as such without intruding any normative considerations whatsoever, and to the fact that human persons (sentient creatures having the capacity to use language and the power of self-reference) are culturally emergent entities whose values cannot be separated from the doctrines, ideologies, and ideals of the societies in which they develop. But the weakness of the usual functional and nonfunctional complaints against homosexuality (as a perversion) is fairly straightforward and hardly requires demonstrating the large conclusions sketched.

The functional complaint may be fairly represented (acknowledging the need for doctrinal adjustments here and there) by the following comment of the liberal Catholic theorist Norman St. John-Stevas, speaking of homosexuality as a distinct perversion (as opposed to "transient homosexuality" in children and adolescents):

> The Catholic natural law tradition accepts as self-evident that the primary purpose of sexual intercourse is procreation, and relegates as secondary

such ends as fostering the mutual love of the spouses and allaying concupiscence. This conclusion is based on two propositions, that man by the use of his reason can discover God's purpose in the Universe, and that God makes known His purpose by certain "given" physical arrangements. Thus, man can deduce that the purpose of sexual activity is procreation, the continuation of the human race; and the physical arrangements God has provided may not be supplanted at man's will. We now know that not every act of *coitus* is conceptual and relational, and others relational only. But to recognize this fact is not to conclude that acts may be rendered conceptual or non-conceptual at man's will. Man is free to act only within the pattern imposed by nature.[23]

But St. John-Stevas also acknowledges Pius XII's *Humani Generis,* to the effect that "divine revelation must be called morally necessary," since though natural law is not beyond the power of human reason, it cannot be known "with ease, with unwavering certitude, and without any admixture of error," due to "the present condition of the human race."[24] St. John-Stevas himself says that "in many controverted moral problems ... the natural law does not provide a certain guide," but he treats this as "a practical difficulty" (*sic*).[25] The simple point remains that in the oldest and most persistent tradition of the West concerned with the specification of perversions, an absolutely critical methodological weakness is freely admitted. Apart from the fiat of the Church there seems to be no reliable way in which to discount otherwise coherent views about the "purpose" of sexual intercourse and sexual relations. Certainly, it seems that the "given" physical arrangements accommodate homosexuality every bit as well as heterosexuality; that the societal "purpose" of procreation is entirely compatible with the mixed personal "purposes" of homosexual, heterosexual, and bisexual behavior (or even of the other so-called sexual perversions); and that on the empirical evidence the reproduction of the species is hardly a sexual concern at the present time (as we approach an unheard-of population of about seven billion by the year 2000). It is even possible that deviant and perverted sexual practice may contribute to procreation, to mutual love, and the allaying of concupiscence.

The nonfunctional complaint may be fairly represented by an essay of Thomas Nagel's.[26] Nagel's view is particularly interesting in that he denies that the concept of sexual perversion depends on a connection between sex and reproduction; he even holds that "social disapprobation or custom ... has no bearing on the concept of sexual perversion."[27] On this extreme view, *if* homosexuality were to be construed as a perversion, it would have to be judged to violate, inherently, some natural or appropriate relationship (in terms either of inclinations or practices or both) between persons. What is essential, Nagel holds, is that "sexual desire has as its characteristic object a certain relation with something in the external world . . . usually a person."[28] The relation, adjusting Nagel's own remarks, must not be "unnatural," "incomplete," "unhealthy," "subhuman," "unsatisfactory," or "imperfect."

As it turns out, Nagel does *not* view homosexuality as a perversion—or at any rate as a perversion like shoe fetishism. Still, in spite of the fact that he avoids the tendentiousness of insisting on the "natural function" of intercourse and sexual relations, he does "exonerate" homosexuality on the basis of an alternative view of some normatively natural relationship between persons—what amounts to a sort of natural justice or natural respect between persons, not to be viewed as a moral matter, though involving evaluations of persons. The point is that Nagel's criterion of perversion *is* designed to justify characterizing certain acts as perverted, and his example may well encourage other critics to postulate alternative criteria on the strength of which his arguments would be overturned. We must, therefore, consider the defensibility of his criterion.

The key to Nagel's view is reciprocity, "the recognition by the sexual object of the subject's desire as the source of his (the object's) sexual self-awareness"; "physical possession must eventuate in creation of the sexual object in the image of one's desire, and not merely in the object's recognition of that desire, or in his or her own private arousal"; natural sexual relations permit "the full range of interpersonal perceptions" or "reflexive mutual recognition."[29] Sara Ruddick has rather conveniently paraphrased this thesis, which may not unfairly be regarded as drawn from an analogue of H. P. Grice's (which Nagel acknowledges[30]) and the contractarian theme of John Rawls's well-known theory,[31] read as a gloss on Sartre's notion of a "double reciprocal incarnation" (which Nagel mentions[32]). On Ruddick's interpretation, sexual completeness obtains "if each partner (1) allows himself to be 'taken over' by desire, which (2) is desire not merely for the other's body but also for his desire, and (3) where each desire is occasioned by a response to the partner's desire."[33] The principal difficulty with this view is that condition 3 seems idiosyncratic, certainly not compellingly linked to judgments of perversion—unless in accord with personal tastes. For one thing, sexual relations that are not "complete" in the respect required by condition 3, or even by condition 2, may be eminently pleasurable and congruent with successful reproduction. For another, failure to be complete, as in seduction or in unsatisfactory but conventional relations, need not—on any familiar view—be seen as a manifestation of perversion. As it turns out, homosexuality, oral-genital intercourse, anal intercourse, bisexuality, and group intercourse need not, on Nagel's view, be perverted; but shoe fetishism and, perhaps, masturbation, sadism and masochism, coprophilia and necrophilia, pedophilia, voyeurism, and exhibitionism would be viewed as perversions.

The most important objection, then, to Nagel's proposal is that it depends ultimately on a moral or quasi-moral criticism of sexual practice and desire, in spite of Nagel's own disclaimer. Though sexually viable, it appears to be relatively remote from common sexual practice—of any variety—and not significantly congruent with sexual pleasure and satisfaction. It supposes, therefore, some overriding consideration bearing on the "natural" development of one's desires and on the "requirement," in sexual matters, as in others, that in treating oneself and another as a "means" one signifies, by reciprocity, that in reality one is treating oneself and another as an "end." That this is a fair reading is supported in part by Nagel's remark that "narcissistic practices and intercourse with animals, infants, and inanimate objects seem to be stuck at some *primitive version* of the first stage [as sketched above]"; also, that "sadism concentrates on the evocation of passive self-awareness in others, but the sadist's engagement is itself active and requires a retention of deliberate control that impedes awareness of himself as a bodily subject of passion *in the required sense*."[34] Nagel regards both sadism and masochism as "disorders" of the second stage.

Nagel does not, however, offer his thesis as entirely certain or entirely adequate. He recognizes that if homosexuality is a perversion, it must be one on grounds quite different from those that would apply, say, to shoe fetishism; he also recognizes that fantasy involving other persons is a familiar ingredient in "natural" sexual relations—one that would appear to be precluded (wrongly, he thinks) by his own criterion. Nevertheless, though he has suggested what may be regarded as "requirements" of (personal) sexual style, his account is curiously indifferent to the element not only of moral condemnation but also of abhorrence associated with standard judgments of perversion.

By a small adjustment we can accommodate the latter in a way that would apply as readily to homosexuality as to the other perversions. Merely assume that a relatively homogeneous society accepts some doctrine about "appropriate" or "admissible" sexual practices, usually incorporated into moral convictions. Then admit that, subscribing to that doctrine, the habits of mind and the tastes and feelings of the members of that society are sensitized and trained congruently. Deviations from the admitted norms will, then, be noted, and relatively extreme departures will be viewed as perverted—in the strong sense that representative members of the society will be disposed to find such extreme practices and inclinations abhorrent. The corollary is obvious: In order to reduce the sense of abhorrence, a society must extend its tolerance from its own normative preference, via intermediary practices, toward the perverted; as it does so, it will inevitably alter its conception of "natural" practices. What the limits of its tolerance may be is difficult to say, but without doubt, they will be substantially in accord with the moral and prudential values prevailing in sectors of community life other than the sexual.[35] There simply is no sense of the perverted without the distasteful, the disgusting, the abhorrent—either morally or "aesthetically" articulated. And there is no way in which the relevant emotions could develop independently of a society's prevailing tastes. It is, therefore, just as tendentious to attempt to specify the perverted in terms of some normative notion of the "proper" sexual relationships that should hold between persons as it is to attempt it in terms of some normative notion of the "proper" function of sexual intercourse and sexual relations. Nagel's tentative approval of homosexuality, then, is just as dubious as the Catholic Church's condemnation. Nagel must be wrong in supposing that "social disapprobation or custom . . . has no bearing on the concept of sexual perversion." It is, in a sense, all there is to the concept of perversion.

The curious thing is that, contrary to widespread belief, homosexuality is almost unknown in the animal world—appearing only under conditions of extreme stress, never consummated in intercourse, and regularly confused with aggressive play.[36] In that sense, fully developed and rationalized among human beings, homosexuality bids fair to being as natural as any other sexual practice. Furthermore, in our own time—possibly as a result of the relative density of human populations, ideological convictions about population growth, and the gradual elimination of fixed differences between male and female social roles—homosexuality (and bisexuality) is clearly being accorded a more hospitable place in the public array of "natural" sexual practices. It is the concept of the perverted that clarifies the natural, and the natural includes, by extended practice and inclination, whatever we no longer find abhorrent or distasteful.[37]

NOTES

1. "Ideas and Trends," *New York Times*, December 23, 1973, p. E5. In April 1974 the membership of the American Psychiatric Association voted, in a referendum, to support the board's vote: 5,854 in favor, 3,810 against, out of 17,910 eligible voters. That vote has now been challenged on the grounds of having been improperly influenced by a letter signed by Association leaders but "conceived and paid for by the National Gay Task Force"! The matter is pending. Cf. *New York Times*, May 26, 1974, p. 39.

2. Third edition (Washington, D.C.: American Psychiatric Association, 1968). The third edition appears to be identical with the second.

3. Cf. Robert L. Spitzer and Paul T. Wilson, "A Guide to the New Nomenclature," *DSM-2*, sec. 7.

4. Cf. *APA Monitor*, vol. 5, no. 2 (February 1974): 1, 9.

5. *Eighth Revision International Classification of Diseases Adapted for Use in the United States*, Public Health Service Publication No. 1693 (Washington, D.C.: U.S. Government Printing Office, 1968).

6. Cf. Morton Kramer, "The Historical Background of *ICD-8*," *DSM-2*, Intro.

7. *DSM-2*, p. 44.

8. *DSM-2*, p. 1.

9. "Ideas and Trends."

10. *APA Monitor*, vol. 5, no. 2.

11. This is undoubtedly related to Thomas Szasz's well-known attack on the concept of mental illness. Cf. *The Myth of Mental Illness* (New York: Harper & Row, 1961).

12. "Ideas and Trends"; also, in criticism of Szasz, see Joseph Margolis, *Psychotherapy and Morality* (New York: Random House, 1966).

13. "Ideas and Trends."

14. Ibid.

15. Ibid.

16. There has been very little published on this issue as yet. The information regarding bisexuality has been collected, informally, from private communications among psychologists, and some psychiatrists, practicing in the Philadelphia area. The point is somewhat surprising since Freud himself definitely held the view that all human beings are bisexual by nature—though, in contemporary terms, he seems to have been particularly ignorant of lesbianism and construed male homosexuality in terms of a limitation of sexual maturity. Cf. *Three Essays on the Theory of Sexuality*, trans. James Strachey (Standard Edition, 1953). Cf. also, Charlotte Wolff, *Love Between Women* (New York: St. Martin's Press, 1971), chaps. 2, 3; and Kate Millett, *Sexual Politics* (New York: Doubleday, 1969).

17. It could, of course, also be said to be a form of insanity. But the charge is too preposterous to have had any significant historical support. Cf. Phyllis Chesler, *Women and Madness* (New York: Doubleday, 1972).

18. An account is provided in Joseph Margolis, *Negativities: The Limits of Life and Death* (Columbus, Ohio: Charles Merrill, 1975). Cf. also, *Psychotherapy and*

Morality; and "Illness and Medical Values," *The Philosophical Forum* (1969): 252-60.

19. Compare Philip Rieff, *Freud: The Mind of a Moralist* (New York: Viking Press, 1959).

20. Cf. Margolis, *Negativities,* chap. 5.

21. Cf. H. L. A. Hart, *Law, Liberty, and Morality* (Stanford, Calif.: Stanford University Press, 1963) on the relationship between law and morality; also, the argument of Lord Devlin, *The Enforcement of Morals* (Oxford: Oxford University Press, 1959). Cf. also, "Report on the Committee on Homosexual Offenses and Prostitution," London, H.M.S.O. Cmd. 247, September 1957, para. 13, cited in Norman St. John-Stevas, *Life, Death and the Law* (Bloomington, Ind.: Indiana University Press, 1961). The essential issue concerns the concept of law as "the enforcement of morality as such."

22. Cf. Joseph Margolis, *Values and Conduct* (New York: Clarendon; and Oxford: Oxford University Press, 1971); *Psychotherapy and Morality; Negativities.*

23. St. John-Stevas, pp. 83-84.

24. Ibid., pp. 29-30.

25. St. John-Stevas.

26. Thomas Nagel, "Sexual Perversion," herein, pp. 247-60.

27. Ibid.

28. Ibid.

29. Ibid.

30. Cf. H. P. Grice, "Meaning," *The Philosophical Review* 66 (1957): 377-88.

31. Cf. John Rawls, *A Theory of Justice* (Cambridge, Mass.: Harvard University Press, 1971).

32. Cf. Jean-Paul Sartre, *Being and Nothingness,* trans. Hazel E. Barnes (New York: Philosophical Library, 1956), part 3.

33. "On Sexual Morality," in James Rachels, ed., *Moral Problems* (New York: Harper & Row, 1971).

34. Nagel, "Sexual Perversion." Italics added. Compare the Freudian orientation of Charlotte Wolff, *Love Between Women:* "What is perversion? I think that it is a fixation of the libido on one organic system only, which may be the sexual organs or other parts of the body. Any fixation of this kind, whether it be in homosexual or heterosexual people, is obsessional. It is a form of fetishism which leads into the blind alley of destructive habits" chap. 1.

35. Cf. Margolis, *Negativities.*

36. Cf. Arno Karlen, *Sexuality and Homosexuality* (New York: W. W. Norton, 1971).

37. *Deviation* is possible in nature, so the "unnatural" occurs in nature. This goes against an argument by Michael Slote in "Inapplicable Concepts and Sexual Perversion," herein, pp. 261-67. Slote argues that whatever has a biologically determinate nature has "a place in nature"; hence the "unnatural" has no application in our world—a fortiori, the perverted.

FEMINISM AND ABORTION

Judith Jarvis Thomson

A Defense of Abortion

Most opposition to abortion relies on the premise that the fetus is a human being, a person, from the moment of conception.[1] The premise is argued for, but, as I think, not well. Take, for example, the most common argument. We are asked to notice that the development of a human being from conception through birth into childhood is continuous; then it is said that to draw a line, to choose a point in this development and say "before this point the thing is not a person, after this point it is a person" is to make an arbitrary choice, a choice for which in the nature of things no good reason can be given. It is concluded that the fetus is, or that we had better say it is, a person from the moment of conception. But this conclusion does not follow. Similar things might be said about the development of an acorn

This article is reprinted with permission from *Philosophy & Public Affairs* 1, no. 1 (copyright © 1971 by Princeton University Press).

into an oak tree, and it does not follow that acorns are oak trees, or that we had better say they are. Arguments of this form are sometimes called "slippery-slope arguments"—the phrase is perhaps self-explanatory—and it is dismaying that opponents of abortion rely on them so heavily and uncritically.

I am inclined to agree, however, that the prospects for "drawing a line" in the development of the fetus look dim. I am inclined to think also that we shall probably have to agree that the fetus has already become a human person well before birth. Indeed, it comes as a surprise when one first learns how early in its life the fetus begins to acquire human characteristics. By the tenth week, for example, it already has a face, arms and legs, fingers and toes; it has internal organs, and brain activity is detectable.[2] On the other hand, I think that the premise is false, that the fetus is not a person from the moment of conception. A newly fertilized ovum, a newly implanted clump of cells, is no more a person than an acorn is an oak tree. But I shall not discuss any of this. For it seems to me to be of greater interest to ask what happens if, for the sake of argument, we allow the premise. How, precisely, are we supposed to get from there to the conclusion that abortion is morally impermissible? Opponents of abortion commonly spend most of their time establishing that the fetus is a person, and hardly any time explaining the step from there to the impermissibility of abortion. Perhaps they think the step too simple and obvious to require much comment. Or perhaps they are simply being economical in argument. Many of those who defend abortion rely on the premise that the fetus is not a person, but only a bit of tissue that will become a person at birth; and why pay out more arguments than you have to? Whatever the explanation, I suggest that the step they take is neither easy nor obvious, that it calls for closer examination than it is commonly given, and that when we do give it this closer examination we shall feel inclined to reject it.

I propose, then, that we grant that the fetus is a person from the moment of conception. How does the argument go from here? Something like this, I take it. Every person has a right to life. So the fetus has a right to life. No doubt the mother has a right to decide what shall happen in and to her body; everyone would grant that. But surely a person's right to life is stronger and more stringent than the mother's right to decide what happens in and to her body, and so outweighs it. So the fetus may not be killed; an abortion may not be performed.

It sounds plausible. But now let me ask you to imagine this. You wake up in the morning and find yourself back to back in bed with an unconscious famous violinist. He has been found to have a fatal kidney ailment, and the Society of Music Lovers has canvassed all the available medical records and found that you alone have the right blood type to help. They have therefore kidnapped you, and last night the violinist's circulatory system was plugged into yours so that your kidneys could be used to extract poisons from his blood as well as your own. The director of the hospital now tells you: "Look, we're sorry the Society of Music Lovers did this to you—we would never have permitted it if we had known. But still, they did it and the violinist now is plugged into you. To unplug you would be to kill him. But never mind, it's only for nine months. By then he will have recovered from his ailment and can safely be unplugged from you." Is it morally incumbent on you to accede to this situation? No doubt it would be very nice of you if you did, a great kindness. But do you *have* to accede to it? What if it were not nine months but nine years? Or longer still? What if the director of the hospital said: "Tough luck, I agree, but you've now got to stay in bed, with the violinist plugged into you, for the rest of your life. Because remember this: All persons have a right to life, and violinists are persons. Granted you have a right to decide what happens in and to your body, but a person's right to life outweighs your right to decide what happens in and to your body. So you cannot ever be unplugged from him." I imagine you would regard this as outrageous, which suggests that something really is wrong with that plausible-sounding argument that was mentioned previously.

In this case, of course, you were kidnapped; you did not volunteer for the operation that plugged the violinist into your kidneys. Can those who oppose abortion on the grounds I mentioned make an exception for a pregnancy due to rape? Certainly. They can say that persons have a right to life only if they did not come into existence because of rape; or they can say that all persons have a right to life, but that some have less of a right to life than others, in particular, that those who came into existence because of rape have less. But these statements have a rather unpleasant sound. Surely the question of whether one has a right to life at all, or how much of a right one has, should not turn on the question of whether or not one is the product of a rape. And in fact the people who oppose abortion on the ground I mentioned do not make this distinction, and hence do not make an exception in case of rape.

Nor do they make an exception for a case in which the mother has to spend the nine months of her pregnancy in bed. They would agree that that would be a great pity and hard on the mother, but would insist all the same that all persons have a right to life, and that the fetus is a person. I suspect, in fact, that they would not make an exception for a case in which, miraculously enough, the pregnancy went on for nine years, or even for the rest of the mother's life.

Some would not even make an exception for a case in which continuation of the pregnancy is likely to shorten the mother's life; they regard abortion as impermissible even to save the mother's life. Such cases are nowadays very rare, and many opponents of abortion do not accept this extreme view. All the same, it is a good place to begin: a number of points of interest come out in respect to it.

1. Let us call the view that abortion is impermissible even to save the mother's life "the extreme view." I want to suggest, first, that it does not issue from the argument I mentioned earlier without the addition of some fairly powerful premises. Suppose a woman has become pregnant, and now learns that she has a cardiac condition such that she will die if she carries the baby to term. What may be done for her? The fetus, being a person, has a right to life; but as the mother is a person too, so has she a right to life. Presumably they have an equal right to life. How is it supposed to come out that an abortion may not be performed? If mother and child have an equal right to life, should not we perhaps flip a coin? Or should we add to the mother's right to life her right to decide what happens in and to her body, which everybody seems to be ready to grant—the sum of her rights now outweighing the fetus' right to life?

The most familiar argument here is the following. We are told that performing the abortion would be directly killing [3] the child, whereas doing nothing would not be killing the mother, but only letting her die. Moreover, in killing the child, one would be killing an innocent person, for the child has committed no crime and is not aiming at his mother's death. And then there are a variety of ways in which this argument might be continued. (1) As directly killing an innocent person is always and absolutely impermissible, an abortion may not be performed. Or, (2) as directly killing an innocent person is murder, and murder is always and absolutely impermissible, an abortion may not be performed.[4] Or, (3) as one's duty to refrain from directly killing an innocent person is more stringent than one's duty to keep a person from dying, an abortion may not be performed. Or, (4) if one's only options are directly killing an innocent person or letting a person die, one must prefer letting the person die, and thus an abortion may not be performed.[5]

Some people seem to have thought that these are not further premises that must be added if the conclusion is to be reached, but that they follow from the very fact that an innocent person has a right to life.[6] But this seems to me a mistake, and perhaps the simplest way to show this is to point out that while we must certainly grant that innocent persons have a right to life, the theses in arguments 1 through 4 are all false. Take argument 2 for example. If directly killing an innocent person is murder, and thus is impermissible, then the mother's directly killing the innocent person inside her is murder, and thus is impermissible. But it cannot seriously be thought to be murder if the mother performs an abortion on herself to save her life. It cannot seriously be said that she *must* refrain, that she *must* sit passively by and wait for her death. Let us look again at the case of you and the violinist. There you are, in bed with the violinist, and the director of the hospital says to you: "It's all most distressing, and I deeply sympathize, but you see this is putting an additional strain on your kidneys, and you'll be dead within the month. But you *have* to stay where you are all the same, because unplugging you would be directly killing an innocent violinist, and that's murder, and that's impermissible." If anything in the world is true, it is that you do not commit murder, you do not do what is impermissible, if you reach around to your back and unplug yourself from that violinist to save your life.

The main focus of attention in writings on abortion has been on what a third party may or may not do in answer to a request from a woman for an abortion. This is in a way understandable. Things being as they are, there is not much a woman can safely do to abort herself. So the question asked is, What may a third party do? And what the mother may do, if it is mentioned at all, is deduced, almost as an afterthought, from what it is concluded that a third party may do. But it seems to me that to treat the matter in this way is to refuse to grant to the mother that very status of person that is so firmly insisted on for the fetus. For we cannot simply read off what a person may do from what a third party may do. Suppose you find yourself trapped in a tiny house with a growing child—I mean a very tiny house, and a rapidly growing child; you are already up against the wall of the house and in a few minutes you'll be crushed to death. The child, on the other hand, will not be crushed to death; if nothing is done to stop him from growing he will be hurt, but in the end he will simply burst open the house and walk out a free man. Now I could well understand it if a bystander were to say: "There's nothing we can do for you. We cannot choose between your life and his, we cannot be the ones to decide who is to live, we cannot intervene." But it cannot be concluded that you too can do nothing, that you cannot attack the child to save your life. However innocent the child may be, you do not have to wait passively while it crushes you to death. Perhaps a pregnant woman is vaguely felt to have the status of a house, which we do not allow the right of self-defense. But if the woman houses the child, it should be remembered that she is a person who houses it.

I should perhaps pause to say explicitly that I am not claiming that people have a right to do anything whatever to save their lives. I think, rather, that there are drastic limits to the right of self-defense. If someone threatens you with death unless you torture someone else to death, I think you have not the right, even to save your life, to do so. But the case under consideration here is very different. In our case there are only two people involved, one whose life is threatened, and one who threatens it. Both are innocent: the one who is threatened is not threatened because of any fault; the one who threatens does not threaten because of any fault. For this reason we may feel that we bystanders cannot intervene. But the person threatened can.

In sum, a woman surely can defend her life against the threat to it posed by the unborn child, even if doing so involves its death. And this shows not merely that the theses in arguments 1 through 4 are false; it shows also that the extreme view of abortion is false, and so we need not canvass any other possible ways of arriving at it from the argument I mentioned at the outset.

2. The extreme view could of course be weakened to say that while abortion is permissible to save the mother's life, it may not be performed by a third party, but only by the mother herself. But this cannot be right either. For what we have to keep in mind is that the mother and the unborn child are not like two tenants in a small house that has, by an unfortunate mistake, been rented to both: the mother *owns* the house. The fact that she does adds to the offensiveness of deducing that the mother can do nothing from the supposition that third parties can do nothing. But it does more than this; it also casts a bright light on the supposition that third parties can do nothing. Certainly it lets us see that a third party who says "I cannot choose between you" is fooling himself if he thinks this is impartiality. If Jones has found and fastened on a certain coat that he needs to keep himself from freezing but that Smith also needs to keep from freezing, then it is not impartiality that says "I cannot choose between you" when Smith owns the coat. Women have said again and again, "This body is my body!" and they have reason to feel angry, reason to feel

that it has been like shouting into the wind. Smith, after all, is hardly likely to bless us if we say to him: "Of course it's your coat; anybody would grant that it is. But no one may choose between you and Jones who is to have it."

We should really ask what it is that says "no one may choose" in the face of the fact that the body that houses the child is the mother's body. It may be simply a failure to appreciate this fact. But it may be something more interesting, namely the sense that one has a right to refuse to lay hands on people, even where it would be just and fair to do so, even where justice seems to require that somebody do so. Thus justice might call for somebody to get Smith's coat back from Jones, and yet you have a right to refuse to be the one to lay hands on Jones, a right to refuse to do physical violence to him. This, I think, must be granted. But then what should be said is not "no one may choose," but only "*I* cannot choose"—indeed not even this, but rather "*I* will not act," leaving it open that somebody else can or should, in particular that anyone in a position of authority, with the job of securing people's rights, both can and should. So this is no difficulty. I have not been arguing that any given third party must accede to the mother's request that he perform an abortion to save her life, but only that he may.

I suppose that in some views of human life the mother's body is only on loan to her, the loan not being one that gives her any prior claim to it. One who held this view might well think it impartiality to say, "I cannot choose." But I shall simply ignore this possibility. My own view is that if a human being has any just, prior claim to anything at all, he has a just, prior claim to his own body. And perhaps this need not be argued for here anyway, since, as I mentioned, the arguments against abortion we are looking at do grant that the woman has a right to decide what happens in and to her body.

But although they do grant it, I have tried to show that they do not take seriously what is done in granting it. I suggest the same thing will reappear even more clearly when we turn away from cases in which the mother's life is at stake and attend, as I propose we now do, to the vastly more common cases in which a woman wants an abortion for some less weighty reason than preserving her own life.

3. Where the mother's life is not at stake the argument I mentioned at the outset seems to have a much stronger pull. "Everyone has a right to life, so the unborn person has a right to life." And isn't the child's right to life weightier than anything other than the mother's own right to life,

which she might put forward as ground for an abortion?

This argument treats the right to life as if it were unproblematic. It is not, and this seems to me to be precisely the source of the mistake.

For we should now, at long last, ask what it comes to, to have a right to life. In some views having a right to life includes having a right to be given at least the bare minimum one needs for continued life. But suppose that what in fact *is* the bare minimum a man needs for continued life is something he has no right at all to be given? If I am sick unto death, and the only thing that will save my life is the touch of Henry Fonda's cool hand on my fevered brow, then all the same, I have no right to be given the touch of Henry Fonda's cool hand on my fevered brow. It would be frightfully nice of him to fly in from the West Coast to provide it. It would be less nice, though no doubt well meant, if my friends flew to the West Coast and carried Henry Fonda back with them. But I have no right at all against anybody that he should do this for me. Or again, to return to the story I told earlier, the fact that for continued life the violinist needs the continued use of your kidneys does not establish that he has a right to be given the continued use of your kidneys. He certainly has no right against you that *you* should give him continued use of your kidneys. For nobody has any right to use your kidneys unless you give him such a right; and nobody has the right against you that you shall give him this right. If you do allow him to go on using your kidneys, this is a kindness on your part, and not something he can claim from you as his due. Nor has he any right against anybody else that they should give him continued use of your kidneys. Certainly he had no right against the Society of Music Lovers that they should plug him into you in the first place. And if you now start to unplug yourself, having learned that you will otherwise have to spend nine years in bed with him, there is nobody in the world who must try to prevent you, in order to see to it that he is given something he has a right to be given.

Some people are rather stricter about the right to life. In their view it does not include the right to be given anything, but amounts to, and only to, the right not to be killed by anybody. But here a related difficulty arises. If everybody is to refrain from killing the violinist, then everybody must refrain from doing a great many different sorts of things. Everybody must refrain from slitting his throat, everybody must refrain from shooting him—and everybody must refrain from unplugging you from him. But does he have a right against everybody that they shall refrain from unplugging you from him? To refrain from doing this is to allow him to continue to use your kidneys. It could be argued that he has a right against us that *we* should allow him to continue to use your kidneys. That is, while he had no right against us that we should give him the use of your kidneys, it might be argued that he anyway has a right against us that we shall not now intervene and deprive him of the use of your kidneys. I shall come back to third-party interventions later. But certainly the violinist has no right against you that *you* shall allow him to continue to use your kidneys. As I said, if you do allow him to use them, it is a kindness on your part, and not something you owe him.

The difficulty I point to here is not peculiar to the right to life. It reappears in connection with all the other natural rights; and it is something that an adequate account of rights must deal with. For present purposes it is enough just to draw attention to it. But I would stress that I am not arguing that people do not have a right to life—quite the contrary, it seems to me that the primary control we must place on the acceptability of an account of rights is that it should turn out in that account to be a truth that all persons have a right to life. I am arguing only that having a right to life does not guarantee having either a right to be given the use of or a right to be allowed continued use of another person's body—even if one needs it for life itself. So the right to life will not serve the opponents of abortion in the very simple and clear way in which they seem to have thought it would.

4. There is another way to bring out the difficulty. In the most ordinary sort of case, to deprive someone of what he has a right to is to treat him unjustly. Suppose a boy and his small brother are jointly given a box of chocolates for Christmas. If the older boy takes the box and refuses to give his brother any of the chocolates, he is unjust to him, for the brother has been given a right to half of them. But suppose that having learned that otherwise it means nine years in bed with that violinist, you unplug yourself from him. You surely are not being unjust to him, for you gave him no right to use your kidneys, and no one else can have given him any such right. But we have to notice that in unplugging yourself you are killing him; and violinists, like everybody else, have a right to life, and thus in the view we are considering, the right not to be killed. So here you do what he supposedly has a right that you shall not do, but you do not act unjustly to him in doing it.

The emendation that may be made at this point is this: the right to life consists not in the right not to be killed but rather in the right not to be killed unjustly. This runs a risk of circularity, but never mind: it would enable us to square the fact that the violinist has a right to life with the fact that you do not act unjustly toward him in unplugging yourself, thereby killing him. For if you do not kill him unjustly, you do not violate his right to life, and so it is no wonder you do him no injustice.

But if this emendation is accepted, the gap in the argument against abortion stares us plainly in the face: it is by no means enough to show that the fetus is a person, and to remind us that all persons have a right to life; we need to be shown also that killing the fetus violates its right to life, that is, that abortion is unjust killing. And is it?

I suppose we may take it as a datum that in a case of pregnancy due to rape the mother has not given the unborn person a right to the use of her body for food and shelter. Indeed, in what pregnancy could it be supposed that the mother has given the unborn person such a right? It is not as if there were unborn persons drifting about the world, to whom a woman who wants a child says "I invite you in."

But it might be argued that there are other ways one can have acquired a right to the use of another person's body than by having been invited to use it by that person. Suppose a woman voluntarily indulges in intercourse, knowing of the chance that it will issue in pregnancy, and then she does become pregnant. Is she not in part responsible for the presence, in fact the very existence, of the unborn person inside her? No doubt she did not invite it in. But doesn't her partial responsibility for its being there itself give it a right to the use of her body?[7] If so, then her aborting it would be more like the boy's taking away the chocolates and less like your unplugging yourself from the violinist—doing so would be depriving it of what it does have a right to, and thus would be doing it an injustice.

And then, too, it might be asked whether or not she can kill it even to save her own life: If she voluntarily called it into existence, how can she now kill it, even in self-defense?

The first thing to be said about this is that it is something new. Opponents of abortion have been so concerned to make out the independence of the fetus, in order to establish that it has a right to life, just as its mother does, that they have tended to overlook the possible support they might gain from making out that the fetus is dependent on the mother, in order to establish that she has a special kind of responsibility for it, a responsibility that gives it rights against her that are not possessed by any independent person—such as an ailing violinist who is a stranger to her.

On the other hand, this argument would give the unborn person a right to its mother's body only if her pregnancy resulted from a voluntary act, undertaken in full knowledge of the chance that a pregnancy might result from it. It would leave out entirely the unborn person whose existence is due to rape. Pending the availability of some further argument, then, we would be left with the conclusion that unborn persons whose existence is due to rape have no right to the use of their mothers' bodies, and thus that aborting them is not depriving them of anything they have a right to and hence is not unjust killing.

And we should also notice that it is not at all plain that this argument really does go even as far as it purports to. For there are different kinds of cases, and the details make a difference. If the room is stuffy and I therefore open a window to air it and a burglar climbs in, it would be absurd to say, "Ah, now he can stay; she's given him a right to the use of her house— for she is partially responsible for his presence there, having voluntarily done what enabled him to get in, in full knowledge that there are such things as burglars, and that burglars burgle." It would be still more absurd to say this if I had had bars installed outside my windows precisely to prevent burglars from getting in, and a burglar got in only because of a defect in the bars. It remains equally absurd if we imagine it is not a burglar who climbs in but an innocent person who blunders or falls in. Again, suppose it were like this: people-seeds drift about in the air like pollen, and if you open your windows one may drift in and take root in your carpet or upholstery. You do not want children, so you fix up your windows with fine mesh screens, the very best you can buy. As can happen, however, and on very rare occasions does happen, one of the screens is defective; and a seed drifts in and takes root. Does the person-plant who now develops have a right to the use of your house? Surely not, despite the fact that you voluntarily opened your windows, that you knowingly kept carpets and upholstered furniture, and that you knew that screens were sometimes defective. Someone may argue that you are responsible for its rooting, that it does have a right to your house because, after all, you *could* have lived out your life with bare floors and furniture, or with sealed windows and doors. But this will not do, for by the same token anyone can avoid a pregnancy due to rape by having a hysterectomy, or by never leaving home without a (reliable!) army.

It seems to me that the argument we are looking at can establish at most that there are some cases in which the unborn person has a right to the use of its mother's body, and therefore some cases in which abortion is unjust killing. There is room for much discussion and argument as to precisely which cases, if any, are unjust. But I think we should sidestep this issue and leave it open, for the argument certainly does not establish that all abortion is unjust killing.

5. There is, however, room for yet another argument here. We all surely must grant that there may be cases in which it would be morally indecent to detach a person from your body at the cost of his life. Suppose you learn that what the violinist needs is not nine years of your life but only one hour: all you need do to save his life is to spend one hour in that bed with him. Suppose also that letting him use your kidneys for that one hour would not affect your health in the slightest. Admittedly you were kidnapped. Admittedly you did not give anyone permission to plug him into you. Nevertheless it seems to me plain you *ought* to allow him to use your kidneys for that hour—it would be indecent to refuse.

Again, suppose pregnancy lasted only an hour and constituted no threat to life or health. And suppose that a woman becomes pregnant as a result of rape. Admittedly she did not voluntarily do anything to bring about the existence of a child. Admittedly she did nothing at all that would give the unborn person a right to the use of her body. All the same it might well be said, as in the newly emended violinist story, that she *ought* to allow it to remain for that hour—that it would be indecent in her to refuse.

Now some people are inclined to use the term "right" in such a way that it follows from the fact that you ought to allow a person to use your body for the hour he needs, that he has a right to use your body for the hour he needs, even though he has not been given that right by any person or act. They may say that it follows also that if you refuse you act unjustly toward him. This use of the term is perhaps so common that it cannot be called wrong; nevertheless it seems to me to be an unfortunate loosening of what we would do better to keep a tight rein on. Suppose that the box of chocolates I mentioned earlier had not been given to both boys jointly, but was given only to the older boy. There he sits, stolidly eating his way through the box, his small brother watching enviously. Here we are likely to say: "You ought not to be so mean. You ought to give your brother some of those chocolates." My own view is that it just does not follow from the truth of this that the brother has any right to any of the chocolates. If the boy refuses to give his brother any, he is greedy, stingy, callous—but not unjust. I suppose that the people I have in mind will say it does follow that the brother has a right to some of the chocolates, and thus that the boy does act unjustly if he refuses to give his brother any. But the effect of saying this is to obscure what we should keep distinct, namely the difference between the boy's refusal in this case and the boy's refusal in the earlier case, in which the box was given to both boys jointly, and in which the small brother thus had what was from any point of view clear title to half.

A further objection to so using the term "right," that from the fact that A ought to do a thing for B it follows that B has a right against A that A do it for him, is that it is going to make the question of whether or not a man has a right to a thing turn on how easy it is to provide him with it; and this seems not merely unfortunate but morally unacceptable. Take the case of Henry Fonda again. I said earlier that I had no right to the touch of his cool hand on my fevered brow, even though I needed it to save my life. I said it would be frightfully nice of him to fly in from the West Coast to provide me with it, but that I had no right against him that he should do so. But suppose he isn't on the West Coast. Suppose he has only to walk across the room and place a hand briefly on my brow—and lo, my life is saved. Then surely he ought to do it; it would be indecent to refuse. Is it to be said, "Ah, well, it follows that in this case she has a right to the touch of his hand on her brow, and so it would be an injustice for him to refuse"? So that I have a right to it when it is easy for him to provide it, though no right when it is hard? It's rather a shocking idea that anyone's rights should fade away and disappear as it gets harder and harder to accord them to him.

So my own view is that even though you ought to let the violinist use your kidneys for the one hour he needs, we should not conclude that he has a right to do so; we should say that if you refuse you are, like the boy who owns all the chocolates and will give none away, self-centered and callous —indecent, in fact—but not unjust. And similarly, that even supposing a case in which a woman pregnant due to rape ought to allow the unborn person to use her body for the hour he needs, we should not conclude that he has a right to do so; we should conclude that she is self-centered, callous, indecent, but not unjust, if she refuses. The complaints are no less grave; they are just different. However, there is no need to insist on this point. If anyone does wish to deduce "he has a right" from "you ought," then all the same he must surely grant that there are cases in which it is not morally required of you that you allow that violinist to use your kidneys, and in which he does not have a right to use them, and in which you do not do him an unjustice if you refuse. And so also for mother and unborn child. Except in such cases as the unborn person has a right to demand it—and we were leaving open the possibility that there may be such cases—nobody is morally *required* to make large sacrifices, of health, of all other interests and concerns, of all other duties and commitments, for nine years, or even for nine months, in order to keep another person alive.

6. We have in fact to distinguish between two kinds of Samaritans: the Good Samaritan and what we might call the Minimally Decent Samaritan. The story of the Good Samaritan, you will remember, goes like this:

> A certain man went down from Jerusalem to Jericho, and fell among thieves, which stripped him of his raiment, and wounded him, and departed, leaving him half dead.
>
> And by chance there came down a certain priest that way; and when he saw him, he passed by on the other side.
>
> And likewise a Levite, when he was at the place, came and looked on him, and passed by the other side.
>
> But a certain Samaritan, as he journeyed, came where he was; and when he saw him he had compassion on him.
>
> And went to him, and bound up his wounds, pouring in oil and wine, and set him on his own beast, and brought him to an inn, and took care of him.
>
> And on the morrow, when he departed, he took out two pence, and gave them to the host, and said unto him, "Take care of him; and whatsoever thou spendest more, when I come again, I will repay thee." (Luke 10:30-35)

The Good Samaritan went out of his way, at some cost to himself, to help one in need of it. We are not told what the options were, that is, whether or not the priest and the Levite could have helped by doing less than the Good Samaritan did; but assuming they could have, then the fact they did nothing at all shows they were not even Minimally Decent Samaritans, not because they were not Samaritans, but because they were not even minimally decent.

These things are a matter of degree, of course, but there is a difference; it comes out perhaps most clearly in the story of Kitty Genovese, who was murdered while thirty-eight people watched or listened and did nothing at all to help her. A Good Samaritan would have rushed out to give direct assistance against the murderer. Or perhaps we had better allow that it would have been a Splendid Samaritan who did this, on the ground that it would have involved a risk of death for himself. But the thirty-eight people not only did not do this; they did not even trouble to pick up a phone to call the police. Minimally Decent Samaritanism would call for doing at least that, and their not having done so was monstrous.

After telling the story of the Good Samaritan Jesus said, "Go, and do thou likewise." Perhaps he meant that we are morally required to act as the Good Samaritan did. Perhaps he was urging people to do more than is morally required of them. At all events it seems plain that it was not morally required of any of the thirty-eight that he rush out to give direct assistance at the risk of his own life and that it is not morally required of anyone that he give long stretches of his life—nine years or nine months—to sustaining the life of a person who has no special right (we were leaving open the possibility of this) to demand it.

Indeed, with one rather striking class of exceptions, no one in any country in the world is *legally* required to do anywhere near as much as this for anyone else. The class of exceptions is obvious. My main concern here is not the state of the law in respect to abortion, but it is worth drawing attention to the fact that in no state in this country is any man compelled by law to be even a Minimally Decent Samaritan to any person; there is no law under which charges could be brought against the thirty-eight people who stood by while Kitty Genovese died. By contrast, in most states in this country women are compelled by law to be not merely Minimally Decent Samaritans, but Good Samaritans, to unborn persons inside them. This does not by itself settle anything, because it may well be argued that there should be laws in this country—as there are in many European countries—compelling at least Minimally Decent Samaritanism.[8] But it does show that there is a gross injustice in the existing state of the law. And it shows also that the groups currently working against liberalization of abortion laws, in fact working toward having it declared unconstitutonal for a state to permit abortion, had better start working for the adoption of Good Samaritan laws generally, or earn the charge that they are acting in bad faith.

I myself think that Minimally Decent Samaritan laws would be one thing, Good Samaritan laws quite another—and in fact highly improper. But we are not here concerned with the law. What we should ask is not whether anybody should be compelled by law to be a Good Samaritan but whether we must accede to a situation in which somebody is being compelled—by nature, perhaps—to be a Good Samaritan. We have, in other words, to look now at third-party interventions. I have been arguing that no person is morally required to make large sacrifices to sustain the life of another who has no right to demand them, and this even where the sacrifices do not include life itself; we are not morally required to be Good Samaritans, or anyway, Very Good Samaritans, to one another. But what if a man cannot extricate himself from such a situation? What if he appeals to us to extricate him? It seems to me plain that there are cases in which we can, cases in which a Good Samaritan would extricate him. There you are: you were kidnapped, and nine years in bed with the violinist lie ahead of you. You have your own life to lead. You are sorry, but you simply cannot see giving up so much of your life to the sustaining of his. You cannot extricate yourself, and ask us to do so. I should have thought that—in light of his having no right to the use of your body—it was obvious that we do not have to accede to your being forced to give up so much. We can do what you ask. There is no injustice to the violinist in our doing so.

7. Following the lead of the opponents of abortion, I have throughout been speaking of the fetus merely as a person; and what I have been asking is whether or not the argument we began with, which proceeds only from the fetus' being a person, really does establish its conclusion. I have argued that it does not.

But of course there are arguments and arguments, and it may be said that I have simply fastened on the wrong one. It may be said that what is important is not merely the fact that the fetus is a person but that it is a person for whom the woman has a special kind of responsibility issuing from the fact that she is its mother. It might be argued that all my analogies are therefore irrelevant—for you do not have that special kind of responsibility for that violinist and Henry Fonda does not have that special kind of responsibility for me. And our attention might be drawn to the fact that men and women both are compelled by law to provide support for their children.

I have in effect dealt (briefly) with this argument in section 4 above; but a (still briefer) recapitulation now may be in order. Surely we do not have any such "special responsibility" for a person unless we have assumed it, explicitly or implicitly. If a set of parents do not try to prevent pregnancy, do not obtain an abortion, and then at the time of birth of the child do not put it up for adoption but rather take it home with them, then they have assumed responsibility for it, they have given it rights, and they cannot now withdraw support from it at the cost of its life because they now find it difficult to go on providing for it. But if they have taken all reasonable precautions against having a child, they do not simply by virtue of their biological relationship to the child who comes into existence have a special responsibility for it. They may wish to assume responsibility for it, or they may not wish to. And I am suggesting that if assuming responsibility for it would require large sacrifices, then they may refuse. A Good

Samaritan would not refuse, or, anyway, a Splendid Samaritan would not, if the sacrifices that had to be made were enormous. But then so would a Good Samaritan assume responsibility for that violinist; so would Henry Fonda, if he is a Good Samaritan, fly in from the West Coast and assume responsibility for me.

8. My argument will be found unsatisfactory on two counts by many of those who want to regard abortion as morally permissible. First, while I do argue that abortion is not impermissible, I do not argue that it is always permissible. There may well be cases in which carrying the child to term requires only Minimally Decent Samaritanism of the mother, and this is a standard we must not fall below. I am inclined to think it a merit of my account precisely that it does *not* give a general yes or a general no. It allows for and supports our sense that, for example, a sick and desperately frightened fourteen-year-old schoolgirl, pregnant due to rape, may *of course* choose abortion, and that any law that rules this out is an insane law. And it also allows for and supports our sense that in other cases resort to abortion is even positively indecent. It would be indecent in the woman to request an abortion, and indecent in a doctor to perform it, if she is in her seventh month and wants the abortion just to avoid the nuisance of postponing a trip abroad. The very fact that the arguments I have been drawing attention to treat all cases of abortion, or even all cases of abortion in which the mother's life is not at stake, as morally on a par ought to have made them suspect at the outset.

Second, while I am arguing for the permissibility of abortion in some cases, I am not arguing for the right to secure the death of the unborn child. It is easy to confuse these two things in that up to a certain point in the life of the fetus it is not able to survive outside the mother's body; hence removing it from her body guarantees its death. But they are different in important ways. I have argued that you are not morally required to spend nine months in bed, sustaining the life of the violinist; but to say this is by no means to say that if when you unplug yourself there is a miracle and he survives, you have a right to turn round and slit his throat. You may detach yourself even if this costs him his life; you have no right to be guaranteed his death by some other means if unplugging yourself does not kill him. There are some people who will feel dissatisfied by this feature of my argument. A woman may be utterly devastated by the thought of a child, a bit of herself, put up for adoption and never seen or heard of again. She may therefore want not merely that the child be detached from her but, more, that it die. Some opponents of abortion are inclined to regard this as beneath contempt, thereby showing insensitivity to what is surely a powerful source of despair. All the same, I agree that the desire for the child's death is not one that anybody may gratify, should it turn out to be possible to detach the child alive.

At this place, however, it should be remembered that we have only been pretending throughout that the fetus is a human being from the moment of conception. A very early abortion is surely not the killing of a person and so is not dealt with by anything I have said here.

NOTES

1. I am very indebted to James Thomson for discussion, criticism, and many helpful suggestions.

2. Daniel Callahan, *Abortion: Law, Choice, and Morality* (New York: Macmillan, 1970), p. 373. This book gives a fascinating survey of the available information on abortion. The Jewish tradition is surveyed in David M. Feldman, *Birth Control in Jewish Law* (New York: New York University Press, 1968), part 5; the Catholic tradition, in John T. Noonan, Jr., "An Almost Absolute Value in History," in *The Morality of Abortion*, ed. John T. Noonan, Jr. (Cambridge, Mass.: Harvard University Press, 1970).

3. The term "direct" in the arguments I refer to is a technical one. Roughly, what is meant by "direct killing" is either killing as an end in itself or killing as a means to some end, for example, the end of saving someone else's life. See note 6 for an example of its use.

4. Cf. *Encyclical Letter of Pope Pius XI on Christian Marriage*, St. Paul Editions (Boston, n.d.), p. 32: "However much we may pity the mother whose health and even life is gravely imperiled in the performance of the duty allotted to her by nature, nevertheless what could ever be a sufficient reason for excusing in any way the direct murder of the innocent? This is precisely what we are dealing with here." Noonan (*The Morality of Abortion*, p. 43) reads this as follows: "What cause can ever avail to excuse in any way the direct killing of the innocent? For it is a question of that."

5. The thesis in argument 4 is in an interesting way weaker than those in 1, 2, and 3: they rule out abortion even in cases in which both mother and child will die if the abortion is not performed. By contrast, one who held the view expressed in 4 could consistently say that one need not prefer letting two persons die to killing one.

6. Cf. the following passage from Pius XII, *Address to the Italian Catholic Society of Midwives:* "The baby in the maternal breast has the right to life immediately from God.—Hence there is no man, no human authority, no science, no medical, eugenic, social, economic or moral 'indication' which can establish or grant a valid juridical ground for a direct deliberate disposition of an innocent human life, that is a disposition which looks to its destruction either as an end or as a means to

another end perhaps in itself not illicit.—The baby, still not born, is a man in the same degree and for the same reason as the mother" (quoted in Noonan, *The Morality of Abortion*, p. 45).

7. The need for a discussion of this argument was brought home to me by members of the Society for Ethical and Legal Philosophy, to whom this paper was originally presented.

8. For a discussion of the difficulties involved, and a survey of the European experience with such laws, see *The Good Samaritan and the Law*, ed. James M. Ratcliffe (New York: Peter Smith, 1966).

Alison Jaggar

Abortion and
a Woman's Right To Decide

I

Philosophical discussions of abortion commonly focus on the question of
how to justify abortion: In what circumstances (if any) is abortion a
morally right course of action, and in what circumstances (if any) is it
morally wrong?[1] Much less frequently discussed is the question concerning the responsibility for applying the results of such reflection to particular cases: given a particular pregnancy, who should decide whether or not
it ought to be terminated? The first is a question in moral philosophy; the
second is a question in social or political philosophy. If everyone were a
totally rational and disinterested moral agent, the second question would
be unimportant, for the same decision would be reached regardless of who
was responsible for making it. But since the answers to the first question
are notoriously diverse, the second question becomes one of great practical

This article is reprinted from *The Philosophical Forum*, volume 5, nos. 1-2 (Fall-
Winter 1973-74) with the permission of the publisher and author.

importance to women. It is to this second question that I will address myself. Specifically, I want to consider whether or not each woman should be
legally guaranteed the sole right to decide whether or not she may have her
own pregnancy terminated.

This problem is not of just narrowly feminist interest: like most feminist issues it raises more-general questions whose resolution is basic for the
formulation of a comprehensive social philosophy. Among the obvious
questions it raises are the extent of individual freedom in society and the
obligation of the state to protect the interests of those who are unable to do
so for themselves. A particularly interesting aspect of this issue is the way
in which it illustrates some fundamental problems with the attempt to
guarantee justice, freedom, and equality through the establishment of
political rights.

In what follows I shall attempt to provide a moral justification for the
claim that each woman should have the sole legal right to decide whether
or not, in her own case, an abortion should be performed. For reasons that
will be given later, I shall ignore utilitarian considerations in my attempt
to establish this conclusion. Instead I shall support my claim that each
woman should have a legal right to abortion by appeal to an underlying
moral right. The moral right to abortion for which I argue, however, is not
a universal or absolute one enjoyed by all women, regardless of their social
situation. Rather, it is a right whose existence depends on certain contingent features of the social situation in which women find themselves.
Within our society, I shall argue, conditions are such that most women
have a moral right to abortion, and, consequently, this right should be
guaranteed by law. However, it is possible to describe other societies in
which women do not have the sole moral right to decide on abortion, and
indeed even within our own society there may be some women who do not
have that right. It will be in our consideration of the reasons why the moral
right to decide on abortion is only a contingent right and does not belong
to all women that we shall gain fresh insight into the difficulties of
attempting to formulate an ideal of the just, free, and egalitarian society in
terms of legal rights.

My argument for the conclusion that each woman should legally be
guaranteed the right to decide whether or not she should abort attempts to
bypass a number of difficult problems that are usually thought to complicate the issue. For example, I do not appeal to the unclear and dubious
"right to one's own body." I skirt the general question of population control. I make no presuppositions about the moral status of unborn human

beings other than to assume they do not have a right to life so absolute that the question of abortion may never be raised; that is, I assume it to be false that there are *no* circumstances that could conceivably justify abortion, but I do not commit myself to any stand on exactly what circumstances might do so. Finally, I avoid the general question of the purposes and limits of state authority. Instead I attempt to short-circuit all these difficulties and to resolve the issue of whether each woman should have a legal right to make her own decision about abortion by appeal to two relatively uncontroversial principles. Thus, if my argument works, it should be acceptable to people of most shades of political opinion and to anyone who will admit that abortion might occasionally be justified. Before presenting my solution, however, I shall briefly survey the claims of the various candidates for the right to judge whether or not a given pregnancy should be terminated.

II

Several grounds are commonly adduced for the pregnant woman's right to decide if she should abort. They include an alleged right to privacy (the basis of the 1973 U.S. Supreme Court decision to liberalize the hitherto very restrictive abortion laws), an alleged right to her own body, and a right to determine her own future. There are also utilitarian arguments for allowing a woman to choose abortion: if a woman is reluctant to have a child, then the refusal to allow her to decide to terminate her pregnancy is said to increase the sum of unhappiness in the world, either by forcing her to seek an illegal, unsafe, and expensive abortion, or by resulting in an unwilling mother and an unwanted child. Other utilitarian arguments concern the general disutility of passing laws restricting a woman's choice when such laws are likely to be disregarded so widely that they will bring the whole legal system into disrespect.

The potential mother, however, is not the only parent with a claim to decide. The potential father also has some grounds to claim at least a share in making the decision. The father's claim rests not so much on possible property rights over the disposition of his semen (although I have heard this argument given!) as on his legal obligation to share in the economic support of the child that will result if the abortion is not performed. He might argue that he should have a choice as to whether or not he undertakes those obligations. He might also make an appeal, parallel to the mother's, to utilitarian arguments about the unwanted children of unwilling fathers.

Many people assume that the doctor or the medical personnel who are asked to perform the abortion should also have some say in deciding whether or not it should occur. In order to justify this claim, it seems necessary to assume either that abortion is a totally nonmoral question of medical technique or, alternatively, that the role of the medical staff is to act as moral rather than as medical authorities. If one rejects these assumptions, then the only other reason that I can think of for allowing the medical personnel to share in deciding whether or not a particular abortion ought to be performed is that they should not have to do something that they believe to be morally wrong.

Much stronger arguments can be brought forward in support of the state's claim to decide on cases of abortion. If the unborn is viewed as having any right to life at all, even a weak one, then it is plausible to suppose that the state has an obligation to protect that right. Additionally, if the birth of a child places a burden on the state by requiring it to provide education, health care, or economic support, then it may be reasonable to grant the state a part in making the decision about whether or not that child should be born. There is also a familiar utilitarian argument for state control of abortion, to the effect that it is for the benefit of all if the state determines the optimum population.

Since demographic decisions ultimately affect the whole world, it is even arguable that decisions about abortion ought to be made by the world community. However, although I believe that in certain circumstances this suggestion might have some merit, it is at present so wildly impractical that I shall not consider it further in this discussion. Should anyone wish to do so, it is easy to construct arguments for world-community control analogous to those that I use for the state.

Given all these conflicting claims and the variety of the grounds on which they rest, it is hard to see how to settle the question of who should decide whether or not a pregnancy should be terminated. Talk of rights is notoriously problematic, and when the alleged rights of different individuals conflict both with each other and with the state, as they do in the case of the abortion decision, the only way to resolve the conflict appears to be by appeal to utilitarian arguments. Even if the utilities and disutilities involved in a complex question such as this could be worked out, however, it is doubtful whether either side would accept them. Antiabortionists refuse to accept utilitarian arguments if they appear to threaten the alleged right to life of the unborn; correspondingly, feminists may well fear that to fall back on utilitarianism would open the way to a fresh call on women for the kind of sacrifices that they have traditionally made. Involuntary abortion and involuntary childbirth are both unacceptable to feminists, but utilitarianism cannot guarantee protection from either.

III

There are two principles that I see as the key to determining whether or not each woman has the right to decide if she should terminate her pregnancy.

The first principle is that the right to life, when it is claimed for a human being, means the right to a full human life and to whatever means are necessary to achieve this. Unfortunately I am not able to spell out precisely the necessary conditions for a full human life. This is a perennial subject of philosophical debate. To some extent, although not entirely, those conditions may be dependent on the level of development of the society in which the right to life is claimed. But certainly they go beyond the requirements for mere physiological survival to the less tangible requirements for full development as a human being, however those requirements should be construed. To be born, then, is only one of the necessary conditions for a full human life; the others presumably include nutritious food, breathable air, warm human companionship, and so on. If anyone has a right to life, she or he must be entitled to all of these.

The second principle to which I shall appeal is the principle that decisions should be made by those, and only by those, who are importantly affected by them. This principle provides the fundamental justification for democracy and is accepted by most shades of political opinion. Ideological differences arise not because of disagreement on the principle but because of disagreement on how to instantiate it.

How do these two principles apply to the issue of each woman's right to decide whether or not she should abort? The first principle suggests that if an individual or an organization does not make a genuine attempt to guarantee all of a child's needs, both before and after its birth, it cannot be viewed as the protector of that child's right to life. The protector of the child's right to life is that individual or organization that attempts to fulfill *all* the conditions necessary to the child's achieving a full human life. If an individual or organization knowingly and willfully neglects some of those necessary conditions, then there is no reason to grant it any special status as the child's protector. Hence, such an individual or organization has no special moral authority that would justify its insistence on just one of the many conditions necessary to a full human life, in circumstances where this would place the burden of fulfilling all the other conditions squarely on the shoulders of some other individual or organization. In particular, it cannot appeal to its special status as defender of the unborn's right to life in order to prohibit abortion, for it has no such special status.

The second principle entails that the decision about abortion should be made by all those whose lives are to be importantly affected by that decision. Which persons are included in that class is determined partly by certain features inherent in the situation (necessarily the lives of the woman and of the unborn are importantly affected), but it is also determined partly by the social context in which the question of abortion arises. For example, in a situation of very short food supply the whole community into which the child is to be born will be affected by the birth in a way in which it would not be affected if food were plentiful.

The two principles together entail that in our society each woman has the right to choose whether or not she should terminate her pregnancy. This conclusion follows from the application of the two principles to certain contingent features of our social organization. These features include the inadequate prenatal and postnatal health care provided by the state, the fact that the main responsibility for raising a child is laid on its biological mother, and the small proportion of the natural resources devoted to welfare.

IV

To explain this, let us look again at the main candidates for a share in making the decision about abortion. Some of those who are eligible on the basis of having their lives affected by the decision are nevertheless unable in principle to participate in making it. They include the unborn child in question and future unborn generations. The world community at large, which is eligible on the same grounds, is also excluded from a share in making the decision—this time because of practical difficulties. This leaves the potential mother, the potential father, the medical staff who are asked to perform the abortion, and the state.

It will be remembered that the father's main claim to being able to decide whether or not his unborn child should be aborted was based on the fact that his life would be affected by the birth of a child. He has a legal obligation to contribute to the child's economic support, and if he happens to be married to the mother, it is conventionally understood that he will take at least a small part in raising the child; if he lives in the same house, he can hardly avoid some contact with it. In fact, however, the father has considerable choice as to how far his life is affected by the birth of his child. He may not live in the same house, and even if he does, present conventions about parenthood indicate that he will take a much smaller part in raising the child than will the mother, perhaps almost no part at all. Again, the father's obligation to provide economic support for the child may not be legally enforced. Finally, he does not have to go through the inconveniences, and even dangers, of pregnancy and childbirth. It is true that many fathers choose voluntarily to share as much as possible in the birth and raising of their children. But the fact remains that the choice is open to the father in a way in which it is not open to the mother. Biology, law, and social conditioning work together to ensure that most women's lives are totally changed as the result of the birth of a child, while men can choose how much they wish to be involved. It is for this reason that the potential mother, rather than the potential father, should have the ultimate responsibility for deciding whether or not an abortion should be performed, although this obviously does not exclude the mother from consulting the father if she wishes. If conventions regarding the degree of parental responsibility assumed by the mother and by the father were to change, or if the law prescribing paternal child support were to be enforced more rigorously, then perhaps we might require that the father share with the mother in making the decision (he could never take over the decision completely, of course, because it is not his body that is involved). But in the present social situation the right of a woman to decide if she should abort is not limited by any right of the father.

Still less should a woman's right to decide be limited by the claims of medical personnel. Their role is to present the medical information that she requests, not to determine the moral weight to be given to that information. They are not concerned in the long-term consequences of the abortion decision except insofar as they are members of the society into which the child will be born. This is not to say that even if the medical practitioners genuinely believe that abortion is morally wrong, they should still be compelled to perform it. But neither should they be able to prevent it. In practice, if there is a difficulty in finding the medical staff prepared to perform abortions, it is an indication that medical practitioners should be drawn from a broader spectrum of the population. Specifically, they should include more women. Generally, people are not slow in recognizing their rights, and if each woman has a right to choose whether or not she should abort, then female medical staff are unlikely to have moral qualms about helping her to exercise that right.

Let us now turn to the more difficult question of the claims of the state to participate in abortion decisions. Ignoring the utilitarian argument, the claim of the state rests on two grounds: the fact that the rest of the community is affected by the birth of new members and the alleged obligation of the state to protect the rights of even its unborn citizens. If our social situation were different, either of these arguments might be strong enough to justify the state's claim. But, as things are now, neither can outweigh the right of each woman to decide.

Certainly this right is not outweighed by the effects of the birth of new members on the rest of the community. While every woman's life is enormously affected by the birth of her child, the effect of new births on the rest of our society is small. Our food supply is ample, neither overpopulation nor underpopulation is as yet a serious problem, and only a very small proportion of our resources is spent on welfare. The birth of more children still has a negligible effect on the lives of everyone except the mother. The father and the siblings may be in some degree exceptions to this, but their involvement is usually minor compared to that of the mother, who has to carry, give birth to, and raise the child. Therefore, the principle that only those who are affected importantly by a decision should share in making it indicates that, in our society, the potential mother rather than the state has the right to decide whether or not she should seek an abortion.

What about the alleged obligation of the state to protect the rights of the unborn? Feminists often try to answer this question by denying that the unborn has any rights. However, I think that this argument for state control of abortion can be answered without having to commit oneself to any stand on the difficult question of the moral status of the unborn or, indeed, to any position on the general justification of abortion. I have already argued that the rights of the unborn child cannot be separated from its rights after it is born; birth is just one necessary condition of an individual's exercising his or her right to life. But an individual's right to life is not fulfilled once she or he is born. She or he then acquires immediately a whole set of complex requirements in order to exercise her or his right to life. In our society the responsibility for fulfilling those needs falls primarily on the mother. The state does indeed provide schooling and a minimal degree of physical care for those children whose mothers are unable to support them. Such children do not usually starve or freeze to death. But, as is shown by the horrifying statistics on "battered" unwanted babies and the stunted physical and emotional development of children in state institutions, the state is far from guaranteeing the fulfillment of all their basic needs. Moreover, the offspring of a poor mother who keeps her children suffer in every way from their mother's poverty: they are malnourished, subject to disease, and perhaps aware that their very existence contributes to her poverty. For our society lays on each woman the bulk of the responsibility for protecting the right to life of her children. The state abandons most of this responsibility by refusing to guarantee for each child the necessary conditions of a full human life. Thus, since in our society the mother and not the state is the primary protector of the child's right to life, it is the pregnant woman and not the state who should decide whether or not, in her own case, abortion is justified.

So far I have ignored the utilitarian arguments surrounding the question of whether each woman has the right to decide to terminate her pregnancy. There are two reasons for this. One is that most utilitarian arguments tend to support the conclusion for which I am arguing. For example, they talk about the suffering caused by illegal abortions or about the danger of promoting a general disrespect for the law, since a law that restricts a woman's right to decide is likely to be widely disobeyed. The main utilitarian argument *against* each woman's having the legal right to decide is that it is in the general interest for the state to control population policy. At this time in history, however, state population control would be more likely to result in forced abortions than in the refusal to terminate a pregnancy; but this proposal is so offensive to the moral intuitions of most people that it would probably be seen as justified only by a dire social emergency. Hence I have ignored that argument here. The other reason why I have avoided utilitarian arguments is that, in this context, they are not usually accepted as conclusive: if they seem to be working against either side in the dispute, then that side invariably reverts to talking about human rights—the antiabortionists appealing to the rights of the unborn, the proabortionists appealing to the rights of women. For myself, I tend to believe that each woman's right to decide if she should abort could be demonstrated very well on utilitarian grounds. But, for the reasons given above, I chose other grounds to defend my claim that, in our society, no individual or group has a justified claim to restrict a woman's right to decide.

To say that each woman in our society has the moral right to decide whether or not she should terminate her pregnancy is not to say that abortion is always justified. It implies nothing about what justifies abortion. Quite possibly, in deciding whether to abort or to bear the child, a woman will make the wrong decision. But the right to decide is hers.

Her right to decide is not derived from some obscure right to her own body; nor is it part of her right to privacy. It is a contingent right rather than an absolute one, resulting from women's situation in our society. In this society each woman is primarily responsible for her own support, for the medical expenses she will incur during pregnancy and childbirth, and for providing her child with both its material and emotional needs. Because of this situation, women's lives are enormously affected by the birth of their children, whereas the community as a whole is affected only slightly. Moreover, because of this situation, each woman finds that she, rather than the state, is the primary protector of her child's right to life. Given these facts, and given the principle that those and only those who are significantly affected by a decision should share in making it, it seems plain that in this society each woman has the sole moral right to determine whether or not, in her case, abortion is justified.

V

That each woman has this moral right is the basis of my claim that our legal system should guarantee to every woman the political right to decide whether or not to terminate her pregnancy. In making this claim, however, I am aware of possible problems: What should be done about very young women? What should be done about those women who are members of minority-group cultures where it is accepted that the family as a whole takes on the responsibility for fulfilling the needs of a child? And even, what should be done about women who are so rich that once a child is born, its existence may not affect their lives in any significant way? Surely circumstances like these would make us hesitate to claim that every woman in our society has the moral right to decide whether to terminate her pregnancy?

It may well be that a few women in these and other circumstances do not have the sole moral right to decide whether or not to seek an abortion. But in our society such women are exceptional, and it is a familiar fact that the law, being general, cannot take account of the unique circumstances of every individual case. I would argue that such cases are so few that they should not be allowed to limit the general conclusion that each woman in our society should be guaranteed the legal right to decide whether or not she should have her own pregnancy terminated. Consideration of such exceptions does indicate, however, a weakness inherent in any attempt to guarantee justice in terms of legal rights. For: "Right by its very nature can consist only in the application of an equal standard; but unequal individuals (and they would not be different individuals if they were not unequal) are measurable only by an equal standard in so far as they are brought under an equal point of view, are taken from one definite side only. . . . To avoid all these defects, right instead of being equal would have to be unequal."[2] And where individuals' moral rights are unequal, it is unjust that their legal rights should be the same.

The right-to-decide issue also shows why freedom and equality cannot be guaranteed simply through the establishment of political rights. As many poor women have pointed out, to grant a woman the legal right to decide whether or not she should seek an abortion does not guarantee that, in a more than trivial sense, a woman has both options open to her. If present social conditions remain unchanged, then the choice remains a merely formal rather than real choice. A real choice about abortion requires that a woman should be able to opt to have her child, as well as to abort it. This means that the full right to life of the child must be guaranteed, either by community aid to the mother who wishes to raise it herself, or by the provision of alternative arrangements that do not put the child who is not raised by its own mother at any significant disadvantage. Conversely, abortions must be made so cheap and convenient that any woman may be able to obtain one without hardship.

The latter condition is not difficult to achieve; indeed, for a number of reasons quite unconnected with women's liberation, it may well be on the way. But the former condition, while it is easy enough to state, would require social changes far-reaching enough to be accurately termed a revolution. Among other things it would require cheap or free medical care for all mothers and children, and probably, if children raised by their mothers are not to have an advantage over the others, the abandonment of the official ideology that sees the nuclear family as the ideal or normal living arrangement. In short, it would require that the community take over the responsibility for the physical and emotional welfare of all mothers and children. Therefore if a woman's right to decide whether or not she should abort is to be translated in practice into a genuine choice, uncoerced by economic stringency, it presupposes fundamental change in our most basic social institutions.

Now arises an apparent paradox. The moral right to decide for which I have been arguing is a right only for women in societies relevantly similar to this one. The existence of that right is contingent on the conditions obtaining in our society. But if these are radically altered, for example by the expenditure of a much greater proportion of our resources on welfare, then a woman's moral right to decide might be restricted. If the whole community were to assume responsibility for the welfare of mothers and children, then the application to the changed social conditions of the two principles that I used in defending the woman's right to decide would surely result in the conclusion that the community as a whole should have a share in judging whether or not a particular abortion should be performed. For the impact of new children on the whole community would be much greater, whereas the impact on the life of the mother would be considerably lessened, and might be reduced to the solely biological. Moreover, the mother's legal and conventional responsibility to protect her child's right to life would be no greater than that of any other member of the community. Of course, to say that the community as a whole should decide about abortions does not mean that the pregnant woman should not have a strong voice in making the decision: she is not just an ordinary member of the community in this matter, for it is still she who must bear and carry the child. Her wishes must therefore be accorded special weight. But she no longer would have the sole right or responsibility, depending on how one views it, for making the decision about whether or not to abort. The paradox, then, is that the attempt to guarantee the conditions in which each woman's right to decide about abortion would become a real option results in the achievement of conditions in which she no longer has that right.

The resolution of this paradox lies in the recognition that the establishment of political rights is inadequate as an ultimate social ideal. As such rights cannot guarantee justice, neither can they guarantee real freedom or equality. Unless our society is fundamentally changed, only a few women will be able to make a choice that is not determined by their economic situation. Hence, except for those fortunate few, the legal freedom to decide whether or not to abort will not result in genuine freedom of choice. And hence women's rights will not really be equal.

The abortion issue shows clearly why, in our search for justice, freedom, and equality, it may well be more fruitful to change our emphasis from the establishment of individual rights to the fulfillment of human needs. To attempt to describe an ideal society in terms of individual rights is to suggest that every society is composed of individuals whose interests inevitably conflict. This picture may be an accurate likeness of our present society, and, so long as it remains accurate, women must be granted the legal right to decide whether or not they should abort. Ultimately, however, when the community as a whole takes on the responsibility for fulfilling the needs of its members and the conflict between the interests of the individual and the interests of the rest of society is reconciled, this right will no longer be necessary. To achieve the legal right to decide about abortion is a first step on the way to women's liberation, but the last step may be the achievement of a society in which the whole notion of individual rights against the community makes no sense at all.

VI

It is sometimes objected that the foregoing argument justifies not only a woman's right to abort but also her right to kill her two-week-old baby or even her six-year-old child. The objectors assume, of course, that if this were indeed a consequence of my account, it would make my claim quite unacceptable.

My answer depends on making a distinction—not a problematic distinction between the moral status of prenatal and postnatal children, but an obvious and uncontroversial distinction between a woman's relation to her unborn child and her relation to it once it is born. She cannot sever the tie between herself and her unborn child in any way short of killing that child. She can, however, cut the connection between herself and a postnatal child without directly killing that child. Psychologically agonizing as it may be (and that empirical fact is not irrelevant to the right to abortion), one can walk away from the crying of a baby as one cannot walk away from the kicking of an unborn child. It is possible, at least in principle, to ignore the needs of a baby, whereas an unborn child will take its needs from a woman's body regardless of her willingness or her ability to give. A mother may, though at tremendous psychological cost, refuse her socially assigned responsibility for raising her child. But there is no way in which a pregnant woman can avoid the discomforts and inconveniences of her condition, nor the experience of childbirth, which not only carries an unavoidable risk to her life, but which, in our society, is sometimes very painful and often humiliating.

I have argued that the pregnant woman's right to decide on abortion results from her finding herself in a social situation that leaves her with the primary responsibility for coping with her pregnancy, the birth, and the child to be. But we must not forget, of course, that only a pregnant woman can ever be in such a situation. It is obvious that a woman's relation to her child is only partly defined by society; it is also determined by biology. It is the conjunction of the biological element with the social one that makes a woman's relation to her unborn child a unique relation of peculiar magnitude and peculiar inevitability. I have already made it clear that if the *social* aspect of the relationship were to change, then we would have to reexamine the claim that women have the sole right to decide on abortion. What I must now make explicit, in order to show that a mother's right to infanticide is not a necessary consequence of a woman's right to abortion, is that when the *biological* aspect of the relationship is changed, as it is when the child is born, then another moral reevaluation must occur, and the rights of the mother must be redefined. (So, indeed, should her responsibilities, together with the rights and responsibilities of the father and of the state, be redefined.) Consequently, it is plain that whether a woman has the right to infanticide is a question quite separate from whether she has the right to abort and must be considered on its own merits.

NOTES

1. The time to write this essay was provided by a Taft grant-in-aid of research. Some of the stimulus to do so was provided by hearing an unpublished paper, "Women's Rights, Population Control, and Marxist Ideology," read by Janet Farrell Smith at a meeting of the midwestern division of the Society for Women in Philosophy, in Chicago, February 1974.

2. Karl Marx, *Critique of the Gotha Programme,* reprinted in Karl Marx and Frederick Engels, *Selected Works of Marx and Engels* (New York: International Publishing Co., 1968), p. 324.

Baruch Brody

Fetal Humanity and the Theory of Essentialism

There is a familiar argument against abortion that runs as follows: (1) From a certain point before birth the fetus is a human being with the same rights to life as any other human being. (2) From that point on, an abortion is—in normal circumstances—an act of murder that cannot be justified morally. (3) Moreover, there should be laws against such abortions.

In a series of earlier papers I have argued that propositions 2 and 3 do indeed follow from proposition 1.[1] But the question still remains as to whether proposition 1 is true. In a recent paper I have tried to show that that question cannot be resolved until we can determine what properties are essential for being human and when the fetus acquires them.[2] No doubt there are many who would prefer to settle the question of fetal humanity without considering such metaphysical questions, but I tried to show that that cannot be done.

In this paper I will present, at least in outline, a general theory of essentialism,[3] and in light of this general theory I will try to determine when the fetus becomes a human being.

AN INTRODUCTION TO ESSENTIALISM

The question that we are concerned with is when the possession of a given property is essential (necessary) for membership in a given class. However, I want to put that question aside for now, for reasons that will emerge shortly, to consider the related question of when a given object has a property essentially (necessarily). These are different questions, since one has to do with the conditions under which an object is a member of a given class, while the other has to do with the conditions under which a given object must have a given property. But an answer to the latter question helps provide an answer to the former.

What is the distinction between the properties that an object has essentially and the properties that an object has accidentally? It is the following: On one hand, there are some properties that an object must have; if the object did not have them, it would not exist at all. These are the properties that an object has essentially. On the other hand, there are some properties that an object has, but might not have.

There are two obvious questions raised by this distinction: (1) What does it mean to say that an object must have a property, as opposed merely to saying that it has the property but might not? (2) How can we tell which properties are possessed by an object essentially and which are possessed by an object accidentally? It is important to keep in mind that these are two different (although obviously related) questions. One is concerned with the meaning of certain claims, the other with how we come to know whether these claims are true or false. And it may be the case (although I think that it is not) that we know what these claims mean without knowing how to tell whether they are true or false.

Many philosophers believe that these questions cannot be answered and therefore reject all talk about essential properties. Some scholars are not so sure and in recent years have attempted to develop answers (especially to the first, crucial question). Many such attempts are based on the Leibnizian idea of a logically possible, but not actual, situation (this is usually called a logically possible, or simply, a possible, world). The assertion is made that an object has a property essentially and necessarily just in case it has that property, not merely in the actual world, but in all possible worlds, or at least in all possible worlds in which the object exists. On the other hand, the argument continues, an object has a property accidentally just in case it has that property in the actual world, but there are possible worlds in which it does not have the property.

Even this attempt is, however, not entirely satisfactory. After all, what does it mean to say that some object, A, has a property, P, in some possible world? Presumably it means that there is some object, B, in that possible world that is identical with A and has P. But what does it mean to say that B is identical with A? In short, what does identity across possible worlds mean? If (as many philosophers believe) that question cannot be answered, then appealing to the idea of an object's having a property in all possible worlds sheds little light on the idea of an object's having a property necessarily. Perhaps an example will help make this point clearer. Consider the big tree on my front lawn. Is it necessarily a tree? Could it have been something else? Well, we can easily imagine a possible world in which there is a big rock on my front lawn but no tree. Is that a world in which my tree is a rock? That depends on whether the big thing on my lawn in that possible world is identical with my tree in the actual world. But since we have no understanding of this cross-world identity, the very meaning of that question (and also, any possible answers to it) is unclear.

For these reasons I have proposed an alternative approach to essential properties. According to this alternative an object has a property necessarily (and essentially) if it cannot lose that property without going out of existence. For example, it is an accidental property of my tree that it has 832 leaves on it. After all, it can grow an additional leaf or a leaf can fall off and the tree will continue to exist. On the other hand, if it were chopped down and cut into lumber so that there was no tree there anymore, my tree would have gone out of existence. On my account, the property of being a tree is essential to the tree on my lawn.

Let us put this definition a little more carefully. If, before a change, there was an object, O, with a property P, then the change is what we can call an alteration (as against a substantial change) if O continues to exist after the change though it no longer possesses P. On the other hand, the change is a substantial change if after its occurrence O no longer exists. Then we shall say that object O has a property P accidentally just in case it has P and its loss of P would be an alteration; but it has P essentially just in case it has P and its loss of P would be a substantial change.

NATURAL KINDS AND ESSENTIAL PROPERTIES

We return now to our original question of how to determine what properties are essential (necessary) for membership in a given class. In order to deal with it, however, one final concept must be introduced. We shall say that any property had essentially by some object and accidentally by none (whether actual or potential) determines a natural kind. In other words, a natural kind is a set of objects each of which has a certain property necessarily (with the proviso that nothing else has that property). The set of trees is one example of a natural kind, since each tree necessarily has the property of being a tree (it would go out of existence if it stopped being a tree) and nothing but trees are trees. But the set of white objects is not a natural kind since not every white object has the property of being white necessarily. Many (perhaps even all) could have their color changed while still continuing to exist.

I should now like to introduce several claims about the properties that are essential for membership in a natural kind: (1) Only the possession of properties had essentially by every member of a natural kind is necessary (essential) for membership in that natural kind. (2) The possession of all properties had essentially by every member of a natural kind is sufficient for membership in that natural kind. Claim 1 tells us which properties are such that their possession is essential (necessary) for membership in natural kinds, while claim 2 tells us which properties are such that their concurrent possession is sufficient for membership in natural kinds.

Both of these claims would be false if they were extended to classes in general. Consider the class of white objects. While being white is not a property had essentially by every member of that class, it is necessary (essential) for membership in that class. So claim 1 would be false if it were extended to cover nonnatural kinds. Similarly, it seems that the only properties had essentially by every member of this class are those had essentially by all colored objects, but the possession of these properties is not sufficient for membership in the class of white objects. What is sufficient is being white. So claim 2 would also be false if it were extended to cover nonnatural kinds.

Intuitively, what is happening here is the following: Assume that for each class there are some properties such that the possession of each of them is necessary and their concurrent possession is sufficient for membership in the class in question. According to claim 1 the only necessary properties are those had essentially by all members of that class, and according to claim 2 their concurrent possession is a sufficient condition for membership in that class. These conclusions must be false in the case of nonnatural kinds for there are no properties that their members, and only their members, have essentially and the possession of which could be the necessary and sufficient conditions for membership in the class in question. But in the case of a natural kind, where there are properties that all members of a class have essentially and nothing else has at all, it is plausible to conjecture that the possession of these properties is necessary and sufficient for membership in the natural kind. This is, of course, precisely what is maintained in claims 1 and 2.

I have no proof that claims 1 and 2 are true. But they are intuitively plausible and no counter-examples seem to be forthcoming. So I will tentatively adopt them and use them to consider the question of the essence of humanity.

HUMANITY AS A NATURAL KIND

We will now use the results of our metaphysical discussion to determine what properties are essential for being human and to determine that point at which the fetus becomes a human being. An important step in this process is to decide whether or not the class of human beings is a natural kind. Obviously all and only the members of the class of human beings have the property of being human. If every member of that class has that property essentially, if no human being can stop being a human being and still exist, then the class of human beings will be a natural kind.

Consider the moment of death. It would be wrong to think of it just as a moment at which the human being undergoes a significant alteration. Rather it is the moment at which he stops being human and goes out of existence. This is why death is so different from anything else that happens to us. We survive other occurrences however they may change us, but we do not survive our deaths. As Wittgenstein put it, "Death is not an event in life: we do not live to experience death."[4] So a human being goes out of existence when he stops being human; being human is therefore an essential property of every human being, and humanity is a natural kind.

It is probably obvious to note that in saying that a human being goes out of existence when he dies (but not, for example, when he loses his memory or experiences a severe change of character) I am not also saying that no part of him continues to exist. His body exists for some time after death, and in some views what is called the soul does also. But the human being has gone out of existence.[5]

The following objection might be raised: It is true that, in the normal course of events, when a human being is no longer a human being, he also no longer exists. But perhaps there are ways in which human beings could stop being human beings but still continue to exist. Consider the case of Gregor in Kafka's *Metamorphosis*. Has he not survived his amazing transformation, although he is no longer a human being? And given that this is so, it follows that being human is not an essential property of human beings.

It is difficult to know what to say about this objection because it is difficult to know what to say about the case of Gregor. Despite its literary strength it is not clear that Kafka's story succeeds in presenting us with a coherent picture of Gregor in an insect's body. But assume that it has. The objector seems to be impressed with the continuities through this change when he assures us that it still is Gregor, and with the discontinuities when he assures us that it is no longer a human being. The justification for this asymmetrical treatment is unclear. To the extent that one thinks that it is still Gregor, should not one also think that it is a human being (even if in the body of a bug); and to the extent that one thinks that it is not a human being, should not one think that it is not Gregor (even if it does have many of his thoughts, feelings, and emotions)?

Moreover there is an important methodological point to note here. I will throughout this essay emphasize the use of self-evident intuitions as a source of knowledge, and will try to elicit intuitions about many unusual cases. But these will be quite closely tied to reality. Those who raise the case of Gregor, however, turn to the fictional and break sharply with reality; and it is just at this point, it seems to me, that a reliance on intuitions is most debatable.

Keeping in mind the two claims about the properties that are necessary and sufficient for membership in a natural kind, we may proceed with our evaluation of essentialist arguments about fetal humanity. The common structure of such arguments is: (a) There is a property, P, that is such that its possession is essential for being human. (b) By the time an entity acquires P, it has every other property, Q, that is essential for being human. (c) When the fetus acquires P, it becomes a human being.

There are two major problems with each of these arguments: How do we tell whether their essentialist claims are true? And how do we modify them so that the appropriate step of type c will follow from the appropriate steps of types a and b? We now see how to solve these problems. Since humanity is a natural kind, the only properties essential for being a human being, given our assumption 1, are those had essentially by every human being—namely, those such that their loss would mean that the human being in question would go out of existence. We can therefore use the going-out-of-existence test to determine the truth of the claims of types a and b in any given argument. And given our assumption 2, the claim of type c does follow straightforwardly from the claims of types a and b.

In short, then, our technical excursus has put us in a position to deal with the problem of the essence of humanity. What we must first see is what properties are such that their loss would mean the going-out-of-existence (the death) of a human being. We turn therefore to an analysis of death.

THE ANALYSIS OF DEATH

The question of when a human being is dead has become one of great importance in recent years. Two factors are primarily responsible. The first is the growing frequency of transplants of vital organs. Given the present state of medical science it is preferable that the organ to be transplanted be removed from the donor's body as soon as possible (organ banks are a conjecturable development for the future). However, there is a strong moral feeling that no matter how definitely incurable the illness of the donor is, and no matter how close to death he may be, it is wrong to remove the organ until the point of natural death has passed. It is therefore extremely important to develop a precise definition of the moment of death so as to satisfy both demands (as much as may be possible) by taking the organ from the donor's body as soon as possible after that point.

The second factor influencing our preoccupation with this definition is the growing technological ability to maintain vital functions by artificial means when they no longer operate naturally. No one feels that we ought to continue to maintain vital functions by artificial means after the person is "dead"; but there is some feeling that, no matter how incurable we may believe his illness to be or how close to death he is, we should continue to supply this artificial maintenance so long as he is alive. Once more, it becomes extremely important to know when "death" occurs.

Because it is these two factors that have given rise to the current emphasis on the issue of defining death, it is important to keep in mind two extremely significant cautionary remarks. The first was made by David

Daube: "The question of at what moment it is in order to discontinue extraordinary or even ordinary measures to keep a person alive should not be confused with the question of at what moment a man is dead. Discontinuation of such measures is often justifiable even while the patient is conscious."[6] Even if Daube's last claim is too strong, there may be cases in which it would be permissible, and perhaps even obligatory, to discontinue medical measures intended to support life even though the person is not yet dead. The relief of human suffering is one obvious motive in such cases. Consequently, although there certainly is a relation between when a person dies and when you can (or should) stop using artificial measures, these are not necessarily identical problems.

The second important cautionary point is Paul Ramsey's: "If no person's death should for this purpose [to remove an organ for use in a transplant] be hastened, then the definition of death should not for this purpose be updated, or the procedures for stating that a man has died be revised as a means of affording easier access to organs."[7] Again, whether or not we agree with the principle of not hastening death for the purpose of organ recovery, we must agree that we should not adopt a definition of death for the purpose of organ recovery; we must agree that we should not adopt a definition of death solely for the sake of making transplant therapy successful. The question of when a person has died has to be settled on independent intellectual grounds.

Traditionally death was defined in terms of a cessation of cardiac and respiratory activity. Doctors would test for such cessation by using mirrors to detect emission of breath and by seeking the pulse to detect continued circulation. It was recognized that death could be brought about by the destruction of other systems and organs (the liver, the kidneys, the brain), but it was generally thought that their destruction brought about death by affecting the functioning of heart and lung. This approach is summarized in the following definition of death: "The cessation of life; the ceasing to exist; defined by physicians as a total stoppage of the circulation of blood, and a cessation of the animal and vital functions consequent thereon, such as respiration, pulsation, etc."[8] This tradition has, of course, come under important challenge in recent years. There is a growing tendency to define death in terms of an irreparable cessation of brain function. It is increasingly felt that this kind of cessation, rather than a cessation of cardiac and respiratory activity, is the essence of death.

A signal place in the development of this revisionist approach is occupied by the report of an ad hoc committee of the Harvard Medical

School that appeared in the *Journal of the American Medical Association* in 1968.[9] That report clearly suggests a movement away from the traditional definition of death and toward the "brain-death" definition (the phrase is a popular one; in using it, we should note that it contains a significant rhetorical load). The authors suggest a variety of clinical tests for determining brain death. These include tests for receptivity and responsitivity, for spontaneous movement, and for reflex activity. They also suggest that a flat (or isoelectric) EEG could serve to confirm brain death.[10]

One point should particularly be noted about their recommendations. They do not suggest that a flat EEG can be taken as definitive of death. They merely offer it as a way of confirming the presence of an irreversible coma. There are good reasons for treating a flat EEG only as an indicator of death; in some well-documented cases a flat EEG reading was obtained for several hours and was followed by complete recovery. The coma was due in those cases to severe barbiturate poisoning, and in such cases, as well as in cases of hypothermia (in which the body temperature may fall below ninety degrees), flat EEG readings are not even good indicators of irreversible coma.

What arguments are offered by the ad hoc committee for its recommendations? They emerge most clearly in its criticism of the traditional definition of death:

> From ancient times down to the recent past it was clear that, when the respiration and heart stopped, the brain would die in a few minutes; so the obvious criterion of no heart beat as synonymous with death was sufficiently accurate. In those times the heart was considered to be the central organ of the body; it is not surprising that its failure marked the onset of death. This is no longer valid when modern resuscitative and supportive measures are used. These improved activities can now restore "life" as judged by the ancient standards of persistent respiration and continuing heart beat. This can be the case even when there is not the remotest possibility of an individual recovering consciousness following massive brain damage. In other situations "life" can be maintained only by means of an artificial respiration and electrical stimulation of the heart beat.[11]

This passage deserves careful attention since it contains the core of the argument for redefining death. Unfortunately it is poorly argued, since it includes three rather different arguments. The first is suggested by the opening passages. There are cases in which the patient's brain has not died, but in which the heart and respiratory system has stopped and will not revive naturally. In such cases, the heart and respiratory system can be revived artificially and will, after a period of time, function naturally and spontaneously. According to the classical definition the patient died but was medically resurrected. It would seem more reasonable to abandon this definition and replace it with one that avoids the element of resurrection. We should therefore adopt the brain-death definition and treat the person as dead only when his brain has died. The second argument is suggested by the closing passages of the quotation: there are cases in which the patient suffers massive brain damage and is clearly dead, though his respiration and circulation can be kept functioning by artificial means. According to the traditional definition such a patient is still alive. Therefore the traditional definition should be rejected in favor of a definition that treats someone as dead when their brain has died.

The second of these arguments is clearly in error. Proponents of the traditional definition, one may reasonably conclude, were talking about spontaneous cardiac and respiratory functions and not artificially supported functions. They were not, therefore, necessarily committed to the view that the patients referred to in the second argument ought to be regarded as still alive. The first argument is not open to this objection, but the argument can be met by modifying the classical definition so that it refers to an irreparable cessation of spontaneous and natural cardiac and respiratory functions. Then the first objection is not valid, for it deals with cases in which spontaneous and natural cardiac and respiratory functions can be revived. According to our revised version of the classical definition, the patient has not died, for those functions have ceased only temporarily, and will resume naturally after interim support.

All of this leads us, however, to still a third argument suggested by the quotation: (1) There are cases in which a person's heart beats spontaneously even though his brain is in irreversible coma. (2) In such cases, even according to the classical definition of death as we have revised it, the person is alive. (3) But he clearly is dead. (4) Therefore, we should revise the definition so that death is the cessation of brain function. This last argument brings us to the crux of the issue: Is proposition 3 true? Paul Ramsey, for one, thinks that it is not:

> It is one thing to declare a person to be obviously still alive so long as he has an indefinitely fully functioning brain in the absence of heart or lung function. It would be quite another thing to declare a person dead (because his brain is past full recovery) in the presence of a still continuing, natural functioning of lungs and/or heart.[12]

These are, I think, very puzzling differentiations. One can easily understand, with Ramsey, that as long as the brain still functions naturally, the absence of spontaneous circulation and respiration does not indicate death (we have had no trouble regarding as alive people who use iron lungs or pacemakers. The traditional definition of death, we could all agree, needs to be modified once again to read: a person is dead only if there has been an irreparable cessation of spontaneous and natural cardiac and respiratory functions and there has been an irreparable cessation of brain function. But suppose we have the latter condition without the former: the brain has ceased to function but the heart and lungs have not. Ramsey is correct in calling attention to this case as different from its reverse. Is the person dead if his brain has suffered irreparable and massive damage, whatever the state of the heart and lungs?

As we use the concept of death to help us determine what is essential for being human, we will remember that there remain some fundamental questions to which we are unable to give precise answers. This is not surprising in light of the complexity of human life. I shall try to reduce this difficulty by continuing my argument in ways compatible with both definitions of death, traditional (as modified in light of our discussion of it) and revisionist.

THE ESSENCE OF HUMANITY

We will first consider the question of what properties are essential to being human if we suppose that death and the passing out of existence occur only if there has been an irreparable cessation of brain function (keeping in mind that that condition itself, as we have noted, is a matter of medical judgment). We shall then consider the same question on the supposition that Ramsey's more complicated theory of death (the modified traditional view) is correct.

According to what is called the brain-death theory, as long as there has not been an irreparable cessation of brain function the person in question continues to exist, no matter what else has happened to him. If so, it seems to follow that there is only one property—leaving aside those entailed by this one property—had essentially by each human being (and therefore that there is only one property that is essential to humanity), namely, the possession of a brain that has not suffered an irreparable cessation of function.[13]

Several consequences follow immediately from this conclusion. We can see that a variety of often-advanced claims about the essence of humanity are false. For example, the claim that movement, or perhaps just the ability to move, is essential for being human is false. A human being who has stopped moving, and even one who has lost the ability to move, has not therefore stopped existing. Being able to move, and a fortiori moving, are not essential properties of human beings and therefore are not essential to being human. Similarly, the claim that being perceivable by other human beings is essential for being human is also false. A human being who has stopped being perceivable by other humans (for example, someone isolated on the other side of the moon, out of reach even of radio communication) has not stopped existing. Being perceivable by other human beings is not an essential property of human beings and is not essential to being human. And the same point can be made about the claims that viability is essential for being human, that independent existence is essential for being human, and that actual interaction with other human beings is essential for being human. The loss of any of these properties would not mean that the human being in question had gone out of existence, so none of them can be essential to that human being and none of them can be essential for being human.

Let us now look at the following argument: (1) A functioning brain (or at least, a brain that, if not functioning, is susceptible of function) is a property that every human being must have because it is essential for being human. (2) By the time an entity acquires that property, it has all the other properties that are essential for being human. (3) The class of human beings is a natural kind. (4) Therefore, when the fetus acquires that property it becomes a human being. It is clear that the property in question is, according to the brain-death theory, one that is had essentially by all human beings. The question that we have to consider is whether the second premise is true. It might appear that its truth does follow from the brain-death theory. After all, we did see that that theory entails that only one property (together with those entailed by it) is essential for being human. Nevertheless, rather than relying solely on my earlier argument, I shall adopt an alternative approach to strengthen the conviction that this second premise it true: I shall note the important ways in which the fetus resembles and differs from an ordinary human being by the time it definitely has a functioning brain (about the end of the sixth week of development). It shall then be evident, in light of our theory of essentialism, that none of these differences involves the lack of some property in the fetus that is essential for its being human.

Structurally there are few features of the human being that are not fully present by the end of the sixth week. Not only are the familiar external features and all the internal organs present, but the contours of the body are nicely rounded. More important, the body is functioning. Not only is the brain functioning, but the heart is beating sturdily (the fetus by this time has its own completely developed vascular system), the stomach is producing digestive juices, the liver is manufacturing blood cells, the kidney is extracting uric acid from the blood, and the nerves and muscles are operating in concert, so that reflex reactions can begin.

What are the properties that a fetus acquires after the sixth week of its development? Certain structures do appear later. These include the fingernails (which appear in the third month), the completed vocal chords (which also appear then), taste buds and salivary glands (again, in the third month), and hair and eyelashes (in the fifth month). In addition, certain functions begin later than the sixth week. The fetus begins to urinate (in the third month), to move spontaneously (in the third month), to respond to external stimuli (at least in the fifth month), and to breathe (in the sixth month). Moreover, there is a constant growth in size. And finally, at the time of birth the fetus ceases to receive its oxygen and food through the placenta and starts receiving them through the mouth and nose.

I will not examine each of these properties (structures and functions) to show that they are not essential for being human. The procedure would be essentially the one used previously to show that various essentialist claims are in error. We might therefore conclude, on the supposition that the brain-death theory is correct, that the fetus becomes a human being about the end of the sixth week after its development.

There is, however, one complication that should be noted here. There are, after all, progressive stages in the physical development and in the functioning of the brain. For example, the fetal brain (and nervous system) does not develop sufficiently to support spontaneous motion until some time in the third month after conception. There is, of course, no doubt that that stage of development is sufficient for the fetus to be human. No one would be likely to maintain that a spontaneously moving human being has died; and similarly, a spontaneously moving fetus would seem to have become human. One might, however, want to claim that the fetus does not become a human being until the point of spontaneous movement. So then, on the supposition that the brain-death theory of death is correct, one ought to conclude that the fetus becomes a human being at some time between the sixth and twelfth week after its conception.

But what if we reject the brain-death theory, and replace it with its equally plausible contender, Ramsey's theory of death? According to that theory—which we can call the brain, heart, and lung theory of death—the human being does not die, does not go out of existence, until such time as the brain, heart, and lungs have irreparably ceased functioning naturally. What are the essential features of being human according to this theory?

Actually, the adoption of Ramsey's theory requires no major modifications. According to that theory, what is essential to being human, what each human being must retain if he is to continue to exist, is the possession of a functioning (actually or potentially) heart, lung, or brain. It is only when a human being possesses none of these that he dies and goes out of existence; and the fetus comes into humanity, so to speak, when he acquires one of these.

On Ramsey's theory, the argument would now run as follows: (1) The property of having a functioning brain, heart, or lungs (or at least organs of the kind that, if not functioning, are susceptible of function) is one that every human being must have because it is essential for being human. (2) By the time that an entity acquires that property it has all the other properties that are essential for being human. (3) The class of human beings is a natural kind. (4) Therefore, when the fetus acquires that property it becomes a human being. There remains, once more, the problem of the second premise. Since the fetal heart starts operating rather early, it is not clear that the second premise is correct. Many systems are not yet operating, and many structures are not yet present. Still, following our theory of essentialism, we should conclude that the fetus becomes a human being when it acquires a functioning heart (the first of the organs to function in the fetus).

There is, however, a further complication here, and it is analogous to the one encountered if we adopt the brain-death theory: When may we properly say that the fetal heart begins to function? At two weeks, when occasional contractions of the primitive fetal heart are present? In the fourth to fifth week, when the heart, although incomplete, is beating regularly and pumping blood cells through a closed vascular system, and when the tracings obtained by an ECG exhibit the classical elements of an adult tracing? Or after the end of the seventh week, when the fetal heart is functionally complete and "normal"?

We have not reached a precise conclusion in our study of the question of when the fetus becomes a human being. We do know that it does so sometime between the end of the second week and the end of the third month. But it surely is not a human being at the moment of conception and it surely is one by the end of the third month. Though we have not come to a final answer to our question, we have narrowed the range of acceptable answers considerably.

IN RESPONSE TO CALLAHAN

It is clear that the position that I have been advocating in this essay places me among the members of the developmental school (as this term is used by Daniel Callahan [14]) and shows my agreement with those who believe that the fetus becomes a human being at some stage in its development. Indeed, the position that I am advocating was first suggested to me by a reading of Callahan's account of that school. But Callahan rejects the whole approach of the school. Let us consider his reasons.

Callahan's first objection is that "if one chooses to use a development criterion, there are any number of stages other than that of brain development that might be chosen. Implantation, gastrulation, the presence of all organs, completion of the brain structure, 'quickening,' viability, birth, and so on have each been suggested as the dividing line by different commentators in recent history. Why choose one rather than another?" [15] In effect, this problem was raised in this essay, and my main concern has been to meet this challenge by defending the reasonableness of a particular dividing line. If my argument has been successful, we need not worry about this objection.

The second, more serious objection has to do with the matter of potentials. Callahan introduces it with the following remark: "Yet it [the developmental approach] is not without its difficulties. One of these is that it does not give wide range to the concept of 'potentiality.' A zygote has, genetically (dependent upon successful development), the potentiality to become a 'person.'" [16] It is not clear why the mere possession of that potential makes the fetus a human being. Callahan, however, goes on to make the following suggestive remark:

> An objection to the use of a common criterion of life for both nascent embryos and dying persons might be based upon one important distinction. In the case of an irreversible coma (signalled by a flat EEG), it is not the coma as such but the irreversibility which is the critical condition. For with the "death" of the brain . . . comes the loss of all potentiality for personhood. . . . In the instance of a zygote or early embryo, however, even before the advent of brain waves—the potentiality for personhood exists. [17]

From our perspective this passage suggests the following argument: The moment at which the human being goes out of existence occurs at that point at which the potential for continued performance of certain functions is no longer present. Brain-death (or brain, heart, and lung death) is considered the moment of death because it is then that this potential ceases. But if that is so, then the property that an entity must have in order to be a human being—the property that is essential for humanity—is the possession of this potential. The fetus has this potential from the moment of conception, and since nothing else is essential for being human the fetus is a human being from the moment of conception. We can therefore view Callahan as attempting to defend the argument of potential by appealing to our own criterion of essentialism.

It seems to me that this point is ultimately in error. In order to see why, let us imagine the following science-fiction case.[18] Imagine that medical technology has reached the stage at which, when brain death occurs, the brain is removed, "liquefied," and "recast" into a new functioning brain. The new brain bears no relation to the old one (it has none of its memory traces, and so on). If the new brain were put back into the old body, would the same human being exist, or a new human being who made use of the body of the old one? I am inclined to suppose the latter. But consider the entity whose brain had died. Is that entity not like the fetus? Both have the potential for developing a functioning brain (we shall call this a weak potential), but neither now has the structure of a functioning brain. We can conclude, it seems to me, that an entity can go out of existence even if it retains a weak potential for having a functioning brain, and analogously, that the fetus is not a human being just because it has this weak potential. What is essential for being human is the possession of the potential for human activities that comes with having the structures required for a functioning brain. It is this potential that the fetus acquires at (or perhaps slightly before) the time that its brain starts functioning, and it is this potential that the newly conceived fetus does not have. We can therefore lay this matter of potential to rest.

CONCLUDING REMARKS

If the argument of this paper is correct, then we can conclude that the fetus becomes a human being between the end of the second week and the end of the twelfth week after conception. I believe that my earlier papers have shown that abortions after the fetus has become a human being cannot be justified morally and should be prohibited by law from that point on.

I recognize that these conclusions are not popular, but I do believe that they are correct. My hope is that this paper will at least convince the reader that these conclusions are worthy of serious consideration.

NOTES:

1. "Abortion and the Law," in *Journal of Philosophy* (1971) and "Abortion and the Sanctity of Human Life," in *American Philosophical Quarterly* (1973). Both are reprinted in Joel Feinberg, *Problems of Abortion* (Belmont, Calif.: Wadsworth. 1973).

2. "On the Humanity of the Fetus," in Robert Perkins, *Abortion: Pro, Con, and Maybe* (Cambridge, Mass.: Schenkman, 1974).

3. For more details see my "De Re and De Dicto Interpretations of Modal Logic," *Philosophia* (1972), and my "Why Settle for Anything Less than Good Old-Fashioned Aristotelean Essentialism," *Nous* (1973).

4. *Tractatus Logico-Philosophicus* (Boston: Routledge and Kegan Paul, 1961), 6. 4311.

5. I am presupposing—for it would take us too far afield to argue the issue here —that the survival of the soul would not be sufficient for the survival of the human being himself. Indeed, from that perception may arise the insistence of many religious people upon the doctrine of resurrection.

6. *Ethics in Medical Progress* (Boston: Little, Brown, 1966), pp. 190-91.

7. *The Patient as Person* (New Haven, Conn.: Yale University Press, 1971), p. 103.

8. *Black's Law Dictionary.*

9. It is conveniently reprinted in Donald Culter, *Updating Life and Death* (Boston: Beacon Press, 1969).

10. Interestingly, a jury in Richmond, Virginia, recently had to deal with a case in which the donor was still breathing, although his brain was destroyed, until his heart was removed. The jury agreed with the doctors that brain-death was the determining factor.

11. Cutler, *Updating Life and Death*, pp. 61-62.

12. Ramsey, *The Patient as Person*, p. 96.

13. Saying this raises, of course, a fundamental problem about the rights of animals, especially their right to life. Unless one is prepared to require what might be called advanced abilities from the brain in question—and that would be likely to exclude infants and brain-damaged or severely retarded adults, as well as fetuses, from the class of human beings—the crucial difference between persons, who have a strong right to life, and animals, who are commonly regarded as having a far weaker one, is the species to which they belong. Can that difference in species

support the differences in rights, especially when we recognize in animals the very property essential for being human?

On this difficult question see my "Morality and Religion Reconsidered," in *Philosophy of Religion: The Analytic Approach* (Englewood Cliffs, N.J.: Prentice-Hall, 1974).

14. In Perkins, *Abortion.*

15. Ibid, pp. 389-90.

16. Ibid, p. 380.

17. Ibid.

18. I shall adopt the brain-death theory to make my point. A similar point can obviously be made using Ramsey's theory.

R. M. Hare

Abortion and the Golden Rule

If philosophers are going to apply ethical theory successfully to practical issues, they must first have a theory. This may seem obvious; but they often proceed as if it were not so. A philosopher's chief contribution to a practical issue should be to show us which are good and which are bad arguments; and to do this he has to have some way of telling one from the other. Moral philosophy therefore needs a basis in philosophical logic—the logic of the moral concepts. But we find, for example, Professor Judith Jarvis Thomson, in an article on abortion which has been justly praised for

This article, which was the 1974 Hurst Lecture at American University, is reprinted with permission from *Philosophy & Public Affairs* 4 (Spring 1975). Copyright © 1975 R. M. Hare.

the ingenuity and liveliness of her examples, proceeding as if this were not necessary at all.[1] She simply parades the examples before us and asks what we would say about them. But how do we know whether what we feel inclined to say has any secure ground? May we not feel inclined to say it just because of the way we were brought up to think? And was this necessarily the right way? It is highly diverting to watch the encounter in the same volume between her and Mr. John Finnis, who, being a devout Roman Catholic, has intuitions which differ from hers (and mine) in the wildest fashion.[2] I just do not know how to tell whether Mr. Finnis is on safe ground when he claims that suicide is "a paradigm case of an action that is always wrong"; nor Professor Thomson when she makes the no doubt more popular claim that we have a right to decide what happens in and to our own bodies.[3] How would we choose between these potentially conflicting intuitions? Is it simply a contest in rhetoric?

In contrast, a philosopher who wishes to contribute to the solution of this and similar practical problems should be trying to develop, on the basis of a study of the moral concepts and their logical properties, a theory of moral reasoning that will determine which arguments we ought to accept. Professor Thomson might be surprised to see me saying this, because she thinks that I am an emotivist,[4] in spite of the fact that I devoted two of the very first papers I ever published to a refutation of emotivism.[5] Her examples are entertaining, and help to show up our prejudices; but they will do no more than that until we have a way of telling which prejudices ought to be abandoned.

II

I shall abjure two approaches to the question of abortion which have proved quite unhelpful. The first puts the question in terms of the "rights" of the fetus or the mother; the second demands, as a necessary condition for solving the problem, an answer to the question, Is the fetus a person? The first is unhelpful at the moment, because nobody has yet proposed an even plausible account of how we might argue conclusively about rights. Rights are the stamping ground of intuitionists, and it would be difficult to find any claim confidently asserted to a right which could not be as confidently countered by a claim to another right, such that both rights cannot simultaneously be complied with. This is plainly true in the present controversy, as it is in the case of rights to property—one man has a right not to starve, another a right to hold on to the money that would buy him food. Professor Thomson evidently believes in property rights, because she curiously bases the right of a woman to decide what happens in and to her own body on her ownership of it. We might ask whether, if this is correct, the property is disposable; could it be held that by the marriage contract a wife and a husband yield up to each other some of their property rights in their own bodies? If so, might we find male chauvinists who were prepared to claim that, if the husband wants to have an heir, the wife cannot claim an absolute liberty to have an abortion? As a question of law, this could be determined by the courts and the legislature; but as a question of morals . . . ?

In the law, cash value can be given to statements about rights by translating them into statements about what it is or is not lawful to do. An analogous translation will have to be effected in morals, with "right" (adjective), "wrong," and "ought" taking the place of "lawful" and "unlawful," before the word "rights" can be a dependable prop for moral arguments. It may be that one day somebody will produce a theory of rights which links the concept firmly to those of "right," "wrong," and "ought" —concepts whose logic is even now a *little* better understood. The simplest such theory would be one which said that A has a right, in one sense of the word, to do X if and only if it is not wrong for A to do X; and that A has a right, in another sense, to do X if and only if it is wrong to prevent A from doing X; and that A has a right to do X in a third sense if and only if it is wrong not to assist A to do X (the extent of the assistance, and the persons from whom it is due, being unspecified and, on many occasions of the use of this ambiguous word "rights," unspecifiable). It is often unclear, when people claim that women have a right to do what they like with their own bodies, which of these senses is being used. (Does it, for example, mean that it is not wrong for them to terminate their own pregnancies, or that it is wrong to stop them doing this, or that it is wrong not to assist them in doing this?) For our present purposes it is best to leave these difficulties on one side and say that *if* at some future time a reliable analysis of the various senses of "rights" in terms of "wrong" or "ought" is forthcoming, then arguments about rights will be restatable in terms of what it is wrong to do, or what we ought or ought not to do. Till that happy day comes, we shall get the issues in better focus if we discuss them directly in terms of what we ought or ought not to do, or what it would be right or wrong to do, to the fetus or the mother in specified circumstances.

III

The other unhelpful approach, that of asking whether the fetus is a person, has been so universally popular that in many of the writings it is assumed that this question is the key to the whole problem. The reason for this is easy to see; if there is a well-established moral principle that the intentional killing of other innocent persons is always murder, and therefore wrong, it looks as if an easy way to determine whether it is wrong to kill fetuses is to determine whether they are persons, and thus settle once for all whether they are subsumable under the principle. But this approach has run into well-known difficulties, the basic reason for which is the following. If a normative or evaluative principle is framed in terms of a predicate which has fuzzy edges (as nearly all predicates in practice have), then we are not going to be able to use the principle to decide cases on the borderline without doing some more normation or evaluation. If we make a law forbidding the use of wheeled vehicles in the park, and somebody thinks he can go in the park on roller skates, no amount of cerebration, and no amount of inspection of roller skates, is going to settle for us the question of whether roller skates are wheeled vehicles "within the meaning of the Act" if the Act has not specified whether they are; the judge has to decide whether they are *to be* counted as such. And this is a further determination of the law.[6] The judge may have very good reasons of public interest or morals for his decision; but he cannot make it by any physical or metaphysical investigation of roller skates to see whether they are *really* wheeled vehicles. If he had not led too sheltered a life, he knew all he needed to know about roller skates before the case ever came into court.

In the same way the decision to say that the fetus becomes a person at conception, or at quickening, or at birth, or whenever takes your fancy, and that thereafter, because it is a person, destruction of it is murder, is inescapably a moral decision, for which we have to have moral reasons. It is not necessary, in order to make this point, to insist that the word "person" is a moral word; though in many contexts there is much to be said for taking this line. It is necessary only to notice that "person," even if descriptive, is not a fully determinate concept; it is loose at the edges, as the abortion controversy only too clearly shows. Therefore, if we decide that, "within the meaning of" the principle about murder, a fetus becomes a person as soon as it is conceived, we are deciding a moral question, and ought to have a moral reason for our decision. It is no use looking more closely at the fetus to satisfy ourselves that it is *really* a person (as the people do who make so much of the fact that it has arms and legs); we already have all the information that we need about the fetus. What is needed is thought about the moral question, How ought a creature, about whose properties, circumstances, and probable future we are quite adequately informed, to be treated? If, in our desire to get out of addressing ourselves to this moral question—to get it settled for us without any moral thought on our part—we go first to the physicians for information about whether the fetus is really a person, and then, when they have told us all they can, to the metaphysicians, we are only indulging in the well-known vice of philosophers (which my fellow linguistic philosophers, at any rate, ought to be on their guard against because that is the mainstay of our training)— the vice of trying to settle substantial questions by verbal maneuvers.

I am not saying that physiological research on the fetus has no bearing on moral questions about abortion. If it brought to light, for example, that fetuses really do suffer on the same scale as adults do, then that would be a good moral reason for not causing them to suffer. It will not do to show that they wriggle when pricked, for so do earthworms; and I do not think that the upholders of the rights of unborn children wish to extend these rights to earthworms. Encephalograms are better; but there are enormous theoretical and practical difficulties in the argument from encephalograms to conscious experiences. In default of these latter, which would have to be of such a sort as to distinguish fetuses radically from other creatures which the antiabortionists would not lift a finger to protect, the main weight of the antiabortionist argument is likely to rest, not on the sufferings of the fetus, but on harms done to the interests of the person into whom the fetus would normally develop. These will be the subject of most of the rest of this paper.

Approaching our moral question in the most general way, let us ask whether there is *anything* about the fetus *or* about the person it may turn into that should make us say that we ought not to kill it. If, instead of asking this question, somebody wants to go on asking, indirectly, whether the fetus is a person, and whether, *therefore*, killing it is wrong, he is at liberty to do so; but I must point out that the reasons he will have to give for saying that it is a person, and that, therefore, killing it is wrong (or that it is not a person and, therefore, killing it is not wrong) will be the very same moral reasons as I shall be giving for the answer to my more direct question. Whichever way one takes it, one cannot avoid giving a reasoned answer to this moral question; so why not take it the simplest way? To say that the fetus is (or is not) a person gives *by itself* no moral reason for or against killing it; it merely encapsulates any reasons we may have for including the fetus within a certain category of creatures that it is, or is not, wrong to kill (that is, persons or nonpersons). The word "person" is doing no work here (other than that of bemusing us).

IV

Is there then anything about the fetus which raises moral problems about the legitimacy of killing it? At this point I must declare that I have no axe to grind—I am not a fervent abortionist nor a fervent antiabortionist—I just want fervently to get to the root of the matter. It will be seen, as the argument goes on, that the first move I shall make is one which will give cheer to the antiabortionists; but, before they have had time to celebrate, it will appear that this move brings with it, inescapably, another move which should encourage the other side. We shall end up somewhere in between, but perhaps with a clearer idea of how, in principle, to set about answering questions about particular abortions.

The single, or at least the main, thing about the fetus that raises the moral question is that, if not terminated, the pregnancy is highly likely to result in the birth and growth to maturity of a person just like the rest of us. The word "person" here reenters the argument, but in a context and with a meaning that does not give rise to the old troubles; for it is clear at least that we ordinary adults are persons. If we knew beyond a peradventure that a fetus was going to miscarry anyway, then little would remain of the moral problem beyond the probably minimal sufferings caused to the mother and just possibly the fetus by terminating the pregnancy now. If, on the other hand, we knew (to use Professor Tooley's science-fiction example[7]) that an embryo kitten would, if not aborted but given a wonder drug, turn into a being with a human mind like ours, then that too would raise a moral problem. Perhaps Tooley thinks not; but we shall see. It is, to use his useful expression, the "potentiality" that the fetus has of becoming a person in the full ordinary sense that creates the problem. It is because Tooley thinks that, once the "potentiality principle" (see below) is admitted, the conservatives or extreme antiabortionists will win the case hands down, that he seeks reasons for rejecting it; but, again, we shall see.

We can explain why the potentiality of the fetus for becoming a person raises a moral problem if we appeal to a type of argument which, in one guise or another, has been the formal basis of almost all theories of moral reasoning that have contributed much that is worthwhile to our understanding of it. I am alluding to the Christian (and indeed pre-Christian) "Golden Rule," the Kantian Categorical Imperative, the ideal-observer theory, the rational-contractor theory, various kinds of utilitarianism, and my own universal prescriptivism.[8] I would claim that the last of these gives the greatest promise of putting what is common to all these theories in a perspicuous way, and so revealing their justification in logic; but it is not the purpose of this paper to give this justification. Instead, since the problem of abortion is discussed as often as not from a Christian standpoint, and since I hope thereby to find a provisional starting point for the argument on which many would agree, I shall use that form of the argument which rests on the Golden Rule that we should do to others as we wish them to do to us.[9] It is a logical extension of this form of argument to say that we should do to others what *we are glad was* done to us. Two (surely readily admissible) changes are involved here. The first is a mere difference in the two tenses which cannot be morally relevant. Instead of saying that we should do to others as we wish them (in the future) to do to us, we say that we should do to others as we wish that they had done to us (in the past). The second is a change from the hypothetical to the actual: instead of saying that we should do to others as we wish that they had done to us, we say that we should do to others as we are glad that they did do to us. I cannot see that this could make any difference to the spirit of the injunction, and logical grounds could in any case be given, based on the universal prescriptivist thesis, for extending the Golden Rule in this way.

The application of this injunction to the problem of abortion is obvious. If we are glad that nobody terminated the pregnancy that resulted in *our* birth, then we are enjoined not, *ceteris paribus*, to terminate any pregnancy which will result in the birth of a person having a life like ours. Close attention obviously needs to be paid to the "*ceteris paribus*" clause, and also to the expression "like ours." The "universalizability" of moral judgments, which is one of the logical bases of the Golden Rule, requires us to make the same moral judgment about qualitatively identical cases, and about cases which are *relevantly* similar. Since no cases in this area are going to be qualitatively *identical*, we shall have to rely on relevant similarity. Without raising a very large topic in moral philosophy, we can perhaps avoid the difficulty by pointing out that the relevant respects here are going to be those things about our life which make us glad that we were born. These can be stated in a general enough way to cover all those persons who are, or who are going to be or would be, glad that they were born. Those who are not glad they were born will still have a reason for not aborting those who would be glad; for even the former wish that, if they had been going to be glad that they were born, nobody should have aborted them. So, although I have, for the sake of simplicity, put the injunction in a way that makes it apply only to the abortion of people who will have a life just like that of the aborter, it is generalizable to cover the abortion of any fetus which will, if not aborted, turn into someone who will be glad to be alive.

I now come back to Professor Tooley's wonder kitten. He says that if it became possible by administering a wonder drug to an embryo kitten to cause it to turn into a being with a human mind like ours, we should still not feel under any obligation either to administer the drug to kittens or to refrain from aborting kittens to whom the drug had been administered by others. He uses this as an argument against the "potentiality principle," which says that if there are any properties which are possessed by adult human beings and which endow any organisms possessing them with a serious right to life, then "at least one of those properties will be such that any organism *potentially* possessing that property has a serious right to life even now, simply by virtue of that potentiality, where an organism possesses a property potentially if it will come to have that property in the normal course of its development." [10] Putting this more briefly and in terms of "wrong" instead of "rights," the potentiality principle says that if it would be wrong to kill an adult human being because he has a certain property, it is wrong to kill an organism (for example, a fetus) which will come to have that property if it develops normally.

There is one minor objection to what Tooley says which we can pass over quickly. The administration of wonder drugs is not normal development; so Tooley ought not to have used the words "in the normal course of its development"; they spoil his "kitten" example. But let us amend our summary of his principle by omitting the words "if it develops normally" and substituting "if we do not kill it." I do not think that this substitution makes Tooley's argument any weaker than it is already.

Now suppose that I discovered that I myself was the result of the administration of the wonder drug to a kitten embryo. To make this extension of the example work, we have to suppose that the drug is even more wonderful and can make kitten embryos grow into beings with human bodies as well as minds; but it is hard to see how this could make any moral difference, especially for Tooley, who rests none of his argument on bodily shape. If this happened, it would not make my reasons for being glad that I was not aborted cease to apply. I certainly prescribe that they should not have aborted an embryo kitten which the wonder drug was going to turn into *me*. And so, by the Golden Rule, I must say that I should not abort an embryo kitten to whom the wonder drug had been administered and which therefore was going to turn into a creature just like me. And, for what it is worth, this is what I would say. The fact that I confidently assert this, whereas Tooley confidently asserts the opposite— so confidently, in fact, that he thinks that this single example is enough to establish his entire case against the potentiality principle, and produces no other—just shows how inadequate intuitions are as a guide to moral con- clusions. The fantastic nature of his example (like that of some of Pro- fessor Thomson's) makes it even more difficult to be certain that we are saying what we *should* say about it. Our intuitions are the result of our up- bringings, and we were not brought up on cases where kittens can be turned into beings with human minds, or where people get kidnapped and have distinguished violinists with kidney failure plugged into their bloodstreams, in Professor Thomson's example.

The problem becomes more difficult if we ask whether the same argu- ment could be used to establish that it would be wrong, if this wonder drug were invented, not to administer it to all the embryo kittens one could get hold of. I shall postpone discussion of this problem until we have discussed the similar problem of whether the potentiality principle, once established, will not force upon us an extreme conservative position not only about abortion but also about contraception, and even forbid chastity. If we allow the potentiality of procreating human beings to place upon us obli- gations to procreate them, shall we not have a duty to procreate all the human beings that we can, and will not even monks and nuns have to obey King Lear's injunction to "let copulation thrive"?[11] To the general prob- lem which this raises I shall return. We shall see that it is simply the familiar problem about the right population policy, which has to be faced whatever view we take of the present question.

V

I propose to take it as established that the potentiality principle is *not* re- futed by Tooley's one example, and that it therefore holds the field until somebody produces a better argument against it—which I do not expect to happen, because the potentiality principle itself can be based on the Golden Rule, as the examples already considered show, and the Golden Rule has a secure logical foundation which I have already mentioned, though I have not had room to expound it.

Why does Tooley think that, if the potentiality principle is once granted, the extreme conservative position on abortion becomes impregnable? Obviously because he has neglected to consider some other potential beings. Take, to start with, the next child that this mother will have if this pregnancy is terminated but will not have if this pregnancy is allowed to continue. Why will she not have it? For a number of alternative reasons. The most knockdown reason would be that the mother would die or be rendered sterile if this pregnancy were allowed to continue. Another would be that the parents had simply decided, perhaps for morally adequate reasons, that their family would be large enough if and when this present fetus was born. I shall be discussing later the morality of family limitation; for the moment I shall assume for the sake of argument that it is morally all right for parents to decide, after they have had, say, fifteen children, not to have any more, and to achieve this modest limitation of their family by remaining completely chaste.

In all these cases there is, in effect, a choice between having this child now and having another child later. Most people who oppose abortion make a great deal of the wrongness of stopping the birth of this child but say nothing about the morality of stopping the birth of the later child. My own intuition (on which I am by no means going to rely) is that they are wrong to make so big a distinction. The basis of the distinction is supposed to be that the fetus already exists as a single living entity all in one place, whereas the possible future child is at the moment represented only by an unfertilized ovum and a sperm which may or may not yet exist in the father's testes. But will this basis support so weighty a distinction?

First, why is it supposed to make a difference that the genetic material which causes the production of the future child and adult is in two different places? If I have a duty to open a certain door, and two keys are required to unlock it, it does not seem to me to make any difference to my duty that one key is already in the lock and the other in my trousers. This, so far, is an intuition, and I place no reliance on it; I introduce the parallel only to remove some prejudices. The real argument is this: when I am glad that I was born (the basis, it will be remembered, of the argument that the Golden Rule therefore places upon me an obligation not to stop others being born) I do not confine this gladness to gladness that they did not abort me. I am glad, also, that my parents copulated in the first place, without contraception. So from my gladness, in conjunction with the extended Golden Rule, I derive not only a duty not to abort, but also a duty not to abstain from procreation. In the choice-situation that I have imagined, in which it is either this child or the next one but not both, I cannot perform both these duties. So, in the words of a wayside pulpit reported to me by Mr. Anthony Kenny, "if you have conflicting duties, one of them isn't your duty." But which?

I do not think that any general answer can be given to this question. If the present fetus is going to be miserably handicapped if it grows into an adult, perhaps because the mother had rubella, but there is every reason to suppose that the next child will be completely normal and as happy as most people, there would be reason to abort this fetus and proceed to bring to birth the next child, in that the next child will be much gladder to be alive than will this one. The Golden Rule does not directly guide us in cases where we cannot help failing to do to *some* others what we wish were done to us, because if we did it to some, we should thereby prevent ourselves from doing it to others. But it can guide us indirectly, if further extended by a simple maneuver, to cover what I have elsewhere called "multilateral" situations. We are to do to the others affected, taken together, what we wish were done to us if we had to be all of them by turns in random order.[12] In this case, by terminating this pregnancy, I get, on this scenario, no life at all in one of my incarnations and a happy life in the other; but by not terminating it, I get a miserable life in one and no life at all in the other. So I should choose to terminate. In order to reach this conclusion it is not necessary to assume, as we did, that the present fetus will turn into a person who will be positively miserable; only that that person's expectation of happiness is so much less than the expectation of the later possible person that the other factors (to be mentioned in a moment) are outweighed.

In most cases, the probability that there will be another child to replace this one is far lower than that this fetus will turn into a living child. The latter probability is said in normal cases to be about 80 percent; the probability of the next child being born may be much lower (the parents may separate; one of them may die or become sterile; or they may just change their minds about having children). If I do not terminate in such a normal case, I get, on the same scenario, an 80 percent chance of a normal happy life in one incarnation, and no chance at all of any life in the other;

but if I do terminate, I get a much lower chance of a normal happy life in the second incarnation and no chance at all in the first. So in this case I should not terminate. By applying this kind of scenario to different cases, we get a way of dramatizing the application of the Golden Rule to them. The cases will all be different, but the relevance of the differences to the moral decision becomes clearer. It is these differences in probabilities of having a life, and of having a happy one, that justify, first of all the presumptive policy, which most people would follow, that abortions in general ought to be avoided, and secondly the exceptions to this policy that many people would now allow—though of course they will differ in their estimation of the probabilities.

I conclude, therefore, that the establishment of the potentiality principle by no means renders impregnable the extreme conservative position, as Tooley thinks it does. It merely creates a rebuttable or defeasible presumption against abortion, which is fairly easily rebutted if there are good indications. The interests of the mother may well, in many cases, provide such good indications, although, because hers is not the only interest, we have also to consider the others. Liberals can, however, get from the present form of argument all that they could reasonably demand, since in the kinds of cases in which they would approve of termination, the interests of the mother will usually be predominant enough to tip the balance between those of the others affected, including potential persons.

The effect of this argument is to bring the morality of contraception and that of abortion somewhat closer together. Important differences will remain, however. There is the fact that the fetus has a very good chance of turning into a normal adult if allowed to develop, whereas the chance that a single coitus will have that result is much lower. Further, if a general duty to produce children be recognized (as the view I have suggested requires), to kill a fetus means the nonfulfillment of this duty for a much longer period (the period from its begetting to the begetting of the next child, if any), whereas, if you do not beget a child now, you may five minutes later. Thirdly, parents become attached to the child in the womb (hence the argument, "We should all think differently if wombs were transparent"), and therefore an abortion may (whatever the compensating good) do some harm to them in addition to that (if any) done to the prospective child that is aborted; this is not so if they merely refrain from procreation. These differences are enough to account for the moral gap between contraception and abortion which will be found in the intuitions of most people; one has to be very extreme in one's views either to consider contraception as sinful as abortion or to think of abortion as *just* another alternative to contraception.

VI

We must now consider some possible objections to this view. Some of these rest on supposed conflicts with received opinion. I shall not deal at great length with these, for a number of reasons. The first is that it would be hard at the moment to point to any at all generally received opinion about abortion. But even if we could, it is a difficult question in moral philosophy, which I have discussed at length elsewhere,[13] how much attention should be paid to received opinion on moral issues. I will sum up my view, without defending it. It is that there are two levels of moral thinking. The first (level 1) consists in the application of learnt principles, which, in order to be learnt, have to be *fairly* general and simple; the second (level 2) consists in the criticism, and possibly the modification, of these general principles in the light of their effect in particular cases, actual and imagined. The purpose of this second, reflective kind of thinking is to select those general principles for use in the first kind of thinking which will lead to the nearest approximation, if generally accepted and inculcated, to the results that would be achieved if we had the time and the information and the freedom from self-deception to make possible the practice of level-2 thinking in every single case. The intuitions which many moral philosophers regard as the final court of appeal are the result of their upbringing—that is, of the fact that just these level-1 principles were accepted by those who most influenced them. In discussing abortion, we ought to be doing some level-2 thinking; it is therefore quite futile to appeal to those level-1 intuitions that we happen to have acquired. It is a question, not of what our intuitions *are*, but of what they *ought to be*—a question which can usefully be dramatized by asking, What opinions about abortion ought we to be teaching to our children?

This may help to answer two objections which often crop up. The first claims that common opinion makes a larger moral distinction between failure to procreate and killing a fetus than the present view would warrant. Sometimes this distinction is said to be founded on the more general one between omissions and acts. There are strong arguments against the moral relevance of this last distinction;[14] and if we are always careful to compare like with like in our examples, and apply the Golden

Rule to them, we shall not obtain any morally relevant difference between acts and omissions, provided that we are engaged in level-2 thinking. However, it may well be that the level-1 principles, which we selected as a result of this thinking, *would* use the distinction between acts and omissions. The reason for this is that, although this distinction is philosophically very puzzling and even suspect, it is operable by the ordinary man at the commonsense level; moreover, it serves to separate from each other classes of cases which a more refined thinking would also separate, but would do so only as a result of a very protracted investigation which did not itself make use of the act-omission distinction. So the act-omission distinction serves as a useful surrogate for distinctions which really are morally relevant, although it itself is not. Thus there may be no morally relevant distinction, so far as the Golden Rule goes, between killing and failing to keep alive *in otherwise identical cases*; but if people have ingrained in them the principle that it is wrong to kill innocent adults, but not always so wrong to fail to keep them alive, they are more likely in practice to do the right thing than if their ingrained principles made no such distinction. This is because most cases of killing differ from most cases of failing to keep alive in *other* crucial ways, such that the former are very much more likely to be wrong than the latter. And in the case of abortion and failure to procreate, it is *possible* (I do not say that it is so) that the best level-1 principles for practical use would make bigger distinctions at birth and at conception than a refined level-2 thinking could possibly support. The reason is that conception and birth are dividing lines that are easily discerned by the ordinary man and that therefore a level-1 principle which uses these dividing lines in order to draw the moral line (what moral line?) *may* lead in practice to the morally best results. But if we are arguing (as we are) whether or not this is so, appeals to the intuitions of the ordinary man are entirely beside the point.

Second, we have the "thin end of the wedge" or "slippery slope" objection. If we sanction contraception, why not abortion; and if abortion, why not infanticide; and if infanticide, why not the murder of adults? As an argument against the too ready abandonment of accepted general level-1 principles this argument has some force; for, psychologically speaking, if the ordinary man or the ordinary doctor has got hold of some general principles about killing, which serve well enough in the ordinary run, and then somebody tells him that these principles ought not to be followed universally, it may well be that he will come to disregard them in cases where he ought not. The argument can be overplayed—I do not think that many doctors who have come to accept abortion are thereby made any more prone to murder their wives) but at this level the argument has *some* force, especially if, in the upbringing of the ordinary man and the ordinary doctor, enormous stress has been laid on general principles of great rigidity—such principles are naturally susceptible to thin ends of wedges. But when we are disputing at level 2 about what our level-1 principles ought to be, the argument has little force. For it may be that we could devise other, equally simple principles which would be wedge-resistant and would draw lines in different places; it may be that we *ought* to do this, if the new places were more likely, if generally recognized, to lead most often to the right results in practice. Tooley recommends such a moral line very shortly *after* birth, and his arguments have a great attraction.[15] For the present, it is enough to say that if the line proved wedge-resistant and if it separated off, in a workable manner, nearly all the cases that would be pronounced wrong by level-2 thinking from nearly all those which would be pronounced permissible, then it would be no argument against this proposal that it conflicted with people's intuitions. These intuitions, like earlier ones which made a big distinction at quickening, are the results of attempts to simplify the issues for a laudable practical purpose; they cannot without circularity be used in an appraisal of themselves. As Tooley implies, we have to find real moral reasons for distinguishing cases. If, as is sure to happen, the distinctions that result are very complicated, we have to simplify them for ordinary use as best we can, and there is no reason to assume that the simplifications which will be best are those which have been current hitherto—certainly not in a context in which circumstances have changed as radically as they have with regard to abortion.

VII

It might be objected, as we have seen, that the view I have advocated would require unlimited procreation, on the ground that not to produce any single child whom one might have produced lays one open to the charge that one is not doing to that child as one is glad has been done to oneself (namely, causing him to be born). But there are, even on the present view, reasons for limiting the population. Let us suppose that fully grown adults were producible ad lib., not by gestation in human mothers or in the wombs of cats or in test tubes, but instantaneously by waving a wand. We should still have to formulate a population policy for the world as a whole, and for particular societies and families. There would be a point at which the additional member of each of these units imposed burdens on the other members great enough in sum to outweigh the advantage gained by the additional member. In utilitarian terms, the classical or total utility principle sets a limit to population which, although higher than the average utility principle, is nevertheless a limit.[16] In terms of the Golden Rule, which is the basis of my present argument, even if the "others" to whom we are to do what we wish, or what we are glad, to have done to us are to include potential people, good done to them may be outweighed by harm done to other actual or potential people. If we had to submit to all their lives or nonlives in turn, we should have a basis for choosing a population policy which would not differ from that yielded by the classical utility principle. How restrictive this policy would be would depend on assumptions about the threshold effects of certain increases in population size and density. I think myself that even if potential people are allowed to be the objects of duties, the policy will be fairly restrictive; but this is obviously not the place to argue for this view.

One big gap in the argument of this paper is my failure to deal with the question of whether, when we are balancing the interests of the potential person into whom this fetus will turn against the interests of other people who might be born, we ought to limit the second class to other members of the same family, or include in it *any* potential person who might in some sense "replace" the first-mentioned potential person. This major question would seem to depend for its answer on a further question: To what extent will the birth or non-birth of *this* person make more or less likely the birth or non-birth of the others? This is a demographic question which at the moment baffles me; but it would obviously have to be gone into in any exhaustive account of the morality of abortion. I have, however, written (possibly too hastily) as if only other potential members of the same family need be considered. That was enough to illustrate the important principle that I was trying to explain.

VIII

Lastly, a logician might object that these potential people do not exist, and cannot be identified or individuated, and therefore cannot be the objects of duties. If I had put my own view in terms of rights or interests, the same objection could be expressed by saying that only actual people have these. Two points can be made against this objection at once. The first is a perhaps superficial one: it would be strange if there were an act whose very performance made it impossible for it to be wrong. But if the objection were correct, the act of aborting a possible person would be such an act; by preventing the existence of the object of the wrongdoing, it would remove its wrongness. This seems too easy a way of avoiding crime.

Second, there seems to be no objection in principle to condemning hypothetical acts: it would have been wrong for Nixon to stay on any longer in the presidency. And it seems a fairly safe principle that if it makes sense to make value judgments about an act that was done, it makes equal sense to make opposite judgments about the hypothetical omission to do that act. "Nixon did right to resign" makes sense; and so, therefore, does "Nixon would have done wrong not to resign." But we do commend actions which resulted in our own existence—every Sunday in thousands of churches we give thanks for our creation as well as for our preservation and all the blessings of this life; and Aristotle says that we ought to show the same gratitude to our earthly fathers as "causes of our being."[17] So it is at least meaningful to say of God or of our fathers that if they had not caused us to exist, they would not have been doing as well for us as they could. And this is all that my argument requires.

Coming now to the purely logical points, we notice that the non-actuality of the potential person (the supposed object of the duty to procreate or not abort) is a separate issue from his nonidentifiability. Unfortunately "identifiable" is an ambiguous word; in one sense I can identify the next man to occupy my carrel at the library by describing him thus, but in another sense I cannot identify him because I have no idea who he is. The person who will be born if these two people start their coitus in precisely five minutes is identified by that description; and so, therefore, is the person who would have been born if they had started it five minutes ago. Moreover (this is an additional point) if we had enough mechanical and other information, we could specify the hair color and all the other traits of that person, if we wished, with as much precision as we could the result of a lottery done on a computer whose randomizing mechanism we could minutely inspect. In this sense, therefore, the potential person is identifiable. We do not know who he will be, in the sense that we do not know what actually now existing person he will be, because he will not be identical with any actually now existing person. But it is hard to see how his inability to meet this logically unmeetable demand for identifiability with some already existing person affects the argument; he is identifiable in the sense that identifying reference can be made to him. So it cannot be nonidentifiability that is the trouble.

Is it then nonactuality? Certainly not *present* nonactuality. We can do harm to, and wrong, succeeding generations by using up all the world's resources or by releasing too much radioactive material. But suppose that this not merely made them miserable, but actually stopped them being born (for example, that the radioactive material made everybody sterile all at once). As before it seems that we can be thankful that our fathers did not do this, thereby stopping us coming into existence; why cannot we say, therefore, that if we behave as well as our fathers, we shall be doing well by our children or grandchildren, or that if we were to behave in this respect worse than our fathers, we would be doing worse by our children or grandchildren. It seems strange to say that if we behaved only a little worse, so that the next generation was half the size it would have been, we had done badly for that generation, but that if we behaved much worse, so that the succeeding generation was reduced to nil, we had not done badly for it at all.

This is obviously a very perplexing matter, and needs much more discussion. All I can hope to do here is to cast doubt on the assumption that some people accept without question, namely, that one cannot harm a person by preventing him coming into existence. True, he does not exist to be harmed; and he is not *deprived* of existence, in the sense of having it taken away from him, though he is *denied* it. But if it would have been a good for him to exist (because this made possible the goods that, once he existed, he was able to enjoy), surely it was a harm to him not to exist, and so not to be able to enjoy these goods. He did not suffer; but there were enjoyments he could have had and did not.

IX

I conclude, then, that a systematic application of the Christian Golden Rule yields the following precepts about abortion. It is prima facie and in general wrong in default of sufficient countervailing reasons. But since the wrongness of it consists, in the main, of stopping a person coming into existence and not in any wrong done to the fetus as such, such countervailing reasons are not too hard to find in many cases. And if the termination of this pregnancy facilitates or renders possible or probable the beginning of another more propitious one, it really does not take much to justify it.

I have not discussed what the law on abortion ought to be; that question would have to be the subject of another paper. I have been speaking only about the morality of terminating individual pregnancies. I will end as I began by saying that my argument has been based on a developed ethical theory, though I have not had room to expound this theory (I have done it in my books). This theory provides the logical basis of the Golden Rule. Though not *founded on* a utilitarian principle, it also provides the basis for a certain sort of utilitarianism that escapes the vices which have been decried in some other sorts.[18] But I shall not now try to defend these last assertions. If they are challenged, and if the view that I have advanced in this paper is challenged, the issue can only be fought out on the terrain of ethical theory itself. That is why it is such a pity that so many people—even philosophers—think that they can discuss abortion without making up their minds about the fundamental problems of moral philosophy.

NOTES

1. Judith Jarvis Thomson, "A Defense of Abortion," *Philosophy & Public Affairs* 1, no. 1 (Fall 1971). Reprinted in *The Rights and Wrongs of Abortion*, ed. Marshall Cohen, Thomas Nagel, and Thomas Scanlon (Princeton, N.J., 1974), hereafter cited as *RWA*; and reprinted herein, pp. 305-23.

2. John Finnis, "The Rights and Wrongs of Abortion: A Reply to Judith Thomson," *Philosophy & Public Affairs* 2, no. 2 (Winter 1973); reprinted in *RWA*.

3. Finnis, "Rights and Wrongs," p. 129; *RWA*, p. 97. Thomson, "Defense," herein, p. 310.

4. Judith Jarvis Thomson and Gerald Dworkin, *Ethics* (New York, 1968), p. 2. Cf. D. A. J. Richards, *Chicago Law Review* 41 (1973): 71, for a similar misunderstanding. I am most grateful to Professor Richards for clearing up this misunderstanding in his article "Free Speech and Obscenity Law," in *University of Pennsylvania Law Review* 123 (1974), fn. 255.

5. "Imperative Sentences," *Mind* 58 (1949), reprinted in my *Practical Inferences* (London, 1971); "Freedom of the Will," *Aristotelian Society Supp.* 25 (1951), reprinted in my *Essays on the Moral Concepts* (London, 1972).

6. Cf. Aristotle, *Nicomachean Ethics* 5, 1137b20. I owe the roller-skate example to H. L. A. Hart.

7. "Abortion and Infanticide," *Philosophy & Public Affairs* 2, no. 1 (Fall 1972): 60; *RWA*, p. 75. It will be clear what a great debt I owe to this article.

8. See my "Rules of War and Moral Reasoning," *Philosophy & Public Affairs* 1, no. 2 (Winter 1972), fn. 3; reprinted in *War and Moral Responsibility*, ed. Marshall Cohen, Thomas Nagel, and Thomas Scanlon (Princeton, N.J., 1974). See also my review of John Rawls, *A Theory of Justice*, in *Philosophical Quarterly* 23 (1973): 154f.; and my "Ethical Theory and Utilitarianism," in *Contemporary British Philosophy*, vol. 3, ed. H. D. Lewis (London, forthcoming).

9. Matthew 7:12. There have been many misunderstandings of the Golden Rule, some of which I discuss in my "Euthanasia: A Christian View," lecture at

the State University College of New York at Brockport (forthcoming).

10. Tooley, "Abortion and Infanticide," p. 55; *RWA*, pp. 70-71 (my italics).

11. Act 4, sc. 6.

12. See C. I. Lewis, *An Analysis of Knowledge and Valuation* (La Salle, Ill., 1946), p. 547; D. Haslett, *Moral Rightness* (The Hague, 1974), chap. 3. Cf. my *Freedom and Reason* (Oxford, 1963), p. 123.

13. See "The Argument from Received Opinion," in my *Essays on Philosophical Method* (London, 1971); "Principles," *Aristotelian Society* 72 (1972-73); and my "Ethical Theory and Utilitarianism."

14. Tooley, "Abortion and Infanticide," p. 59; *RWA*, p. 74. See also J. C. B. Glover's forthcoming book on the morality of killing.

15. Tooley, p. 64; *RWA*, p. 79. If the potentiality principle be granted, the number of permissible infanticides is greatly reduced, but not to nothing. See my "Survival of the Weakest," in *Documentation in Medical Ethics* 2 (1973); reprinted in *Moral Problems in Medicine*, ed. S. Gorovitz et al. (New York, forthcoming).

16. See my review of Rawls, pp. 244f.

17. *Nicomachean Ethics* 8, 1161a17, 1163a6, 1165a23.

18. See my "Ethical Theory and Utilitarianism."

Bibliography

The following bibliography is neither comprehensive nor selective: not all relevant works have been listed, for no doubt some have accidentally been omitted; and many nonphilosophical works that are nevertheless useful to philosophers have been included. Those entries more narrowly philosophical have been indicated by an asterisk.

Adams, Mildred. *The Right To Be People.* New York: Lippincott, 1967.

*Alexander, W. M. "Philosophers Have Avoided Sex." *Diogenes,* No. 72 (1970): 56-74.

*Aquinas, Thomas. *On the Truth of the Catholic Faith.* Book 3, parts 1 and 2. Translated by Vernon J. Bourke. New York: Doubleday, 1956.

Archbishop of Canterbury (Fisher). *The Church and Marriage.* London: Church Information Board, 1954.

*Ardley, Gavin. "The Meaning of Plato's Marital Communism." *Philosophical Studies* (Ireland) 18 (1969): 36-47.

*Aristotle. "Politica." Book 2, chaps. 1-4, in Vol. 10. Translated by Benjamin Jowett. *The Works of Aristotle.* Edited by W. D. Ross. Oxford: Clarendon Press, 1921.

———. *De Generatione Animalium.* Book 1-4. Translated by A. L. Peck. Boston: Harvard University Press, 1943.

Astell, Mary. *A Serious Proposal to the Ladies, for the Advancement of their true and greatest Interest.* London, 1694.

———. *An Essay in Defense of the Female Sex.* London, 1697.

———. *Reflections on Marriage.* London, 1706.

*Atkinson, Ronald. *Sexual Morality.* New York: Harcourt, Brace and World, 1965.

*Augustine. *City of God.* Translated by P. Levine. Cambridge Mass.: Harvard University Press, 1966. Book 1, chaps. 16-19; Book 12, chap. 24; Book 14, chaps. 17-28; Book 15, chap. 16; Book 22, chap. 24.

Auvinen, Riita. "Women and Work (II): Social Attitudes and Women's Careers." *Impact* 20 (1970): 73-83.

Babbage, S. B. *Sex and Sanity.* Philadelphia: Westminster Press, 1965.

Bailey, Derrick S. *Sexual Ethics.* New York: Macmillan, 1963.

Banks, J. A., and Olive Banks. "List of Relevant Books and Pamphlets to the Woman Question Published in Britain in the Period 1792-1880." An Appendix to *Feminism and Family Planning.* New York: Schocken, 1964.

Bardèche, Maurice. *Histoire des Femmes.* 2 vols. Paris: Stock, 1968.

*Barnhart, J. E., and M. A. Barnhart. "Marital Faithfulness and Unfaithfulness." *Journal of Social Philosophy* 4 (1973): 10-15.

*Beardsley, Elizabeth. "Referential Genderization." *The Philosophical Forum* 5 (1973): 285-93.

Bebel, August. *Woman and Socialism* (1885). Translated by Meta L. Stern. New York: Socialist Literature Company, 1910.

Bell, Robert R. *Premarital Sex in a Changing Society.* Englewood Cliffs, N.J.: Prentice-Hall, 1966.

Belok, M. V. "A Forgotten Minority." *Journal of Thought* 4 (1969): 273-77.

Benjamin, Harry. *The Transsexual Phenomenon.* New York: Julian Press, 1966.

Benston, Margaret. "The Political Economy of Women's Liberation." *Monthly Review* 21 (1969): 13-27.

Berge, André, et al. *Body and Spirit: Essays in Sexuality.* Translated by Donald Attwater. New York: Longmans, 1939.

*Berkeley, George. Letter to Percival, July 29, 1710. *The Works of George Berkeley,* Vol. 8. Edited by A. A. Luce and T. E. Jessop. London: Nelson, 1948. Pp. 34-35.

Bernard, Jessie. *The Sex Game.* Englewood Cliffs, N.J.: Prentice-Hall, 1968.

*Bertocci, Peter Anthony. *The Human Venture in Sex, Love and Marriage.* New York: Association Press, 1949.

————. *Sex, Love, and the Person.* New York: Sheed and Ward, 1967.

Bieber, Irving, et al. *Homosexuality.* New York: Basic Books, 1962.

Bird, Caroline. *Born Female: The High Cost of Keeping Women Down.* New York: McKay, 1968.

Blanshard, Paul. "Christianity and Sex." *The Humanist* 34 (1974): 27-33.

Blanshard, Paul, and Edd Doerr. "Is Abortion Murder?" *The Humanist* 32 (1972): 8-9.

*Blum, Larry, Marcia Homiak, Judy Housman, and Naomi Scheman. "Altruism and Women's Oppression." *The Philosophical Forum* 5 (1973): 222-47.

Boston Women's Health Collective. *Our Bodies, Ourselves.* New York: Simon and Schuster, 1971.

British Council of Churches. *Sex and Morality* (A Report to the British Council of Churches). Philadelphia: Fortress Press, 1966.

Broderick, C. B., and J. Bernard, eds. *The Individual, Sex and Society.* Baltimore: Johns Hopkins Press, 1969.

Brown, Rita Mae. "Living With Other Women." *Women: A Journal of Liberation* (Winter 1971): 33-34.

*Bruch, Robert W. "The Commandability of Pathological Love." *Southwestern Journal of Philosophy* 3 (1972): 131-40.

*Buckley, M. J. *Morality and the Homosexual: A Catholic Approach to a Moral Problem.* Westminster, Md.: Newman Press, 1960.

Bullough, Vern L. *The History of Prostitution.* New York: University Books, 1964.

*Callahan, Daniel. *Abortion: Law, Choice and Morality.* New York: Macmillan, 1970.

Carpenter, Edward. *Sex-Love and Its Place In a Free Society.* England: Labour Press, 1894.

Casler, Lawrence. "Permissive Matrimony: Proposals for the Future." *The Humanist* 34 (1974): 4-9.

Chapman, J. D. *The Feminine Mind and Body.* New York: Philosophical Library, 1967.

Chasteen, Edgar R. *The Case for Compulsory Birth Control.* Englewood Cliffs, N.J.: Prentice-Hall, 1971.

Chesser, Eustace. *Is Chastity Outmoded?* London: Heinemann, 1960.

————. *Unmarried Love.* New York: David McKay, 1965.

Christensen, H. T. *Sex, Science, and Values.* SIECUS Study Guide No. 9. New York: SIECUS, 1969.

Clinton, Richard L., and R. Kenneth Godwin. *Political Science in Population Studies.* Lexington, Mass.: Lexington Books, 1972.

Cole, William Graham. *Sex in Christianity and Psychoanalysis.* New York: Oxford University Press, 1955.

Comfort, Alexander. *Barbarism and Sexual Freedom. Lectures on the Sociology of*

Sex from the Standpoint of Anarchism. London: Freedom Press, 1948.

——. *Sexual Behaviour in Society.* London: Duckworth, 1950.

*Connell, Richard J. "A Defense of 'Humanae Vitae.'" *Laval Théologique et Philosophique* 26 (1970): 57-87.

Cox, Harvey. "Evangelical Ethics and the Ideal of Chastity." *Christianity and Crisis* 24 (1964): 75-80.

Craig, Alec. *Sex and Revolution.* London: Allen and Unwin, 1934.

Cumming, Alan. "Pauline Christianity and Greek Philosophy: A Study of the Status of Women." *Journal of the History of Ideas* 34 (1973): 517-28.

*Curran, Charles E. "Homosexuality and Moral Theology: Methodological and Substantive Considerations." *The Thomist* 35 (1971): 447-81.

*de Beauvoir, Simone, *The Second Sex* (1949). Translated by H. M. Parshley. New York: Knopf, 1952.

Decter, Midge. *The New Chastity and Other Arguments Against Women's Liberation.* New York: Coward, McCann and Geoghegan, 1972.

Dedek, John F. *Contemporary Sexual Morality.* New York: Sheed and Ward, 1971.

Demant, V. A. *Christian Sex Ethics.* New York: Harper and Row, 1963.

De Rham, Edith. *The Love Fraud.* New York: Clarkson Potter, 1965.

de Rougemont, Denis. *Love in the Western World.* Translated by M. Belgion. New York: Pantheon, 1970.

de Sade, Donatien Alphonse-François. *Justine; Philosophy in the Bedroom; Eugenie de Franval and Other Writings* (1791). Translated by R. Seaver and A. Wainhouse. New York: Grove Press, 1965.

*Dewar, Lindsay. *Marriage without Morals: A Reply to Mr. Bertrand Russell.* London: Society for Promoting Christian Knowledge, 1931.

*Dickason, Anne. "Anatomy and Destiny: The Role of Biology in Plato's Views of Women." *The Philosophical Forum* 5 (1973): 45-53.

Ditzion, Sidney. *Marriage, Morals, and Sex in America: A History of Ideas.* New York: Bookman Associates, 1953.

Dixon, Marlene. "Why Women's Liberation?" *Ramparts* 7 (December 1969): 57-63.

*Dolan, Joseph V. "'Humanae Vitae' and Nature." *Thought* 44 (1969): 358-76.

*Dupré, Louis. *Contraception and Catholics.* Baltimore: Helicon Press, 1964.

Duvall, Sylvanus Milne. *Men, Women, and Morals.* New York: Association Press, 1952.

Edwards, John N., et al. *Sex and Society.* Chicago: Markham Publishing Co., 1972.

Eller, Vernard. *The Sex Manual for Puritans.* Foreward by Richard Armour. Nashville: Abingdon, 1971.

Ellis, Albert. *Sex Without Guilt.* New York: Lyle Stuart, 1958.

————. "Rationality in Sexual Morality." *The Humanist* 29 (1969): 17-21.

Ellis, Albert, and Albert Abarbanel, eds. *The Encyclopedia of Sexual Behaviour.* London: W. Heinemann Medical Books, 1961.

Ellis, Albert, and Ralph Brancale. *The Psychology of Sex Offenders.* Springfield, Ill.: Charles C. Thomas, 1956.

Ellis, Havelock. *Studies in the Psychology of Sex.* New York: Random House, 1936.

Ellmann, Mary. *Thinking about Women.* New York: Harcourt, Brace and World, 1968.

*Engels, Friedrich. *The Origin of the Family, Private Property, and the State.* New York: International Publishers, 1942.

Engler, Barbara. "Sexuality and Knowledge in Sigmund Freud." *Philosophy Today* 13 (1969): 214-24.

*Epictetus. *The Discourses and Manual.* Book 2, chaps. 18, 22. Translated by P. E. Matheson. Oxford: Clarendon Press, 1916.

Farber, Seymour, and Roger H. L. Wilson, eds. *The Potential of Women.* New York: McGraw-Hill, 1963.

Fast, Julius. *Body Language.* New York: M. Evans & Co., 1970.

Fawcett, Millicent Garrett. *Women's Suffrage.* London: The People's Books, 1912.

*Feinberg, Joel, ed. *The Problem of Abortion.* Belmont, Calif.: Wadsworth, 1973.

*Fichte, Johann Gottlieb. *The Science of Rights* (1795). First Appendix: "Fundamental Principles of the Rights of the Family." Translated by A. Eger Kreger, Philadelphia: J. B. Lippincott, 1869.

*Finnis, John M. "Natural Law and Unnatural Acts." *Heythrop Journal* 11 (1970): 365-87.

Firestone, Shulamith. *The Dialectic of Sex: The Case for Feminist Revolution.* New York: William Morrow, 1970.

Fisher, P. R. *The Gay Mystique.* New York: Stein and Day, 1972.

Fletcher, Joseph. *Situation Ethics: The New Morality.* Philadelphia: Westminster Press, 1966.

————. *Moral Responsibility: Situation Ethics at Work.* Philadelphia: Westminster Press, 1967.

Flexner, Eleanor. *Century of Struggle: The Women's Rights Movements in the United States.* Cambridge, Mass.: Belknap Press, Harvard University, 1966.

Foote, Nelson. "Sex as Play." *Social Problems* 1 (1954): 159-63.

*Fourier, Charles. *Harmonian Man: Selected Writings of Charles Fourier.* Edited by Mark Poster. New York: Anchor, 1971.

Fremantle, Anne, ed. *The Papal Encyclicals.* New York: Mentor, 1956.

Freud, Sigmund. "'Civilized' Sexual Morality and Modern Nervous Illness." *The Standard Edition of the Complete Psychological Works of Sigmund Freud.* Vol. 9. London: Hogarth Press, 1959.

————. *Three Contributions to the Theory of Sex.* New York: Dutton, 1962.

*Fried, Marlene Garber. "In Defense of Preferential Hiring." *The Philosophical Forum* 5 (1973): 309-19.

Friedan, Betty. *The Feminine Mystique.* New York: Dell, 1962.

Fromm, Erich. *The Art of Loving.* New York: Harper and Row, 1956.

Fulford, Roger. *Votes for Women.* London: Faber and Faber, 1957.

Furness, C. F. *The Genteel Female: An Anthology.* New York: Knopf, 1931.

Gagnon, John H., and William Simon, eds. *Sexual Deviance.* New York: Harper and Row, 1967.

Garskoff, Michele H. *Roles Women Play: Readings Towards Women's Liberation.* Belmont, Calif.: Brooks/Cole Publishing Co., 1971.

Gilman, Charlotte Perkins. *The Man-made World: Our Androcentric Culture.* New York: Charlton, 1914.

*Godwin, William. *Enquiry Concerning Political Justice and Its Influence on Morals and Happiness* (1793). Edited by F. E. L. Priestley. Toronto: University of Toronto Press, 1946. Book 8, chap. 8, pp. 506-13.

Gornick, Vivian, and Barbara Movan, eds. *Women in Sexist Society: Studies in Power and Powerlessness.* New York: Basic Books, 1971.

*Gould, Carol. "The Woman Question: Philosophy of Liberation and the Liberation of Philosophy." *The Philosophical Forum* 5 (1973): 5-44.

Graham, Abbie. *Ladies in Revolt.* New York: The Women's Press, 1934.

Greer, Germaine. *The Female Eunuch.* London: MacGibbon & Kee, 1970.

Grimes, Alan P. *The Puritan Ethic and Woman Suffrage.* New York: Oxford, 1967.

Grummon, Donald L., and Andrew M. Barclay. *Sexuality: A Search for Perspective.* New York: Van Nostrand, 1971.

Guilbert, Madeleine. "Women and Work (III): The Effects of Technological Change." *Impact* 20 (1970): 85-91.

Guttmacher, Alan. *Birth Control and Love.* New York: Macmillan, 1969.

Guyon, Rene. *Sex Life and Sex Ethics.* London: John Lane, The Bodley Head, 1933.

———. *The Ethics of Sexual Acts.* New York: Knopf, 1948.

———. *Studies in Sexual Ethics.* 2 vols. New York: Knopf, 1948-50.

Haire, Norman, ed. *Encyclopedia of Sexual Knowledge.* 2nd ed. London: Encyclopedic Press, 1965.

*Hall, Diana Long. "Biology, Sex Hormones, and Sexism in the 1920's." *The Philosophical Forum* 5 (1973): 81-96.

Hall, Gladys M. *Prostitution in the Modern World.* New York: Emerson Books, 1936.

Hall, Robert, et al. *Abortion in a Changing World.* New York: Columbia University Press, 1970.

*Harding, Sandra. "Feminism: Reform or Revolution." *The Philosophical Forum* 5 (1973): 271-84.

Hart, Harold H., ed. *Sexual Latitude: For and Against.* New York: Hart Publishing Co., 1971.

Hauser, Philip M., et al. *The Population Dilemma.* Englewood Cliffs, N.J.: Prentice-Hall, 1963.

Heer, David M., et al. *Readings on Population.* Englewood Cliffs, N.J.: Prentice-Hall, 1968.

Hefner, Hugh M. "The Playboy Philosophy." *Playboy Magazine,* 1962-65. Chicago: HMH Publishing Company.

*Hegel, G. W. F. *The Phenomenology of Mind* (1807). Translated by J. B. Baillie. London: Allen and Unwin, 1910. Chap. 6, sec. Aa, "The Ethical World."

———. *Philosophy of Right* (1821). Translated by T. M. Knox. London: Oxford University Press, 1942. Part 3, sec. 1, pp. 105-21.

———. *On Christianity: Early Theological Writings.* Translated by T. M. Knox. New York: Harper and Row, 1961. Pp. 304-08.

*Hein, Hilde. "On Reaction and the Women's Movement." *The Philosophical Forum* 5 (1973): 248-70.

*Held, Virginia. "Marx, Sex, and the Transformation of Society." *The Philosophical Forum* 5 (1973): 168-84.

Herbert, Solomon. *Fundamentals in Sexual Ethics: An Inquiry into Modern Tendencies.* London: Black, 1920.

Heron, Alastair, ed. *Towards a Quaker View of Sex.* London: Friends Home Service Committee, 1964.

Herschberger, Ruth. *Adam's Rib.* New York: Pellegrini and Cudahy, 1948.

Hiltner, Seward. *Sex Ethics and the Kinsey Reports.* New York: Association Press, 1953.

Himes, Norman E. *Medical History of Contraception.* New York: Schocken Books, 1963.

Hodann, Max. *History of Modern Morals.* Translated by Stella Browne. London: Heinemann, 1937.

Hoffman, Martin. *The Gay World.* New York: Basic Books, 1968.

Hofmann, Hans F. *Sex Incorporated: A Positive View of the Sexual Revolution.* Boston: Beacon Press, 1967.

Holmes, Ronald M. *Sexual Behavior.* Berkeley, Calif.: McCutcham Publishing Co., 1971.

Hooker, E. *Final Report of the Task Force on Homosexuality.* Bethesda, Md.: National Institute of Mental Health, 1969.

Horney, Karen. *Feminine Psychology* New York: W. W. Norton, 1967.

*Hume, David. "Of Polygamy and Divorces." *Essays Moral, Political, and Literary.* Vol. 2. Edited by T. H. Green and T. H. Grose. London: Longmans, Green, 1875.

Hunt, Morton M. *The Affair: A Portrait of Extra-Marital Love in Contemporary America.* Cleveland: The World Publishing Co., 1969.

Hutchinson, Evaline D. S. *Creative Sex.* London: Allen and Unwin, 1936.

Ingram, Kenneth. *Sex Morality Tomorrow.* London: Allen and Unwin, 1940.

Jeffs, C. *Sex and Salvation: The World's Master Pet Sin-God Defeated.* London: Page and Thomas, 1950.

Kanowitz, Leo. *Women and the Law: The Unfinished Revolution.* Albuquerque, N.M.: University of New Mexico Press, 1969.

*Kant, Immanuel. *Observations on the Feeling of the Sublime and the Beautiful* (1763). Sec. 3, "Of the Distinction Between the Beautiful and the Sublime in the Interrelations of the Two Sexes." Berkeley, Calif.: University of California Press, 1960.

*————. *The Philosophy of Law* (1797). Translated by W. Hastie. Edinburgh, 1887. Part 1, sec. 1.

————. *Lectures on Ethics.* Translated by Louis Infield. London: Methuen and Co., 1930. Pp. 162-71.

Kardiner, Abram. *Sex and Morality*. London: Routledge and Kegan Paul, 1955.

Kennedy, Eugene. *The New Sexuality: Myths, Fables, and Hang-ups*. New York: Doubleday, 1972.

*Kierkegaard, Soren. *The Diary of a Seducer* (1843). Translated by Fick. Ithaca N.Y.: The Dragon Press, 1932.

*———. *Works of Love* (1847). Translated by David F. Swenson and Lilian Marvin Swenson. Princeton, N.J.: Princeton University Press, 1946.

*———. "The Aesthetic Validity of Marriage." *Either/Or*. Vol 2. Translated by W. Lowrie. New York: Anchor, 1959.

Kinsey, Alfred C. *Sexual Behavior in the Human Male*. Philadelphia: W. B. Saunders Co., 1948.

———, et al. *Sexual Behavior in the Human Female*. New York: Pocket Books, 1965.

Kirkendall, Lester A. *Premarital Intercourse and Interpersonal Relationships*. New York: Julian Press, 1961.

———. *Sex Education*. New York: Julian Press, 1965.

———. "Reflections on Sexual Morality." *The Humanist* 32 (1972): 11-13.

———. "Applying Conscience to Sexual Morality." *The Humanist* 32 (1972): 30-32.

Kirkendall, Lester A., and Robert N. Whitehurst. *The New Sexual Revolution*. New York: D. W. Brown, 1971.

Klein, Viola. *The Feminine Character: History of an Ideology*. London: Routledge and Kegan Paul, 1946.

Köhn-Behrens, Charlotte. *Eros at Bay: The Illusion of Modern Love*. Translated by D. and E. L. Rewald. London: Putnam, 1962.

Komisar, Lucy. *The New Feminism*. New York: Franklin Watts, 1971.

Kopp, Marie E. *Birth Control in Practice*. New York: Arno Press, 1972.

*Korsmeyer, Carolyn. "Reason and Morals in the Early Feminist Movement: Mary Wollstonecraft." *The Philosophical Forum* 5 (1973): 97-111.

*Kosok, Michael. "Phenomenology of Fucking." *Telos*, No. 8 (1971): 64-76.

Kraditor, Aileen. *The Ideas of the Woman Suffrage Movement*. New York: Columbia University Press, 1965.

———, ed. *Up from the Pedestal: Landmark Writings in the American Woman's Struggle for Equality*. Chicago: Quadrangle, 1968.

Krich, A. M., ed. *The Homosexuals*. New York: Citadel Press, 1954.

———, ed. *The Sexual Revolution*. New York: Dell, 1964.

Kurtz, Paul. "Tolerance Versus Repression." *The Humanist* 32 (1972): 34-35.

Landau, Rom. *Sex, Life, and Faith: A Modern Philosophy of Sex.* London: Faber, 1946.

*Leiser, Burton M. *Liberty, Justice and Morals.* New York: Macmillan, 1973.

Lemert, Edwin M. *Human Deviance, Social Problems and Social Control.* Englewood Cliffs, N.J.: Prentice-Hall, 1967.

Lewin, S. A., and John Gilmore. *Sex Without Fear.* New York: Medical Research Press, 1950. Rev. ed. 1962.

Lifton, Robert Jay, ed. *The Woman in America.* Boston: Beacon Press, 1964.

*Lindsey, B. B., and W. Evans. *The Companionate Marriage* (1927). New York: Arno, 1972.

Lonsdale, Kathleen. "Women in Science: Reminiscences and Reflections." *Impact* 20 (1970): 45-59.

*Lucas, J. R. "Because You Are a Woman." *Philosophy* 48 (1973): 161-71.

Luther, Martin. *What Luther Says.* St. Louis: Concordia Publishing House, 1959. Pp. 132-34, 884-86, 902, 906, 1457-59.

Maccoby, E. "Woman's Intellect." *The Potential of Women.* Edited by Seymour M. Farber and Roger H. Wilson. New York: McGraw-Hill, 1963.

———. "Feminine Intellect and the Demands of Science." *Impact* 20 (1970): 13-28.

Mace, David R. *Does Sex Morality Matter?* London: Rich and Cowan, 1943.

*Macguigan, Maryellen. "Is Woman A Question?" *International Philosophical Quarterly* 13 (1973): 485-505.

MacKinnon, D. M., et al. *God, Sex and War.* Philadelphia: Westminster Press, 1965.

MacMurray, John. *Reason and Emotion* (1935). London: Faber and Faber, 1962. Chaps. 6 and 7.

*Margolis, Clorinda, and Joseph Margolis. "Alternative Life-Styles and Sexual Tolerance." *The Humanist* 33 (1973): 19-20.

Márkus, Maria, "Women and Work (I): Feminine Emancipation at an Impasse." *Impact* 20 (1970): 61-72.

Marmor, Judd, ed. *Sexual Inversion: The Multiple Roots of Homosexuality.* New York: Basic Books, 1965.

*Martin, Michael. "Pedagogical Arguments for Preferential Hiring and Tenuring of Women Teachers in the University." *The Philosophical Forum* 5 (1973): 325-33.

*Marx, Karl, and Friedrich Engels. *Manifesto of the Communist Party.* London: W. Reeves, 1888.

Masters, R. E. L. *Forbidden Sexual Behavior and Morality.* New York: Matrix House, 1966.

Masters, William H., and Virginia E. Johnson. *Human Sexual Response.* Boston: Little, Brown, 1966.

————. *Human Sexual Inadequacy.* Boston: Little, Brown, 1970.

May, Rollo. "Paradoxes of Sex and Love." *Love and Will.* New York: W. W. Norton, 1969.

McCaffrey, Joseph, ed. *The Homosexual Dialectic.* Englewood Cliffs, N.J.: Prentice-Hall, 1972.

McDermott, John F., ed. *The Sex Problem in Modern Society: An Anthology.* New York: Modern Library, 1931.

McFadden, William C. "Conscience and Sexuality." *The Humanist* 32 (1972): 32-33.

*Merleau-Ponty, Maurice. "The Body in Its Sexual Being." *Phenomenology of Perception.* New York: Humanities Press, 1965.

*Milhaven, John Giles. "The Grounds of Opposition to 'Humanae Vitae.'" *Thought* 44 (1969): 343-57.

*Mill, John Stuart. *On the Subjection of Women.* London, 1869. Republished by Fawcett Books, New York, 1973.

*Millett, Kate. *Sexual Politics.* New York: Avon, 1969.

Mitchell, Juliet. "Women: The Longest Revolution." *New Left Review* (November-December 1966): 11-37.

Mohr, J. W., R. E. Turner, and M. B. Jerry. *Paedophilia and Exhibitionism.* Toronto: University of Toronto Press, 1964.

Montagu, Ashley. *Sex, Man and Society.* New York: G. P. Putnam's Sons, 1969.

Morgan, Robin, ed. *Sisterhood Is Powerful.* New York: Random House, 1970.

Morrison, Eleanor S., and Vera Borosage, eds. *Human Sexuality: Contemporary Perspectives.* Palo Alto, Calif.: National Press Books, 1973.

*Nagel, Thomas. "Equal Treatment and Compensatory Discrimination." *Philosophy and Public Affairs* 2 (1973): 348-63.

Neff, Wanda Fraiken. *Victorian Working Women.* New York: Columbia University Press, 1929.

Neubeck, Gerhard. *Extra-Marital Relations.* Englewood Cliffs, N.J.: Prentice-Hall, 1969.

Newsom, George E. *The New Morality.* London: Nicholson, 1932.

*Nietzsche, Friedrich. *Thus Spake Zarathustra* (1885). Part 1, secs. 13, 18, 20 in *The Portable Nietzsche.* Translated by Walter Kaufmann. New York: Viking Press, 1954.

*——. *Beyond Good and Evil* (1886). Secs. 79, 84, 85, 86, 102, 120, 123, 126, 131, 139, 144, 145, 148, 167, 168, 172 in *The Philosophy of Nietzsche*. Translated by H. Zimmern. New York: Random House, 1954.

*Noonan, John T., Jr. *Contraception: A History of Its Treatment by the Catholic Theologians and Canonists*. New York: Mentor Press, 1965.

Novak, Michael, ed. *The Experience of Marriage*. New York: Macmillan and Co., 1964.

*Nowell-Smith, P. H. "Morality: Religious and Secular." *Rationalist Annual* (1961): 5-22.

O'Faolain, Julia, and Lauro Martines, eds. *Not in God's Image: Women in History from the Greeks to the Victorians*. New York: Harper and Row, 1973.

Olford, Stephen F., and F. A. Lawes. *The Sanctity of Sex*. Westwood, N.J.: Revell, 1963.

O'Neil, Robert P., and M. A. Donovan. *Sexuality and Moral Responsibility*. Washington, D.C.: Corpus, 1968.

O'Neill, Nena, and George O'Neill. *Open Marriage: A New Life Style for Couples*. New York: M. Evans and Co., 1972.

O'Neill, William L. *Everyone Was Brave: The Rise and Fall of Feminism in America*. Chicago: Quadrangle, 1969.

Oraison, Marc. *The Human Mystery of Sexuality*. New York: Sheed and Ward, 1967.

*Ortega y Gasset, José. *On Love* (1939). Translated by Toby Talbot. New York: Meridian, 1957.

Ostermann, Robert, and Mark R. Arnold. *"The Pill" and Its Impact*. Princeton, N.J.: Dow Jones and Co., 1967.

Ovid. *The Art of Love and Other Poems*. Translated by J. H. Motzley. Cambridge, Mass: Harvard University Press, 1939. 1:13-17; 2:111-17; 3:123-124, 173-175.

Parkhurst, Sylvia. *The Suffragette Movement*. New York: Longmans, Green, 1931.

Patai, Raphael, ed. *Women in the Modern World*. New York: Free Press, 1967.

*Pierce, Christine. "Equality: Republic V." *Monist* 57 (1973): 1-11.

*Pierce, Christine, and Margery Collins. "Holes and Slime: Sexism in Sartre's Psychoanalysis." *The Philosophical Forum* 5 (1973): 112-27.

*Plato. "Symposium." *The Dialogues of Plato*. Third edition. Translated by Benjamin Jowett. New York and London: Oxford University Press, 1892.

*——. "Republic." *The Dialogues of Plato*. Third edition. Translated by Benjamin Jowett. New York and London: Oxford University Press, 1892.

Pomerai, Ralph De. *The Future of Sex Relationships*. London: Paul, 1936.

Pomeroy, Hiram S. *The Ethics of Marriage*. New York: Funk and Wagnalls, 1888.

Pope Pius XI. *Casti Connubii*. Encyclical, 1930. Reprinted in Anne Fremantle, ed., *The Papal Encyclicals*. New York: Mentor, 1956.

Post, Louis F. *Ethical Principles of Marriage and Divorce*. Chicago: Public Publishing Co., 1906.

Radzinowicz, Leon. *Sexual Offences*. London: Macmillan, 1957.

*Rapaport, Elizabeth. "On the Future of Love: Rousseau and the Radical Feminists." *The Philosophical Forum* 5 (1973): 185-205.

Ree-Bartlett, Lucy. *Sex and Sanctity*. London: Longmans, 1912.

Reed, Evelyn. "Women: Caste, Class or Oppressed Sex." *Problems of Women's Liberation*. New York: Pathfinder Press, 1971.

Reich, Wilhelm. *The Sexual Revolution: Towards a Self-Governing Character Structure*. New York: Orgone Press, 1945.

————. *The Invasion of Compulsory Sex-Morality*. New York: Farrar, Straus & Giroux, 1971.

Reiche, Reimut. *Sexuality and Class Struggle*. Translated by S. Bennett. New York: Praeger, 1971.

Rhymes, D. *No New Morality*. Indianapolis, Ind.: Bobbs-Merrill, 1964.

*Ricoeur, Paul. "Wonder, Eroticism and Enigma." *Cross Currents* 14 (1964): 133-41.

Rimmer, Robert H. *Proposition Thirty-One*. New York: New American Library, 1969.

————. *Harrad Letters to Robert H. Rimmer*. New York: Signet, 1969.

————. *The Harrad Experiment*. New York: Bantam, 1970.

————. *Thursday, My Love*. New York: Signet, 1973.

————. *You and I Searching for Tomorrow*. New York: Signet, 1973.

————. *Adventures in Loving*. New York: Signet, 1974.

Robinson, J. A. T. *Christian Morals Today*. Philadelphia: Westminster Press, 1964.

Robinson, William J., et al. *Sex Morality: Past, Present, and Future*. New York: Critic Guide Co., 1912.

Rogers, Katherine M. *The Troublesome Helpmate: A History of Misogyny in Literature*. Seattle: University of Washington Press, 1966.

*Rosenthal, Abigail. "Feminism Without Contradictions." *Monist* 57 (1973): 28-42

Rossi, Alice. "Sex Equality: The Beginnings of Ideology." *The Humanist* 29 (1969): 3-6.

*————, ed. *The Feminist Papers: From Adams to Beauvoir.* New York: Bantam, 1973.

Roszak, Theodore, and Betty Roszak, eds. *Masculine/Feminine.* New York: Harper and Row, 1969.

Rothman, David, et al. *Birth Control and Morality in Nineteenth Century America.* New York: Arno Press, 1972.

Rover, Constance. *Love, Morals and the Feminists.* London: Routledge and Kegan Paul, 1970.

Roy, Rustum, and Della Roy. *Honest Sex.* New York: New American Library, 1968.

————. "Is Monogamy Outdated?" *The Humanist* 30 (1970): 19-26.

Royal Commission on Marriage and Divorce. Report. Cmd. 9678. London: H.M.S.O., 1956.

*Ruddick, Sara. "On Sexual Morality." *Moral Problems.* Edited by James Rachaels. New York: Harper and Row, 1971. Pp. 85-105.

Rubin, Theodore Isaac. *In the Life.* New York: Macmillan, 1961.

Ruether, Rosemary Radford. *Religion and Sexism.* New York: Simon and Schuster, 1974.

Ruitenbeek, Hendrik M., ed. *Sexuality and Identity.* New York: Delta, 1970.

*Russell, Bertrand. "Liberalism and Women's Suffrage." *Contemporary Review* 94 (July 1908): 11-16.

*————. *Anti-Suffragist Anxieties.* London: People's Suffrage Federation, 1910.

*————. "When Should Marriage Be Dissolved?" *The English Review* 12 (August 1912): 133-41.

*————. "Marriage and the Population Question." *International Journal of Ethics* 26 (1916): 443-61.

*————. *Principles of Social Reconstruction.* London: Allen and Unwin, 1916.

*————. "Sex Education." Chapter 12 of Bertrand Russell, *On Education.* London: Allen and Unwin, 1926.

*————. "Education Without Sex-Taboos." *The New Republic* 52 (November 16, 1927): 346-48.

*————. *Marriage and Morals.* New York: Liveright Publishers, 1928.

*————. "Ostrich Code of Marriage." *Forum* 80 (July 1928): 7-10.

*————. "My Own View of Marriage." *The Outlook* 148 (March 7, 1928): 376-77.

*———. "Shall the Home be Abolished?" *Literary Digest* 8 (November 28, 1931): 25-26.

*———. "Our Sexual Ethics." *The American Mercury* 38 (1936): 36-41.

Sanger, William W. *History of Prostitution: Its Extent, Causes, and Effects Throughout the World.* New York: Harper & Brothers, 1858.

*Sartre, Jean-Paul. "First Attitude Toward Others: Love, Language, Masochism." *Being and Nothingness.* Translated by Hazel E. Barnes. New York: Philosophical Library, 1956. Pp. 478-91.

Sarvis, Betty, and Hyman Rodman. *The Abortion Controversy.* New York: Columbia University Press, 1973.

Schneir, Miriam. *Feminism: The Essential Historical Writings.* New York: Random House, 1972.

Schofield, Michael. *Sociological Aspects of Homosexuality.* Boston: Little, Brown, 1965.

*Schopenhauer, Arthur. "Essay on Women." *Parega and Paralipomena* (1851). Available in translation. William Durant, ed. *The Works of Schopenhauer.* New York: Simon and Schuster, 1928.

*———. "The Metaphysics of Sexual Love." *The World as Will and Representation.* Vol. 2. New York: Dover Publications, 1958.

Schur, Edwin M., ed. *The Family and the Sexual Revolution.* Bloomington, Ind.: Indiana University Press, 1964.

*Schwarz, Oswald. *The Psychology of Sex.* Baltimore: Penguin, 1949.

Seaman, Barbara. *Free and Female.* New York: Fawcett, 1973.

Shainess, Natalie. Panel Discussion in *Abortion in a Changing World.* Vol. 2. Edited by Robert Hall. New York: Columbia University Press, 1970.

Sherwin, Robert V. "Laws on Sex Crimes." *The Encyclopedia of Sexual Behavior.* New York: Hawthorn Books, 1961. Vol. 2, pp. 622-30.

Shope, David F. *Interpersonal Sexuality.* Philadelphia: Saunders, 1975.

*Shrag, Francis. "Rights over Children." *Journal of Value Inquiry* 7 (1973): 95-105.

Sinclair, Andrew. *The Emancipation of the American Woman.* New York: Harper and Row, 1965.

Slater, Philip. *The Pursuit of Loneliness.* Boston: Beacon Press, 1970.

Sloane, R. Bruce, and Diana Frank Horutz. *A General Guide to Abortion.* Chicago: Nelson-Hall Company, 1973.

*Solomon, Robert. "Sexual Paradigms." *Journal of Philosophy* 71 (1974): 336-45.

Solovyov, Vladimir Sergeyevich. *The Meaning of Love.* Translated by Jane Marshall. London: Geoffrey Bles, 1945.

Stekel, Wilhelm. *Sexual Aberrations*. New York: Liveright, 1930.

Stoller, Robert J. *Sex and Gender: On the Development of Masculinity and Femininity*. New York: Science House, 1968.

Stopes, M. C. *Married Love*. New York: The Critic & Guide Co. 1918.

Storr, Anthony. *Sexual Deviation*. Baltimore: Penguin Books, 1964.

Strachey, Ray. *The Cause: A Short History of the Women's Movement in Great Britain*. London: G. Bell, 1928.

Szasz, Thomas S. "Legal and Moral Aspects of Homosexuality." *Sexual Inversion*. Edited by J. Marmor. New York: Basic Books, 1965.

Tanner, Leslie, ed. *Voices from Women's Liberation*. New York: Signet, 1970.

Taylor, Gordon. *Sex in History*. Revised edition. London: Panther Books, 1965.

*Taylor, Roger L. "Sexual Experience." *Aristotelean Society* (New Series) 68 (1967): 87-104.

Tereshkova-Nikolayeva, Valentina. "Women in Space." *Impact* 20 (1970): 5-12.

*Thalberg, Irving. "Reverse Discrimination and the Future." *The Philosophical Forum* 5 (1973): 294-308.

Thielicke, Helmut. *The Ethics of Sex*. Translated by John Doberstein. New York: Harper and Row, 1964.

*Thompson, William. *Appeal of One Half of the Human Race, Women, Against the Pretensions of the Other Half, Men, to Retain Them in Political and Thence in Civil and Domestic Slavery; in Reply to a Paragraph of Mr. (James) Mill's Celebrated "Article on Government."* London, 1825.

Thomson, Judith Jarvis. "Preferential Hiring." *Philosophy and Public Affairs* 2 (1973): 364-84.

Tiger, Lionel. "The Possible Biological Origins of Sexual Discrimination." *Impact* 20 (1970): 29-44.

*Toon, Mark. *The Philosophy of Sex According to St. Thomas Aquinas*. Catholic University of America Philosophical Studies No. 156. Washington, D.C.: Catholic University of America, 1954.

*Tormey, Judith. "Exploitation, Oppression and Self-Sacrifice." *The Philosophical Forum* 5 (1973): 206-21.

Tucker, Robert, ed. *Marx-Engels Reader*. New York: Norton, 1972. Pp. 331-63.

*Verene, D. P., ed. *Sexual Love and Western Morality: A Philosophical Anthology*. New York: Harper and Row, 1972.

*Vetterling, Mary. "Some Common Sense Notes on Preferential Hiring." *The Philosophical Forum* 5 (1973): 320-24.

Walker, Kenneth, and P. Fletcher. *Sex and Society.* London: Penguin, 1955.

Walsh, Correa Moylan. *Feminism.* New York: Sturgis and Watton, 1917.

Ward, Barbara E. "Women and Technology in Developing Countries." *Impact* 20 (1970): 93-101.

Ware, Cellestine. *Woman Power.* New York: Tower Books, 1970.

*Watt, E. D. "Professor Cohen's Encyclical." *Ethics* 80 (1970): 218-21.

Wayne, T. G. *Morals and Marriage: The Catholic Background to Sex.* New York: Longmans, 1936.

West, D. J. *Homosexuality.* London: Pelican, 1955.

*Whitbeck, Carolyn. "Theories of Sex Differences." *The Philosophical Forum* 5 (1973): 54-80.

White, Douglas. *Modern Light on Sex and Marriage.* London: Skeffington, 1932.

White, Lynn. *Educating Our Daughters.* New York: Harper, 1950.

Whitehurst, Robert N. "Sex—In and Out of Marriage." *The Humanist* 30 (1970): 27-28.

Whiteley, Charles H., and W. M. Whiteley. *Sex and Morals.* New York: Basic Books, 1967.

Wilson, Colin. *Origins of the Sexual Impulse.* London: Panther, 1963.

Wilson, J. B., with Everett Meyers. *Wife Swapping: A Complete Eight Year Survey of Morals in North America.* New York: Counterpoint, Inc., 1965.

*Wilson, John. *Logic and Sexual Morality.* Baltimore: Penguin, 1956.

Winick, Charles. "The Desexualized Society." *The Humanist* 29 (1969): 6-8.

"Wolfenden Report, The." *Report of the Committee on Homosexual Offences and Prostitution.* Cmd. 247. London: H.M.S.O., 1957.

*Wolff, Robert Paul. "There's Nobody Here But Us Persons." *The Philosophical Forum* 5 (1973): 128-44.

*Wollstonecraft, Mary. *A Vindication of the Rights of Woman* (1792). New York: W. W. Norton, 1967.

The Woman Question: Selections from the Writings of Karl Marx, Frederick Engels, V. I. Lenin, and Joseph Stalin. New York: International Publishing Co., 1951.

Women's Caucus Newsletter. The New University Conference, Chicago.

"Women's Manifesto" *New Left Notes.* July 10, 1967.

*Wood, Frederick C. *Sex and the New Morality.* New York: Association Press, 1968.

Wright, Helena. *Sex and Society.* Seattle: University of Washington Press, 1969.

Wynn, John C., ed. *Sexual Ethics and Christian Responsibility: Some Divergent Views.* New York: Association Press, 1970.

Contributors

Robert Baker has taught philosophy at the University of Iowa and Wayne State University. He is now at Union College (Schenectady, New York). In addition to coediting *A Workbook in Logic*, he has published papers in epistemology and social philosophy.

Bernard H. Baumrin is professor of philosophy, City University of New York (the Graduate School and Lehman College) and a member of the New York State Bar. He is the author of the two-volume *Philosophy of Science: The Delaware Seminar* (1963).

Michael D. Bayles, professor of philosophy at the University of Kentucky, was a fellow in law and philosophy at Harvard Law School, 1974-75. Author of articles on ethics and political-legal philosophy, he is the editor of *Ethics and Population* (1975).

Chairman of the philosophy department at Rice University, **Baruch Brody** is the author of *Abortion and the Sanctity of Human Life* (1975).

Carl Cohen is professor of philosophy in the Residential College of the University of Michigan, Ann Arbor. He is a member of the national board of directors of the American Civil Liberties Union and is the author of *Civil Disobedience* (1972) and *Democracy* (1973).

Frederick Elliston has taught at Trinity College and York University. He now teaches at Union College (Schenectady, New York). He is coeditor of *Husserl Expositions and Appraisals* (forthcoming).

Marilyn Frye, formerly assistant professor at the University of Pittsburgh, has held visiting appointments at several universities, most recently at Michigan State University. Ms. Frye focuses on topics pertaining to feminism and related social and political issues.

R. M. Hare is professor of moral philosophy at Corpus Christi College, Oxford University. He is the author of three volumes in the "New Studies in Practical Philosophy" series, published by the University of California Press in 1972, and of *The Language of Morals* (1952).

Assistant professor of philosophy at the University of Cincinnati, **Alison Jaggar** has done her most recent work on normative problems in moral and political philosophy, particularly the philosophical aspects of feminism.

Barbara Lawrence is associate professor of humanities at the State University College of New York at Old Westbury. A former editor, she has written for the *New York Times*, the *New Yorker*, and *Columbia Poetry*.

Joseph Margolis, professor of philosophy at Temple University, is the author of *Negativities: The Limits of Life and Death* (1975) and of *Knowledge and Existence* (1973).

Lecturer in philosophy at the University of Guelph (Ontario), **John McMurtry** has published in the *Monist*, the *Canadian Journal of Philosophy*, the *Atlantic Monthly*, and the *Nation*.

Janice Moulton has taught philosophy at the University of North Carolina and Temple University. Ms. Moulton heads the eastern division of the Society for Women in Philosophy. She has written papers in the areas of linguistic theory and the philosophy of language, reference, and causation.

Thomas Nagel, professor of philosophy at Princeton University and author of *The Possibility of Altruism* (1970), has written on the philosophy of mind, social philosophy, and ethics.

Assistant professor of philosophy at the State University College of New York at Fredonia, **David Palmer** has published articles on Locke and Kant, among others, in the *American Philosophical Quarterly* and the *Proceedings of the Fourth International Kant Congress*.

Sara Ruddick has taught philosophy at New York University and the New School for Social Research. She has written on Virginia Woolf, Jurgen Habermas, and cultural anthropology.

Michael Slote, associate professor of philosophy at the State University of New York at Stony Brook, is the author of *Reason and Scepticism* (1970) and *Metaphysics and Essence* (1974).

Robert Solomon has taught philosophy at several American universities, most recently at the University of Texas and the University of Michigan. He is the author of *From Rationalism to Existentialism* (1972) and editor of *Nietzsche* (1973) and *Phenomenology and Existentialism.* (1972).

Professor of philosophy at Massachusetts Institute of Technology, **Judith Jarvis Thomson** is the author of a number of articles on issues in ethics and the philosophy of mind.

D.P. Verene is associate professor of philosophy at Pennsylvania State University. Author of essays on Hegel, Ernest Cassirer, and topics in the philosophy of culture, he is the editor of *Sexual Love and Western Morality* (1972) and coeditor of *Giambattista Vico's Science of Humanity* (1975).

Richard Wasserstrom, professor of law and philosophy at the University of California, Los Angeles, is the author of *The Judicial Decision* (1961) and editor of *Today's Moral Problems* (1974).